MODERNISM AND THE CHOREOGRAPHIC IMAGINATION

Edinburgh Critical Studies in Modernism, Drama and Performance

Published in the series
The Speech-Gesture Complex: Modernism, Theatre, Cinema
Anthony Paraskeva

Irish Drama and the Other Revolutions: Irish Playwrights, Sexual Politics, and the International Left, 1892–1964
Susan Cannon Harris

Modernism and the Theatre of the Baroque
Kate Armond

Beckett's Breath: Anti-Theatricality and the Visual Arts
Sozita Goudouna

Russian Futurist Theatre: Theory and Practice
Robert Leach

Pina Bausch's Dance Theatre: Tracing the Evolution of Tanztheatre
Lucy Weir

The Federal Theatre Project, 1935–1939: Engagement and Experimentation
Rania Karoula

Modernist Disguise: Masquerade in Modern Performance and Visual Culture
Ron J. Popenhagen

Greek Tragedy and Modernist Performance
Olga Taxidou

Modernism and the Choreographic Imagination: Salome's Dance after 1890
Megan Girdwood

www.edinburghuniversitypress.com/series/ecsmdp

MODERNISM AND THE CHOREOGRAPHIC IMAGINATION
Salome's Dance after 1890

Megan Girdwood

EDINBURGH
University Press

Edinburgh University Press is one of the leading university presses in the UK. We publish academic books and journals in our selected subject areas across the humanities and social sciences, combining cutting-edge scholarship with high editorial and production values to produce academic works of lasting importance. For more information visit our website: edinburghuniversitypress.com

© Megan Girdwood, 2021, 2023

Edinburgh University Press Ltd
The Tun – Holyrood Road
12(2f) Jackson's Entry
Edinburgh EH8 8PJ

First published in hardback by Edinburgh University Press 2021

Typeset in Sabon and Gill Sans by
Servis Filmsetting Ltd, Stockport, Cheshire

A CIP record for this book is available from the British Library

ISBN 978 1 4744 8162 5 (hardback)
ISBN 978 1 4744 8163 2 (paperback)
ISBN 978 1 4744 8164 9 (webready PDF)
ISBN 978 1 4744 8165 6 (epub)

The right of Megan Girdwood to be identified as the author of this work has been asserted in accordance with the Copyright, Designs and Patents Act 1988, and the Copyright and Related Rights Regulations 2003 (SI No. 2498).

CONTENTS

List of Illustrations	vi
Abbreviations	vii
Acknowledgements	viii
Series Editor's Preface	x
Introduction	1
1. 'Unlocatable Bodies': Modernist Veiled Dancers from Loïe Fuller to Maud Allan	33
2. 'That Invisible Dance': Symbolism, *Salomé* and Oscar Wilde's Choreographic Aesthetics	73
3. 'Harmonies of Light': Ciné-dances and Women's Silent Film	111
4. 'Herodias' Daughters Have Returned Again': W. B. Yeats and the Ideal Body	153
Epilogue: 'Danced through its Seven Phases': Samuel Beckett and the Late Modernist Salome	189
Bibliography	210
Index	233

ILLUSTRATIONS

I.1	Gustave Moreau, *Orphée* (1865). © Musée d'Orsay, Paris	10
I.2	Gustave Moreau, *The Apparition* (1876–77). © Harvard Art Museums/Fogg Museum, Bequest of Grenville L. Winthrop	11
1.1	Jules Chéret, *Folies Bergère, La Loïe Fuller* (1893). Bibliothèque nationale de France	37
1.2	Loïe Fuller, photographed by Frederick W. Glasier (1902). Library of Congress	43
1.3	Ruth St Denis in *Radha* (1906). Library of Congress	55
1.4	Maud Allan as Salome (1908). National Portrait Gallery, London	61
2.1	*The Harlot's House: A Poem by Oscar Wilde; with Five Illustrations by Althea Gyles.* London: Mathurin Press, 1904. © The British Library	87
2.2	'The Stomach Dance'. From a portfolio of Aubrey Beardsley's drawings illustrating *Salomé* by Oscar Wilde. © The British Library	100
3.1	'In the Beardsley Manner: The Salomé of the Russian Ballet'. *The Illustrated London News*, 28 June 1913. National Library of Scotland. Reproduced under Creative Commons License CC-BY 4.0	128
3.2	'Salome'. *The Picturegoer* 4 (August 1922). National Library of Scotland. Reproduced under Creative Commons License CC-BY 4.0	130
3.3	Still from *Salomé: An Historical Phantasy by Oscar Wilde* (dir. Charles Bryant, 1922)	132
3.4	Stasia Napierkowska (c. 1910). Library of Congress	138
3.5	Still from *Thèmes et Variations* (dir. Germaine Dulac, 1929)	143
3.6	Still from *Thèmes et Variations* (dir. Germaine Dulac, 1929)	143
4.1	Michio Ito as 'the Hawk' in W. B. Yeats's play *At the Hawk's Well* (1916). Photograph by Alvin Langdon Coburn. George Eastman Museum	172

ABBREVIATIONS

CDW   *The Complete Dramatic Works of Samuel Beckett.* London: Faber and Faber, 2006
CP   *The Collected Plays of W. B. Yeats.* 2nd edition. London: Macmillan, 1952. Reprinted 1960
CW   *The Complete Works of Oscar Wilde.* 5th edition. Edited by Merlin Holland. London: Harper Collins, 1948. Reprinted 2003
PI   *The Complete Works of Oscar Wilde.* Volume 5, *Plays I: The Duchess of Padua, Salomé: Drame en un Acte, Salome: Tragedy in One Act.* Edited by Joseph Donohue. Oxford: Oxford University Press, 2013
VP   *The Variorum Edition of the Poems of W. B. Yeats.* Edited by Peter Allt and Russell K. Alspach. New York: Macmillan, 1957

ACKNOWLEDGEMENTS

I could not have completed this project without the support of a wide community of scholars, friends and family over the years. I am enormously grateful to Emilie Morin for her kind and rigorous reflections on my work from its early stages, and for her guidance and encouragement throughout the process of writing this book. I would also like to thank Erica Sheen, who offered probing questions and sensitive feedback at critical moments in my research, as well as Laura Marcus and Hugh Haughton for generous responses that helped to shape the direction of the book at a vital juncture. As series editor, Olga Taxidou has expertly steered this project from manuscript proposal to final version and I am very grateful for her thoughtful advice. Thanks must also go to my anonymous readers and to the team at Edinburgh University Press for their care and attention in helping me prepare this monograph: Jackie Jones, Fiona Conn, Ersev Ersoy, and my copy-editor Andrew Kirk.

I am very grateful to good friends and colleagues who read and commented on portions of this work in its various forms: Francesca Bratton, Natalie Ferris, Susan Jones, Jack Quin, Hannah Simpson and Séan Richardson. As is the case with any major research project, many of the book's key ideas and arguments were sharpened and improved through conversations with fellow researchers at conferences and seminars, and I would like to thank the organisers of the 2017 Modernist Studies Association Conference, held in Amsterdam, for allowing me to organise a panel on Modernism and Movement (particular thanks to fellow speakers Carrie Preston and Hannah Simpson). Over the years, this project has migrated with me between various institutions, and I am especially thankful for the vibrant band of researchers at the University of York, who brought levity and camaraderie, as well as intellectual stimulation, to this enriching but often challenging process. Special thanks to Marie Allitt, Alex Alonso, Laura Blomvall, Sarah Cawthorne, Jennie England, Julia Erdosy, Karl O'Hanlon, Anna Reynolds, Phillip Roberts, Tim Rowbotham and Carla Suthren. I would also like to thank my early mentors at Cambridge, Leo Mellor and Raphael Lyne, as well as the English Department at York St John University and the School of Literatures, Languages and Cultures at the University of Edinburgh for ensuring my continued growth as a teacher and scholar. I am very grateful to my colleagues at Edinburgh for welcoming me into their department, and to my students for their insights and enthusiasm.

The research for this project was made possible by funding from the Arts and Humanities Research Council, administered through the White Rose College of the Arts and Humanities. Particular thanks go to Caryn Douglas and Clare Meadley for their warm encouragement and administrative assistance. Additional funding from WRoCAH enabled me to undertake important research trips to Emory University, the Cinémathèque française, Light Cone Film, the British Film Institute, and Trinity College Dublin. I am grateful to the librarians, archivists and academics at those institutions for their guidance and support. I would like to thank the Musée d'Orsay and the Fogg Museum at Harvard for granting permission and supplying the images of Gustave Moreau's *Orphée* and *The Apparition*; the British Library for granting me permission to reproduce two illustrations by Althea Gyles and Aubrey Beardsley; and the Universal Order for permission to reproduce Alvin Langdon Coburn's photograph of Michio Itō in costume for *At the Hawk's Well*, supplied by the collections of the George Eastman Museum. Material from the epilogue was originally published as an article in the *Journal of Modern Literature* 42.4 (2019): 74–92. Parts of it are reproduced here with permission from Johns Hopkins University Press. Every effort has been made to trace all other copyright holders, but if any have been inadvertently overlooked the publisher will be pleased to make arrangements to rectify this at the first opportunity.

Finally, I must thank my family for their love and encouragement: my parents-in-law, Caroline and Harold Mozley, and Olivia, Neil and Lily Johnson; my wonderful parents – David and Lisa – and my sister Caitlin, who gave me unwavering support and a sense of perspective when I needed it. Most of all, I am grateful to Fiona Mozley, whose enduring love, patience and good humour sustained me throughout this process.

SERIES EDITOR'S PREFACE

Edinburgh Critical Studies in Modernism, Drama and Performance addresses the somewhat neglected areas of drama and performance within Modernist Studies, and is in many ways conceived of in response to a number of intellectual and institutional shifts that have taken place over the past ten to fifteen years. On the one hand, Modernist Studies has moved considerably from the strictly literary approaches, to encompass engagements with the everyday, the body, the political, while also extending its geopolitical reach. On the other hand, Performance Studies itself could be seen as acquiring a distinct epistemology and methodology within Modernism. Indeed, the autonomy of Performance as a distinct aesthetic trope is sometimes located at the exciting intersections between genres and media; intersections that this series sets out to explore within the more general modernist concerns about the relationships between textuality, visuality and embodiment. This series locates the theoretical, methodological and pedagogical contours of Performance Studies within the formal, aesthetic and political concerns of Modernism. It claims that the 'linguistic turn' within Modernism is always shadowed and accompanied by an equally formative 'performance/performative turn'. It aims to highlight the significance of performance for the general study of modernism by bringing together two fields of scholarly research which have traditionally remained quite distinct – Performance/Theatre Studies and Modernism. In turn this emphasis will inflect and help to reconceptualise our understanding of both Performance Studies and Modernist Studies. And in doing so, the series will initiate new conversations between scholars, theatre and performance artists and students.

Olga Taxidou

INTRODUCTION

The lively gesture; antiquity has permitted it.

—Aby Warburg

An Obsessive Myth

On 15 March 1914, the *Washington Post* printed an article by an American academic, Professor David Edgar Rice of Columbia University, who was anxious to alert readers to an alarming rise in cases of adultery and divorce involving dancers: women whose profession seemed to signal their moral disrepute.[1] After spearheading an inquiry into the matter and compiling some questionable statistics, Rice had discovered that 'dancers as a class are fully 20 per cent ahead of any other class in furnishing domestic and undomestic upheavals'.[2] The sight of a woman dancing, according to Rice, 'kindled [the] sluggish imagination' of the average American man, leading to all manner of romantic improprieties. It was believed that this problem derived from a long-standing association between dance and the human creative instinct: throughout history, he wrote, 'the dancer was the only key to lands of imagination from which mankind drew power and inspiration'.[3] Such stimulation, however, could be sexually improper, and dancers had since gained an extraordinary power over the minds of their audiences, resulting in this recent spate of adulterous trysts. Turning his discursive instincts to sources drawn from religion and mythology, Rice unsurprisingly alighted upon the historical figure whose reputation preceded her in this respect:

> [T]he habit of the ages has given the dancer a power over man's subconscious that she still retains today. There was a sound psychological reason for the gift of St. John the Baptist's head to Salome. And the man of today who sacrifices home, family, or throne to the dancer is simply swept away by primitive impulses which have persisted in him for thousands of years.[4]

This article's broad psychologising would have resonated with its early twentieth-century readership. By 1914, Salome, the daughter of Herodias, had obtained an unparalleled degree of notoriety, largely in the wake of Oscar Wilde's controversial play *Salomé*, written in 1891. The bones of Salome's biblical story are well known: after performing a dance at the request of her stepfather and uncle Tetrarch Herod Antipas, Salome used her influence to demand that the severed head of John the Baptist be brought to her on a platter. A reluctant but captivated Herod acquiesced, ordering the execution of his prisoner in order to satisfy Salome's perverse desire. Operating as a cautionary tale for the author of the *Washington Post* article, and for many cultural commentators at the time, Salome apparently demonstrated the ability of dancers to weave their hypnotic effects on the minds of helpless men, often to violent or sexually immoral ends. Submitting to his irrational instincts, a man might be persuaded into a self-destructive action, willingly dismantling the patriarchal order and its enduring symbols of stability: 'home, family, or throne'. Dancers were not merely sources of temptation for the men who watched them, Rice reasoned, but also representative of a greater, more pernicious threat to the social fabric and the moral values it transcribed, piercing the rational surface of modernity with their 'primitive' energies.

While reflecting a widespread concern about Salome's popularity as a choreographic theme, this article also alludes to the important relationship, suggested by writers and artists during this period, between the art of dance and the creative energies of the imagination. In the late nineteenth and twentieth centuries, Salome's dance was reinvented by numerous poets, playwrights, painters, dancers and film-makers, who sought to render the elusive movements of her body – and her myth – through the power of their craft. It is Salome's body that this book foregrounds in new terms, revealing the multiple sites of both individual and collaborative artistic ingenuity constellated around her dance, crossing the permeable boundaries between different disciplines and modes of artistic production. During and after the *fin de siècle*, Salome's dance was gradually refashioned as an unlikely but influential site of female authorship as performers offered their own versions of this figure, shaping her textual representations in the work of modernist writers and signalling new formal and aesthetic connections between the domains of literature and dance. Before reviewing the range of scholarly debates that have informed this book's approach and conceptual framework, it is necessary to offer a brief history of the Salome myth in order to give a sense of the diverse and complex forms she adopted in the age of modernism.

'There are certainly obsessive myths that return in writing', observes Françoise Meltzer, cautioning that such narrative 'returns' are invariably shaped by their own historical specificities, which subject such myths to continual revision.[5] Salome is one such 'obsessive' figure, whose dance was invoked in a wealth of contexts across nineteenth- and twentieth-century literature and culture. She first appears, however, in the Gospels according to Mark (c. AD 65) and Matthew (c. AD 75), and in the nearly contemporaneous *Antiquities of the Jews* (c. AD 93) by the Roman historian Flavius Josephus.[6] The biblical texts do not name Salome, but record the dance of the daughter of Herodias at Herod's birthday feast, and her request for the severed head of John the Baptist to be presented to her on a platter. Both Matthew (14:1–12) and Mark (6:14–29) suggest that Herodias encouraged her daughter's gruesome demand, thereby framing Salome as a pawn in her mother's schemes. Herod Antipas had divorced his first wife in order to marry Herodias – the wife of his half-brother Philip – a forbidden act that embroils Salome in a torrid history of adultery and incest, prompting the Baptist's vocal criticisms of her mother. Alice Bach observes that it is likely that the only woman present at Herod's feast would have been a *hetaira* (a courtesan), suggesting that even the brief biblical accounts connect Salome's dance to illicit sexuality, despite omitting further details of the performance.[7] In Josephus's *Antiquities*, Salome is named for the first time as the daughter of Herodias, but there is no mention of a dance, or, indeed, of a severed head. Somewhat confusingly, this text also presents us with more than one Salome: the daughter of Herodias is named as the great granddaughter (and grandniece) of Salome I, and Josephus names another earlier Salome, known to the Greeks as Alexandra, thus adding a further layer of uncertainty to this shifting genealogy. In her assessment of the textual corpus surrounding Salome, Megan Becker-Leckrone cogently surmises that in the Gospels 'we had a deed without a name [. . .] [in the *Antiquities*] we have a name without a deed'.[8] These gaps and discrepancies characterise Salome's story: 'the narrative effects of the intricate intertextuality which has not only perpetuated but actually constituted the Salome myth from the first (at least) to the twentieth century'.[9] By the late nineteenth century, Salome was a composite and flexible figure, open to considerable reinterpretation.

Consolidated by the catalogue of alluring and monstrous women produced by nineteenth-century art – from Judith and Cleopatra to Dante Gabriel Rossetti's Lilith – Salome has traditionally been taken as a sign of male horror in the face of modern womanhood. In particular, she has been aligned with the figure of the *femme fatale*, and thereby linked to unconventional desires and sexual mores, as well as the slightly different threat posed by the politicised, emboldened New Woman. Salome's various nineteenth-century images emerged too from a broader fetishising of the East, emblematically linked to empires at once expanding and under threat.[10] Edward Said has shown that emergent ideas about the orient and the occident tended to feminise and exoticise the former, while conceptualising the latter as a literal and imagined space of masculine power.[11] With her dance decoded as a means of soliciting erotic attention, Salome's body was readily translated into a far-flung territory awaiting male conquest, although she was also thought to be capable of unnatural brutality, thereby covertly signalling the latent prospect of revolt. The *fin de siècle* that gave rise to these visions was itself a period of startling innovation, conflicting values, and beginnings and ends. As Vincent Sherry contends in *Modernism and the Reinvention of Decadence*: 'there was an intense sense of possibility and novelty in the air, but it was not detachable from the feeling of current civilization being at its end and a concomitant sense of dissolution in norms ranging from the literary to the moral'.[12] Supposedly prone to unbridled sexual longings, and the violent urge to impair the man she desired, Salome's dancing body was framed in a stream of portraits as a source of dangerous excess to be contained by the creative vision of the artist, but also, conversely, as a site of aesthetic possibility and transformation.

What persisted across later versions of the Salome figure was the dance so briefly alluded to in the Gospels. Although images of Salome had appeared frequently in medieval and Renaissance art, she became a ubiquitous figure in nineteenth-century French writing, reinvented as an oriental temptress, sexually ravenous and scantily clad; one of the many 'perverse virgins' represented in the art of the period.[13] The historian Peter Gay has shown that the nineteenth century was overrun with portrayals of vicious femininity, embodied by 'the vengeful female, the murderous courtesan, the immortal vampire' and 'the castrating sisterhood' – associated with Salome in particular.[14] Stéphane Mallarmé's *Hérodiade* (1867–98) offers one of the more influential renderings of the theme, though the fragments of his incomplete dramatic poem do not foreground the dance, instead presenting Salome as remote, frigid and unyielding, enamoured of 'the horror of virginity'.[15] Subtly interweaving tropes of awe and dread, Mallarmé aligns his Salome with the concept of the sublime and evokes the transfixed states that often arise in response to sublime objects, presenting the female body as a source of deathly stillness rather than the lively movement associated with later interpreters of her dance. Beyond Mallarmé's unfinished poem, Salome was evoked in Joris-Karl Huysmans's novel *À Rebours* (*Against Nature*, 1884), Gustave Flaubert's short story 'Hérodias' (1887), Jules Laforgue's satirical 'Salomé' in his *Moralités légendaires* (*Moral Tales*, 1887), and the paintings of Henri Regnault, Puvis de Chavannes and Gustave Moreau, to cite only a selection.[16] Although these sources undoubtedly left their mark on the dense Symbolist language of Oscar Wilde's *Salomé*, his play introduced critical new elements to the story, namely the 'dance of the seven veils' and the shocking final consummation, in which Salome kisses the lips of John the Baptist's (Iokanaan's) severed head, before an aghast Herod orders her execution.[17] While rehearsals in London were underway for its first production in 1892, Wilde's play was banned by the English censor, who was shocked by the text's blasphemous treatment of its religious theme. However, published versions of the play in French and English gained an extraordinary grip on the popular imagination, exacerbated by the added controversy surrounding Wilde's trials in 1895. Inspired by this range of *fin-de-siècle* sources, countless writers, performers and film-makers then went on to reimagine Salome, and her dance in particular, prompting the eruption of a phenomenon that commentators anxiously termed 'Salomania'.[18]

In this way, Salome's imaginative reach extended well beyond the Symbolist and Decadent circles of the 1880s and 1890s. Her popularity coincided with the development of modern dance and, I argue, played a formative role in shaping the careers of the women at the forefront of this new art form, as well as in the spheres of theatre and film. Loïe Fuller, Sarah Bernhardt, Maud Allan, Ida Rubinstein, Theda Bara, Martha Graham and Rita Hayworth were just a few of the performers who came to be associated with Salome's veiled dance. In 1905, Richard Strauss composed his famous opera *Salome*, using the translated text of Wilde's play for the libretto. Numerous silent films dedicated to the Salome theme were released, of which James Stuart Blackton's *Salome* (1908) appears to have been the first.[19] Salome also enjoyed extensive literary afterlives in the early twentieth century, materialising in the Michael Field poem 'A Dance of Death' (1912), Ezra Pound's playful divagation from Laforgue, 'Our Tetrarchal Précieuse' (1918), and Anzia Yezierska's *Salome of the Tenements* (1923). For W. B. Yeats, Salome seems to have been something of an obsession, recurring in his works 'Nineteen Hundred and Nineteen' (1921) and *A Vision* (1925), while also making a shadowy appearance in his experimental dance-dramas, from *At the Hawk's Well* (1916) to *The Death of Cuchulain* (1939). Salome endures as a kernel of an idea in many twentieth-century literary meditations on dance and bodily severance, leaving her signature on John Berryman's image of 'violent and formal dancers / [. . .] shaking their pithless heads' and Samuel Beckett's *Not I* (1972), a play inspired by Caravaggio's *Decollation of St John the Baptist* (1608).[20] The poet Jorie Graham described Salome as the central figure in her collection *Region of Unlikeness* (1991), claiming in an interview that she would 'write until suddenly what felt opaque turned transparent', taking Salome's dance as a metaphor for the paradoxes of poetic creation and that unsettling moment when the veil of language is pierced.[21] These latter examples point towards a more diffuse and capacious interpretation of Salome's veiled movements, one that allows her to move outside the stricter parameters of adaptation, translation and homage. While many artists engaged with her theme in very direct terms, this book is also interested in Salome's more covert and opaque forms, which reveal her important place in the wider visual constellation of women-in-movement during this period. As part of this conceptual paradigm, Salome signified a fraught and evolving dynamic between dancing women and their spectators, especially the artists and poets who attempted to crystallise her choreographic movements in other (textual, visual, plastic, cinematographic) forms.

Wilde's *Salomé*, however, remains the best-known version of this narrative and it forms the cornerstone of one of the most recent and extensive critiques of the Salome theme: Petra Dierkes-Thrun's *Salome's Modernity: Oscar Wilde and the Aesthetics of Transgression*. Exploring the aesthetic and philosophical frameworks of Wilde's play through readings of Nietzsche, Bataille and Foucault, Dierkes-Thrun traces the fascinating emergence of 'utopian erotic and aesthetic visions of individual transgression' across different adaptations of Wilde's *Salomé*, from the Strauss opera and performances by Maud Allan and Alla Nazimova, to Ken Russell's outrageous Wildean riposte, *Salome's Last Dance* (1988).[22] Dierkes-Thrun importantly shows how twentieth-century fantasies concentrated around Wilde and his sexuality repurposed the disruptive vision of his play, which she reads as a forward-looking modernist text immersed in a secular philosophy of individualism and aesthetic pleasure, with clear debts to the currents of French Symbolism. By foregrounding Wilde as the progenitor of Salome's twentieth-century afterlives, Dierkes-Thrun centres her modernist 'transgressive' aesthetic in *Salomé*'s particular formulation of *fin-de-siècle* aestheticism and, crucially, homoeroticism, embodied also in Aubrey Beardsley's famous illustrations for the published English text. While many critics have productively read Wilde's sexuality into the permutations of Salome's veils, these readings have often resulted in a conceptual conflation of the dancing woman's body with that of the male author, a model this book seeks to unsettle by focusing specifically on engagements with her dance, asking what such engagements can tell us about modernism's broader choreographic fixations. Influential as Wilde's rendering of Salome proved to be for later interpreters – as I discuss in Chapter 2 – this is not a study grounded in adaptations of a single play, nor does it take Wilde as its starting point. In some ways, I understand Salome to be a less stable subject, not wholly reducible to her own literary and cultural contexts but rather embedded in a broader iconography of movement that reaches its tendrils outwards, into disparate but interrelated images of the feminine body from antiquity to the twentieth century.

In this sense, my approach has more in common with Anne-Gaëlle Saliot's recent cultural history of the anonymous French drowning victim known as *l'inconnue de la Seine* (the unknown woman of the Seine), whose many 'metamorphoses [. . .] constitute points of negotiation through which to understand modernity', despite lacking, like Salome, a stable 'original story', but rather appearing in masks, busts, texts and images from the late nineteenth century onwards.[23] Recurring as a kind of spectral presence and reaching the height of her popularity in the 1930s, the *Inconnue* is 'often so discreetly encoded in texts and images that she can, at times, be present without being visible', possessing rather 'multilayered visual and discursive functions'.[24] In a related vein, my study takes Salome as a lynchpin – a figure to think through – whose narrative percolates various modernist sources as a visual metaphor, or as a set of recurring concepts, rather than a fixed cultural object or source of adaptation. It is necessary, therefore, to look through and beyond Salome's veils in order to understand the protean nature of her genealogy, which extends into the fascinating and diverse iconography of dancers seeking severed heads at the turn of the century.

Choreographic Imaginations: Nietzsche, Warburg, Bergson

In using the term 'choreographic imagination', this book aims to investigate the way in which dance permeated modernist performance and literary cultures both in terms of its figurative function – through symbolism and stage imagery – and its methods of movement. Dance emerged as a model for other art forms and new modes of perception in the late nineteenth and twentieth centuries. If there was a philosopher of dance during this period, then the title surely belongs to Friedrich Nietzsche, whose interventions in the study of Greek tragedy were hugely influential for dancers, choreographers and writers interested in the revival of classical aesthetics and forms of movement. For Nietzsche, dance had the capacity to act as a model for writing, which he felt had become degenerate by the late nineteenth century. In *Twilight of the Idols* (1889), he criticised his German precursors and contemporaries for what he perceived to be their lack of training in logic and graceful prose, arguing that cognitive functions must be learned and practised, much as a performer rehearses choreography:

> [T]hinking has to be learned in the way dancing has to be learned, *as* a form of dancing [. . .] For dancing in any form cannot be divorced from a *noble education*, being able to dance with the feet, with concepts, with words: do I still have to say that one has to be able to dance with the pen – that writing has to be learned?[25]

For Nietzsche, dance ideally combined rhythmic fluency with corporeal dexterity, using the body to perform a progression of positions and movements that could be replicated by the philosophical mind. There was, however, another side to dance: Nietzsche also considered it to be expressive of art's Dionysian elements, declaring in *The Birth of Tragedy* (1872) that the 'whole symbolism of the body' was engaged by the Greek dithyramb: 'the rhythmic motions of all the limbs of the body in the complete gesture of dance'.[26] The dancer offered a vivid, vital challenge to the 'veil' of 'Apolline consciousness', a veil of form that Nietzsche expected the Dionysian figure to destroy. Nietzsche's reading of the Apollonian/Dionysian dialectic bled into the vocabulary of modern dance, and Isadora Duncan even took to describing him as a 'dance teacher' after being introduced to his work in 1902.[27] Certainly, Nietzsche's conceptualising of the dancer as a force of expressive intensity resonates with depictions of Salome's dance as a monstrous and excessive performance, which threatens to cast aside the veils that conceal her body – veils that '[hide] that Dionysian world from [. . .] view'.[28] Whereas Mallarmé, another key advocate of dance in the period, promoted the aesthetic beauty and formal grace of dance as a kind of poetry in motion, Nietzsche admired the primitive energies and physical struggles expressed by the dancer, rooted in a language that was wholly of the body, erupting through any available linguistic categories. In this respect, Nietzsche's work introduced an alternative conception of antiquity to modern readers, creating an index of pre-classical, bacchanalian gestures seemingly in tension with the more restrained and formally static models of classical sculpture and art (though the eventual unification of these forms was crucial to his reading of Greek tragedy).

Modern dance was shaped by this broader set of intertextual negotiations with ancient myth: while performers such as Duncan saw the maenads, the murderous women of Euripides' *The Bacchae*, as embodying the sensuous, chaotic force of the Dionysian, the Apollonian was often associated with the musician Orpheus, whom Maurice Blanchot classes as the archetypal artist.[29] These contrasting but interrelated myths might provide us with an important way of thinking about the paradox of the dancer as both the author and the object of her art; her body operating as an expressive, self-directed instrument that nonetheless submits itself to the gaze of her spectators. While not dealing explicitly with dance, the Orphic narrative places a similar emphasis on the destructive force of the gaze to that found in Wilde's *Salomé*: Orpheus's descent into the underworld to rescue his wife Eurydice ends in failure when he cannot resist his impulse to look back at her during their climb to the earth's surface. In her form as a shade, Eurydice, according to Blanchot, has a veiled Salomean quality: she is 'the limit of what art can attain; concealed behind a name and covered by a veil, she is the profoundly dark point towards which art, desire, death, and the night all seem to lead'.[30] It is Orpheus's 'work' to bring her to the light, but his gaze signals an impulse to see Eurydice, 'not when she is visible, but when she is invisible'.[31] The Orphic impulse relegates Eurydice to the status of a terrible absence; an invisible presence at the centre of the night.

This idea of an 'invisible' yet irresistible spectacle frames many of the late nineteenth-century accounts of dance considered in this book, including those of Mallarmé and Wilde, who repeatedly articulate their desire to gaze at 'invisible' women, often modern dancers, as part of their larger aesthetic projects.

Perhaps the most ephemeral of art forms, dance 'fades' like Eurydice, and it has often faded from histories and critical accounts of modernism, not least because of its strong association with female creativity. Yet, as this book shows, pioneers of new choreographic forms, such as Loïe Fuller, often used this very concept of 'invisibility' to challenge extant models of performance and spectatorship in their quest for artistic autonomy, discovering power in that 'profoundly dark point' that the Orphic artist cannot reach.

Eurydice's story therefore holds a lesson for interpreters of Salome. In a challenge to Blanchot, Karen Jacobs notes that Eurydice's perspective is lost when Blanchot 'represents [her] annihilation as a loss sustained only by Orpheus, and only measurable in terms of his artistic project'.[32] Like many readers of the Orphic myth, Blanchot focuses on the pivotal moment between Orpheus and Eurydice but neglects to confront the death of the artist: in Ovid's *Metamorphoses* and other sources, Orpheus is finally killed and dismembered by the maenads, the dancing followers of Dionysus. The maenads' violent force, while represented ambiguously by Ovid, marks an important 'attempt to achieve symbolic dominance' over the Orphic song.[33] In many operatic interpretations, including Gluck's *Orfeo ed Euridice* (1762), Ovid's destructive conclusion is either omitted or conspicuously reworked.[34] Orpheus's death was, however, a prominent theme in Ancient Greek art and it was later represented by painters including Albrecht Dürer, Andrea Mantegna, Giovanni Battista and Gustave Moreau, the French Symbolist best remembered for his paintings of Salome. Indeed, the narrative of Salome and John the Baptist shares striking similarities with that of Orpheus and the maenads. In Moreau's *Orphée* (1865), a young woman in oriental finery holds the severed head of Orpheus on his lyre, while the maenads lurk in the background (Fig. I.1). Moreau's pictorial arrangement foregrounds the lone figure of the nineteenth-century *femme fragile*, presented in the style of a Pre-Raphaelite muse, while the Dionysian dancers are shown in typical Greek poses at a distance, spatially representing the classical myth as a spectral precursor to Moreau's Symbolist interpretation. The following decade, Moreau returned to the motif of the sensuous head-hunter, creating his two famous paintings of Salome: *Salomé dansant devant Hérode* (1876) and *L'Apparition* (1876) (Fig. I.2).

For the purposes of this introduction, it is important to establish a conceptual framework that allows us to read these images of head-hunters, from the maenads who dismember Orpheus to the dancing Salome who requests the head of John the Baptist, as part of an interrelated genealogy. The German art historian Aby Warburg's reflections on the death of Orpheus in his landmark essay 'Dürer and Italian Antiquity' (1905) provide a valuable paradigm for such an inquiry. This essay importantly clarified Warburg's concept of the 'pathos formula' (*Pathosformel*), which he defined as the re-emergence of a classical 'emotive gestural language' in Quattrocento and Renaissance

1.1 Gustave Moreau, *Orphée* (1865). © Musée d'Orsay, Paris

1.2 Gustave Moreau, *The Apparition* (1876–77).
© Harvard Art Museums/Fogg Museum, Bequest of Grenville L. Winthrop

painting.[35] Comparing Ancient Greek illustrations of Orpheus and the maenads to Mantegna's and Dürer's treatment of the same theme, Warburg observed the return of specific forms of movement, or what Georges Didi-Huberman calls 'a characteristic use of gesture' in his book on Warburg, *The Surviving Image*.[36] Influenced by Nietzsche's philosophical construction of the concept of eternal return, Warburg maps the 'eternal return of ancient resemblances' across these gestural iterations, although, as Didi-Huberman notes, these gestures are changed and transformed through each repetition: 'The maenad who returns by virtue of the survival of certain forms in the Quattrocento is not the Greek figure as such, but an image marked by what we might call the metamorphic phantom of this figure.'[37] Crucially, it is a 'resemblance' that returns for Warburg in these images of Orpheus and the maenads, not an exact copy. Warburg's 'pathos formula', which he later reconstituted as 'engrams of affective experience',[38] provides a fruitful model for the iconography of dancing head-hunters traced across the following chapters, which Warburg himself might term 'a genealogy of resemblances'.[39]

The critical reiteration of particular images and forms of movement, revolving around the interlinking of female dancers with violence, is at the heart of this book, which offers a reading of Salome's dance and her modernist 'metamorphic phantoms', to borrow Didi-Huberman's term. As his focus on the maenads suggests, such figures were of special interest to Warburg. Long before attempting to constellate these formulae in his hugely ambitious *Mnemosyne Atlas* (1924–29), Warburg chronicled his fascination with a particular recurring image at the *fin de siècle*: that of the woman-in-movement, whom he termed the 'Nympha'. In correspondence with his friend André Jolles, Warburg discussed the emergence of the Nympha in Quattrocento art, commenting particularly on the Domenico Ghirlandaio frescoes in Santa Maria Novella's Tornabuoni chapel in Florence. One letter from Jolles describes the Nympha of these frescoes as 'A fantastic figure [. . .] with a billowing veil [. . .] Sometimes she was Salome dancing with her death-dealing charm in front of the licentious Tetrarch; sometimes she was Judith carrying proudly and triumphantly with a gay step the head of the murdered commander.'[40] In the Ghirlandaio fresco depicting the birth of John the Baptist, this Nympha is the female servant dressed in flowing diaphanous veils who enters carrying a basket of fruit above her head. In a note on 'head-hunting', Warburg articulated the visual consonance between such images of female fruit-bearers and maenads: 'Judith, Salome, maenad, via the Nymph as bringer of fruit'.[41] The symmetry is underlined by the fact that an early sinopia drawing for Ghirlandaio's fresco in fact depicted the fruit-bearer as Salome carrying the Baptist's head, an iconographic doubling later repeated in Titian's nearly identical oil paintings of *Girl with Fruit Peel* (c. 1555) and *Salome* (c. 1550).

In these visions of the Nympha, Warburg traces 'the new gestural language of pathos from the world of pagan forms'.[42] The veiled servants whom Ghirlandaio depicts at the nativities of the Virgin and the Baptist, along with Salome dancing in the image of Herod's feast, suggest that the pagan movements of the maenads, and their impulse to decapitate, have been incorporated into a Christian context. Warburg collected various incarnations of the Nympha (including Ghirlandaio's frescoes) for one of the plates in the *Mnemosyne Atlas* (Plate 46), which forms an important case study in Giorgio Agamben's influential essay 'What is a Paradigm?' Here, Agamben argues that we would be wrong to see this plate as merely an 'iconographic repertory' that can be decoded chronologically; instead, he claims that Warburg's pathos formulae – of which the Nympha is a key example – are 'hybrids of archetype and phenomenon, first-timeness (*primavoltità*) and repetition'.[43] 'This means', Agamben writes, 'that the nymph is the paradigm of the single images, and the single images are the paradigms of the nymph.'[44] Thinking genealogically with Foucault, Agamben develops a theory of the paradigm that means there is 'no origin or *archē*; every phenomenon is the origin, every image archaic'.[45] Warburg's Nympha offers one such paradigm of interlinking visual gestures that are repeated and transformed with each iteration.

The approach taken in this book draws on Warburg's formulation of the Nympha, read as paradigmatic by Agamben. In this respect, Salome's dance can be viewed as part of a larger matrix of repeated gestures that includes the violent impulses of the Dionysian maenads, Judith with the head of Holofernes, and other similar figures who were enthusiastically represented at the *fin de siècle* and incorporated into the new language of modern dance. Warburg crucially reads the Nympha as a figure who *brings* or *bears* an offering of some kind, a gesture which, read in the context of his wider thought, might be linked to the way images themselves carry repeated symbols and associations, as well as dynamic forms. Didi-Huberman is keen to stress that Warburg's project is not merely about constructing an iconology of symbols, but about theorising an 'ancient dynamorphic memory' that 'bears forces and transforms forms more than it transforms meanings'.[46] Warburg was not just interested in the revival of antique images for their own sake but in the complex relationship between these revivals and the specific historical forces that contextualised their re-emergence; in the process of 'grafting' that saw the 'eternal shoots of pagan antiquity' implanted into the 'rootstock' of a new set of cultural and aesthetic codes.[47] Dancers at the forefront of changes in conventional choreographic methods were crucially inspired by the visual archives of classical and Renaissance art that underpin Warburg's theory of images. As Gabriele Brandstetter puts it in her seminal interdisciplinary study, *Poetics of Dance*:

> While modernist writers experienced the break with the tradition of bourgeois learning as a liberating step [. . .] the modern dancer explored the museum as a storehouse of images. Dance's pursuit of the new at the turn of the century is inconceivable without the visual archives of occidental (and oriental) culture.[48]

Coining the term 'topos formula' to differentiate between the pictorial and spatial systems at work in modern dance, Brandstetter argues that the specific topos formulae instrumentalised by dancers, including movement figures of the 'labyrinth' and the 'spiral', were central to the projects of modernism.[49] The object of the veil is crucial to the construction of these spatial forms, marking 'the boundary between expressiveness and impenetrability, between the dynamics of transient movement and the motionless structure of the body in space'.[50] Brandstetter draws on Warburg's concepts to construct a wide-ranging reading of such early twentieth-century bodily forms, although she distinguishes between the 'Greek model' – which includes images of the maenads – and what she calls the 'exotic model', emblematised by the *femme fatale* and Salome in particular. Operating in line with Warburg's original observations about the consonance between such models, my study stresses crucial points of overlap between the corporeal idioms of this period, since the philhellenism of modern dance often bled into representations of Salome's libidinous orientalism, merging these apparently divergent visual registers.

Even in Warburg's earliest commentaries on the Nympha, he stresses that she appeared in both the 'visual arts' of the Quattrocento and 'as a living figure – in the performing arts'; in processions, pastoral dramas and productions concerning mythical subjects.[51] It seems significant too that he became fixated with this figure in the 1890s, a decade that witnessed the earliest performances of modern dancers such as Loïe Fuller, as well as the Lumière brothers' invention of the *cinématographe*, which inscribed her dancing movements in light. Warburg certainly saw Isadora Duncan dance in the early years of the next century, perhaps offering him a modern incarnation of the veiled Nympha that he found everywhere in Renaissance art.[52] Didi-Huberman has directly observed the close relationship between the Nympha and the modern dancers who were so popular during this period:

> [H]ow can one fail to observe that this paradox of the *Pathosformel* encompasses a contemporary phenomenon which is manifest, on the one hand, in the abstract and oversized dynamograms deployed by Loïe Fuller, with her fabric volutes, and on the other, in the dynamograms produced by the chronophotography of Étienne-Jules Marey, which are purified and abstract but also organic?[53]

This phenomenon can be perceived in the work of figures as diverse as Ruskin, Proust, Hofmannsthal, Mallarmé, Fuller and Duncan: it might be termed a *fin-de-siècle* 'maenadism', underlining the significance of the Dionysian dancers to this historical and cultural moment.[54] While critics have identified a strong affiliation between the Orphic myth and Symbolist poetics, especially in the work of Rilke, Nerval, Novalis and Mallarmé, the *fin de siècle* also signals the return of the maenads, whose dance enters into explosive contact with such a mode of Orphic singularity.[55] These dancing figures may constitute a blind spot in Blanchot's model of the Orphic gaze, but they appear at the close of the nineteenth century in the dynamic movements of female performers, often in suggestive reinventions of the Salome narrative.

The pathos formula emblematised by Warburg's Nympha is visible in the aesthetics and movement register of modern dance. To varying degrees and in different ways, Fuller, Duncan, Ruth St Denis and their peers employed flowing textiles, light technologies and fluid dance movements that accommodated the pull of gravity to create an impression of continuous transformation in opposition to ballet's fixed positions, coupled with a movement repertory that included spiralling torsions, arm rotations and *arc en cercle*. This last technique – an arching backwards of the torso – was commonly associated with both the maenads and Salome, who is frequently shown in this position in medieval depictions of her dance. At the same time as it was being used in performance, this pose was closely tied to the iconography of hysteria, most famously diagnosed by the nineteenth-century French physician Jean-Martin Charcot through his work with female patients at the Salpêtrière hospital in Paris. Performing in Schmitt's *La Tragédie de Salomé* in 1912, Natalia Trouhanowa, who also danced the role in Strauss's opera, concluded the choreography with a deep back-bend in the vein of a 'Charcotesque hysteric'.[56] Similarly, in Flaubert's 'Hérodias', Salome dances 'up on her hands [. . .] like some great beetle', invoking the Salome depicted on the tympanum in the Cathedral of Rouen,[57] a choice of pose that Brandstetter describes as 'a pathos formula of erotic exaltation'.[58] Agamben traces the evolution of this particular grammar of movement in his 'Notes on Gesture', arguing that the discourses around hysteria, made into a spectacle by the use of visual technologies such as photography and film, fomented the conditions for an excess and disintegration of gestural meaning in the late nineteenth century. 'An era that has lost its gestures is, for that very reason', Agamben asserts, 'obsessed with them.'[59] Agamben's theorising of gesture is valuable to the connections this book maps between the languages of different art forms, which underwent critical formal change during this period of unstable or 'lost' gestures. Indeed, dance, like cinema, was a crucial sphere of gestural transformation: according to Agamben, the choreographies of Isadora Duncan and Sergei Diaghilev appeared to signal 'the headlong attempt to regain *in extremis* those lost gestures', opening up the possibility that dance might recover the connection between the human body and systems of meaning, restabilising the vertiginously fragmented modern subject.[60]

While Nietzsche and Warburg show how dance came to be understood as an expression of Dionysian energy in art, other philosophers were more interested in the way dance facilitated new aesthetic categories and modes of perception at this fraught historical moment. In his influential essay *Time and Free Will* (1889), Henri Bergson illustrated his theory of 'aesthetic feeling' by examining how grace, specifically the grace of the dancer, elicits a sensory response from the spectator based on 'the perception of ease in motion'.[61] The apparently natural facility of the dancer's gestures gradually allows the viewer to anticipate the progress of the dance, creating the impression that the flow of time has been mastered:

> For the rhythm and measure, by allowing us to foresee to a still greater extent the movements of the dancer, make us believe that we now control them. As we guess almost the exact attitude which the dancer is going to take, he seems to obey us when he really takes it: the regularity of the rhythm establishes a kind of communication between him and us, and the periodic returns of the measure are like so many invisible threads by means of which we set in motion this imaginary puppet.[62]

For Bergson, the movements of the dancer, here termed a 'puppet', allow the spectator to feel a sense of control: the pleasure derived from the perception of grace is rooted in a feeling of mastery, as the performance is predicted and contained by the spectator's imagination. Narratives dealing with relationships of domination, often between a male artist and a mechanised female body, can be found across nineteenth-century fiction; for instance, in E. T. A. Hoffmann's *Der Sandmann* (1816) and Auguste Villiers de l'Isle-Adam's *L'Eve Future* (1886), which tells of a scientist, the fictionalised Thomas Edison, creating automata to replace the novel's real female characters. Reflecting Charcot's performative manipulation of his female hysterics, this widespread interest in uncanny, automated and subordinate bodies shaped the literary culture into which Wilde's *Salomé* emerged, reflected in the suggestions of hypnosis and predetermination that permeate his play.

This formulation of the dancer also taps into the conceptual tensions at the heart of modern dance's various movement philosophies, which seemed to prioritise ideas of spontaneity, natural motion and 'involuntary choreography' on the one hand, yet also conceived of the dancing body as a type of autonomous machine.[63] Indeed, women's bodies, especially on stage, were frequently presented as controllable and submissive objects, despite (or perhaps as a result of) the formation of political positions that opposed patriarchal conceptions of femininity, represented by figures such as the New Woman, and politically engaged dancers such as Isadora Duncan and Maud Allan. While the reproductive and body-altering capacities of technology unseated the notion that women's bodies were the 'last remaining site of redemptive nature', they also fed, according to Rita Felski, 'a patriarchal desire for technological mastery over woman, expressed in the fantasy of a compliant female automaton'.[64] The Bergsonian dancer reflects the earlier interest in machine-like bodies expressed in Heinrich von Kleist's *Über das marionettentheater* (*On the Marionette Theatre*, 1810), which shaped late nineteenth- and twentieth-century theories of acting and performance, particularly for dramatists such as Yeats, Maurice

Maeterlinck and Edward Gordon Craig, as I explore in subsequent chapters. Although modern dancers such as Fuller and Duncan largely retained authority over the content of their performances, a range of modernist theatre practitioners conceptualised the dancing body as a controllable stage element that might perfectly communicate their larger dramatic visions, often taking these very dancers as key sources of inspiration.

Dancing Modernisms

Covering a range of artistic forms and practices from the *fin de siècle* to what might traditionally be considered modernism's closing years, this book combines perspectives from a number of interrelated fields. This interdisciplinary project is underpinned by Jacques Rancière's recent work in the sphere of aesthetic philosophy, which provides substantial tools for examining the crossovers between different art forms. In his book *Aisthesis: Scenes from the Aesthetic Regime of Art*, Rancière importantly defines his concept of the 'aesthetic regime of art' as a modern phenomenon, distinct from the 'ethical' and 'representational' regimes he also identifies.[65] Between the eighteenth and twentieth centuries, the hierarchies established by the so-called 'representational regime' of images were destabilised as art 'ceaselessly redefined itself – exchanging, for example, the idealities of plot, form and painting for those of movement, light, and the gaze'.[66] The 'movement belonging to the aesthetic regime', which Rancière associates with the development of aesthetic philosophy, tended to 'erase the specificities of the arts and to blur the boundaries that separate them from each other and from ordinary experience'.[67] Ephemeral forms conjured by the moving body and the play of light in space were newly juxtaposed with the printed word and the proscenium arch.

Such an exchange between art forms and aesthetic principles is charged with political possibility, since it diminishes the biases that once determined 'which subjects and forms of expression were deemed worthy of inclusion in the domain of a given art'.[68] A non-hierarchical approach is therefore a precondition of Rancière's aesthetic theory, and he demonstrates this approach in *Aisthesis* through a selection of case studies – 'scenes' – that undo notions of canonicity or high art, offering what he calls 'a counter-history of artistic modernity', in which artists such as Loïe Fuller and Charlie Chaplin occupy a more influential position in 'the modernist paradigm' than Mondrian or Kandinsky.[69] The crossovers that my book maps between literature and dance, traditionally differentiated within the hierarchy of the arts, as well as the crucially related hierarchy of gender, are supported by Rancière's insights into the emergence of new notions of art at particular historical moments. For instance, Fuller's 1893 performance of her serpentine dance, discussed at length in Chapter 1 and also taken as one of Rancière's key 'scenes', reflected a contemporary belief among certain poets that dance could 'invent a new power of artifice' and 'a new idea of fiction'.[70] Daniel Albright also recognises that 'the arts themselves have no power to aggregate or to separate' and yet they 'will gladly assume the poses of unity or diversity according to the desire of the artist or the thinker'.[71] The interdisciplinary framework of my book is not retroactively imposed upon disparate texts, objects and performances; rather, it shows how the cultural ferment of ideas and practices in the late nineteenth and twentieth centuries stimulated real crossovers between the arts, notably and profoundly between literature and dance.

These exchanges became particularly acute during the period that witnessed the movement we call modernism. Although some of the individuals considered across these chapters had a profoundly ambivalent relationship with modernism, the ideas, practices and works associated with this movement provide vital points of reference for the materials discussed throughout, many of which were formulated as responses to or reactions against modernism's projects. W. B. Yeats may have felt an opposition between the 'ancient sect' of Irish myth and 'that filthy modern tide' (*VP*, 611), but his own attitudes towards art often coincided directly with those of his modernist peers, including Ezra Pound and Constantin Brancusi. Modernist scholars have long been preoccupied with the complex relationship between modernism and modernity, influentially critiqued by Theodor Adorno as a negative interplay between modernist aesthetics and mass culture.[72] Contrary narratives, such as the reading advanced in Andreas Huyssen's *After the Great Divide*, have formulated new ways of interpreting the cultural purposes of modernism and the historical avant-garde, showing how artists sought various ways to reintegrate their work into life praxis.[73] Indeed, for Sara Danius, the distinction Adorno draws is related to 'a whole series of recurring dichotomies such as the opposition of art to society, of beauty to utility, of the organic to the mechanical, of aesthetic discourse to communicative discourse'.[74] In this vein, my book attempts to navigate away from these binaries, embracing the interdisciplinary outlook of the 'new modernist studies', a field alert to the resonances between literature and the changing conditions wrought under modernity in areas including technology, industry, media and popular culture.[75] Such work has sought to redistribute the emphases between high art and 'lower' forms of cultural activity in order to show how modernism was intimately embroiled in the workings of history and culture.

Naturally, one of the key concepts underpinning my readings of the modernist choreographic imagination is that of movement. The period spanning the *fin de siècle* to the much-debated end of modernism seems itself to be a period in perpetual movement, marked by advances, reversals and shifting epochal boundaries. The recent collection *Late Victorian into Modern* stresses the mobility of the transitional decades between 1880 and 1920, emphasising the continuities that bear out during a time seen as both 'modern and archaic, as a beginning and a *fin*'.[76] Moreover, critical debates have long revolved around the question of modernism's status as a so-called movement: its historical and cultural specificities; its periodisation and geographies; the discrete schools, ideologies and movements – Futurism, Imagism, Vorticism – that constitute its broader apparatus. As part of a growing scholarly interest in moving forms and bodies, the essays collected in *Moving Modernisms* have reframed issues of regionalism, globalism and scale, while probing into the complex relation between motion and emotion, which was radically affected by the dynamic new technologies of the twentieth century.[77] Modernism was also shaped by the spectre of immobility: the temporal and physical ruptures of war; inert, fragile and inelastic bodies; moments of stillness and silence in performance. An important subset of this broader academic field has included a direct interest in the moving (often dancing) bodies that permeate modernist texts, demonstrating, in Tim Armstrong's words, 'a particular fascination with the limits of the body, either in terms of its mechanical functioning, its energy levels, or its abilities as a perceptual system'.[78]

Nowhere was this fascination more clearly concentrated than in the sphere of dance. During the late nineteenth and early twentieth centuries, a range of individuals declared dance an ideal model for the exigencies of literary practice. For Mallarmé, Loïe Fuller was 'la forme théâtrale de poésie par excellence' [the ideal theatrical form of poetry], her dance creating lyrical movements with the human body that the written word struggled to match.[79] Years later, in 'A Dialogue on Dramatic Poetry' (1928), T. S. Eliot praised the literary potential of a different form of dance, asking: 'if there is a future for drama and particularly for poetic drama, will it not be in the direction indicated by the ballet?'[80] Eliot's question alludes to both the stylistic parallels and the collaborative practices that developed between the ballet and the theatre in the first decades of the twentieth century, underlined by experimental productions such as *Parade* (1917), and the establishment of a School of Ballet at Yeats's Abbey Theatre in 1927. The impact of Sergei Diaghilev's Ballets Russes on the cultural landscape of modernism was far-reaching, and modern dancers – Fuller and Duncan especially – had a profound influence on the artists and writers they knew, including Mallarmé, Auguste Rodin and Edward Gordon Craig.[81] Dance also became a favourite subject for silent film pioneers, and some of the earliest films recorded by the Lumière brothers captured the performances of the skirt dancers who took Paris by storm in the 1890s.

Although there is a strong critical tradition pertaining to modernism and the body, dance has long been a neglected aspect of modernist studies. This is in spite of the many exchanges that occurred between artists of various disciplines as a result of modernism's collaborative spirit, reflected in the accounts of non-textual forms such as music, film and painting by scholars in the field.[82] A number of recent studies have sought, speaking more broadly, to rethink modernism's vexed relationship with the body in terms of acting techniques and body training methods, philosophies of movement and systems of notation.[83] 'The battle between the word and the body', Olga Taxidou argues in her landmark study *Modernism and Performance*, 'is primarily fought through and on the body of the modernist performer.' 'The category of dance', she later suggests, 'is crucial in most debates about the efficacy of the poetic word on stage and its relationship to the actor.'[84] Locating the body's expressive power in its precisely orchestrated or seemingly spontaneous movements, dance gave artists a means of challenging the (often gendered) Cartesian hierarchy of mind and body, forming new interplays between written and corporeal languages in dramatic performance. With these interplays in view, Amy Koritz's *Gendering Bodies/Performing Art* forges crucial dialogues between dance history in England and early twentieth-century drama, arguing that the marginalisation of dance in academic circles has stemmed from its characterisation as a 'feminine' art form. She places dancers including Isadora Duncan and Maud Allan at the heart of the period's performance cultures, while showing how a critical reluctance to recognise the creative input of female dancers often led to them being denied authorial status in relation to their art.[85] Beyond this important intervention, although dance was occasionally discussed in relation to broader assessments of twentieth-century performance, the rich reciprocal connections between literary modernism and choreography were not explored in full until the publication of Susan Jones's *Literature, Modernism and Dance*. My own work is indebted to Jones's illuminating evaluation of the ties formed between these arts in the twentieth century, which reveals how extensively modernist approaches to language, gender and embodiment were shaped by the formal and aesthetic practices of dancers. This book has also been informed by the larger claim her study makes: that we can learn much about dance and literature by reconfiguring the traditional hierarchies governing the arts, which in turn will allow for the emergence of new cultural histories.[86]

As a figure whose history is inseparable from her dance, Salome has received considerable attention from scholars interested in the crossovers between dance and other art forms.[87] Frank Kermode described Salome as 'an emblem of the perfect work of art' in his important study *Romantic Image*, demonstrating her significance as a symbolic device for poets such as Yeats and Mallarmé, both of whom engaged substantially with the dance cultures of their day. Focusing on imagery rather than performance, Kermode employs the particular emblems of 'dancer' and 'tree' as analogies for the self-contained, 'self-begotten' unity of the poetic image and the 'organic' life of the work of art in romantic doctrine, which he follows through to the late nineteenth and twentieth centuries.[88] His choice of images, crystallising in the famous final stanza of Yeats's 'Among School Children', aligns quite specifically with the pathos formula informing the outlook of the present study, though Kermode does not trace the Yeatsian Salome dancer back to the Greek model. In Ovid's version of 'The Death of Orpheus', Dionysus, regretting the bard's murder, punishes the dancing maenads by transforming them into trees: 'He fastened in the woods by twisting roots / All the women who had seen that wickedness, / Each at the place of her pursuit, their toes / Drawn down to points forced deep in the firm soil'.[89] The head-hunting maenads, who ghost later versions of this feminine type in Salome and Judith, might thus be read as embodying the dynamic tensions at the heart of Kermode's conceptualisation of the Image as it manifests in the work of poets such as Yeats, for whom the Image must be 'all movement, yet with a kind of stillness'.[90] This is certainly a tension that underwrites Warburg's theory of images and their capacity to bear dynamic energies; as Agamben writes of the Nympha, '[she] is always already in the process of dividing herself according to her opposed polarities – at once too alive and too inanimate – while the poet no longer succeeds in granting her a unified existence'.[91]

Although Kermode's work has been rightly influential for other accounts of Salome, his reading of her as an 'impassive' figure – contained by the poet's symbolic order and largely divorced from the realities of performance – risks erasing the creative industry of the many women who interpreted her dance on their own terms. It is the poet's language, Kermode claims, that resolves the tension between fixity and motion embodied by the dancing woman; 'The beauty [. . .] of a woman in movement', he writes, 'is the emblem of the work of art or Image.'[92] This translation from choreographic movement to still image seems to hinge on a form of conceptual ossification that fixes the female body into an emblem. Rosi Braidotti warns of 'the mental habit of translating women into metaphor', arguing further that 'the valorisation of woman as textual body' conceals a formidable kind of prejudice against female creative autonomy.[93] Symbolism, despite its celebration of dance, often rested on this form of translation; as Koritz observes, the language of Symbolism 'enabled a separation of a dance from the aesthetically suspect materiality of the dancer's body', ultimately permitting 'the marginalization of the performer and the containment of the female body'.[94] Salome's role as a Symbolist muse clearly forms a crucial part of her history, but I place this aspect in dialogue with the interventions of the performers and choreographers who communicated primarily through the moving language of dance or in written commentaries on their practice.

Grounded though it is in the methods and debates of literary criticism, this book makes a consistent effort to discuss dance on its own terms, rather than using it simply as a lens through which to understand modernist texts. A valuable framework for bridging the different vocabularies of literature and dance is provided by Brandstetter, who contends that the revolutionary methods of modern dance – specifically early twentieth-century 'free dance' (*freier Tanz*)

– were linked to similar 'ruptures' signalled by the programmes of literary modernism and the historical avant-garde, revolving around the instability of the modern subject.[95] The very notion of the 'dance work' also became precarious during this period, as solo dancer-choreographers such as Fuller, Duncan and Allan largely disavowed the documentation or notation of their dances, and prioritised concepts of 'natural' movement and spontaneity, writing about their practice with a kind of expressive lyricism, rather than committing to the more systematised vocabularies of ballet.[96] At the same time, there exists a wealth of peripheral material contextualising their performances, including reviews, film recordings, illustrations, memoirs, interviews, photographs, and poetic and fictional responses, all of which I call upon in the chapters that follow, since such materials provide crucial evidence of the ways in which dance permeated broader literary and cultural discourses. Following Brandstetter, this study does not attempt to intervene in debates about dance reconstruction, but engages instead with the 'visual paradigms' of choreographic modernism, tracing the evolutions of a particular type of bodily imagery and its realisation in performance, which Salome embodies most explicitly.[97]

In part, this research takes its lead from the approaches to Salome's dance explored through the lens of feminist performance.[98] In a chapter on Salome dancers in her study *Female Spectacle*, Susan Glenn stresses that most critics 'miss Salome's transformation into a pliant figure of entertainment', and she opens up the marginalised histories of female (and male drag) performers dancing as Salome on the early twentieth-century stage.[99] Similarly, Mary Simonson argues that, unlike literary texts, 'performance offers a site of resistance and female authorship' that undermines the conventional treatment of 'Salome's dance as a phantom-like, mystical "truth"'.[100] Although these accounts of Salome's dance have clarified the importance of performance to feminist readings of this dancer, I make a consistent effort to complicate Simonson's contention that the literary tradition formed around Salome does not 'seem to allow any feminist wiggle room'.[101] Rather, the works that this book considers reveal a series of complex engagements between writers and performers, through which dancers were able to assert their corporeal agency within texts, inform the shape of dramatic material, and recalibrate the hierarchy of author and actor.

Salome dances at the centre of these conflicting approaches to choreographic performance and female creativity. Her 'dance of the seven veils' is most often read as a kind of striptease; indeed, the symbol of the veil appears to demarcate a porous boundary between the naked female body and the gaze of the spectator, though this is a boundary in perpetual movement. The fine line between revelation and concealment structures and defines her dance: as Roland Barthes writes in *The Pleasure of the Text*, 'Is not the most erotic portion of the body *where the garment gapes?*'[102] While one reading of Salome's veils might have her dancing form reduced to an object of male desire, the veils also create a space cut off from the spectator's gaze into which the dancer can retreat, suggesting a position from which the performer might both engineer the dance and assert control of her body. It was this zone of (in)visibility that appealed most strongly to her modernist interpreters, and Sally Banes argues that dance has the power to facilitate precisely this kind of feminist reckoning: 'through dance, men's attitudes toward women and women's attitudes about themselves are literally given body on stage'.[103] Salome's dance might seem to be rooted in the sensual allure of the body, in libidinous female nature submitting to the demands of a masculine authority, but Salome crucially asks for something in return: her dance compels Herod into an irrational exchange, and she obtains, through her performance, the broken body of the man she desires. While Herod wins only the fleeting pleasure of her dance, Salome secures a capital prize: the severed head, with its long cultural and historical lineage, comes to signify a rupture in the political order of the state, the destabilising of patriarchal integrity and the violent feminine conquest of the male form. In what follows, I seek to recover these sites of ambivalent seduction and exchange, mapping the transformation of a persuasive myth across its moving modernist forms.

The first chapter examines how the Salome theme infiltrated the sphere of modern dance, focusing on the careers of the American performer Loïe Fuller and her one-time pupil Maud Allan, both of whom gained fame in the theatres of Europe for their very different solo performances and their interpretations of Salome. Interrogating Rancière's reading of Fuller's dancing body as 'unlocatable' beneath her diaphanous veils, I explore how Fuller's orchestration of her own corporeal absence critically influenced literary uses of dance, especially in the output of the Symbolist movement, considered here through the work of Stéphane Mallarmé, Georges Rodenbach and Jean Lorrain. Through my discussion of Fuller's early performances at the Folies Bergère and her two specific 'Salome' dances, I show how she cultivated a movement aesthetics based on the serpentine line – theorised as a 'line of beauty' by William Hogarth and Edmund Burke – that encapsulated both the philhellenism of modern dance and an emergent modernist kinaesthetics of torsion, as conceptualised in the work of Hillel Schwartz. This chapter then considers how these strategies were reformulated in Allan's more controversial and conspicuously erotic *Vision of Salome* (1907), arguing that Fuller and Allan shared a feminist interest in the individualism of the solo performer, both adopting the *fin-de-siècle* stage actress Sarah Bernhardt as a crucial model. In these very different modernist 'dances of veils', the flowing textiles and whirling motions of Warburg's Nympha – 'a pagan goddess in exile' – were deployed to reinvent the Salome myth as a source of creative individualism and feminist emancipatory possibility, at once evading and clarifying early twentieth-century anxieties about the moving female body and its disruptive gestures.

Returning to the *fin de siècle*, Chapter 2 considers how Wilde's play *Salomé*, first performed at the Théâtre de l'Oeuvre in February 1896, was shaped by modern dance practices, body cultures and other late nineteenth-century theories of performance, especially in relation to the concepts of grace and mechanical gesture developed in the work of Heinrich von Kleist, Alfred Jarry and Maurice Maeterlinck. Following his French precursors, Wilde stressed Salome's role as the passive object of the aesthete's gaze, while paradoxically imagining his heroine's capacity for bodily agency, erotic transgression and disturbing violence. Although *Salomé* is often read as reproducing concealed signals of male homosexual longing and pejorative nineteenth-century tropes of femininity, such as the *femme fatale*, this chapter closely analyses Wilde's play in order to highlight a rhetoric of bodily absence that replicates, through its ardent assertions of linguistic hollowness, the absent centre particular to Fuller's veiled performances. Wilde's description of Salome's 'invisible dance' in a note to his illustrator Aubrey Beardsley therefore signals both the idiosyncratic queerness of his Salome figure and her connections to the movement aesthetics of modern dance. I show how Wilde's depiction of this dancer was further grounded in his evolving ideas about women's dress and social reform, evidenced through his work at the late Victorian magazine *Woman's World* and his celebration of stage actors such as Bernhardt and Ellen Terry. Through exploring Bernhardt's ultimately frustrated attempt to play Salome, and the possibilities Wilde imagined for her dance, this chapter demonstrates how *Salomé* contributed to the radical corporeal language of the woman-in-movement, later realised in Ida Rubinstein's famous staging of the play in St Petersburg (1908). Deploying her abilities in mime to evade the Russian censors, Rubinstein transformed Wilde's unuttered text into the 'invisible' axis of the performance, using her body as an instrument of textual as well as corporeal meaning.

In Chapter 3, I examine how modernist choreographic forms intersected with the development of silent film in both Hollywood and France, analysing the emergence of new grammars of movement theorised in 1920s cinematic discourse. This chapter shows how popular conceptions of the celebrated Russian performer Alla Nazimova – once the highest-paid actress in Hollywood – were shaped by the categories of exotic and kinetic femininity that similarly defined Salome's representations in the Symbolist and Art Nouveau movements, suggesting a connection that Nazimova would make explicit in her own queer avant-garde screen adaptation of Wilde's play, *Salomé: An Historical Phantasy by Oscar Wilde* (1922), which drew too on the aesthetics of ballet modernism, especially the Ballets Russes' *La Tragédie de Salomé* (1913). Nazimova was one of many prominent actors and dancers interviewed by the modernist writer Djuna Barnes, whose encounters with Salome performers – including Nazimova and Mimi Aguglia – are read closely in this chapter, with a focus on Barnes's satirical deconstruction of female celebrity and her neo-decadent revision of Salome's dance in the short story, 'What Do You See, Madam?' (1915). I argue that the points of contact between these women, and their different renderings of this particular dance, collude in the formation of a feminine modernist aesthetic that extends back to Fuller, whose 'harmonies of light' offered a blueprint of cinematographic movement to the French film-maker Germaine Dulac. A pioneer of women's experimental film-making in her native France, Dulac was crucially influenced by the bodily techniques of performers such as Nazimova, Rubinstein, Fuller and Stasia Napierkowska, all of whom danced as Salome. As this chapter shows, Nazimova's 'serpentine weavings' and the 'leaping line' of Dulac's 'cineographic expression' offer filmic realisations of Fuller's signature kinaesthetic, described by Dulac, in terms resonant of Mallarmé and Wilde, as *'un corps invisible'*.

Chapter 4 turns to the place of dance in W. B. Yeats's poetry and work for the theatre, tracing Yeats's long-standing interest in Salome through two case studies: the dance-dramas *At the Hawk's Well* (1916) and *The King of the Great Clock Tower* (1934). Reflecting on his youthful engagement with the Symbolist poetics of Mallarmé, Verlaine and other *fin-de-siècle* writers, Yeats articulated his own desire to create 'some Herodiade of our theatre', an ambition, I argue, that focused his attempts to integrate components of dance into his works for the Irish dramatic movement, even in early plays such as *Deirdre* (1907). These choreographic inclinations were not satisfied in isolation: Yeats's various negotiations with dance were indebted to the concepts of the modernist theatre practitioner Edward Gordon Craig and, furthermore, brought him into close contact with the dancers Michio Ito and Ninette de Valois, with whom he collaborated on productions of his plays for dancers. The input of these dancers, who emerged from rather different trans-national training systems and performance traditions, shaped both the 'ideal' image of the dancer that Yeats revered and also the realisation of these plays as performance texts. For Yeats, as this chapter shows, Salome's dance was not merely reducible to the contexts of Symbolism, or classical images of Greek head-hunters, but was also embedded in the Irish national mythology that so crucially undergirded his experimental stage-texts. Aligned with the spectral legendary figures of the *Sidhe*, Salome is transfigured, across Yeats's oeuvre, into a source of disruptive erotic and political energies, embodying his own ambivalent responses to Irish cultural nationalism in his last play, *The Death of Cuchulain* (1939).

Finally, in an epilogue, I consider how the choreographic forms and images constellated around Salome's dance were both absorbed and radically reconfigured by the late modernist Irish playwright Samuel Beckett. Salome persists as a trace in Beckett's texts; her myth – in its many varied and altered contexts – reached Beckett through a range of sources, from the Yeatsian dance-dramas that he saw at the Abbey Theatre in the 1930s, to poems by Mallarmé and Guillaume Apollinaire that he read with interest. He told his biographer James Knowlson that his late play *Not I* (1972) was inspired by one of Caravaggio's vivid pictorial responses to the Salome myth, *The Decollation of St John the Baptist*, which he saw on a trip to Malta. Scattered and disparate though they may be, these traces nonetheless point to Beckett's deeper absorption of this paradigmatic modernist dance as a 'metamorphic phantom' that he would harness to the demands of his own theatre. If his late nineteenth- and early twentieth-century precursors imagined the modernist dancer to be 'invisible' beneath her veils, Beckett at once deconstructed and paradoxically re-embodied this dancer in his abstract stage choreographies, organising his works around dramatically reduced gestures and forms of movement. His stageworld frequently pivots on the very tension between rhythmic continuity and dismemberment that underpins Salome's narrative, rendering it one of the definitive bodily fantasies of the period. This epilogue ultimately reads Beckett's dance play *Quad I + II* as a minimalist and dramatically pared-back manifestation of the pathos formula examined in preceding chapters, stripped of most of its specifying traits and symbols but crucially bearing the same dynamic forces. Beckett therefore provides us with one way of recovering the often-underplayed continuities between late nineteenth-century Symbolism and modernist theatre at its most abstract, showing how the forms associated with Salome's dance were adopted and transformed in the second half of the twentieth century.

Readers will no doubt call to mind other versions of the Salome dance that are not given prominence in what follows. While productions involving Loïe Fuller, Maud Allan, Ida Rubinstein, Tamara Karsavina and Ninette de Valois are discussed at length, there were other dancers – not considered in this study – who placed Salome at the centre of their choreographic projects, such as Gertrude Hoffmann, a well-known Maud Allan imitator, and the Harlem Renaissance performer Aida Overton Walker, who incorporated a Salome dance into her popular production *Bandanna Land*. Dozens of Salomes moved across the stages of theatres and music halls in the early twentieth century and, while it is not possible to name them all here, other critics have covered much important ground in this respect.[104] In order to retain a sense of specificity and conceptual clarity in the following chapters – as well as imposing necessary limits on the number of case studies – I have devoted particular attention to 'scenes' and performance events that sit at the junctures of literary and choreographic modernisms, making visible the links – collaborative, imaginative and even speculative – between writers and performers in their handling of this particular thematic material. There were, of course, many other significant stage versions of Wilde's text that did much to restore his play to theatrical repertoires on a global scale, including Lindsay Kemp's various reworkings of *Salome* between 1973 and 1984, and Steven Berkoff's *Salome*, first staged at Dublin's Gate Theatre in 1988. While contemporaneous with Beckett's late plays, these productions reorient our Salomean lore around the similarly mythologised person of Oscar Wilde, a rhetorical custom that this book attempts both to accommodate and complicate from the outset. Focusing attention on the figure of Herod, and making the legacy of Wilde's sexuality the source of the play's spectacular appeal, these stage versions take us away from the dancer herself, especially as she might be understood within the particular contexts of modernism and its vital nexus of bodily concerns, around which Beckett's drama continued to orbit.

It has certainly not been my aim to catalogue every one of Salome's appearances in late nineteenth- and twentieth-century literature, art and performance; indeed, such a project would be both methodologically unwieldy and, in practical terms, impossible, since her manifestations during this period are so numerous and, in many instances, tethered only loosely to the 'original' myth and therefore difficult to pin down. In any case, it is these latter versions that become of interest in the closing chapters of this project, as I turn to the work of Yeats and Beckett in order to understand how the dynamic visual and spatial components of experimental theatre reconfigure the elemental forms of this modernist dance of veils, in which Salome herself becomes an increasingly ghostly and elusive antecedent. When Vladimir, one of the protagonists in Beckett's best-known play *Waiting for Godot* (1953), is affected by the sight of Lucky's dance, he is strikingly described as 'squirming like an aesthete' (*CDW*, 39), providing evidence of a sensory receptiveness grounded in a form of kinaesthetic empathy. The specificity of Beckett's comparison frames this involuntary movement as a diminished repetition of a decadent gesture, recalling the 'hidden nerve' of Wilde's aesthete Dorian Gray who feels 'each delicate fibre of his nature quiver' before his portrait.[105]

It is through this language of the body – of gesture, movement and dance – that the imaginative energies focused around Salome migrate across the texts and performances considered in this book, suggesting resonances not only between *fin-de-siècle* aesthetic movements and early twentieth-century modernism at its zenith, but also between modernist performance in its formative and later stages, thus complicating the narratives of breakage or rupture that have become increasingly subject to scrutiny in the field. Calling attention to the long afterlife of the *fin de siècle* in modernist writing and performance, *Modernism and the Choreographic Imagination* thus aims to contribute to ongoing efforts to dismantle the aesthetic and sexual hierarchies that once governed our histories of modernism, showing how this subtle dancer and her many interpreters produced a web of unexpected but enduring connections between literature and dance, pioneered by the women who adopted her as a powerful modern muse.

Notes

1. David Edgar Rice, 'Why Danger Lurks in Nimble Toes of Dancing Stage Beauties', *Washington Post*, 15 March 1914.
2. Ibid.
3. Ibid.
4. Ibid.
5. Françoise Meltzer, *Salome and the Dance of Writing: Portraits of Mimesis in Literature* (Chicago: University of Chicago Press, 1987), 2.
6. Matthew 14:1–12; Mark 6:14–29; Flavius Josephus, 'Jewish Antiquities: Book XVIII, Chapter VIII', in *The Genuine Works of Flavius Josephus* (Birmingham: Christopher Earl, 1770), 604–5, Gale Eighteenth Century Collections Online.
7. Alice Bach, *Women, Seduction, and Betrayal in Biblical Narrative* (Cambridge: Cambridge University Press, 1997), 227.
8. Megan Becker-Leckrone, 'Salome: The Fetishization of a Textual Corpus', *New Literary History* 26.2 (1995): 244.
9. Ibid., 250–1. Anthony Pym has also explicated the difficulties of defining a Salome canon in 'The Importance of Salomé: Approaches to a *Fin de Siècle* Theme', *French Forum* 14 (September 1989): 311–22. Becker-Leckrone rightly takes issue, however, with Pym's clear 'privileging [. . .] of texts that turn the whole "theme" into an exchange between men, where the body of the woman is valued by men, and the woman at the heart of the story is ultimately displaced' ('Salome', 246–7).
10. For discussion of Salome and the construction of the *femme fatale*, see Jess Sully, 'Challenging the Stereotype: The *Femme Fatale* in *Fin-de-siècle* Art and Early Cinema', in *The Femme Fatale: Images, Histories, Contexts*, ed. H. Hanson and C. O'Rawe (Basingstoke: Palgrave Macmillan, 2010), 46–59. See also Rebecca Stott, *The Fabrication of the Late-Victorian Femme Fatale: The Kiss of Death* (Basingstoke: Palgrave Macmillan, 1992).
11. Said also refers to Salome specifically as typifying the sensuous, dangerous womanhood that fascinated writers such as Flaubert, Swinburne and Baudelaire, shaping their perception of 'the Orient'; Edward W. Said, *Orientalism* (London: Penguin, 2003), 180. See also Peter Wollen, 'Fashion/Orientalism/The Body', *New Formations* 1 (1987): 5–33.
12. Vincent Sherry, *Modernism and the Reinvention of Decadence* (Cambridge: Cambridge University Press, 2015), 7.
13. Bram Dijkstra, *Idols of Perversity: Fantasies of Feminine Evil in Fin-de-Siècle Culture* (Oxford: Oxford University Press, 1989), 352–402.
14. Peter Gay, *Education of the Senses: The Bourgeois Experience: Victoria to Freud* (New York: W. W. Norton, 1999), 201.
15. Stéphane Mallarmé, 'Herodiade', trans. David Lenson, *The Massachusetts Review* 30.4 (1989): 586.
16. Along with Anthony Pym and Megan Becker-Leckrone's articles, these nineteenth-century literary and artistic versions of Salome have been catalogued in a number of earlier studies including Helen Zagona, *The Legend of Salome and the Principle of Art for Art's Sake* (Geneva: Droz, 1960); Mario Praz, *The Romantic Agony*, trans. Angus Davidson (New York: Meridian, 1956).
17. As Praz notes, Heinrich Heine also had his Herodias kiss the head of John the Baptist in *Atta Troll* (1843), but this poem crucially conflates the desires of mother and daughter and makes Herodias the key figure. See *The Romantic Agony*, 299–302.

18. Richard Bizot, 'The Turn-of-the-Century Salome Era: High- and Pop-Culture Variations on the Dance of the Seven Veils', *Choreography and Dance* 2 (1992): 71–87.
19. A number of scholars have compared Strauss's treatment of the Salome theme to other versions; see, for example, Lawrence Kramer, 'Culture and Musical Hermeneutics: The Salome Complex', *The Cambridge Opera Journal* 2 (1990): 269–94; Petra Dierkes-Thrun, '"The Brutal Music and the Delicate Text?": The Aesthetic Relationship between Wilde's and Strauss's *Salome* Reconsidered', *Modern Language Quarterly* 69.3 (2008): 367–89.
20. John Berryman, 'The Song of the Demented Priest', in *The Heart is Strange: New Selected Poems* (New York: Farrar, Straus and Giroux, 2014), 28. Beckett commented to Avigdor Arikha and James Knowlson that *Not I* was inspired by the Caravaggio painting he saw in Malta; see Knowlson, *Damned to Fame: The Life of Samuel Beckett* (London: Bloomsbury, 1996), 588.
21. Jorie Graham, quoted in Thomas Gardner, 'An Interview with Jorie Graham', in *Regions of Unlikeness: Explaining Contemporary Poetry* (Lincoln, NE: University of Nebraska Press, 1999), 217–18.
22. Petra Dierkes-Thrun, *Salome's Modernity: Oscar Wilde and the Aesthetics of Transgression* (Ann Arbor, MI: University of Michigan Press, 2011), 2.
23. Anne-Gaëlle Saliot, *The Drowned Muse: The Unknown Woman of the Seine's Survivals from Nineteenth-century Modernity to the Present* (Oxford: Oxford University Press, 2015), 27–8.
24. Ibid., 24–5.
25. Friedrich Nietzsche, *Twilight of the Idols and The Anti-Christ*, trans. R. J. Hollingdale (London: Penguin, 1990), 76–7.
26. Friedrich Nietzsche, *The Birth of Tragedy: Out of the Spirit of Music*, trans. Shaun Whiteside (London: Penguin, 1993), 21.
27. Gabriele Brandstetter, *Poetics of Dance: Body, Image, and Space in the Historical Avant-Gardes*, trans. Elena Polzer and Mark Franko (Oxford: Oxford University Press, 2015), 53.
28. Nietzsche, *The Birth of Tragedy*, 21.
29. Maurice Blanchot, 'The Gaze of Orpheus', in *The Gaze of Orpheus and Other Literary Essays*, trans. Lydia Davis (New York: Station Hill, 1981).
30. Ibid., 99.
31. Ibid., 100.
32. Karen Jacobs, 'Two Mirrors Facing: Freud, Blanchot, and the Logic of Invisibility', *Qui Parle* 4.1 (1990): 35.
33. Ibid., 35.
34. For a discussion of this subject, see Jeffrey L. Buller, 'Looking Backwards: Baroque Opera and the Ending of the Orpheus Myth', *International Journal of the Classical Tradition* 1.3 (1995): 57–79.
35. Aby Warburg, 'Dürer and Italian Antiquity', in *The Renewal of Pagan Antiquity: Contributions to the Cultural History of the European Renaissance*, trans. David Britt (Los Angeles: Getty Research Institute, 1999), 553.
36. Georges Didi-Huberman, *The Surviving Image: Phantoms of Time and Time of Phantoms: Aby Warburg's History of Art*, trans. Harvey L. Mendelsohn (Philadelphia: Pennsylvania State University Press, 2017), 117.
37. Ibid., 105.
38. Aby Warburg, 'The Absorption of the Expressive Values of the Past (Introduction to the *Mnemosyne Atlas*)', trans. Matthew Rampley, *Art in Translation* 1.2 (2009): 278.
39. Warburg, quoted in Didi-Huberman, *The Surviving Image*, 106.

40. André Jolles, quoted in E. H. Gombrich, *Aby Warburg: An Intellectual Biography* (Oxford: Phaidon, 1986), 107.
41. Warburg, quoted in ibid., 287.
42. Warburg, 'The Absorption of the Expressive Values of the Past', 281.
43. Giorgio Agamben, 'What is a Paradigm?', in *The Signature of All Things: On Method*, trans. Luca D'Isanto with Kevin Attell (New York: Zone Books, 2009), 29.
44. Ibid., 29.
45. Ibid., 31.
46. Didi-Huberman, *The Surviving Image*, 110.
47. Warburg, 'On *Imprese Amorose* in the Earliest Florentine Engravings' (1905), in *The Renewal of Pagan Antiquity*, 174.
48. Brandstetter, *Poetics of Dance*, 41.
49. Ibid., 17–18.
50. Ibid., 97.
51. Warburg, 'The Theatrical Costumes for the Intermedi of 1589' (1895), in *The Renewal of Pagan Antiquity*, 381.
52. Gombrich, *Aby Warburg*, 110.
53. Didi-Huberman, *The Surviving Image*, 163.
54. Ibid., 166.
55. Walter A. Strauss, *Descent and Return: The Orphic Theme in Modern Literature* (Cambridge, MA: Harvard University Press, 1971).
56. Clair Rowden, 'Whose/Who's Salome? Natalia Trouhanowa, a Dancing Diva', in *Performing Salome, Revealing Stories*, ed. Clair Rowden (Farnham: Ashgate, 2013), 91.
57. Gustave Flaubert, 'Herodias', in *Three Tales*, trans. A. J. Krailsheimer (Oxford: Oxford University Press, 1991), 103.
58. Brandstetter, *Poetics of Dance*, 184.
59. Giorgio Agamben, 'Notes on Gesture', in *Infancy and History: The Destruction of Experience*, trans. Liz Heron (London: Verso, 1993), 137.
60. Ibid., 138.
61. Henri Bergson, *Time and Free Will: An Essay on the Immediate Data of Consciousness*, trans. F. L. Pogson (Mineola, NY: Dover Publications, 2001), 12.
62. Ibid., 12.
63. Mark Franko, *Dancing Modernism/Performing Politics* (Bloomington, IN: Indiana University Press, 1995), 9–10.
64. Rita Felski, *The Gender of Modernity* (Cambridge, MA: Harvard University Press, 1995), 19–20.
65. A full discussion of these different regimes can also be found in Jacques Rancière, *Aesthetics and its Discontents*, trans. Steven Corcoran (Cambridge: Polity, 2009).
66. Jacques Rancière, *Aisthesis: Scenes from the Aesthetic Regime of Art*, trans. Zakir Paul (London: Verso, 2013), x–xi.
67. Ibid., xii.
68. Rancière, *Aesthetics and its Discontents*, 10.
69. Rancière, *Aisthesis*, xiii.
70. Ibid., 96; 100.
71. Daniel Albright, *Panaesthetics: On the Unity and Diversity of the Arts* (New Haven, CT: Yale University Press, 2014), 3–4.
72. Most influential in this regard was Adorno and Horkenheimer's analysis of the 'culture industry' in *Dialectic of Enlightenment* (1944). See Theodor W. Adorno and Max Horkheimer, *Dialectic of Enlightenment: Philosophical Fragments*,

ed. Gunzelin Schmid Noerr, trans. Edmund Jephcott (Stanford, CA: Stanford University Press, 2002), 94–136.
73. Andreas Huyssen, *After the Great Divide: Modernism, Mass Culture and Postmodernism* (Bloomington, IN: Indiana University Press, 1986).
74. Sara Danius, *The Senses of Modernism: Technology, Perception, and Aesthetics* (Ithaca, NY: Cornell University Press, 2002), 7–8.
75. Douglas Mao and Rebecca Walkowitz, 'The New Modernist Studies', *PMLA* 123.3 (2008): 737–48.
76. Laura Marcus, Michèle Mendelssohn and Kirsten E. Shepherd-Barr, eds, 'Introduction', in *Late Victorian into Modern* (Oxford: Oxford University Press, 2016), 1–2.
77. David Bradshaw, Laura Marcus and Rebecca Roach, eds, *Moving Modernisms: Motion, Technology, Modernity* (Oxford: Oxford University Press, 2016).
78. Tim Armstrong, *Modernism, Technology and the Body: A Cultural Study* (Cambridge: Cambridge University Press, 1998), 4–5.
79. Stéphane Mallarmé, 'Autre étude de danse: les fonds dans le ballet d'après une indication recent', in *Igitur, Divagations, Un Coup de dés*, ed. Bertrand Marchal (Paris: Gallimard, 2003), 207.
80. T. S. Eliot, 'A Dialogue on Dramatic Poetry', in *Selected Essays, 1917–1932* (New York: Harcourt, Brace, 1932), 34.
81. See Juliet Bellow, *Modernism on Stage: The Ballets Russes and the Parisian Avant-Garde* (London: Routledge, 2013); Davinia Caddy, *The Ballets Russes and Beyond: Music and Dance in Belle-Époque Paris* (Cambridge: Cambridge University Press, 2012).
82. See, for example, Daniel Albright, *Untwisting the Serpent: Modernism in Music, Literature and Other Arts* (Chicago: University of Chicago Press, 2000); Daniel Albright, ed., *Modernism and Music: An Anthology of Sources* (Chicago: University of Chicago Press, 2003); David Trotter, *Cinema and Modernism* (Oxford: Blackwell, 2007).
83. An important recent example of this work is Carrie J. Preston, *Modernism's Mythic Pose: Gender, Genre, Solo Performance* (Oxford: Oxford University Press, 2011).
84. Olga Taxidou, *Modernism and Performance: Jarry to Brecht* (Basingstoke: Palgrave Macmillan, 2007), 5, 194.
85. Amy Koritz, *Gendering Bodies/Performing Art: Dance and Literature in Early Twentieth-Century Culture* (Ann Arbor, MI: University of Michigan Press, 1995).
86. Susan Jones, *Literature, Modernism and Dance* (Oxford: Oxford University Press, 2013). Earlier work in the field includes Felicia McCarren, *Dancing Machines: Choreographies of the Age of Mechanical Reproduction* (Stanford, CA: Stanford University Press, 2003); Teri A. Mester, *Movement and Modernism: Yeats, Eliot, Lawrence, Williams and Early Twentieth-Century Dance* (Fayetteville, AK: University of Arkansas Press, 1997).
87. See Peter Cooke, 'It Isn't a Dance: Gustave Moreau's *Salome* and *The Apparition*', *Dance Research* 29 (2011): 214–32; Daria Santini, 'That Invisible Dance: Reflections on the "Dance of the Seven Veils" in Richard Strauss's *Salome*', *Dance Research* 29 (2011): 233–45.
88. Frank Kermode, *Romantic Image* (London: Routledge, 2002), 111, 120.
89. Ovid, 'The Death of Orpheus', in *Metamorphoses*, trans. A. D. Melville (Oxford: Oxford University Press, 2008), 251.
90. Kermode, *Romantic Image*, 102.
91. Giorgio Agamben, *Nymphs*, trans. Amanda Minervini (London: Seagull Books, 2013), 52–3.

92. Ibid., 69.
93. Rosi Braidotti, quoted in Teresa de Lauretis, *Technologies of Gender: Essays on Theory, Film and Fiction* (Bloomington, IN: Indiana University Press, 1987), 24; Rosi Braidotti, *Patterns of Dissonance: A Study of Women and Contemporary Philosophy* (Cambridge: Polity, 1991), 134.
94. Koritz, *Gendering Bodies/Performing Art*, 5.
95. Brandstetter, *Poetics of Dance*, 5–7.
96. Ibid., 12.
97. Ibid., 13.
98. Susan A. Glenn, 'The Americanization of Salome: Sexuality, Race, and the Careers of the Vulgar Princess', in *Female Spectacle: The Theatrical Roots of Modern Feminism* (Cambridge, MA: Harvard University Press, 2000), 96–125; Julie Townsend, 'Staking Salomé: The Literary Forefathers and Choreographic Daughters of Oscar Wilde's "Hysterical and Perverted Creature"', in *Oscar Wilde and Modern Culture: The Making of a Legend*, ed. J. Bristow (Athens, OH: Ohio University Press, 2008), 154–79.
99. Glenn, *Female Spectacle*, 97.
100. Mary Simonson, 'Choreographing Salome: Re-creating the Female Body', in *Body Knowledge: Performance, Intermediality and American Entertainment at the Turn of the Twentieth Century* (Oxford: Oxford University Press, 2013), 28–9.
101. Ibid., 29.
102. Roland Barthes, *The Pleasure of the Text*, trans. Richard Miller (New York: Hill and Wang, 1975), 9.
103. Sally Banes, *Dancing Women: Female Bodies on Stage* (Abingdon: Routledge, 1998), 1.
104. For a discussion of Aida Overton Walker's Salome dance, see David Krasner, *A Beautiful Pageant: African American Theatre, Drama and Performance in the Harlem Renaissance, 1910–1927* (Basingstoke: Palgrave Macmillan, 2002), 63–7. See also Toni Bentley, *Sisters of Salome* (New Haven, CT: Yale University Press, 2002).
105. Oscar Wilde, *The Picture of Dorian Gray*, ed. Joseph Bristow (Oxford: Oxford World's Classics, 2006), 21, 25.

I

'UNLOCATABLE BODIES': MODERNIST VEILED DANCERS FROM LOÏE FULLER TO MAUD ALLAN

When the actor Gwendolen Bishop wrote to enquire about performance rights for the first London production of Oscar Wilde's *Salomé* in May 1905, Wilde's close friend Robert Ross expressed some concerns about the realisation of the late author's dramatic vision. He asked that the group organising the production, the New Stage Club, ensure that 'none of the male parts [...] be taken by a lady' and further requested that the actor playing the role of Salome 'abstain from introducing in the dancing scene anything of the nature of Loïe Fuller's performances'.[1] Ross's scepticism about Loïe Fuller is somewhat surprising in light of the unprecedented success that the dancer in question had achieved throughout the 1890s, not least as a modern interpreter of the Salome myth.[2] A Chicago-born performer with very little formal training, Fuller was rapturously celebrated by French artists and writers of the *fin de siècle*, who saw her luminous serpentine dance as the emblem of an exciting new strain of technological modernity: a Salomean dance of veils for a critical moment of epochal transition. Even prior to the first production of Wilde's *Salomé*, Fuller had placed Salome at the centre of her own creative agenda. From the time of Fuller's arrival in Paris in 1892 until at least the mid-twentieth century, Salome's dance was the subject of numerous reinventions across the spheres of literature, dance, film, music and art, circumscribing the porous boundaries between these different forms with the movements of her veils. Through their dances, and their commentaries on their choreographic practice, Fuller and her peers crucially challenged and redefined conventional methods of representing this biblical figure in the art and literature of their time.

It is now a critical commonplace to note that the course of modern dance was effectively directed by women, including Fuller, Isadora Duncan, and, in America, Ruth St Denis. Referring to their dance practice as 'aesthetic' or 'interpretive', these women did not, for the most part, receive a classical ballet training, but they harboured ambitions to turn their own choreographic creations into 'high art'.[3] Manipulating large diaphanous veils using hand-held poles, Fuller had coloured lights projected on to her continuously moving body, creating a luminous morphology rooted in the evolutions of her dancing form. As Sally Sommer put it in one of the earliest critiques of Fuller's contribution to dance history: 'As light hit the material, it was fractured and diffused by the movement. The effect was one of colour washing, bleeding, running, across a shimmering and iridescent surface.'[4] Moving beneath these billowing materials, Fuller's body was largely hidden from her spectators: it existed at the centre of the serpentine dance as a point of vital yet unsettled energy, constantly slipping in and out of view. The ambiguity of Fuller's presence was heightened by the fact that her dances inspired legions of imitators, many of whom masqueraded as Fuller, adopting both her name and her choreographic style. Not only was Fuller's body a site of visual and rhetorical veiling, inspiring associations with Salome, but there was also doubt as to whether it was even her body at all.

A revolutionary in the world of dance, Fuller's ideas crystallised around the figure of Salome, whose veils she alluded to in her serpentine dance even before she created two specific Salome choreographies in 1895 and 1907. Much as Salome became culturally ubiquitous during this period, Fuller's itinerant body navigated the faultlines between different art forms and disciplines. Rancière has claimed that Fuller's serpentine dance, performed at the Folies Bergère in 1893, invested the human body with powers of artifice that surpassed those of Symbolist poetics, mobilising aesthetic forms that had previously been rendered in the static moulds of paint and clay. Yet he also describes Fuller's body as a problematic element in the choreography, writing of her dance technique:

> It does not reveal the body; it renders it 'unlocatable'. It does not express inner energy; it makes it an instrument fit to draw forms in space through movement, forms that the painter's brush left on the canvas in two dimensions and the sculptor's knife fixed in immobile forms.[5]

This critical register accords with historical reviews of Fuller's dances, often described by journalists as elusive and spectral. Yet in his choice of the word 'unlocatable' [*introuvable*], Rancière displaces the body of the dancing woman in order to convey the apparent ephemerality of her performance, and her body's unstable location within it.[6] Such terminology reflects the subtle rejections of the dancer's gendered bodily form expressed by key theorists of dance including Stéphane Mallarmé, who preferred to emphasise the ungraspable nature of the dance, denying, on some level, the dancer's individual control and bodily power.[7]

Taking the vexed formula of the 'unlocatable body' as a point of departure, this chapter explores Fuller's ability to engineer her own physical displacement, rendering her body a site of imagistic, sexual and material variability beneath her Salomean veils. Influenced by Fuller and other modern dancers, the performer Maud Allan used Salome's dance in a different way to challenge previous incarnations of this figure, and to imagine a space for female spectators in her audience. Considering these dancers within the wider history of modernist performance, I suggest that these 'modern Salomes' constructed veiled dances that privileged the body as a site of creative power, reclaiming the figure of Salome as an artist whose expressive capabilities rested in her movement.[8]

The very idea of the modern, Sally Banes explains, was often gendered as female in the *fin de siècle*, and ambitious dancers such as Fuller carved a space for women as not merely performers but also inventors, who could engage with the vibrant 'new beauty' of electricity, cinema and science.[9] Moreover, the freer, self-directed forms of movement demonstrated by Fuller and her peers engaged with early feminist politics, just as they embraced the aesthetic potential of new styles of performance and stage design. The body of the female head-hunter, represented in these dances, operated as a site of sexual inscrutability in the 1890s and afterwards, suggesting that dancing women, following in this controversial icon's wake, might also unsettle patriarchal and heterosexual conceptions of the female body.

Certainly, scholars have drawn on the methodologies of feminist and queer studies to interpret Fuller's dance technique. Although reviews and profiles tended to emphasise Fuller's apparently chaste disposition, commentators repeatedly observed a disembodied quality to her performances, employing a rhetoric of ghostliness that has often been ascribed to queer women. Even when she stands 'in plain view', Terry Castle reminds us, the queer woman is characterised as 'elusive, vaporous, difficult to spot'.[10] This is certainly true of Fuller, who lived with her female partner Gabrielle Bloch (known professionally as Gab Sorère) for two decades, and yet was commonly portrayed as a cheerful American matron in contemporary profiles, devoid of any allusive erotic life.[11] Fuller's queerness has been read back into the transformative permutations of her dances, while Allan, known for the undisguised eroticism of her *Vision of Salome*, ended her career defending herself against accusations of lesbianism in a trial that combined erotic intrigue and wartime politics.

This chapter foregrounds these selected choreographic engagements with Salome's astonishingly popular myth, showing how modern dancers crucially altered Salomean iconographies and intervened in the shifting genealogy of modernist performance. Reading the important sexual and choreographic interventions staged by these performers alongside Symbolist texts in thrall to the image of the veiled dancer, this chapter traces her evolution as a figure invested with the ambivalent qualities of poetic muse and augury of twentieth-century feminist performance.

Mallarmé's Furious Dancer

Fuller, who is often considered a 'pioneer' or a 'detonator' in the history of modern dance, was also, Rhonda Garelick contends, an 'interlocutor': she formed a point of communication between culturally highbrow forms of dance and the more popular styles of the music hall.[12] During this period, Fuller and her imitators were widely celebrated. Parisians frequenting the city's theatres would see Jules Chéret's colourful posters advertising her performances at the Folies Bergère (Fig. 1.1), and her dances were preserved in paintings and sculptures by Henri de Toulouse-Lautrec and François-Raoul Larche. Diners at French restaurants might even find themselves ordering 'Glace Loïe-Fuller' for dessert: a Fuller-themed ice cream that appeared on a number of menus across the country. As one of the best-known performers on the French stage, Fuller often danced as part of a variety show, delivering her serpentine dance and other routines as turns alongside different acts, such as illusionists and magic lantern shows. The magic lantern itself was an instrument she sometimes used in performances, with her veils acting as a moving screen for the projection of brilliantly rendered images. Perhaps unusually, Fuller's dances were held in high esteem by the French literati as well as the general public: Auguste Rodin and Anatole France considered her a great cultural innovator of the period, and she also inspired Mallarmé to compose a lyrical reflection on her art in 1893, comparing her dancing form to his own creative labours with language.[13]

This was not, however, Mallarmé's first critical response to dance. Writing about Fuller allowed the poet to revisit themes that he had already developed in his influential essay on the 'Ballets' (1886). In this earlier piece, Mallarmé holds up the ballerina Elena Cornalba as a sublime embodiment of poetic expression, describing her performance in the ballet *Les Deux Pigeons* as a form of corporeal writing:

> [T]*he dancer is not a woman dancing*, for these juxtaposed reasons: that *she is not a woman*, but a metaphor summing up one of the elementary aspects of our form: knife, goblet, flower, etc., and that *she is not dancing*, but suggesting, through the miracle of bends and leaps, a kind of corporeal writing, what it would take pages of prose, dialogue, and description to express, if it were transcribed: a poem independent of any scribal apparatus.[14]

1.1 Jules Chéret, *Folies Bergère, La Loïe Fuller* (1893). Bibliothèque nationale de France

For Mallarmé, the dancer's punctuated movements work like an inscription, tracing the course of the body through space in a manner analogous to language. Quoting from this passage, Jones has argued that Mallarmé 'shifts the aesthetics of dance away from a purely mimetic tradition, emphasising instead the creative input of the dancer who "suggests" form as she moves'.[15] It is difficult to reconcile this reading entirely with Mallarmé's subtle eclipsing of the dancer's creative authorship within her chosen discipline: he describes the dancing figure as an 'unlettered ballerina', and later asserts, using Salomean imagery, that 'she hastily delivers up, through the ultimate veil that always remains, the nudity of your concepts, and writes your vision silently like a sign, which she is'.[16] The dancer, then, works as an 'unconscious' mirror for the creative vision of the poet-spectator, returning his 'concepts' through her symbolic performance. Although Mallarmé places the poet in a position of 'submissive' worship before the dancer, he insists upon the poet's ability to read the dance through 'the Flower *of [his] poetic instinct*', whereas the dancer remains 'unlettered', diminished within a body–intellect paradigm that aligns women with purely sensual or physical concerns.[17]

The body of the female dancer recurs in Mallarmé's work, according to Dee Reynolds, as a 'focal point for contradictions and paradoxes in myths of femininity' that persisted across French literature and culture.[18] Several years after penning his influential statement on Elena Cornalba, Mallarmé attended one of Fuller's performances at the Folies Bergère and, entranced by what he witnessed, recorded his impressions in prose. This later essay offers a sustained exploration of Mallarmé's changing approach to the relationship between literary and choreographic aesthetics.[19] Although he presents a modern dancer, rather than a ballerina, as the epitome of Symbolist form, Mallarmé again suggests that Fuller's performance surpasses the effects of verse:

> To protest that this dazzling illuminate satisfies a pensive delicacy like that attained, for example, by the reading of verse, shows one's ignorance of the subtleties included in the mysteries of Dance. A fully restored aesthetic will surpass the notes scribbled in haste, where, at least, I denounce, taking a closer look, an error common to any staging: aided as I am, unexpectedly, by the sudden solution given by my muse with a tiny shiver of her dress, my almost unconscious, or not voluntarily in question here, inspiration.[20]

Fuller's body elides stable descriptors, moving in and around traditional conceptions of gender, performance and language. Frank Kermode contends that Fuller's dance, as Mallarmé understands it, 'is more perfectly devoid of ideas, less hampered by its means, than poetry [...] yet it is not absolutely pure; the dancer is not inhuman'.[21] This response invokes the aesthetic judgements conferred upon female bodies by Symbolist writers who commonly associated women with nature, pleasure and feeling, as opposed to masculine reason or logic. Indeed, Mallarmé reaches for literary tropes to anchor Fuller in an aesthetic tradition privileging the inspired vision of the writer, interpreting the female body as an art object. The notion of dance as a 'mystery' serves a vital purpose as it shrouds the performer in rhetorical uncertainty, proffering instead a vagueness that obscures the specificity of the dancer's technique and her artistic agency. Although he professes to resist the lure of analogy, the arts of poetry and dance are deeply interconnected in Mallarmé's writing, and he ultimately reads Loïe Fuller as his 'muse' in relation to his own imaginative impulses.

In this sense, as Felicia McCarren observes, Mallarmé's critique performs a 'simultaneous idealization of the dance and dehumanization of the dancer'.[22] Mallarmé's descriptions of Fuller show him reaching for appropriate metaphors that are never far away from paradox, repeatedly illustrating the limits of language when it is placed at the service of dance. At one point, Fuller 'appears, like a snowflake', delicate and impermanent, yet quickly transforms into 'the furious dancer', enlivened with a seething tangibility.[23] The thought of a snowflake turned to sudden violence is jarring, as are Mallarmé's comments on Fuller's curiously fragile and chilling radiance: 'In the terrible cascade of cloth, the figure swoons, radiant, cold.'[24] What emerges from this essay is a sense of the difficulty Mallarmé experienced as a spectator (and a poet) in attempting to articulate his thinking about the body of the dancer in prose. Resistant to stable meanings, Fuller dances, according to Julie Townsend, outside traditional conceptions of performance and its 'available categories'.[25] For Mallarmé, the movements of Fuller's veils and the gestures of her body both 'clear' and 'instate' the stage, sweeping away the tired modes of mimetic drama and creating an art that is 'all movement' and 'pure' expression.[26] Dance is here construed as both the destruction of an old aesthetic order and the building of a new one, importantly represented by the movements of the veil.

Fuller's dance offered poets a 'new idea of fiction', changing the conditions of art and its forms of expression, rooting meaning in the body and in its movements through space.[27] Intriguingly, Mallarmé imagines the stage beneath the dancer's feet as another body, possessed of a 'spatial virginity', which Fuller alone handles and 'make[s] flower'.[28] The presentation of the stage as a body of warm flesh awaiting attention and of Fuller as a life-bringing force disrupts the writer's earlier portrayal of the dancer as his muse, or as a mere symbol awaiting the poet's creative interpretation. Here, Fuller is the master of the space surrounding her: her dance enlivens the static, untouched body of the theatre, making it blossom through her physical presence. Although Mallarmé does not allow Fuller to emerge completely from her metaphorical trappings – she remains a simile, a 'figure' – he does imagine her as a creative, rejuvenating force who breathes life into the inert form of the stage. Bringing a warm blush to the 'virginal' site beneath her feet, she is also ambivalently gendered, stimulating the ground with her 'hard [. . .] points', as she 'build[s]' and 'make[s]' art, 'instituting a place'.[29]

This contradictory account reflects the oppositional impulses associated with the concept of a veiled dance in many late nineteenth-century texts. Mallarmé briefly imagines Fuller's body to be nude, slowly revealed by the gradual 'peeling away' of veils, but at the core of her dance, where her body should be, there emerges only 'a central nothingness, all volition'.[30] It is as if her body has been emptied of its animating force, leaving it 'dead' and inert at the centre, while the dance happens *around* it, bestowing her energy upon the space of the stage and creating a new fiction outside the parameters of the body. It is, however, the body of the woman that remains ambiguous in Mallarmé's text: where Fuller is given physical meaning, it is through a language that frames her as a virile creator enlivening the virginal body of the stage. There is a queerness to her artistry as she is reconceived by Mallarmé in masculine terms, commanding her space in an act of erotic conquest. Yet as a dancing woman, she is also a muse, a 'naked statue' and a 'dead' centre, whose powerful form remains a source of bewilderment for the poet. Mallarmé's response to Fuller shows that her body continued to be a knotty problem at the heart of his critical appreciation of dance. His writing demonstrates a reluctance to admit to the physical might of the modern dancer, who is both the creator and the object of her art.

Elsewhere in his critical writings, however, Mallarmé encouraged his contemporaries to see the imaginative potential of dance and its value as a model for literary praxis. In another brief essay, he praised the work of the Belgian Symbolist poet Georges Rodenbach using choreographic analogies, comparing Rodenbach's writing to the 'gauze' of the dancer's costume: 'he gathers, lengthens, and creases the cloth, holds it out like living folds'.[31] Rodenbach's Symbolist idiom is here aligned with the luminous materials expertly animated by Loïe Fuller and also, more widely, with the image of the veiled dancer that had recently taken centre stage in paintings of Salome by Henri Regnault and Gustave Moreau at the annual salon of the Académie des Beaux-Arts. Using choreographic imagery to furnish his critique of Rodenbach, Mallarmé subtly reverses the terms of the analogy between text and performance posed in his essays on Fuller and Elena Cornalba. In doing so, he apprehends the qualities of dance as they emerge from the eloquent forms of the writing in question, arguing for a dance of language to mirror a poetics of movement.[32]

The idea of Fuller as an 'unlocatable' dancer in fact originally came from Rodenbach, who used the term *introuvable* to describe Fuller's dance in an article for Le Figaro in May 1895.[33] For Rodenbach, the figure of the dancer clearly held magnetic promise as a literary subject, although he also dealt in the sinister and misogynistic archetypes that fed the late nineteenth-century visual iconography of dancing maenads and 'head-hunters' like Salome. In Rodenbach's largely neglected Symbolist novel *Bruges la Morte* (1892), the widowed aesthete Hugues Viane becomes enchanted with a dancer who bears an unnerving resemblance to his dead wife, around whose image he has formed an all-consuming cult of grief. The dancer, Jane, initially appears to the protagonist as a spectral Salome, rising into Hugues's hallucinatory vision in 'a blur of white muslin, bridal veils, girls in procession to their first communion'.[34] Similar images of veils appear elsewhere to underline the precarious quality of Hugues's perceptions, and to construct a sense of the dancer's opacity as a projection of his morbid psychology. For Hugues, Jane is a Nympha-like creature, who possesses Salome's sensuous immorality – 'a loose woman [. . .] from the theatre' – but also her pallid coldness: on the stage, she is 'a dead woman coming down from the slab of her tomb', who seems to be a faithful resurrection; 'truly his dead wife'.[35] In naming this dancer, Rodenbach may have been consciously alluding to the Moulin Rouge soloist Jane Avril, whose performances were vividly captured in a famous series of posters by Henri de Toulouse-Lautrec and in the writings of Arthur Symons. In the poem 'La Mélinite: Moulin Rouge' (1895), Symons writes of Avril's 'morbid, vague, ambiguous grace' as 'she dances for her own delight', framing the dancer's creative individualism as a source of decadent, almost narcissistic pleasure that both seduces and disturbs her viewers.[36]

A pivotal scene in *Bruges la Morte* reproduces these macabre associations as Jane, wearing the dress of Hugues's dead wife, performs a dance: 'in a fit of wild exuberance, [she] started to dance with a multiplicity of entrechats, slipping back into the choreography of the stage'.[37] Jane's body (veiled as the body of another woman through the acquisition of her clothing) is framed as a fount of disruptive excess, taking on the 'polluted, vulgar' semblance of the *femme fatale*. This dancing figure appals Rodenbach's protagonist precisely because she lays bare the extent of his self-deception: Jane, alive and animated where his wife was perfectly still, escapes his aestheticising vision, constructing her own corporeal performance. Much as modern dancers proved resistant to existing aesthetic categories, Jane's dance marks an expression of her creative power, performed by an alert, mobile body that evades Hugues's attempts to consecrate it as a *memento mori*. In the novel's final moments, however, Rodenbach punishes this expression of feminine agency with violence, as Hugues exacts a brutal revenge on his dancer, strangling her with a strand of his deceased wife's hair. After dancing beyond the paralysing vision Hugues accords to her, it is the moving body of Jane that is cruelly immobilised and conquered by the pernicious control of the aesthete, a moment of retribution that Wilde also enacts at the end of *Salomé*.

Fuller and other modern dancers sought to alter precisely this kind of representational framework with their choreographic innovations, prioritising the transformational properties of the moving body. As Mallarmé and Rodenbach strained to recognise in their various accounts of dance, Fuller developed a corporeal aesthetic that elevated the dancer's work from its prosaic conditions and the seemingly more restrictive forms of the ballet, granting the dancing body a capacity for revolution. This radical approach signals Fuller's place at the forefront of a modernism characterised, in Tim Armstrong's words, 'by the desire to intervene in the body; to render it part of modernity', although her serpentine dance was not merely preoccupied with the 'fragmentation and augmentation of the body in relation to technology', but also with the body co-opting technology to enlarge the effects of both, mutating the human form out into the world of artifice.[38] Fuller's innovations enhanced her body's capacities through the use of stage effects and lighting, but, as Mallarmé seems to recognise in his essay, Fuller also transformed the technologised space around her into an embodied entity, itself part of the dance. It is in this sense that 'movement itself becomes', as Mark Franko asserts, 'a modernist object'.[39] By suggesting her body's potential to transfer its sensory and particularly its kinaesthetic effects beyond skeletal constraints, Fuller tapped into the literary and cultural formations concentrated around the vexed status of the body of the dancer, which took on related forms in the work of Mallarmé, Wilde and other artists of the *fin de siècle*.

Loïe Fuller's Vanishing Form

Even before she choreographed her own version of the Salome dance, Loïe Fuller was commonly associated with this figure in the popular imagination, probably as a result of their shared predilection for veiled dances. As one commentator put it, 'Loie Fuller is full of the idea of Salome. She talks Salome; almost thinks Salome.'[40] Recalling in part the skirt dances that filled Parisian music halls during the 1890s, Fuller transformed the veil into her central choreographic motif, making it a billowing, amorphous extension of her body rather than a mere element of her costume (Fig. 1.2). As such, her dances differed entirely from the stripteases that came to shape Salome's legacy in the popular music hall repertoire. Figured in the press as an innocent and asexual alternative to the *femme fatale* whose image she seemed to invoke through her affiliation with Salome, Fuller's modern choreographies deployed a visual rhetoric of veiling that made her body elusive and sexually ambiguous.[41] Her serpentine dance was not structured around the removal of the veil and the exposure of a hidden body, but rather the creative collusion between these forms to *produce* images, placing the dancer's body behind a continuously unfolding screen of illuminated materials. As I show in the next chapter, the intricate web of influences and artistic concerns concentrated around the figure of Salome and the development of modern dance draws Wilde and Fuller into

1.2 Loïe Fuller, photographed by Frederick W. Glasier (1902). Library of Congress

close proximity, and Katharine Worth has even suggested that Wilde may have had Fuller's costumes in mind when he described his Salome as clothed in 'green, like a curious, poisonous lizard'.[42]

The full extent of Fuller's contribution to the aesthetics of modernist performance has often been under-appreciated. Her cultivation of a 'serpentine' aesthetic was enormously influential for other modern dancers, pioneering a shift towards a specific style of movement. 'Serpentine' is a key term in aesthetic philosophy that illustrates, in Rancière's words, 'a certain idea of the body and what makes for its aesthetic potential: the curved line'.[43] It has its conceptual roots in the serpentine 'line of grace' that William Hogarth identifies in *The Analysis of Beauty* (1753):

> The eye hath this sort of enjoyment in winding walks, and serpentine rivers, and all sorts of objects, whose forms, as we shall see hereafter, are composed principally of what, I call, the *waving* and *serpentine* lines.
>
> Intricacy in form, therefore, I shall define to be that peculiarity in the lines, which compose it, that *leads the eye a wanton kind of chase*, and from the pleasure that gives the mind, intitles [sic] it to the name of beautiful: and it may be justly said, that the cause of the idea of grace more immediately resides in this principle...[44]

Hogarth's description of the viewer's ocular 'chase' as 'wanton', and therefore unfulfilled, resonates with the type of fleeting pleasure recorded by Fuller's admirers, who sought to glimpse her body among the serpentine lines of her veils. Later in the *Analysis of Beauty*, Hogarth reflects on the type of dance that might accord with his understanding of beauty and grace, describing the French minuet as achieving 'the greatest variety of movements in serpentine lines imaginable'.[45] He further identifies Shakespeare's description of Perdita's dance as 'a wave o' th' sea' in *The Winter's Tale* as a model of ideal beauty, which chimes with the way modern dancers often sought to ground their own movements in the rhythms of the natural world, as was the case for Isadora Duncan, who expressed an affinity for the undulations of the sea: 'my first idea of movement, of the dance, certainly came from the rhythm of the waves'.[46] Writing over a century before the tenets of modern dance began to take shape, Hogarth sketches out a theory of choreographic beauty predicated on the serpentine form that would become Fuller's signature.

Following Hogarth, Edmund Burke also considered the 'varied line' to be the structural principle of beautiful forms. In a familiar rhetorical manoeuvre, however, Burke illustrated his theory of the varied line with recourse to the image of a woman's naked skin:

> Observe that part of a beautiful woman where she is perhaps most beautiful, about the neck and breasts; the smoothness; the softness; the easy and insensible swell; the variety of the surface, which is never for the smallest space the same; the deceitful maze, through which the unsteady eye slides giddily, without knowing where to fix, or whither it is carried. Is not this a demonstration of that change of surface continual and yet hardly perceptible at any point which forms one of the great constituents of beauty?[47]

Burke's writing on the varied line anticipates later approaches to dance, imagining the elusive body of the woman-in-movement to be a source of disruptive and decadent pleasure. This surface of infinite variety is, for Burke, the epitome of serpentine beauty, and he notes that 'perfectly beautiful bodies [. . .] vary their direction every moment, and they change under the eye by a deviation continually carrying on, but for whose beginning or end you will find it hard to ascertain a point'.[48] This account of continuous variation in movement certainly describes Mallarmé's experience of watching Fuller dance, yet Burke's writing also lends this body an unruly quality. It is a 'deceitful maze', designed to unsettle the 'giddy' spectator who cannot contain its restless form with a single look. Indeed, the body of the woman is here framed as a resistant and unconquerable territory, eliding the colonising impulses of the lustful viewer with her oceanic swells and variform geography.

The dancer's veils seem to delineate the continuous 'change of surface' that

Burke identifies with the serpentine line, and such moving garments are central to Warburg's Nympha, emblematised by individual modern dancers such as Isadora Duncan. Discussing Greek and 'exotic' forms of bodily imagery in modern performance, Brandstetter identifies the motif of the veil – the dancer's flowing drapes and textiles – as a crucial point of intersection between these two visual models. The veil, she writes, 'signifies a zone of transition [. . .] [it] unfurls a transitory act of creating and relocating meaning in motion'.[49] There are two distinct functions of the veil within this definition: in the case of Fuller and her imitators, Brandstetter argues, the veil works to conceal and dematerialise the dancer's body; in performances of Salome's dance, on the other hand, the contours of the body are emphasised and sexualised. Fuller's movement aesthetics are thus placed in stark opposition to traditional choreographic interpretations of Salome, and comparable orientalist themes such as 'the dance of the bee'. Yet while many renderings of Salome's dance undoubtedly stressed the veil's erotic potential, Fuller's contributions to the index of bodily imagery at the *fin de siècle* marked a shift in approaches to both the dance of Salome and the idea of a 'dance of veils' more broadly. Fuller drew on a range of visual idioms, including classical and 'exotic' forms, to construct her idiosyncratic dance style, which was repeatedly linked to the dance of Salome by contemporary commentators. Fuller's 'serpentine' aesthetic not only signalled her debt to the serpentine dances typically associated with Eastern visual and spiritual cultures, such as the Indian *nautch* dancers she saw at the 1889 Paris Exposition, but also aligned her with the key spatial models of modern performance, especially the kinetic figure of the spiral produced by her use of expansive textiles.[50]

The revival of classical gestures in modern dance, as documented by Brandstetter and more recently in the work of Carrie Preston, was encouraged by movement philosophies such as American Delsartism, pioneered by Steele MacKaye and Genevieve Stebbins in the 1880s and 1890s. Stebbins developed a vitalist conception of movement that proved formative for dancers including Duncan and Ruth St Denis, while also reflecting contemporary theories of consciousness and evolution, such as Henri Bergson's *élan vital*. Crucially, Stebbins privileged the 'spiral' as an ideal principle of motion, writing in *Dynamic Breathing and Harmonic Gymnastics* (1892): 'Every form of creative dynamic energy, be it that of intellectual effort, of spiritual aspiration, or of physical life, is transmitted by a spiral wave-motion [. . .] nature works in the spiral wave'.[51] While there is no evidence that Fuller, unlike some of her contemporaries, directly adhered to the practice of classical 'statue posing', there are clear overlaps between her 'serpentine' movements and Stebbins's 'spiral' paradigm, which placed a similar emphasis on the core of the body as the source of dynamic energy, and encouraged 'natural' and 'harmonious' movement patterns based on spiralling and circular gestures. Fuller's movement repertory relied on the interplay between what Ann Cooper Albright calls the 'outside visual effect and the inside torque': the relation between the torso's 'percussive twist[s]' and the cresting of the fabrics, manipulated by her hand-held poles.[52] The contemporary serpentine dancer Jody Sperling has also stressed the significance of the fabric's texture and density, since Fuller often used silk of the lightest weight. 'With a heavier weave', Sperling writes, 'there is more torque, resistance and effort as part of the play.'[53] Since her performance's visual effect depended upon the creation of images with the veils, the strength of Fuller's arms was of paramount importance, as they had to produce a series of extended rotations to keep the silks mobile and aloft.

Fuller's techniques, and the similar movement styles of her peers, have prompted Hillel Schwartz to claim that modern dancers were 'enamoured of torsion', the new kinaesthetic ideal that encouraged performers to engage with the natural pull of gravity, perform fluid motions emanating from the solar plexus, and execute spontaneous and natural gestures in accordance with a Grecian model of grace.[54] Fuller's own descriptions of her style, like popular reports on her performances, were largely poetic and impressionistic, expressing a sense of wonder at her continuous transformation and a disregard for the traditional vocabulary of ballet. Yet the figure of the 'spiral' recurs as a key descriptor in both the historical sources and in more recent scholarship, which delineates the 'extravagant spiral effects as [Fuller] performed a series of vertiginous *châinées*, sometimes travelling, sometimes spinning on the spot'.[55] Brandstetter describes how Fuller 'moved the fabric in spirals, circles, waves, loops, and twists to form ephemeral sculptural figuration, which partly resembled natural shapes, partly abstract sculpture'.[56] In both Fuller and Duncan's choreographies, and the related Greek dance styles of Margaret Morris and Ruby Ginner, the veil proved a vital accessory to this new kinaesthetic of torsion.

Given this study's focus on the recurring emblem of the 'dance of veils', I am interested in how Fuller's performances exploited the veil's dramatic potential as a choreographic object, reclaiming it for feminist purposes. Her performances were far removed from more obviously erotic forms of dance that have become familiar in the context of Salome's story. 'Loïe Fuller's body', argues Dana Mills, 'inscribed on the veil and made it communicate, thus giving it a place in the history of modernist aesthetics.'[57] Apparently transfixed by the way her outline flickered beneath the more substantial presence of the materials, reviewers of Fuller's performances offered accounts that repeatedly insisted upon her body's disappearance. 'Now Loïe Fuller swoops around, turning, her skirt swelling and enclosing her like a flower's calyx', wrote Roger Marx in 1893.[58] The terms used to describe Fuller by spectators and reviewers often betrayed a sense of wonder at the quasi-spiritual quality of her dance, coupled with an appreciation for her technological wizardry. Townsend has argued that Fuller 'prefigured modernist concerns with the decentred or impersonal subject' and a related interest in mechanised bodies.[59] The idea of Fuller as a 'gigantic screw' suggests an intimate correspondence between Fuller's dancing form and the images of machines at work that flooded twentieth-century literary culture, which can be traced through the recurring fascination with marionettes, dolls and automata demonstrated by a range of writers and film-makers.[60] While Fuller's movements were not themselves rigid or mechanical, critics and practitioners of dance during this period borrowed elements from industry's rhetorical index, since, as McCarren reasons, 'dance offers ways of thinking both about the movement possible with machines and about machines moving themselves'.[61]

Fuller's stage innovations influenced film-makers including Thomas Edison, Georges Méliès and the Lumière brothers, and her choreographic style incorporated mechanical registers that struck a chord with the technological aesthetics of the period.[62] She was known as *'la fée éléctricité'*, and she experimented with radium, carbon-arc lights and phosphorescent salts to produce unearthly shows of intermingled lights and colours.[63] Jones has observed, however, that despite the 'apparent sensuousness of her performances', the image Fuller cultivated was largely non-erotic and based upon a sense of what was natural and harmonious in movement.[64] In her autobiography, *Fifteen Years of a Dancer's Life* (1913), Fuller claimed to have 'discovered' her serpentine dance in Chicago during the rehearsals for a play called *Quack, M.D.* in 1890. Her account emphasises the spontaneity of her choreographic creations. Indeed, she claims that her body moved 'unconsciously', following a path of its own instinctive making. 'Gently, almost religiously, I set the silk in motion', she declares; 'I saw that I had obtained undulations of a character heretofore unknown. I had created a new dance.'[65] In opposition to the rigour of the ballet with its established vocabulary of gestures and positions, Fuller's dance practice was contingent on a sense of spiritual feeling and a deep concern for the expression of movement for its own sake.[66] She set movement in opposition to language, and asserted that 'motion has been the starting point of all effort at self-expression, and it is faithful to nature'.[67] Critics have reasoned that the essential place of movement in Fuller's art muted the cultural and physical particularities of her dance, 'dissolv[ing] the shape of her body into a whirl of fabric and light', and rendering her 'a force of performativity itself, mutating into vast and ephemeral decorative forms'.[68]

Although this interpretation affirms the centrality of organic, fluid motion to Fuller's choreographic technique, it also reverts to the narrative of disappearance and dissolution so often attached to the dancer's body, which this chapter has critiqued. Rancière adopts a similar critical stance in his reading of Fuller, stating that the 'new art' she instates 'comes from a new body, relieved of the weight of its flesh, reduced to a play of lines and tones, whirling in space'.[69]

One might surmise from this that the physical properties of the dancer's body – her strong bones, perspiring skin and straining muscles – are incompatible with the delicate 'lines' of the art she creates, suggesting that the dance emerges, ethereal, *despite* the exertions of her definable physique. Yet this is precisely where critics conflate the performance effects of Fuller's art with the performance itself, declaring her body to be absent when it in fact only appears to have vanished behind her veils. In response to Rancière, Mills argues that while '[t]he body may be perceived as without a space [...] it is a perception that arises through the dancer's manipulation of her body spatiality'.[70] With her dynamic, working body at the centre of her silk cocoon, Fuller deliberately orchestrates her own vanishing point in order to rewrite her body's limits, rendering the veil 'not a supplement to the body but an extension of its movement'.[71] This is how Fuller contributes to the changing conditions of dance as an art form, not through the eradication of her presence, as some critics have suggested, but through the reinvention of her spatial frontiers, collapsing the distinction between skin and veil.

Fuller's style absorbed forms of movement derived from new technologies, but she also harked back to more traditional narrative modes and symbols, taken from French Symbolism and its debts to Romanticism.[72] Reviewers expressed astonishment that this creature of metamorphosis could be human beneath her veils:

> Again she emerges from the darkness, her airy evaluations now tinted with blue and purple and crimson, and again the audience rise at her and insist on seeing her pretty, piquant face before they can believe that the lovely apparition is really a woman.[73]

It is the profound ambiguity of Fuller's bodily self, hinted at in such accounts, that has led a number of scholars to consider her performance style as articulating a queer subjectivity. Using Teresa de Lauretis's concept of a 'technology of gender', which posits gender as 'the product of various social technologies [...] and institutionalized discourses', Townsend has read Fuller's experiments with stage effects and movement styles as probing into the interplays between technology, gender and sexuality, arguing that Fuller's 'lesbian identity and her work as an artist [...] are inextricably linked'.[74] More recently, Penny Farfan has interpreted Fuller's 'Fire Dance', initially created for her 1895 *Salomé*, as an uncanny compendium of erotic allusions that encompasses the spectres of Wilde, Salome and witchcraft, 'arising from repressed affiliations and eerie doubles [...] layered incrementally in a queer and feminist genealogy'.[75] By withholding her body from the gaze of her spectators, Fuller, it might be reasoned, retreated from a space of known or conventional erotic possibility, orchestrating her dance from the very site of physical absence and invisibility in which queer female sexuality was imagined to take place.

In this sense, there are connections to be drawn between Fuller's subtle choreographing of sexual difference and the literary and artistic traditions that represented dancing women as figures imbued with heterodox sexual meaning, from the maenads of Greek myth to Judith and Salome. According to Dierkes-Thrun, in many Western portrayals of Salome and of Wilde, 'transgressions of the female body – both the straight one and [. . .] the lesbian or bisexual one – intersect with those of the male homosexual body'.[76] The kind of queer reading Fuller invites perhaps sits between the thresholds of these different categories, retaining a sense of the multiple forms of desire and intimacy that collate in the veiled body of the dancer, a force of ambiguous gender and longing. 'Queer is a continuing moment, movement, motive – recurrent, eddying, *troublant*', writes Eve Sedgwick, noting that the word 'queer' itself has links to the Latin *torquere*, meaning 'to twist'.[77] Fuller's spiralling, serpentine dance movements might therefore be read as queer in the sense that they perform a continuous act of decentring; indeed, Fuller herself proposed a suggestive connection between her dance technique and her relationship with Gabrielle Bloch, writing in her autobiography: 'I wonder if her friendship, so well founded and positive, is not intimately mingled with the love of form, of colour and of light, which I interpreted synthetically before her eyes when I appeared to her for the first time.'[78] Muting any obvious erotic content, this recollection nonetheless stirs with queer possibility, evoking a relationship of intimate mingling between bodily forms, prompted by an almost epiphanic apparition of colour and light.

While some scholars have objected to queer interpretations of Fuller's dance that dismiss the importance of her body and render 'lesbian sexuality an absence, a refusal of eros', it is possible to read Fuller back into her choreographies on her own terms.[79] Fuller conceptualised dance as a sensual enactment of inner feeling, but also as a means of staging the single body's expansive connectedness among other bodies, phenomena and aesthetic forms. She imagines herself as a plastic 'interpreter' of the lines, colours and lights that frame and define her dance, thereby decoding the language of the stage for her spectators using her body, and perhaps also the language of queer intimacy for her female partner. This is the kind of double function that the veiled dance imaginatively permits, and it is telling that so many of the women who were drawn to it in the late nineteenth and early twentieth centuries were queer or at least perceived in such terms.[80] The 'apparitional' nature of Fuller's dance – read in some cases as signalling a queer aesthetic – was crucially engineered by her body, which operated as a powerful interpretative instrument constructing the choreography along with its many possible sexual meanings.

Salome: An Unhappy Acrobat

When Fuller first travelled to Paris in 1892, after performing with various touring groups and shows in the US, she arrived in a city already thoroughly preoccupied with the image of Salome.⁸¹ The Symbolist and Decadent movements, led by Salome enthusiasts such as Flaubert, Huysmans and Moreau, had stimulated a cultural fascination with this oriental dancer, whetted by western Europe's broader imperial ambitions, and the risqué performances of popular dancers at the Moulin Rouge and similar venues. Following the immediate success of her serpentine dance, which revitalised the potential of veiled choreographies, it seemed certain that Fuller would make an innovative contribution to this catalogue of Salomes. Indeed, it was upon witnessing Fuller's serpentine dance that the French poet Armand Silvestre encouraged her to adapt the dance of Salome, declaring when he saw her: 'I dreamed of Salome before Herod.'⁸²

Fuller did not delay in satisfying this particular vision. Her first *Salomé* opened in early March 1895 at the Comédie Parisienne. For this self-styled '*pantomime lyrique*', Fuller worked with the set designer Georges Rochegrosse, the composer Gabriel Pierné, who wrote the score, and the librettist C. H. Meltzer. The production was structured as four tableaux, designed to convey the altering tones and mood of the biblical tale, as Salome relinquishes her initial chastity and dances for Herod in a futile attempt to save the life of the Baptist. While Fuller's serpentine dances had emphasised her singular, luminous presence on an otherwise deserted stage, this *Salomé* was a lavish production, influenced perhaps by the Symbolist paintings of Moreau.⁸³ The *New York Times* hailed it as 'the talk of Europe' and reported that it was 'a marvel of beauty and grace'.⁸⁴ Fuller's 'Fire Dance', incorporated into one of the tableaux, was a particular success, and, like her serpentine dance, it depended upon her technological ambition: six holes were cut into the stage and overlaid with glass, and lights were then projected on to Fuller's dancing body from below.⁸⁵ As for the style of her movements, Fuller herself described the choreography to the *Chicago Tribune* as 'not new. It is the old dance of Bible times.'⁸⁶ It appears that Fuller was eager to root her approach to Salome's dance in the biblical sources rather than more recent literary versions, although she did draw out the sublime, hypnotic strains suggested by Mallarmé and others, declaring, 'I can fairly feel the awful horror of the thing, then I move in a dazed way through that frightful dance.' According to the journalist who interviewed Fuller, this involved her circling the room 'in a slow, weird manner'.⁸⁷

Fuller's measured, deliberate steps suggest a hieratic movement vocabulary that disavowed the erotic gyrations of the striptease to make the woman's body a source of remote and portentous action. This complex operation was also, in Fuller's words, entirely of her own making:

> I am not going to do 'Salome' here [in New York]. I couldn't; there isn't time enough. It would take a month to get the stage ready for it, and I should have to spend weeks training the auxiliaries. It takes seventy-five

> people to do it [. . .] I want you to understand that the dances are all my own [. . .] in my own dances the gas man can't do anything until I teach him how. I invented the dances myself, every one of them.[88]

As this statement suggests, Fuller was a thoughtful interpreter of her own creative process, and she repeatedly underlined her role as the orchestrator of her creative projects. She cast herself as the star talent in *Salomé*, of course, but also as a teacher, who '[left] nothing to chance. I drill my light men, drill them to throw the light so, or so.' Under Fuller's direction, the movements of the stage crew were strictly choreographed, and 'they [had] to do their business with the exactitude of clockwork'.[89] Implicit in these reflections is a strong sense that Fuller was not merely interested in painting herself as a celebrity performer, but in expanding the remit of the female dancer to encompass the roles of choreographer, director and pedagogue as well.

There was a gap of twelve years between Fuller's dynamic and stylistically experimental *Salomé* dance, and her second attempt at the same theme: *La Tragédie de Salomé* (1907). This production was set to a score by Florent Schmitt and a libretto by Robert d'Humières, and seems to have more closely reflected Wilde's rendering of Salome as a sexually provocative New Woman.[90] Certainly, the costumes and set design were fantastic: Fuller emerged on to the stage like a peacock, resplendent in more than four thousand real feathers, while the severed head of John the Baptist glowed eerily, bathed in the light of six hundred lamps.[91] Yet for the writer and director Jules Claretie, who watched Fuller's rehearsals, it was not an erotic spectacle that materialised from Salome's veils, but rather the body of an expressive artist, 'whose hands – mobile, expressive, tender or threatening hands, white hands, hands like the tips of bird's wings – emerged from the clothes, imparted to them all the poetry of the dance'.[92] By rooting the meaning of Fuller's movements in the instrumental power of her hands, Claretie recognised Fuller's presence as the author and creator of the performance: she was not an erotic object to be dissected as a composite of almost bared flesh, but rather, the maker of her art, tracing symbols in the air with her beautiful gestures.

In Claretie's opinion, Fuller's decision to adapt the dance of Salome was not merely a case of aesthetic suitability, but of 'destiny'. Writing of her rehearsals for the 1907 production, he observed:

> I can well believe that Loie Fuller's Salome is destined to add a Salome unforeseen of all the Salomes we have been privileged to see [. . .] This woman, who has so profoundly influenced the modes, the tones of materials, has discovered still further effects, and I can imagine the picturesqueness of the movements when she envelops herself with the black serpents which she used the other evening only among the accessories behind the scenes.[93]

Claretie's praise, celebrating Fuller's fondness for striking props and effects, also alludes to the serpentine metaphors long associated with both Fuller and the figure of Salome. Physically entwining herself with the black serpents that recall Cleopatra's fateful asps, Fuller also 'envelops' her choreographic aesthetic into a larger iconographic paradigm of powerful, 'serpentine' women whose movements transfix. There is a Medusan subtext to these 'serpents'; indeed, the Gorgon's severed head, encircled by snakes, might be read as a classical inversion of the Baptist's decapitation, with these images representing alternative forms of gendered violence, prompted in each case by an assertion of female power. While the Gorgon's serpentine gaze might have immobilised the men who looked at her – reversing the Orphic impulse – the serpentine variations of modern dancers privileged an aesthetics of continuous movement rather than paralysis. Walking among her statues, Medusa is a curator of fossilised aesthetic forms, whereas Fuller's adaptations of the Salome myth transfer the 'serpentine' metaphor into the realm of the choreographic. The Salome theme might have seemed an unusual choice for Fuller at this moment in her career, since it invoked a recent tradition of carnal desire and female powerlessness in the face of violence firmly at odds with the reputation she had built as a dancer. However, as Albright observes, Fuller's Salome dances demonstrated 'different feminist [strategies] for confronting and intervening in misogynist representations of sexualised women'.[94] It was the characterisation of Salome as a *femme fatale* that Fuller construed differently, in her first performance particularly, which diffused the erotic energy of the dance and presented Salome's love for John the Baptist as a form of deep loyalty motivated by religious feeling and self-sacrifice.

In this sense, Fuller's work signals a critical intervention in the long history of nineteenth-century representations of dancing head-hunters (or, like Medusa, women whose heads are sought). Asserting her authority over every aspect of the show and evading the *femme fatale* type through a careful revision of the role, Fuller forged strong associations between the figure of Salome and that of the modern dancer as a creator, rather than merely the object of a spectacle. Perhaps unsurprisingly, this interpretation of the biblical tale was not to the taste of all of her spectators, and the comments of the decadent writer Jean Lorrain in particular have fed the widely accepted notion that her 1895 *Salomé* was a failure.[95] In a scathing review, Lorrain emphasised the physicality of Fuller's performance, which, unlike her serpentine dance, allowed her body to partially emerge from its veils: 'One perceives too late that the unhappy acrobat is neither mime nor dancer; heavy, ungraceful, sweating [...] she manoeuvres her veils and her mass of materials like a laundress misusing her paddle.'[96] Lorrain magnifies the details of Fuller's exertions, noting her weight and her perspiring skin. Here, the 'unlocatable' body is firmly discovered, but it is framed as an object of excess – of disgust – rather than the delicate, unfixable form praised by other reviewers. Although recent work, by Albright in particular, has done much to revise the history of Fuller's first *Salomé*, Lorrain's comments must be contextualised with reference to his own literary strategies for representing the female form. His dismissive reaction to Fuller's *Salomé* was crucially embedded in broader discourses framing the bodies of dancing women, which he had already addressed in his accounts of physically demonstrative, sensual women with a fondness for technological spectacle.

In his short story 'Magic Lantern' (1891), first published in *L'Echo de Paris*, Lorrain muses at length on the dangerous, alluring prevalence of 'the Fantastic' in modern life, a phenomenon that 'invades us, chokes us, and obsesses us'.[97] The unnamed narrator of the story enters into an exchange at a magic lantern show with another audience member, the physicist André Forbster, who attempts to convince him that the artistic and technological cultures of modernity do not signal the end of 'illusion' but rather the opposite, pointing to the evidence of spiritual and necromantic practices in the theatre itself. Most of his observations revolve around the women in the audience, including 'three elegant women on the balcony' with 'chalky complexions [. . .] eyes blackened with kohl and the scarlet stains on their pained lips, like bloody wounds'.[98] These 'damnable cadavers' are strikingly predictive of Bram Stoker's three 'weird sisters' in *Dracula* (1897), while in another part of the audience, Forbster spies 'the beautiful Madame G—', an articulated porcelain doll 'produced for export', who resembles 'the Olympia of Doctor Coppelius' in Hoffmann's *Der Sandmann*.[99] These women are case studies in *fin-de-siècle* degeneracy as diagnosed by Max Nordau, exemplifying distortions of 'natural' womanhood made possible by new technologies and apparently perverse forms of desire.

The genre of the fantastic, for Lorrain, was deeply connected to late nineteenth-century spiritual and neurological discourses around 'Hypnotism, magnetism, suggestion and hysteria'. In 'Magic Lantern', the narrator and his companion link these maladies to Charcot's patients at the Salpêtrière: 'the wild women who stretch themselves out on their hands and merrily make hoops of themselves'.[100] Framing these female hysterics as dancers, Lorrain draws on the same index of gestures that the French composer Maurice Emmanuel specifically associates with the Dionysian maenads in his contemporaneous study of Greek dance, *La Danse grecque antique* (*The Antique Greek Dance*, 1896). Like the 'merry hoops' described in 'Magic Lantern', an 'extreme' backward bend, Emmanuel claims, is characteristic of 'those mad with hysteria', and can only be understood 'on pathological grounds'.[101] This pose, an *arc en cercle*, was also wholly or partially reproduced by modern dancers, becoming a 'signature gesture' of both free-dance and *Ausdruckstanz* (German Expressionist dance), as seen in Grete Wiesenthal's *Danube Waltz* (1908) and Mary Wigman's *Allegro con Brio* (1920).[102] Ruth St Denis's Indian *nautch* turn in *Radha* (1906) seems to carry the ghost of the *arc en cercle* (Fig. 1.3), and the pose is also later remembered in Louise Bourgeois's (suggestively headless) bronze sculpture *Arch of Hysteria* (1993).

Lorrain thus accesses a complex set of visual associations in his short story, which finally focuses on one particular member of the audience: 'an exquisite young woman' who, with the sinister intent of a modern head-hunter, 'never misses an execution' and 'shivers with profound sensuality every time she sees the fall of a severed head – eternally young though, as if kept fresh by the sight of blood!'[103] The optical technology of the magic lantern becomes the source of the woman's degenerate beauty, collapsing the distinction between the spectacle of a public beheading and the ephemeral projections that were the hallmark of an age of technological reproduction. Popular conceptions of female self-expression as a dangerous and modern spectacle, evident in Lorrain's work, shaped the emerging relationship between hysteria and photography, reflected in Charcot's eagerness to capture and display photographs of his female patients at his famous Tuesday lectures.[104] 'One reason women love dancing', Havelock Ellis claimed, 'is very probably because it enables them to give harmonious and legitimate emotional expression to this neuro-muscular irritability which might otherwise escape in more explosive forms.'[105] Crucially, Lorrain's eccentric interweaving of the magic lantern exhibition and the lustful, vampiric *femme fatale* figure exploits the very connections between technology and misogynistic representations of the female body that Fuller challenged so creatively in her choreographies. Lorrain's critique of Fuller's *Salomé* was thus clearly part of a complex landscape of nineteenth-century psychological theories and practices, in which suspicions of the female body and its spectacular appeal ran deep.

By revising the decadent tropes Lorrain expected from his sensual head-hunters, and refusing to revel in their perverse eroticism, Fuller invited Lorrain's disappointment, but accessed a mode of corporeal agency that had always been latent in the Salome story. Fuller was certainly embroiled in the mechanics of the modern spectacle described in Lorrain's 'Magic Lantern', but she was no mere decorative oddity: she took on the role of both illusion and illusionist, designing her own costumes and stage instruments. There were a number of critics who recognised the extent of Fuller's creative autonomy, and her mastery of her own technological reproducibility. Claretie, for instance, celebrated Fuller as 'a unique personality, an independent creator, a revolutionist in art', whose work was not merely aesthetically distinct but politically transformative. Enthusing about the rehearsals for her second Salome dance, he wrote:

> I had, as it were, a vision of a theatre of the future, something of the nature of a feministic theatre.

'UNLOCATABLE BODIES'

1.3 Ruth St Denis in *Radha* (1906). Library of Congress

> Women are more and more taking men's places. They are steadily supplanting the so-called stronger sex [...] Just watch and you will see women growing in influence and power; and if, as in Gladstone's phrase, the nineteenth century was the working-man's century, the twentieth will be the women's century.[106]

This is a powerful statement on the effects of Fuller's choreographic interventions. It is worth noting that Fuller quotes at length from this article in her autobiography, suggesting that she was eager to emphasise the political elements of her praxis, therefore engaging in a revealing self-fashioning that illuminates much about her particular relationship to the revolutionary iconography of dancers seeking severed heads. For Claretie, her technological accomplishments and bewitching spectacles rendered her a force of singular creative authority, whose work crucially redefined the place of women in theatre, and in political life more widely.

Tellingly, of all the performers Fuller admired, Sarah Bernhardt, who was initially attached to the thwarted London production of Wilde's *Salomé*, was the one she sought to emulate most keenly. In *Fifteen Years of a Dancer's Life*, she recalls watching Bernhardt performing in New York when she was only sixteen years old. Her breathless prose reformulates the descriptive style that was so common in reviews of her own choreographies, as she imagines Bernhardt's body as curiously weightless and unearthly: 'She came forward lightly, appearing barely to brush the earth.'[107] This 'lightness' does not, however, minimise the impact of Bernhardt's stage presence; on the contrary, Fuller recalls how the French actor advanced to the 'middle of the stage, and surveyed this audience of actors'.[108] Looking decisively at her audience (composed of dancers and performers), Bernhardt unsettles the demarcations of the theatrical space, dismantling her own position as the object of the audience's gaze and subjecting them to a critical dissection of her own. Capturing this transformative moment of kinaesthetic affinity between two pioneers of the nineteenth-century stage, Fuller's autobiography is an important record of the theatrical space enabling a potent exchange between women. Her writing destabilises any straightforward understanding of the spectator's gaze in either Bernhardt's performances or, indeed, Fuller's choreographies, which were perhaps influenced by the elder French actor's carefully contrived 'lightness'; her ease of movement.[109]

Fuller's account suggests a corporeal symmetry between herself and Bernhardt, another inheritor of Salome's legacy, which reflects extant discourses surrounding the kinaesthetic effects of modern dance and the role of the viewer in such performances. Dance historians have debated about the extent to which modern dancers fully achieved their capacity to unsettle the gender dynamics of spectatorship and the voyeuristic position of their male observers.[110] Noting a 'dynamic tension' underpinning modern dance, Susan Manning perceives a dissonance between 'representational frames [that] reiterated and updated pre-existent images of gender' and 'the kinesthetic dimension [that] introduced a new image of the female body in motion'.[111] Acknowledging that many early twentieth-century modern dancers, including Maud Allan and Ruth St Denis, reproduced essentialist visions of gender and race in their dances, Manning nonetheless argues that the kinaesthetic element of these choreographies provided an alternative mode of aesthetic engagement, creating an empowering space for the female spectator. This tension is manifest in Fuller's adaptations of the Salome myth, which naturally drew on a representational frame grounded in the essentialist visions of women formed in nineteenth-century portraits of the figure, whereas the kinaesthetic elements of her choreographies disturbed such gendered modes, reinventing Salome on different terms. Embodying Schwartz's new kinaesthetic of torsion, Fuller and her contemporaries developed grammars of movement that drew on styles and methods of physical expression that were were deeply integrated into popular conceptions of health and well-being, early feminist politics, and modernist aesthetics in the twentieth century.[112]

These connections between kinaesthetic experience and gender politics are shored up by Fuller's own reflections on her developing practice. In her autobiography, Fuller intimated that her career was modelled in part on that of her 'idol' Bernhardt, who was famously embroiled in the controversy surrounding *Salomé* and its censorship in England. Fuller enthused repeatedly about Bernhardt in interviews and recalled an occasion when Bernhardt saw her perform at the Folies Bergère: 'I danced and, although she could not know, I danced for her. I forgot everything else. I lived again through the famous day in New York, and I seemed to see her once more, marvellous as she was at the matinee.'[113] Even when their roles are reversed, Fuller recasts herself as a spectator to Bernhardt's performance, and imaginatively entwines her choreographic technique with her memory of Bernhardt's movements. At the sight of the French actor in the audience, the historic moment of kinaesthetic empathy returns to Fuller, merging her own dancing with the image of her idol and thus creating an intense sensory connection between the two women, built around their shared role as spectators to each other's performances. It is fascinating that Salome should form a point of connection between these performers, whose ideas and methods of movement enabled a freer kind of female body to emerge on stage.

Dancing for Women: Maud Allan's *Vision*

Although Fuller is widely considered to be the first modern dancer to choreograph the role of Salome, she was by no means the last, nor, indeed, the most famous. By the time she began preparing *La Tragédie de Salomé* in

1907, Salome's transformation into a transatlantic cultural phenomenon was already well underway. That same year, the New York Theatre opened a 'School for Salomes', preparing its dancers to take the notorious princess on to the vaudeville circuit.[114] Perhaps unsurprisingly, the conspicuous arrival of Salome on American soil instilled a sense of outrage in more conservative quarters: the actor Marie Cahill penned angry letters to President Roosevelt and others, warning that 'pernicious subjects of the "Salome" kind' would poison the minds of impressionable theatregoers.[115] Lois Cucullu has shown that *Salomé* 'spawn[ed] an entire industry that, under the banner of Salomania, attract[ed] and produc[ed] willing converts on and off stage and screen' on an unprecedented scale.[116]

One of the triggers for Salome's surge in popularity on both sides of the Atlantic during this period was the success of the Canadian performer Maud Allan. A number of scholars have excavated the history of Allan's solo dance *The Vision of Salome* and the subsequent scandal surrounding her libel trial in 1918, when she was also set to play the lead role in J. T. Grein's production of Wilde's *Salomé*.[117] In a very different vein to Loïe Fuller, whose choreographies have been coded as queer in later academic expositions, Allan's dancing body was often interpreted at the time as a site of sexual deviancy, 'just as Wilde's queer body was read and traced in hindsight through his aesthetic creed'.[118] It was widely believed, for instance, that her Sapphic influence extended into the highest echelons of political life: there were rumours that she was the lover of Margot Asquith, wife to the British Prime Minister Herbert Asquith. For this reason, her *Vision of Salome*, which premiered in Vienna's Carl-Theatre in 1906, stimulated ideas about Salome's potential as both a progressive and a revolutionary icon, emblematic of contemporaneous political movements such as the struggle for women's suffrage, and alternative conceptions of femininity previously embodied by the image of the New Woman.

Although Allan departed from Fuller's example and embraced the more conspicuously erotic orientalism associated with traditional nineteenth-century Salome images, she shared Fuller's sense of choreographic authorship, going to great lengths to assert her self-control and individualism as a dancer. For this reason, she invites comparison with her former mentor. Tellingly, like Fuller, she also cited Sarah Bernhardt as a formative influence, recalling, in her autobiography, the effect of watching Bernhardt perform in San Francisco: 'My ambitious little heart burned within me. She was the one woman in the world I wanted to rival, and I have not lost the feeling yet [. . .] I think the turning point in my career came from my first sight of that great woman.'[119] Historians of the theatre may not often remember Bernhardt and Allan in the same breath, but it is significant that Allan articulated her aspirations in these terms, aligning herself very directly with the woman Wilde most sincerely hoped would play his Salome. In this way, she was also affiliating herself with

Bernhardt's success, her formidable control of the stage, and her unrivalled command of her uncorseted, equivocally gendered body, thereby joining the community of female performers kinaesthetically connected by the memory of Bernhardt's presence.

In a similar manner to Isadora Duncan, Allan styled her dance technique as a return to classical aesthetic principles and poses, in tune with antique modes of beauty and grace. She also characterised her dance practice as an elegant realisation of the world's natural rhythms, inspired by 'the poetry of motion in the running brooks and the rhythm of the tossing branches that gave [her] a desire to express something within [herself] by the grace of motion'.[120] Like Fuller, Allan drew on a wealth of sources taken from history and the arts to devise her performance philosophy, incorporating organic, technological and classical registers into her choreographies, despite her lack of formal training. She was also influenced by Delsartism, declaring that 'Delsarte's theories teach us that every fibre, every vigorous impulse, every muscle, and every feeling should have its existence so well defined that at any moment it can actually assert itself.'[121] This comprehensive approach to physical movement as a means of self-expression enabled Allan and other dancers impressed by Delsarte's theories to approach their bodies as sites of power and creativity.

Crucially, Allan disputed the 'impression in some quarters that whatever success [she] may have achieved has been obtained by a kind of floating, airy, effortless, butterfly kind of process'. Here, she explicitly takes issue with the (now familiar) rhetoric that dehumanises the dancer and undermines her labour and bodily technique. As Allan points out, she '[has] worked, and still continues to work and study, quite apart from the physical and mental strain of public performances, very, very hard'.[122] The conditions of professional dance, despite encouraging the kinds of infantilising critiques to which Allan objected, also allowed her to challenge contemporary attitudes towards women by emphasising the physical strength of her dancing body and her independence as a practitioner. It is perhaps for this reason that feminist critics have reclaimed Allan's *Vision of Salome* as an intervention in the chequered and misogynistic histories of modern dancers interested in both Greek models of feminine movement – represented by the dancing maenads – and 'oriental' dancers such as Salome.

Allan's *Vision of Salome* opened at London's Palace Theatre on 6 March 1908, and Allan, initially scheduled to dance for two weeks, performed the piece for over eighteen months. It was set to Marcel Rémy's score, composed after the pair of them saw performances of Max Reinhardt's avant-garde production of Wilde's *Salomé* in 1903. It has been suggested that Allan's choice of Salome as a theme for her new dance 'gave [her] a chance to make her mark as an avant-garde artist by following in the footsteps of Wilde, Reinhardt, and Strauss'.[123] It seems likely, however, that Allan was strategically aligning herself with Fuller and Bernhardt as well, since they had specifically claimed Salome as an icon of female individualism, albeit without a dramatic realisation in Bernhardt's case.[124] Although certain strands of feminist thought have sometimes proved resistant to the concept of individualism, preferring to emphasise the idea of the collective, twentieth-century avant-garde feminists, Lucy Delap contends, 'used [the term individualism] in ways that complemented or were integral to their "feminism"'.[125] In Allan's case, the choice of Salome as a choreographic role was an act of solidarity as well as a solo pursuit, integrating her into this particular imaginative community of performers.

Moreover, Allan reflected on Salome's character in a manner reminiscent of Fuller's approach over a decade earlier: she envisaged her Salome as an innocent child with a divine gift for dance and a desire to please her mother, Herodias. The choreography for the *Vision* was, however, arranged in two parts, which Allan describes in her autobiography as the 'Dance of Salome' and the 'Vision of Salome'. The latter presents a more complex and decidedly less chaste understanding of Salome's motives and expression, drawing on the qualities Wilde bestowed upon his dancer:

> She is horror stricken! Suddenly a wild desire takes possession of her. Why, ah! Why, should her mother have longed for this man's end? Salomé feels a strange longing, compelling her once more to hold in her hands this awful reward of her obedience, and slowly, very slowly, and with ecstasy mingled with dread, she seems to grasp the vision of her prize and lay it on the floor before her.[126]

Allan's colourful intermingling of horror, desire, wildness and ecstasy explicitly reformulates the attributes pressed upon Salome in a string of nineteenth-century portraits, from Mallarmé to Huysmans and Wilde, which have, according to Mary Simonson, 'come to stand for anxieties about cultural disorder, describing a desire to legitimize male control of female bodies and behaviour'.[127] Allan's contemporaries waxed lyrical about the erotic elements of the *Vision*, euphorically describing her as the most enticing of degenerates: 'Swaying like a white witch with yearning arms and hands that plead, Miss Allan is such a delicious embodiment of lust that she might win forgiveness with the sins of her wonderful flesh.'[128] Barely concealed beneath scant panels of jewels like Moreau's hypnotic dancer, Allan's body trembled and swayed on stage, embracing Salome's intense and unearthly sexuality (Fig. 1.4).

Yet in performance, Allan's reclaiming of Salome's perceived sordidness – her anguished and violent lust – did more than simply repeat the stereotypes implicit in earlier incarnations of this figure. The mere fact of her near exposure did not by any means disqualify her as the creator of the dance or turn her control over to the hungry gaze of her audience. Writing about the evolution of the striptease, Rachel Shteir identifies the craze for Salome dances as an

1.4 Maud Allan as Salome (1908). National Portrait Gallery, London

important 'phase in the history of undressing', pointing out the contradictions inherent in Allan's carefully crafted self-image and the descriptions of her dance as lascivious and explicit.[129] Throughout the twentieth century, this dance form retained an ability to provoke and infuriate, whether its detractors were Prohibition-era reformers or second-wave feminists. The striptease had various lives as a model of Jazz Age decadence and women's liberation, as well as a more politically fraught symptom of criminal subcultures, prostitution and the commercialisation of female sexuality. Importantly, it could also function as a critique of sexual desire: the striptease artist made eroticism a spectacle, yet often parodied or satirised the very conditions of performative excess she embraced.[130]

In an essay on 'Striptease' in his *Mythologies* (1957), Roland Barthes argues that the erotic illusion of the dancer's performance is contingent on the sustained veiling of her body. 'Woman', he writes, 'is desexualized at the very moment when she is stripped naked.'[131] Crucially, in his reading of the striptease, Barthes also recognises the singular power of the dancer, whose technique allows her to assert control over the spectacle, creating a critical distance between her dancing body and the voyeuristic gaze of the spectator:

> Thus we see the professionals of striptease wrap themselves in the miraculous ease which constantly clothes them, makes them remote, gives them the icy indifference of skilful practitioners, haughtily taking refuge in the sureness of their technique: their science clothes them like a garment.[132]

Barthes's description of the dancer's technique draws on the Ancient Greek notion of *technē*, a term for craftsmanship that aligns ideas about embodied practice with those of knowledge and learning.[133] While his reading of the striptease reiterates its primarily erotic appeal, it also complicates the notion that a veiled dance merely turns the body of the performer into a passive spectacle, thus providing a more nuanced way of reading Allan's *Vision of Salome* as a vehicle for her own technical and creative abilities.

Although she depended upon rather different styles of self-presentation and choreography, Allan, like Bernhardt and Fuller before her, also contrived an unlikely space for the female spectator among her hushed and enthralled audience members. Many of Allan's most ardent fans during this period were young, respectable, middle-class women, who responded to her *Vision* by throwing parties in her honour, to which, unsurprisingly, no men were invited. At these gatherings, some of which Allan herself attended, the women present dressed up as Salome, listened to music, and enthused about the power of her dance. The women's suffrage movement also quickly adopted Allan as a symbol of 'rebellion, individualism, and violence'.[134] Judith Walkowitz has shown that Salome's dance appealed to this generation of young feminists because they were able to claim it as 'their own cultural form' and thereby also regain control of 'their own erotic gaze', challenging the assumption that Salome's veiled body was oriented towards the desires of men alone.[135]

Of course, Allan's surge in popularity among women was met by stern objections about the morally corrosive influence of her dances. A particularly concerned journalist at the *New York Times* chronicled a worrying 'spread of Bohemianism in English society', and cited Allan as an instigator of this trend, even suggesting that the British monarch had been forced to combat Salome's insidious presence in the domestic sphere:

> From the presentation of the Salome dance in English homes, and the lionising of the performer as an honoured and gushed-over guest, to the appearance of some of these feminine enthusiasts of rank and lineage in the same role, is but a step. It is bound to come unless a halt is called. Indeed, it is insisted by popular rumour that Miss Allan has already found adept imitators among her titled friends, gossip pointing in this connection to the married daughter of a Ducal House, renowned for her extravagances and eccentricities, though no word of reproach has ever been brought against her character.[136]

The forms of 'imitation' alluded to in this article loosely implicate Allan and her circle in the unnamed sexual proclivities associated with Wilde and Salome as cultural figures. 'Extravagances and eccentricities' obliquely suggest all kinds of extraordinary and unorthodox habits, without, of course, explicitly detailing the practices they hint at. The language used to describe Salome's insatiable reach into every aspect of cultural life in Britain (and elsewhere) reflects the rhetorical strategies deployed to announce, identify and condemn homosexuality in the late nineteenth century, exploiting the mutability of meaning and the openness of suggestion, rather than direct treatment of the act. It is in this way that queerness could be construed as pernicious, widespread and contagious.

Wilde's spectre, liable to reappear throughout the early decades of the twentieth century, certainly overshadowed Allan's dancing, and his image was resurrected once again when Allan became embroiled in a scandalous court case that effectively placed the figure of Salome on trial.[137] In February 1918, while Allan was preparing to play the lead role in J. T. Grein's production of *Salomé*, the right-wing MP Noel Pemberton Billing implicitly accused her of participating in homosexual subcultures in his journal *The Vigilante*, in an article entitled 'The Cult of the Clitoris'. This elliptical paragraph not only suggested that there was an active circle of Salome enthusiasts engaged in clitoral worship, constellated around the magnetic figure of Maud Allan, but that these individuals were additionally immersed in acts of political subversion and treason:

> The Cult of the Clitoris
> To be a member of Miss Maud Allan's performances in Oscar Wilde's Salome one has to apply to a Miss Valetta, of 9, Duke Street ... If Scotland Yard were to seize the list of these members I have no doubt they would secure the names of several thousand of the first 47,000.[138]

The reference to the '47,000' alludes to an elaborate and fantastically strange conspiracy theory advanced by Billing in an earlier article for *The Vigilante*, in which he described a German plot to spread homosexuality throughout British society and, at the same time, turn civilians into informants. The guilty parties – 'forty-seven thousand English men and women' – were apparently listed in a mysterious book belonging to 'a certain German Prince'.[139] In the court case that commenced when Allan and Grein sued Billing for libel, 'the threat of Wilde', Jodie Medd declares, 'was supplemented and perhaps exceeded by the threat of lesbian sexual espionage'.[140] This fraught interweaving of treasonous action and erotic transgression was not unique: just two years previously, the scandalous circulation of the Irish nationalist Roger Casement's diaries, containing details of his own homosexual affairs, had emerged from a similar context, coinciding with Casement's support for the Easter Rising and his criticism of British colonial brutality, which ultimately led to his execution.

These anxieties about sexual and political sedition connect in the figure of Salome, a woman born into royalty who lived in Roman-occupied Judea, a region riven along racial and religious faultlines. Salome's dance was portrayed as an erotic offence of monstrous proportions, incestuously designed to seduce her uncle, but it was further open to interpretation as an act of political subterfuge, deceiving the Tetrarch into the politically dubious execution of his hostage, Iokanaan. Wartime Britain, alert to the threat of espionage, betrayal and unpatriotic feeling, had a heightened susceptibility to such myths, which appeared to connect unorthodox bodies to unpredictable politics. Just as Allan was imagined to be part of this coterie of homosexual spies, Salome too might be perceived as an enemy of the state: the lover of a prophet-prisoner and beguiler of kings.

Moreover, across its many forms in literature and the visual arts, Salome's dance was grounded in the kind of uncertain language that governed representations of the female body, brought into sharp relief by the confusion surrounding the word 'clitoris' in the Pemberton Billing trial. Medd argues: 'It is precisely the language of the female body – the female non-productive but desiring body – that simultaneously demands and refuses interpretative attention, inciting scandal through its very resistance to representation.'[141] Indeed, those who interpreted Salome's veiled dance as a striptease might have imagined that what lay beneath her final veil was the unknown site of female pleasure, or, in an imaginative collapsing of dancer and author, a body conjured by Wilde's own transgressive desires: the transvestic body, what Marjorie Garber terms 'a space of possibility structuring and confounding culture'.[142] While the figurative displacement of the woman at the moment of revelation seems to risk the erasure of her bodily presence, Salome's dance is structured by precisely these kinds of sexual ambiguities, in Wilde's play and other texts, which allowed the distinctions between the deceased male author, the lesbian dancer and the veiled muse they shared to be erased so comprehensively during the 1918 trial.

The sense that the Pemberton Billing case was essentially reviving the history of Wilde's trials was enhanced by the presence of Lord Alfred Douglas as a witness. Disparaging his relationship with Wilde, Douglas viciously denounced the author of *Salomé* as 'the greatest force for evil in Europe in the last 350 years. Not only sexual evil [. . .] He was an agent for the devil in every possible way.'[143] Contriving Wilde in such terms, Douglas emphasised the potential of his literature to breed chaos 'in Europe', subtly overwriting *Salomé*'s Hiberno-French heritage and the legacies of transnational Symbolism, and resituating the play within the larger, more prescient context of a continent at war. Furthermore, he characterised himself as an interpreter of the text's allusions and motifs, claiming that Wilde 'intended it to be an exhibition of perverted sexual passion', and even arguing that the prominent image of the moon was a symbol of 'unnatural vice'.[144]

In this way, the trial became a stage for closely reading the text of *Salomé* against the imagined proclivities and anatomical intricacies of Maud Allan.[145] It was, Lucy Bland argues, 'the British war years' most visible attack on the morality of a lone woman'.[146] Allan's rumoured desires were thought to be confirmed by her knowledge of her own body: the medical expert Dr Serrell Cooke declared that only a doctor or a 'pervert' could possibly understand the meaning of the word 'clitoris'.[147] The fact that her brother Theo had been executed for a pair of gruesome murders decades before was also used as evidence of Allan's 'hereditary vice',[148] although the other key 'relative' in this case was certainly Wilde, who bound the dancer into a community of artists privy to unsanctioned practices and forms of knowledge.

Allan's attempt to prosecute Pemberton Billing for libel ultimately failed, and the trial rekindled, in the most public way, feverish concerns about the cultural legacy left by Salome, and also the perceived proximities between literature, performance and private lives. In authoring her own version of the Salome dance, Maud Allan had built on Loïe Fuller's efforts to carve an imaginative space for the women in her audience, using modern dance as a means of disrupting conventional modes of spectatorship and female performance. She was aligned repeatedly with the suffragettes during her career, and although she distanced herself from this particular group, she was very much a part of the progressive politics and 'rebellious cultural modernism' of Margot Asquith and her group, despite disapproving of the more radical and violent aspects of the suffrage campaign.[149] It was when she returned to Wilde's play in 1918 that Allan was punished most severely for her long association with the figure of Salome, and her dancing body was unceremoniously critiqued as a site of sexual and political betrayal, complicit in the veiled sins of the original text.

The Cult of Salome

The women who interpreted Salome's dance in the *fin de siècle* and early twentieth century imagined the dance, taken out of its literary and painterly forms, as a vessel for individual authorship on stage, which corresponded with their desire to create a distinct role for the female choreographer. Loïe Fuller and Maud Allan took two very different approaches to the modernist dance of veils, but each nonetheless used this theme to orchestrate their own art, fashioning themselves as the dance's singular creative force in their interviews and autobiographical writings. As we shall see in later chapters, when the Ballets Russes premiered *La Tragédie de Salomé* in 1913 with Tamara Karsavina dancing in the lead role, they recalled Fuller's lavish 1907 production, even using the original score devised by Florent Schmitt.[150] That Diaghilev's company, the experimental, avant-garde face of choreographic modernism, should allude to Loïe Fuller's version of *Salomé* in the early years of its rampant European success testifies to Fuller's lasting cultural legacy as a dance pioneer and, moreover, her ability to communicate between 'high art' and the popular stage.

Fuller's and Allan's careers in dance spanned the decades between the nineteenth and twentieth centuries, and their contributions to modern dance not only altered perceptions of the female dancer as a creative force, but also intervened in larger aesthetic debates concerning the status afforded to women and their bodies in art, and the imaginative possibilities for female spectators at the modern theatre. It is perhaps no surprise that Salome's dance was fanatically reproduced during this period across Europe and the USA, building on the triumphs of Fuller and Allan, as well as the controversy mustered around Wilde's play. Gertrude Hoffmann, a Maud Allan imitator, enjoyed real success on the American stage, alongside Eve Tanguay, Aida Overton Walker, and drag performers such as Eddie Cantor.[151] 'Salomania', whetted by an occidental fascination for the East, also reflected modern conceptions of the dancer as 'a mobile European subject', whose moving body could engage spectators in 'a synecdochic, kinaesthetic experience of other cultures', even refiguring the performer as 'a portable world's fair'.[152] Salome's enduring popularity reflected the continued relevance of *fin-de-siècle* aesthetic movements to the burgeoning projects of modernism, despite claims to the contrary in some quarters. The Pemberton Billing trial energised concerns about Wilde's phantasmic grip on the throat of modern British culture, and the tenets of

Decadence and Symbolism continued to preoccupy writers who responded to the 1890s as both a decaying, lethargic end point, and a period of radicalism and artistic freedom. In the next chapter, we return to 1890s Paris – the setting of Fuller's choreographic revolution – to explore Oscar Wilde's remarkable intervention in this history, which took shape alongside these transformations in dance practice and related debates concerning the forms and techniques of modernist theatre.

NOTES

1. Robert Ross, quoted in William Tydeman and Steven Price, *Wilde: Salome* (Cambridge: Cambridge University Press, 1996), 29–30.
2. Fuller's career has been the subject of a number of studies, including Rhonda K. Garelick, *Electric Salome: Loïe Fuller's Performance of Modernism* (Princeton, NJ: Princeton University Press, 2007); Ann Cooper Albright, *Traces of Light: Absence and Presence in the Work of Loïe Fuller* (Middletown, CT: Wesleyan University Press, 2007); Giovanni Lista, *Loïe Fuller: Danseuse de la Belle Époque* (Paris: Somogy-Stock/La Librairie de la Danse et le Centre de national du livre, 1995); Richard Current and Marcia Ewing Current, *Loïe Fuller: Goddess of Light* (Boston, MA: Northeastern University Press, 1997).
3. Banes, *Dancing Women*, 67.
4. Sally Sommer, 'Loïe Fuller', *The Drama Review* 19 (1975): 54.
5. Rancière, *Aisthesis*, 105.
6. Rancière uses the word *introuvable* ('unfindable') in the original French version of *Aisthesis*. The verb *trouver*, commonly translated as 'to find', also connotes forms of intellectual apprehension and feeling, suggesting that Fuller's body cannot be found in a literal sense, but also that it evades stable thought and categorisation. See Jacques Rancière, *Aisthesis: Scènes du régime esthétique de l'art* (Paris: Éditions Galilée, 2011), 123.
7. As Dana Mills has shown, although Rancière's critique of Fuller threatens to eclipse the body of the woman on stage, his aesthetic theories also institute modes of thinking that allow for a gendered reading of the dancing form. See Dana Mills, 'The Dancing Woman is the Woman Who Dances into the Future: Rancière, Dance, Politics', *Philosophy and Rhetoric* 49.4 (2016): 482–99.
8. The press called Fuller the 'modern Salome'. See Rhonda K. Garelick, 'Electric Salome: Loïe Fuller at the Exposition Universelle of 1900', in *Imperialism and Theater: Essays on World Theater, Drama, and Performance*, ed. J. Ellen Gainor (New York: Routledge, 1995), 86.
9. Banes, *Dancing Women*, 67–9.
10. Terry Castle, *The Apparitional Lesbian: Female Homosexuality and Modern Culture* (New York: Columbia University Press, 1993), 2.
11. Comments of this nature include: 'She is a hard working, plucky, good little woman whom success has not spoiled', in 'Loie Fuller's European Career', *Chicago Daily Tribune*, 30 July 1893. A later review of a performance by Fuller's dance company concluded: 'it cannot be charged that erotic incitation characterizes any of the music or the spirit in which the dancers of the present repertoire are interpreted'. See 'La National: La Loie Fuller and Her Company', *Washington Post*, 12 October 1909.
12. Garelick, *Electric Salome*, 16.
13. An English translation of Mallarmé's essay on Fuller appears as 'Another Study of Dance: The Fundamentals of Ballet', in *Divagations*, trans. Barbara Johnson

(Cambridge, MA: Harvard University Press, 2007), 135–7. This essay revises an article that first appeared as 'Considérations sur l'art du ballet et la Loïe Fuller' in the *National Observer*, 13 May 1893.
14. Stéphane Mallarmé, 'Ballets', in *Divagations*, 130.
15. Jones, *Literature, Modernism and Dance*, 15.
16. Mallarmé, 'Ballets', 134.
17. Ibid., 134.
18. Dee Reynolds, 'The Dancer as Woman: Loïe Fuller and Stéphane Mallarmé', in *Impressions of French Modernity: Art and Literature in France, 1850–1900*, ed. Richard Hobbs (Manchester: Manchester University Press, 1995), 155.
19. See Frank Kermode, 'Poet and Dancer before Diaghilev', *Salmagundi* 33/34 (1976): 23–47; Susan Jones, '"Une écriture corporelle": The Dancer in the Text of Mallarmé and Yeats', in *The Body and the Arts*, ed. Corinne Saunders, Ulrika Maude and Jane Macnaughton (Basingstoke: Palgrave Macmillan, 2009), 237–46; Julie Townsend, 'Synaesthetics: Symbolism, Dance and the Failure of Metaphor', *The Yale Journal of Criticism* 18 (2005): 126–48.
20. Mallarmé, 'Another Study of Dance', 136.
21. Kermode, 'Poet and Dancer before Diaghilev', 44.
22. Felicia McCarren, 'Stéphane Mallarmé, Loïe Fuller and the Theater of Femininity', in *Bodies of the Text: Dance as Theory, Literature as Dance*, ed. Ellen W. Goellner and Jacqueline Shea Murphy (New Brunswick, NJ: Rutgers University Press, 1995), 217.
23. Mallarmé, 'Another Study of Dance', 136.
24. Ibid., 136.
25. Julie Townsend, 'Alchemic Visions and Technological Advances: Sexual Morphology in Loie Fuller's Dance', in *Dancing Desires: Choreographing Sexualities On and Off the Stage*, ed. Jane C. Desmond (Madison, WI: University of Wisconsin Press, 2001), 78.
26. Mallarmé, 'Another Study of Dance', 136–7.
27. Rancière, *Aisthesis*, 100.
28. Mallarmé, 'Another Study of Dance', 136.
29. Ibid., 136.
30. Ibid., 136. Auguste Rodin's watercolour of Fuller is one of the few images from the period to imagine her as naked beneath her veils.
31. Mallarmé, 'The Only One Would Have to Be as Fluid', in *Divagations*, 138.
32. Mallarmé himself experimented with the physical properties of language and *mise en scène* in this way, especially in his unfinished inter-medial project *Livre* (1842–98), which Kélina Gotman has recently described as a 'choreotext'. Like his incomplete *Hérodiade*, this was an unstaged, perhaps unstageable dramatic work that nonetheless initiated a form of dance between reader, author and text. See Kélina Gotman, 'Mallarmé's "*Livre*": Notes towards a Schizotheatre', *Textual Practice* 33.1 (2017): 175–94, DOI: 10.1080/0950236X.2017.1308963.
33. Georges Rodenbach, 'Danseuses', *Le Figaro*, 5 May 1896.
34. Georges Rodenbach, *Bruges La Morte*, trans. Mike Mitchell (Sawtry: Dedalus European Classics, 2005), 40.
35. Ibid., 80, 46.
36. Arthur Symons, 'La Mélinite: Moulin Rouge', in *Poems by Arthur Symons*, vol. 1 (London: William Heinemann, 1902), 99.
37. Rodenbach, *Bruges La Morte*, 69.
38. Armstrong, *Modernism, Technology and the Body*, 6, 3.
39. Franko, *Dancing Modernism/Performing Politics*, x–xi.
40. Unidentified journalist, quoted in Garelick, *Electric Salome*, 120.

41. Fuller's serpentine dance was created during a hypnotism scene in the play *Quack, M.D*. Garelick also discusses Fuller's 'longstanding notion of herself as not just a performer, but a *hypnotizer*, a supernatural force'. See *Electric Salome*, 22. See also Felicia McCarren, 'The "Symptomatic Act" circa 1900: Hysteria, Hypnosis, Electricity, Dance', *Critical Enquiry* 21 (1995): 748–74.
42. Katharine Worth, *Oscar Wilde* (Basingstoke: Macmillan, 1983), 64–5.
43. Rancière, *Aisthesis*, 95.
44. William Hogarth, *The Analysis of Beauty* (London: W. Strahan, 1772), 25.
45. Ibid., 148.
46. Isadora Duncan, *My Life* (New York: Liveright, 2013), 2.
47. Edmund Burke, *A Philosophical Enquiry into the Sublime and Beautiful*, ed. Paul Guyer (Oxford: Oxford University Press, 2015), 93.
48. Ibid., 92.
49. Brandstetter, *Poetics of Dance*, 97.
50. Ibid., 97.
51. Genevieve Stebbins, *Dynamic Breathing and Harmonic Gymnastics* (New York: Edgar S. Werner, 1892), 61.
52. Albright, *Traces of Light*, 15.
53. Jody Sperling, 'Book Reviews', *Dance Films Association: Annual Review* (2008): 17.
54. Hillel Schwartz, 'Torque: The New Kinaesthetic of the Twentieth Century', in *Incorporations*, ed. Jonathan Crary and Sanford Kwinter (New York: Zone Books, 1992), 73.
55. Jones, *Literature, Modernism and Dance*, 17.
56. Brandstetter, *Poetics of Dance*, 272.
57. Mills, 'The Dancing Woman', 488.
58. Roger Marx, quoted in Albright, *Traces of Light*, 42.
59. Townsend, 'Alchemic Visions and Technological Advances', 78–9.
60. Albright cites these reviews in *Traces of Light*, 20, 26.
61. McCarren, *Dancing Machines*, 5.
62. Tom Gunning claims that early film-making, with its 'magical and illogical transformations', performs 'the syntax of Fuller's constant metamorphoses out of a matrix of movement'. See 'Loïe Fuller and the Art of Motion: Body, Light, Electricity, and the Origins of the Cinema', in *Camera Obscura, Camera Lucida: Essays in Honour of Annette Michelson*, ed. Richard Allen and Malcolm Turvey (Amsterdam: Amsterdam University Press, 2003), 85–6.
63. Banes, *Dancing Women*, 69–70; Garelick, *Electric Salome*, 6.
64. Jones, 'Une écriture corporelle', 240.
65. Loïe Fuller, *Fifteen Years of a Dancer's Life: With Some Account of her Distinguished Friends* (Boston, MA: Maynard, 1913), 33.
66. For Fuller, this was a feminist issue, and she criticised ballet's attempts to control the female body, declaring that any practice that 'deforms the body an iota should not, cannot be justified as art'. Fuller, quoted in Garelick, *Electric Salome*, 120.
67. Fuller, *Fifteen Years*, 72.
68. Garelick, *Electric Salome*, 34.
69. Rancière, *Aisthesis*, 94.
70. Mills, 'The Dancing Woman', 487.
71. Ibid., 488.
72. Garelick, *Electric Salome*, 32.
73. Anonymous reviewer, quoted in Gunning, 'Loïe Fuller and the Art of Motion', 79.
74. de Lauretis, *Technologies of Gender*, 2; Townsend, 'Alchemic Visions and

Technological Advances', 74. Tirza True Latimer claims that Fuller 'staged a presence that was specifically lesbian'; see 'Loie Fuller: Butch Femme Fatale', in *Proceedings of the Society of Dance History Scholars, 22nd Annual Conference* (Albuquerque, NM: University of New Mexico Press, 1999), 86.
75. Penny Farfan, *Performing Queer Modernism* (Oxford: Oxford University Press, 2017), 39.
76. Dierkes-Thrun, *Salome's Modernity*, 10.
77. Eve Kosofsky Sedgwick, *Tendencies* (Durham, NC: Duke University Press, 1993), xii.
78. Fuller, *Fifteen Years*, 266.
79. Garelick, *Electric Salome*, 10. Albright also doubts the value of such queer interpretations, criticising the 'reductive reading of the equation of performance with life' (*Traces of Light*, 123). Her response misconstrues the value of this kind of project by perceiving its aim to be purely biographical, rather than a powerful challenge to dominant modes of interpretation and spectatorship.
80. Maud Allan, to whom I return in this chapter, is a key example, but the opera singer Mary Garden, the actor Alla Nazimova, and the writers Michael Field, Djuna Barnes and Claude Cahun responded, in various ways, to the story of Salome, and were also connected to the history of lesbian literature and performance.
81. Garelick has described Fuller's experiences touring with William 'Buffalo Bill' Cody's *Wild West Show* in the 1880s, and her experiments dancing with light and veils while playing the title role in *Aladdin's Wonderful Lamp* in 1887. See *Electric Salome*, 24–7.
82. 'Miss Fuller's New Dance', *New York Times*, 24 January 1896.
83. Albright, *Traces of Light*, 126; Tydeman and Price, *Wilde: Salome*, 138.
84. 'Miss Fuller's New Dance'.
85. Ibid. Albright also discusses the set for the 'Fire Dance' in *Traces of Light*, 126.
86. 'La Loie in Perihelion', *Chicago Daily Tribune*, 12 April 1896.
87. Ibid.
88. 'Coming Back to Dance', *New York Tribune*, 23 February 1896.
89. '"La Loie" Talks of Her Art', *New York Times*, 1 March 1896.
90. Bentley, *Sisters of Salome*, 44.
91. Ibid., 44.
92. Jules Claretie, quoted in Albright, *Traces of Light*, 139.
93. This is taken from an article that Claretie wrote for *Le Temps*, which Fuller cites extensively in her autobiography. See *Fifteen Years*, 288.
94. Albright, *Traces of Light*, 116.
95. This narrative has been comprehensively challenged by Albright, who draws on a wealth of historical reports and reviews to paint a more balanced picture of the critical response. See *Traces of Light*, 125–34.
96. Jean Lorrain, quoted in ibid., 127.
97. Jean Lorrain, 'Magic Lantern', in *Late Victorian Gothic Tales*, ed. Roger Luckhurst (Oxford: Oxford University Press, 2009), 174.
98. Ibid., 174.
99. Ibid., 174.
100. Ibid., 172.
101. Maurice Emmanuel, *The Antique Greek Dance, After Sculptured and Painted Figures*, trans. Harriet Jean Beauley (London: John Lane, 1913), 173.
102. Brandstetter, *Poetics of Dance*, 152.
103. Ibid., 175.
104. For a cultural history of hysteria, see Georges Didi-Hubermann, *Invention of*

Hysteria: Charcot and the Photographic Iconography of the Salpêtrière, trans. Alisa Hartz (Cambridge, MA: MIT Press, 2004).
105. Havelock Ellis, *Man and Woman: A Study of Human Secondary Sexual Characters* (London: Walter Scott, 1894), 307.
106. Jules Claretie, quoted in Fuller, *Fifteen Years*, 282.
107. Fuller, *Fifteen Years*, 91.
108. Ibid., 91.
109. Fuller was not the only female performer to be struck by Bernhardt's unearthly appearance and style of movement. Ellen Terry used extraordinary metaphors to describe Bernhardt in her memoir, declaring her 'transparent as an azalea, only more so; like a cloud, only not so thick'. See Ellen Terry, *The Story of My Life: Recollections and Reflections* (New York: Doubleday, 1908), 237.
110. Susan Manning, 'The Female Dancer and the Male Gaze: Feminist Critiques of Early Modern Dance', in *Meaning in Motion: New Cultural Studies of Dance*, ed. Jane C. Desmond (Durham, NC: Duke University Press, 1997), 154.
111. Ibid., 164.
112. Preston, *Modernism's Mythic Pose*, 11–14.
113. Fuller, *Fifteen Years*, 92.
114. Davinia Caddy, 'Variations on the Dance of the Seven Veils', *Cambridge Opera Journal* 17.1 (2005): 37.
115. 'The Salome Dance Gets into Politics', *New York Times*, 24 August 1908.
116. Lois Cucullu, 'Wilde and Wilder Salomés: Modernising Wilde's Nubile Princess from Sarah Bernhardt to Norma Desmond', *Modernism/modernity* 18 (2011): 497.
117. See, for example, Lucy Bland, 'Trial by Sexology? Maud Allan, *Salome* and the "Cult of the Clitoris" Case', in *Sexology in Culture: Labelling Bodies and Desires*, ed. Lucy Bland and Laura Doan (Chicago: University of Chicago Press, 1998), 183–98; Judith R. Walkowitz, 'The "Vision of Salome": Cosmopolitanism and Erotic Dancing in Central London 1908–1918', *The American Historical Review* 108.2 (2003): 337–76; Amy Koritz, 'Dancing the Orient for England: Maud Allan's "The Vision of Salome"', *Theatre Journal* 46 (1994): 63–78.
118. Dierkes-Thrun, *Salome's Modernity*, 96.
119. Maud Allan, *My Life and Dancing* (London: Everett, 1908), 36.
120. Ibid., 45.
121. Ibid., 65.
122. Ibid., 75.
123. Dierkes-Thrun, *Salome's Modernity*, 83.
124. Allan knew Loïe Fuller and toured with her troupe in France in 1907. See Felix Cherniavsky, *The Salome Dancer: The Life and Times of Maud Allan* (Toronto: McClelland and Stewart, 1991), 148.
125. Lucy Delap, *The Feminist Avant-Garde: Transatlantic Encounters of the Early Twentieth Century* (Cambridge: Cambridge University Press, 2007), 103.
126. Allan, *My Life and Dancing*, 126.
127. Simonson, *Body Knowledge*, 27.
128. Journalist quoted in Cherniavsky, *The Salome Dancer*, 163.
129. Rachel Shteir, *Striptease: The Untold History of the Girlie Show* (New York: Oxford University Press, 2004), 45.
130. Ibid., 4–8.
131. Roland Barthes, 'Striptease', in *Mythologies*, trans. Annette Lavers (London: Vintage, 2009), 97.
132. Ibid., 99.
133. In 'The Question Concerning Technology' (1954) Martin Heidegger defines

technē as 'the name not only for the activities and skills of the craftsman, but also for the arts of the mind and the fine arts. *Technē* belongs to bringing-forth, to *poiēsis*.' See *The Question Concerning Technology and Other Essays*, trans. William Lovitt (New York: Garland, 1977), 13.
134. Dierkes-Thrun, *Salome's Modernity*, 100.
135. Judith Walkowitz, *Nights Out: Life in Cosmopolitan London* (New Haven, CT: Yale University Press, 2012), 65.
136. 'The Spread of Bohemianism in English Society', *New York Times*, 16 August 1908.
137. Kristin Mahoney has shown how Wilde's 'ghost' continued to exert a grip on the popular imagination after his death: the *Los Angeles Times* and *New York Times* devoted articles to alleged 'sightings' of the author, and Wilde's nephew, Arthur Cravan (who himself disappeared mysteriously), published a posthumous interview with Wilde in the Surrealist magazine *Maintenant* in 1913. See Kristin Mahoney, *Literature and the Politics of Post-Victorian Decadence* (Cambridge: Cambridge University Press, 2015), 6.
138. *The Vigilante*, 16 February 1918, reprinted in Noel Pemberton Billing, ed., *Verbatim Report of the Trial of Noel Pemberton Billing M.P. On a charge of Criminal Libel Before Mr Justice Darling at the Central Criminal Court, Old Bailey* (London: Vigilante Office, 1918), 455. Quoted in Michael Kettle, *Salome's Last Veil: The Libel Case of the Century* (London: Hart-Davis, 1977), 18–19.
139. *The Vigilante*, 26 January 1918, quoted in Philip Hoare, *Oscar Wilde's Last Stand: Decadence, Conspiracy, and the Most Outrageous Trial of the Century* (New York: Arcade, 1997), 57–8.
140. Jodie Medd, '"The Cult of the Clitoris": Anatomy of a National Scandal', *Modernism/modernity* 9 (2002): 29.
141. Ibid., 32.
142. Marjorie Garber, *Vested Interests: Cross-Dressing and Cultural Anxiety* (New York: Routledge, 1992), 342.
143. 'The Billing Case', *Manchester Guardian*, 3 June 1918.
144. Ibid.
145. Allan had previously illustrated a German sex manual for women entitled *Illustrated Dictionary of the Woman* (1900). As Toni Bentley notes, Pemberton Billing never found out about this or he would certainly have used it at her trial to prove an 'unnatural' knowledge of the female body. See Bentley, *Sisters of Salome*, 55.
146. Lucy Bland, *Modern Women on Trial: Sexual Transgression in the Age of the Flapper* (Manchester: Manchester University Press, 2013), 17.
147. Medd, 'Anatomy of a Scandal', 37.
148. 'Mr Pemberton Billing and Miss Maud Allan: The Opening', *Manchester Guardian*, 30 May 1918.
149. Walkowitz, *Nights Out*, 64–5.
150. 'The Russian Ballet', *The Observer*, 6 July 1913.
151. Glenn, *Female Spectacle*, 101–17.
152. Michelle Clayton, 'Modernism's Moving Bodies', *Modernist Cultures* 9.1 (2014): 30.

2

'THAT INVISIBLE DANCE': SYMBOLISM, *SALOMÉ* AND OSCAR WILDE'S CHOREOGRAPHIC AESTHETICS

A copy of Oscar Wilde's *Salomé* in the original French, addressed to the artist Aubrey Beardsley, bears the following inscription in Wilde's hand: 'For Aubrey: for the only artist who, besides myself, knows what the dance of the seven veils is, and can see that invisible dance.'[1] Beardsley, a co-founder of the provocative periodical *The Yellow Book* (1894–97), supplied the illustrations for the English version of Wilde's play, published in 1894 using a somewhat loose translation by Lord Alfred Douglas.[2] Associated with this particular group of late Victorian men, Wilde's 'invisible dance' might plausibly be read as an allusion to the secret and protected language they shared with each other, a subtle coda for J. A. Symonds's *l'amour de l'impossible*, or Lord Alfred Douglas's oft-repeated 'love that dare not speak its name'.[3] Animated by these well-known and much-discussed aspects of Wilde's biography, the 'dance of the seven veils' that occurs at the climax of *Salomé* has often been read as a cryptic shorthand for the dramatist's own aesthetic and erotic interest in the male form. Marjorie Garber, for instance, sees Salome as a transvestic figure, whose veils circumscribe the hidden body always apparently masked in Wilde's literary system: 'The cultural Imaginary of the Salome story is the veiled phallus and the masquerade. This is the latent dream behind the manifest content of Salome.'[4] Retaining a rich awareness of the highly ambiguous gender constructions at work in Wilde's text, this reading has become popular with later interpreters of *Salomé*, since it underscores the play's undoubted homoeroticism and corresponds with Wilde's dedicated interest in both personal self-fashioning and the aesthetic interplay between surface and depth, theorised in works such as *The Decay of Lying* (1891) and 'The Truth of Masks' (1891). Yet such an approach also makes a bold critical move by figuratively (and, in some stage productions, literally) inserting a male presence into the space supposedly vacated by the dancer's body, thereby colluding in the same mystification of the female form that characterised the *fin-de-siècle* responses to dance discussed in the previous chapter. Once again, dancing women are construed as unseen and unknowable, and Salome's body becomes a point of absence or lack for Wilde's audience, conceivable only in relation to her author and often at the expense of the performer's creative work.

As we have seen in the case of Fuller, however, such a mode of disembodiment was in fact purposefully cultivated by modern dancers as part of a radical attempt to rewrite the body's limits, often through the strategic use of costume materials and visual technologies. While Wilde's use of the term 'invisible' acknowledges the puzzling opacity of the dance that ostensibly sits at the heart of his drama, it also aligns *Salomé*'s choreographic aesthetics with contemporary dance practices. Garber's argument is most interesting when she claims that 'Salome and her dance became a figure for that which can – and cannot – be represented'; her dance suspends fixed categories to the point where the terms of dramatic representation itself are at stake.[5] What critical responses to Wilde's play have not always fully appreciated is the extent to which the implicit homoeroticism of Salome's 'invisible' performance – and the instability of her physical presence – intersect with the aesthetics of women's modern dance and related modes of theatrical performance that formulated new types of gesture and movement in the late nineteenth century. Like Fuller's signature use of drapes, and other forms of skirt dance popularised during this period, the central performance in *Salomé* is contingent on the use of multiple veils, and it resists, by its very nature, secure representation in visual or verbal terms. Exploring how Wilde both adapted and departed from the Symbolist and Decadent texts often cited as his key sources, this chapter explores the multiple ways in which Salome's dance was imagined by Wilde and his contemporaries, rendering it a site of interpretative possibility for the female performer and opening it up to other experiments in choreography and dramatic writing.

Although Wilde composed the first version of *Salomé* in 1891, prior to the modern dance performances that Mallarmé witnessed at the Folies Bergère, the play was not staged until February 1896. By that point, Wilde and his collaborators had apparently discussed various possibilities for a theatrical realisation of the dance of the seven veils, transforming it from a brief stage direction into the play's dramatic apex. But Wilde's (fairly inconsistent) intentions for the performance, outlined in the recollections of his friend Gomez Carrillo, are not the only relevant contexts. The dance itself had also taken on a range of forms in the public imagination, stimulated by the controversy surrounding the play's censorship in England and Beardsley's singular illustrations, as well as a vogue for veiled dancers led by Fuller and her imitators. Previous accounts of *Salomé* have not always fully explored the connections between the play's emphasis on the dancing body as spectacle and the theories of corporeal movement that shaped Symbolist and avant-garde theatre, including an acute interest in depersonalised and mechanical acting styles, and a growing (not unrelated) appreciation for the graceful, fluid styles of motion embodied by powerful female actors such as Sarah Bernhardt, Ellen Terry and Eleanora Duse, whose careers were augmented by the work of early feminist movements and debates about the New Woman.

Placing Wilde's literary project in dialogue with this constellation of bodily practices, this chapter examines the aesthetic and cultural contexts of the first performance of *Salomé* at the Théâtre de l'Oeuvre, an institution managed by the director Aurélien Marie Lugné-Poe. This event came in the aftermath of the play's disastrous encounter with the English Lord Chamberlain and, stoking further controversy, Wilde's trials and incarceration.[6] Lugné-Poe's production meant a good deal to Wilde, who believed it had 'turned the scale in his favour', at least in terms of the treatment he received while imprisoned.[7] Wilde has often been characterised as a popular dramatist who sacrificed his political radicalism for commercial success, but *Salomé* marks a clear departure from his comedies of manners, given its debts to the more experimental facets of *fin-de-siècle* French drama advanced by playwrights including Alfred Jarry and Maurice Maeterlinck. Salome's dance of the seven veils built on a crucial shift in understandings of the relationship between performer and dramatist, and Wilde's text can be read alongside the growing fascination with choreographed and mechanised bodies in the work of these playwrights. In Katharine Worth's opinion, a dramatist such as Wilde, an Irishman in Paris writing through the various strains of the theatrical avant-garde, was 'holding out his hand across fifty years to Beckett', anticipating trends in performance that would later take hold in the twentieth century.[8]

Salome, as Wilde imagined her, emerged on to a stage already coming to terms with the changing cultural landscape of modernity, shaped by the rise of new technologies and forms of rhythm and movement. At the *fin de siècle*, Parisian theatres witnessed an explosion of innovative performances across different genres, and *Salomé* was not the only striking new play performed in the French capital in 1896. The year's second major theatrical event took place on 9 December, again under the auspices of Lugné-Poe's theatre company. Jarry's *Ubu Roi*, a provocative interpretation of *Macbeth* featuring puppet-like actors, had its *répétition générale*, a public dress rehearsal for critics, writers and other privileged members of the artistic community. Irreverent, blasphemous, parodic and obscene, both Wilde's and Jarry's work engaged with and troubled existing methods of dramatic representation, drawing on Symbolist and avant-garde strategies of aesthetic estrangement, political critique and sexual difference. 1896 was also the year in which the Lumière brothers patented their *cinématographe*, and some of their earliest work includes recordings of serpentine dancers such as Fuller, illustrating the fervent hold that seemingly free and wild dancers had gained on the popular imagination.[9] Such technologies seemed to open up new possibilities for the human (or inhuman) body, transforming it into an object that could be reconstrued, recaptured, supplanted and supplemented by machines. Salome, a seductively veiled and autonomous figure, fuelled concerns about the legitimacy of fixed perceptions of the female body, and about the kind of exchanges that might occur between spectators and performers in the theatre. In Flaubert's version of the story, for instance, Salome's dance precipitates an alarming sensory response in her spectators, as 'invisible sparks [shoot] out' from her body, 'firing the men with excitement'.[10] Transformed from a lustful and sensuous vision into something electrically charged, Salome's body stands at the permeable interstices of nineteenth-century aesthetic movements and the mechanised, volatile impulses represented by new technologies and modern forms of desire.

'This very unattractive tragedy': Symbolism, Decadence and *Salomé* on Stage

Salomé had already caused Wilde considerable trouble by the time it premiered in February 1896. Several years previously, a planned production in London with Sarah Bernhardt in the lead role had been cancelled by the Lord Chamberlain on the grounds of the play's religious subject matter (the ban on theatrical representations of biblical material was not lifted in England until 1931).[11] Edward Pigott, the London Examiner of Plays at the time, described *Salomé* as a 'miracle of impudence' and articulated in florid terms his alarm at the princess's demonstrations of desire for Iokanaan's severed head, which seemed to approach the realm of necrophilia.[12] Beardsley's illustrations did little to ease the controversy surrounding the work. Populated by bodies of indeterminate sex and in various states of exposure, Beardsley's drawings were interpreted as visual confirmation of the perversely erotic strain of Decadence, although their dark beauty was appreciated in some quarters. In *The Trembling of the Veil* (1922), W. B. Yeats recalled telling Beardsley that he had never equalled his depiction of Salome revelling before her capital prize; the artist allegedly responded, 'Yes, yes; but beauty is so difficult.'[13] It was certainly a difficult beauty that Wilde created in *Salomé*, a play that contributed to the iconography of threatening sexuality associated with previous versions of this figure in nineteenth-century art and literature.

Wilde's initial decision to compose his play in French strategically affiliated him with the interconnected schools of Decadence and Symbolism. Writers associated with these schools, as we have seen, took inspiration from the modern dance performances of Fuller, while also conjuring visions of voluptuous, degenerate head-hunters in their art and writing. The aesthetic outlooks of these movements were continuously theorised and redefined during this period, and the task of defining them is only further complicated by the inconsistencies of their best-known theorist, the English critic Arthur Symons. In his essay 'The Decadent Movement in Literature' (1893), Symons termed Symbolism a mere 'branch' of Decadence, with the latter 'most precisely expressing the general sense of the newest movement in literature', a movement of 'intense self-consciousness, a restless curiosity in research, an over-subtilising refinement upon refinement, a spiritual and moral perversity'.[14] This defiantly morbid school found admirers beyond France, and Wilde, influenced by the Aestheticism of his Oxford tutor Walter Pater, was its most notable evangelist in the English language (a connection eagerly diagnosed by *Salomé*'s outraged detractors). By 1899, however, Symons had experienced a change of heart. In *The Symbolist Movement in Literature*, he disparaged Decadence as a 'straying aside from the main road of literature', a 'mock interlude [. . .] [that] diverted the attention of the critics while something more serious was in preparation'.[15] This more sober form was Symbolism, and it was, in Symons's opinion, grave and spiritual whereas Decadence encouraged only degeneracy of the sort embodied by Wilde and his associates. The falling fortunes of Decadence, a movement fundamentally entwined with notions of decay and corruption, saw Symbolism embraced as a term endowed with boundless possibility, aspiring towards the kind of novelty that was thought to characterise the modernist imagination. This critical shift, Vincent Sherry has shown, allowed Symbolism to be co-opted as a forerunner of modernist innovation, while Decadence was prematurely dismissed as overly stylised and saturnine, irreversibly affixed to the sense of an ending.[16] Developed in the work of poets such as Mallarmé and Arthur Rimbaud, Symbolism signalled 'a revolt against exteriority, against rhetoric, against a materialistic tradition; in this endeavour to disengage the ultimate essence, the soul' of things.[17] Firmly opposed to realism and naturalism, it sought, through symbols, to grant literature 'its authentic speech'.[18]

Symons's reversals and qualifications in his commentaries blur any straightforward distinction between these movements, compounded by the fact that he discusses a number of the same writers in both works, including Verlaine, Mallarmé and Huysmans, all of whom were fascinated by Salome and other nineteenth-century incarnations of female corruption. While the historic entanglements of their coteries have often led to the conflation of these terms, they were subsequently taken up in alternative ways, with Symbolism emerging as a more dominant 'theory' while Decadence endured a lesser status as a 'mood'.[19] Both, however, were central to the projects of modernism, and to the work that Wilde produced in the 1890s. It is perhaps no coincidence that Symons shifted his allegiance to Symbolism in the wake of Wilde's imprisonment and the very public prosecution of Decadent sensibilities. *Salomé*, Wilde's clearest nod to contemporaneous French literary forms, traced the contours of these aesthetic variations and continuities, and it is interesting that Symons himself would rework Wilde's themes in his poem 'The Dance of the Daughters of Herodias' (1897) and his cycle *Studies in Strange Sins* (1923), inspired by Beardsley's art.

The outraged responses to *Salomé* in England, if not in France, were hardly surprising given the public persona of its author.[20] Even prior to the scandal of Wilde's trials, newspapers responded to *Salomé* with palpable fear and disgust, as demonstrated in this 1894 review of the English text:

> To our thinking this very unattractive tragedy is even less attractive in its English rendering than it was in the original French. As for the illustrations by Mr. Aubrey Beardsley we hardly know what to say of them. They are fantastic, grotesque, unintelligible for the most part, and, so far as they are intelligible, repulsive. They would seem to represent the manners of Judaea as conceived by Mr. Oscar Wilde portrayed in the style of Japanese grotesque as conceived by a French *décadent*. The whole thing must be a joke, and it seems to us a very poor joke.[21]

A lack of comprehension appears to be at the heart of this reviewer's unease, suggesting that the repulsive content of Wilde's play was obscured by its style; the ostentatious similes and sensual, evocative language. Tropes associated with French (and loosely 'subversive') literature, signalled by the term *décadent*, render the work 'unintelligible' in the main, disclosing only dissident meanings when any meaning is disclosed at all. This reviewer's fervent interpretation of the play's elliptical qualities betrays an underlying anxiety about the capacities of language to veil unorthodox desires, particularly as they relate to sexuality. Wilde's interest in masks and veils was read against him during his prosecution, a rhetorical strategy that was also used at Maud Allan's libel trial, as we have seen.[22] The 'invisible' nature of the dance of the seven veils was therefore viewed as a shorthand for the text itself, which deals in seemingly 'unintelligible' ideas.

Salome's body, and her dance in particular, operated as a locus for these anxieties. If Wilde was capable of spreading his perceived immorality, *Salomé* was seen as a vessel for such deviant communications, strengthened by the cultural legacy of his muse. While Fuller may have challenged the more grotesque and erotically explicit elements of Salome's story, many of Wilde's sources were fully conversant with these themes, embracing the pathos formula of Salome as a sexually motivated head-hunter. Gustave Moreau's famous Symbolist artwork *L'Apparition* (1876–77) clearly demonstrates these qualities, with its sensuous coupling of a near-naked Salome and the elevated, luminous head of John the Baptist.[23] In Huysmans's novel *À Rebours*, one of Wilde's key sources, this painting sends the protagonist Des Esseintes into raptures as he revels in the horror of Salome's beauty:

> She became, in a sense, the symbolic deity of indestructible Lechery, the goddess of immortal Hysteria, the accursed Beauty singled out from all others by the cataleptic paroxysm that stiffens her flesh and hardens her muscles; the monstrous, indiscriminate, irresponsible, unfeeling Beast who, like the Helen of antiquity, poisons everything that comes near her, everything that sees her, everything that she touches.[24]

Des Esseintes is a consummate aesthete, indulging in the corrupt beauty of his art as much as he luxuriates in the excesses of language, offering endless taxonomies of his aesthetic environment while remaining passive and physically inert at its centre. In the character of Des Esseintes, 'we see', according to Symons, 'the sensations and ideas of the effeminate, over-civilised, deliberately abnormal creature who is [. . .] partly the father, partly the offspring, of the perverse art that he adores'.[25] It is little surprise that the 'yellow book' eagerly consulted by Wilde's Dorian Gray, another purveyor of 'perverse art', should turn out to be *À Rebours*. The sentences seem to dance for him with the 'subtle monotony of their music', full of 'complex refrains and movements elaborately repeated'.[26]

While Decadent men such as Des Esseintes and Dorian Gray were regarded as queerly feminine, the women they depicted were typically imbued with a pseudo-masculine erotic presence, writ large in their libidinous gazes and imposing sexual power. Salome was often construed in such pathological terms, as suggested by the appalled phrasing of the Examiner of Plays, who expressed his disgust at Salome's climactic 'paroxysm of sexual despair' before the severed head of Iokanaan.[27] As the 'goddess of immortal Hysteria', she is subtly affiliated with the patients at Charcot's Salpêtrière, an institution Foucault describes as a 'theatre of ritual crises' designed to incite public anxieties.[28] Salome's stiff and hardened muscles even reflect Charcot's practice of casting the bodies of his hysterics in wax, preserving their contorted forms in aesthetic moulds.[29] Figured as an aberrant subject, transfixed by the grotesque object of her desire, Salome is bound up in strategies for staging the female body across the period's scientific and aesthetic cultures, and the resulting anxieties about the contaminating effects of witnessing such performances.

This was the fervent climate that shaped Wilde's early thinking about the subject of his play. Salome was clearly associated with the possible dangers of hysteria and enchantment, stimulated by the 'misogynistic revery' of Huysmans.[30] In *À Rebours*, Moreau's painting is used to invoke the dancer's body, not as a source of transformative female creativity, but as a stiffly sculpted *femme fatale*, whose powerful desires are ultimately subsumed by the ecstasy of the male aesthete. Wilde was certainly influenced by the Symbolist

Salomes that proliferated during this period, and Yeats, immersed in the cultural climate of *fin-de-siècle* Paris, described his own desire to create 'some Herodiade of our theatre, dancing seemingly alone in her narrow moving luminous circle'.[31] Reflecting on the creative imperatives of the period, Yeats saw Salome as emblematic of a particular set of ideals and practices, 'separate from everything heterogeneous and casual, from all character and circumstance'.[32] His understanding of the dancer's place in the Symbolist imagination was shaped by his friendship with Symons, who recited to him the poetry of Verlaine and Mallarmé, apparently to great effect. 'My thoughts gained in richness and in clearness from his sympathy, nor shall I ever know how much my practice and theory owe to the passages that he read me', mused Yeats, describing the lingering impact of Symbolist poetics on his own dramatic philosophy, and also undoubtedly on the Salome-themed plays for dancers that he wrote in the 1930s.[33] As Yeats's reflections suggest, Salome, or 'Herodiade', was an elemental symbol for the aesthetic movements of the late nineteenth century.

While Wilde's imagination may have been stimulated by his French contemporaries, he did not seek simply to replicate their interpretations of this myth; according to Jane Marcus, his *Salomé* 'de-mystifies' the image of Salome created by the Symbolists.[34] In Wilde's play, this veiled dancer was ostensibly freed from the catalepsy of Huysmans's and Moreau's visions, transferred instead to the mobile arena of the stage, which allowed Wilde to access new theatrical discourses and related developments in dance. There are debates about the extent to which *Salomé* was originally meant for the theatre: Robert Ross felt that the dance of the seven veils disrupted the 'dramatic unity of the play'; others have suggested that Wilde may have been writing in the relatively obscure tradition of the closet drama – a form of 'reading drama' with which Mallarmé's *Hérodiade* is often associated.[35] Discussing the ambiguities inherent in *Salomé*'s staging requirements, Joseph Donohue points to a prevalent late nineteenth-century conflict between 'a pure, unsullied, "perfect" kind of drama [. . .] and a more material, contingent kind of theatre intended for both eye and ear'.[36] It seems clear, however, that Wilde conceived of *Salomé* as a performance text: plays would be his dominant and most successful form in the 1890s and his early attempt to find a theatre to produce *Salomé* suggests that he was deeply invested in its dramatic realisation.

Wilde thought in detail about what a production of *Salomé* might constitute. The performance histories of *Salomé*, and the artistic loyalties of the institutions affiliated with Wilde's play, reveal much about the aesthetic and dramaturgic debates framing her dance. Even prior to Bernhardt's failed attempt to bring the play to London, Wilde and his friend Charles Ricketts originally planned a French production, together conceiving an immersive theatrical experience with the different groups of characters visually designated by bright blocks of colour, and a 'rich turquoise' sky 'cut by the perpendicular fall of gilded strips of Japanese matting forming an aerial tint above the terraces'.[37] Wilde also wanted to release perfumes into the theatre to reflect the mood of different scenes. These plans for a synaesthetic staging, informed by a craze for *Japonisme*, did not come to fruition, although Ricketts did later stage *Salomé* at the King's Hall in Covent Garden in 1906. It was therefore left to Lugné-Poe to unveil Wilde's play for the first time at his Théâtre de l'Oeuvre, an independent theatre founded in 1893 with the objective of staging works perceived as experimental or provocative, criteria that Wilde's play certainly satisfied.

The Théâtre de l'Oeuvre was one of a number of theatres in Paris that provided a space for Symbolism's dramatic projects. Paul Fort's Théâtre d'Art was another, and it had briefly been attached to a possible production of *Salomé* prior to Lugné-Poe.[38] Through the Théâtre d'Art, Fort had associated himself with other major French-language dramatists pushing the boundaries of theatrical convention: in 1891, he had staged Maurice Maeterlinck's *L'Intruse* (*The Intruder*, 1890) and *Les Aveugles* (*The Blind*, 1890), introducing the Belgian playwright's concept of 'static theatre' to Parisian audiences.[39] Maeterlinck was an important theorist of Symbolist performance and his approach to the acting body influenced a range of practitioners from Jarry to Yeats and Edward Gordon Craig, all of whom differently incorporated aspects of his thinking into their dramatic systems. Providential forces and uncertain boundaries shadow Maeterlinck's plays: these works are populated by marionette-like characters that reflect the dramatist's ambition to turn the actor's body into a controllable stage element. Patrick McGuinness has observed that Maeterlinck saw the body as a 'rogue by-product, a kind of uncleansable residue in the process of performance', yet he turned these anxieties into a coherent dramatic philosophy, suggesting that marionettes, or performers mimicking marionette behaviours, might remedy the issue of subjective expression in the actor, thereby enhancing the authority of the playwright.[40] This approach to the dynamic between performer and dramatist reflected and cultivated broader thinking about choreographed movements, technologically augmented bodies, and the relationship between acting and free will.

Although the prophetic tones and Symbolist register of *Salomé* seem to reflect aspects of Maeterlinck's work, Lugné-Poe's theatre was not as strictly invested in the Symbolist agenda as the Théâtre d'Art. After Fort's purist loyalty to Symbolism led to his institution's ruin, Lugné-Poe took a less faithful but more productive approach.[41] His staging of *Salomé* handled some of the play's more controversial material through a tactics of evasion; for instance, Lugné-Poe cast the Page of Herodias (who utters the play's most controversial homoerotic line) as a woman (his wife Suzanne Després) and thereby avoided creating further scandal in the wake of Wilde's trial.[42] It is also significant that the play was quietly rehearsed and barely promoted, suggesting that the director was keen to resist both a theatrical controversy and the very real threat of censorship, which had already put paid to efforts to stage the play in England. It is difficult to ascertain how the dance of the seven veils was performed by Lina Munte, although Jean de Tinan's celebration of her role as 'more beautiful and more terrible than [Wilde] had imagined' suggests that her Salome was invested with the qualities of horror and awe embodied by Mallarmé's Hérodiade.[43] Receiving a mixed critical response, this 1896 production of *Salomé* nonetheless integrated Wilde's play into the French theatrical culture of the *fin de siècle*, alluding to parallels between his work and the radical theatres of Maeterlinck and Jarry.

The thematic and stylistic overlaps between these dramatists are striking, particularly in terms of their approach to the role of the actor and qualities of gesture and movement. Theatre historians have long described Jarry's *Ubu Roi* – also first produced by Lugné-Poe in 1896 – as a pivotal moment for the avant-garde, when a proto-modernist theatre emerged, raging with expletives, from the vestiges of the dramatic tradition. Partly conceived as a burlesque of Shakespearean tragedy, *Ubu Roi* is written in the mode of a farce, though its infantile protagonist – King Ubu – might be seen as offering a scathing critique of the age's covetous materialism and degenerate morality. Allegedly, a riot broke out among members of the audience following the profane opening line, although competing accounts of the play's reception have created some dispute as to what actually occurred at the two performances on 9 and 10 December 1896. Some of the confusion regarding the extent of the public outcry originates from Yeats's account of watching *Ubu Roi* in *The Trembling of the Veil*, which he composed and published decades after the event:

> The audience shake their fists at one another, and the Rhymer whispers to me, 'There are often duels after these performances', and he explains to me what is happening on stage [. . .] I am very sad, for comedy, objectivity, has displayed its growing power once more.[44]

Yeats acknowledges the possible imprecision of his account, admitting that 'many pictures come before me without date or order'.[45] Discussing the historiographies of *Ubu Roi*, Thomas Postlewait has identified a tendency among scholars to use this premiere as a key example of avant-garde rebellion, without fully accounting for the existing conditions that fomented such a work.[46] Maeterlinck's 'static theatre', for instance, had previously dramatised the marionette-like performance techniques deployed by Jarry, and Maurice Bouchor's *Petit Théâtre des Marionettes* similarly extolled the virtues of puppetry. Importantly, Wilde's *Salomé* had been staged at the same theatre ten months earlier, paving the way for Jarry's bodily grotesquerie and experimental style. Yeats probably attended the *répétition générale* rather than the premiere, and the make-up of the audience, with its diverse vested interests and critical biases, made controversy inevitable, which was ultimately what Jarry worked for as a playwright, designer and director. As Günter Berghaus has pointed out, Jarry's utter disdain for bourgeois values meant that *Ubu Roi* was largely conceived as 'dynamite thrown at an audience who visited play-houses only to parade their dresses and jewels'.[47]

Putting aside its possible imprecisions, Yeats's account of *Ubu Roi* does capture the broader sense that this performance, like Wilde's *Salomé*, was a critical moment in theatre history. The *fin-de-siècle* stage was not usually a space for such radical work, given its reliance on dilapidated traditions and economic imperatives.[48] In both form and content, Jarry's play refused to conform to this system, much as Wilde's *Salomé* was a seeming anomaly in the context of his popular dramatic oeuvre. Yeats appears to have been less disturbed by the profanities of *Ubu Roi*'s dialogue than by the methods of performance, which included players dressed as overgrown puppets; in his words, 'dolls, toys, marionettes, and now they are all hopping like wooden frogs'. In these jerky, unnatural movements, Yeats discerns the loss of a human aspect, figured as a postlapsarian fall from grace:

> After Stéphane Mallarmé, after Paul Verlaine, after Gustave Moreau, after Puvis de Chavannes, after our own verse, after all our subtle colour and nervous rhythm, after the faint mixed tints of Conder, what more is possible? After us the Savage God.[49]

This is Yeats coming to terms with the sight of the dramatic tradition passed, in Taxidou's words, 'through the modernist shredder'.[50] The formal beauty and spiritual ideals associated with Symbolism were threatened by the aggressive creatures populating the modernist stage, which looked towards the machine worship of later writers such as F. T. Marinetti and Wyndham Lewis. The shifting performance cultures brought into relief by the two key premieres of 1896 show that Wilde's dancer was not merely a product of Symbolist fantasies, but a figure in tune with modernist theatre practices and related approaches to the moving body on stage. The controversial receptions accorded to Wilde's and Jarry's works, and their shared history at Lugné-Poe's Théâtre de l'Oeuvre, drew them into proximity at a particularly fertile moment for the theatre, as did their adjacent interests in marionettes and dance movement. However, while Jarry's 'savage' performers introduced audiences to the more degenerate possibilities of machine-like bodies, other modernist uses of marionettes foregrounded their unexpected capacity for grace.

Proto-modernist Puppets from Kleist to Wilde

If *Salomé* and *Ubu Roi* unsettled traditional means of representing the body on stage, they also pioneered new aesthetic crossovers between different performance cultures and art forms: dance, puppetry, music, painting and poetic drama. Like Mallarmé and Valéry, Jarry was an influential theorist of dance, although he spurned the image of the graceful female ballerina celebrated by Mallarmé and sought instead to carve a new place for the athletic male dancer on stage, an aim later realised by Diaghilev and Nijinsky at the Ballets Russes.[51] In this way, Jarry perhaps anticipated the rejection of ballet by modernists such as Ezra Pound, for whom it represented 'a decadent romanticism' connected to the insipid beauty of the *prima ballerina*.[52] This was a model of feminine grace that modern dancers such as Fuller, Duncan and Ruth St Denis were already creatively challenging, inspired by role models from mythical and religious sources. The head-hunters that danced across the modernist stage posed a challenge to external forms of control over the bodies of women, offering an image of the female dancer as a desiring, autonomous performer, whose dance exceeded the frames of language, gender and mimetic representation. As such, Wilde's understanding of nineteenth-century approaches to movement in performance provides an important context for reading the 'dance of the seven veils' and other choreographic forms in his work.

Heinrich von Kleist's essay *On the Marionette Theatre*, written in 1810, offered a vital theoretical model for modernist responses to dance: Wilde, Yeats and Beckett were all familiar with the work, and incorporated some of Kleist's ideas about grace and movement into their dramatic systems.[53] In this brief but complex essay, Kleist writes that pure 'grace' and freedom of movement are only possible for a form which either has 'no consciousness at all – or has infinite consciousness – that is, in the mechanical puppet or in the god'.[54] The uncanny capacities and movements of the puppet seem at times to surpass the skills of the human actor: as Kleist speculates, 'a marionette constructed by a craftsman according to his requirements could perform a dance that neither he [the dancer] nor any other outstanding dancer [. . .] could equal'.[55] Lucia Ruprecht has shown that Kleist's thinking on the question of grace was influenced by Schiller, especially his treatise *Über Anmut und Würde* (*Gracefulness and Dignity*, 1793). Schiller developed a framework for thinking about grace as a property of movement, praising the figure of the serpentine line as an example of graceful variation (probably taken from Hogarth's 'line of grace' discussed in the previous chapter). As Ruprecht explains, however, Schiller struggled to accommodate the paradox of the graceful body, which must perfect an action learned artificially so that it appears to be 'natural', rather than 'affected'.[56] For Kleist, writing in Schiller's wake, human self-consciousness prohibits the repeated realisation of an absolutely graceful movement, whereas the marionette, somewhat counter-intuitively, is able to execute a graceful choreography beyond human capability: it possesses an articulated form that is at once more perfect and more degenerate than the body of a real dancer. 'The price for the puppet's extreme perfection is high', writes Ruprecht; 'it has lost, or more precisely, never had, any humanity.'[57]

Kleist departs from Schiller in understanding that grace must necessarily have an artificial quality: he considers it a consequence of the postlapsarian condition that human dancers have lost their 'unity of bodily movement'.[58] The marionette, who lacks desire, gender or self-consciousness, provides a depersonalised model of choreographic grace.

Although Kleist's essay seemed to undermine the abilities of human dancers, modernist choreographers and directors took much from his theories, Carrie Preston argues, since they believed that marionettes might allow them to 'perfect human movement'.[59] Divorced from the messiness of personality, the puppet provided a model of submission that some dramaturgs hoped their actors would be able to adopt. Following a renewed interest in Kleist's theories, the marionette was often invoked to protect the hierarchy determining the relationship between playwright and actor. 'The puppet', Taxidou claims, 'is conscripted into the argument that tries to maintain the power of the playwright. It becomes the purest form of mediation for the playwright's voice.'[60] In his biography of Wilde, Richard Ellmann suggests that Wilde, who initially believed the actor to be of equal importance to the playwright, decided upon the latter's superiority once he was actually writing plays himself.[61]

Wilde, however, had a complex understanding of the figure of the marionette, which he contemplated at various points in his creative works and essays. This is perhaps most evident in 'The Harlot's House', first published in *The Dramatic Review* in 1885. In this poem, Wilde uses the figure of the marionette to explore the tension between submission and creative release inherent in the art of dance; a conflict that manifests frequently across the choreographic images considered in this book. Describing the titular harlot as a kind of marionette, Wilde suggests parallels between the harlot's sexual currency and the dance of the puppet, with its automatic gestures and responses:

> Sometimes a clockwork puppet pressed
> A phantom lover to her breast,
> Sometimes they seemed to try to sing.
>
> Sometimes a horrible marionette
> Came out, and smoked its cigarette
> Upon the steps like a live thing. (CW, 867)

These automata approximate human forms, but their cold clockwork movements produce a grotesque performance of true desire. Wilde grounds these images in the language of dance from the opening lines: 'We caught the tread of dancing feet, / We loitered down the moonlit street' (CW, 867). The simple rhyme links the progress of the dance to the illumination of the moon, a connection that anticipates the visual register of *Salomé* with its repeated insinuations of lunar influence. Wilde's marionettes are not solid machines but spectral apparitions: 'phantom[s]', 'slim silhouetted skeletons', 'shadows' (*CW*, 867). These insubstantial presences seem closer to the forms of Eastern shadow-puppet theatre, such as the *ombres chinoises*, than to hand or wooden puppetry.[62] This is perhaps unsurprising, given the popularity of the *théâtre d'ombres* during the 1880s and 1890s, when Montmartre's cabaret Chat Noir was famous for its shadow plays, directed by Henri Rivière. Wilde may well have discovered his 'strange mechanical grotesques / Making fantastic arabesques' (*CW*, 867) in the flat silhouettes of Rivière's puppets, 'shadows [racing] across the blind' of the cabaret's illuminated screen (*CW*, 867). Lugné-Poe, a friend to both Rivière and Wilde, was keen to emulate the Chat Noir's success at the Théâtre de l'Oeuvre, and even speculated about bringing shadow plays to the theatre during the 1893 season.[63] The 'ghostly dancers' of 'The Harlot's House' strongly evoke this minor form of theatre, conjuring the sense of an ambiguously constituted dance in which the body of the performer is subsumed by the play of light on stage materials: a strategy that, of course, became Loïe Fuller's hallmark during this same period.

In her illustrations for the 1904 version of 'The Harlot's House', Wilde's close friend Althea Gyles, an Irish artist and occultist, embraced the poem's spectral imagery. Gyles, who also designed the covers for several of Yeats's poetry collections, turns to the model of the *théâtre d'ombres* to accompany Wilde's text: each of her five ghostly scenes is framed by what appears to be a proscenium arch, with Grecian-style columns in the foreground. These subtle neoclassical tropes are developed by the appearance of a satyr-like creature – possibly Pan – playing the violin in two of the images, while the shadows of dancing women are framed by leaves and flowers 'wheeling in the wind' (*CW*, 867), redolent of the three Graces in Botticelli's *Primavera* (1482). Gyles's imagery not only gestures towards Wilde's well-documented philhellenism, but also reproduces the aesthetic idiom of Warburg's Nympha with her distinctive flowing drapes and curving movements; 'an embodiment of pagan life', whose 'billowing veils [. . .] were the embodiment of worldly wantonness'.[64] These figures, however, are threatened by Wilde's macabre vision: the final screen (Fig. 2.1) shows a pair of animalistic skeletons capturing a fleeing dancer using nets and long, rope-like cords that visually echo Wilde's 'wire-pulled automatons'. Under the violent control of these skeletal actors, the female dancer is wrestled from her classical context and transformed into a marionette.

Reading the text of 'The Harlot's House' in dialogue with Gyles's illustrations produces a multifaceted impression of Wilde's individual approach to dance. Rather than the three Graces, the dancer in Gyles's last illustration resembles Botticelli's Chloris, the nymph pursued and abducted by Zephyrus, the spirit of the March winds, on the right-hand side of *Primavera*. The imbrication of Gyles's Greek symbolism with the marionettes of the *théâtre d'ombres* offers a particular mutation of the classical Nympha, whose serpentine grace is here

2.1 *The Harlot's House: A Poem by Oscar Wilde; with Five Illustrations by Althea Gyles.*
London: Mathurin Press, 1904. © The British Library

rather darkly co-opted by the spectral projections of the modern age: the apparitional images conjured by the magic lantern and *cinématographe* combine in 'The Harlot's House' with the speaker's anxieties about 'mechanical' and automated forms of human behaviour, especially as they fit into his critique of sexual exchange. Kleist's marionette becomes emblematic of a troubling strain of modernity, in which the graceful movements of antiquity are overlaid with the death-like, 'phantom' reproductions filling the modern stage.

Wilde's poetic formulation of these dancers, accompanied by Gyles's artistic interpretations, sheds new light on *Salomé*, which has been read in quite different terms as creating 'a utopian opening for human agency'.[65] Certainly, 'The Harlot's House' suggests a crisis of autonomy underpinning the dancer's movements that illuminates the dynamics of Salome's dance and the play's wider approaches to creativity and control. As we have seen, dance was philosophically construed in the late nineteenth and twentieth centuries as emblematic, on the one hand, of Dionysian wildness and physical ecstasy; and on the other, as a graceful embodiment of control and fastidious restraint. These conceptual tensions underpin Wilde's understanding of dance movement. Elsewhere, he discusses the benefits of using mechanical performers who entirely conform to the will of the dramatist; for instance, in this 1892 letter to the *Daily Telegraph*, Wilde describes his delight at Maurice Bouchor's puppet version of *The Tempest*, suggesting that puppets might prove to be ideal actors:

> There are many advantages in puppets. They never argue. They have no crude views about art. They have no private lives. We are never bothered by accounts of their virtues, or bored by recitals of their vices; and when they are out of an engagement they never do good in public or save people from drowning, nor do they speak more than is set down for them. They recognise the presiding intellect of the dramatist, and have never been known to ask for their parts to be written up. They are admirably docile, and have no personalities at all.[66]

Wilde's wry endorsement of the puppet accords with the opinions of other writers interested in marionette choreography, from Kleist to the Bauhaus director Oskar Schlemmer, who speculated about the advantages of using automata in his *Triadisches Ballett* (1922): 'Why should not the dancers actually be marionettes, controlled by wires, or, better still, by a device of perfect mechanical precision which would work automatically?'[67] Such commentaries can be traced back to Wilde's approval of the dramatist's 'presiding intellect', which privileges the dominant vision of the author in a way that Yeats and Beckett would later promote in their own experiments with dance. Yet Wilde's enthusiasm for supplanting the human performer with the marionette was tempered by a contrary anxiety, felt by many at the time, regarding the possible rebellion of such machines and their subversive potential for self-realisation.

These conflicting impressions regarding mechanised and depersonalised performing bodies found expression elsewhere in Wilde's writing. Imprisoned in Reading Gaol in 1897, Wilde considered this alternative side to the puppet in *De Profundis*, his long letter to Lord Alfred Douglas:

> It makes me feel sometimes as if you yourself had been merely a puppet worked by some secret and unseen hand to bring terrible events to a terrible issue. But puppets themselves have passions. They will bring a new plot into what they are presenting, and twist the ordered issue of vicissitude to suit some whim or appetite of their own. To be entirely free, and at the same time entirely dominated by law, is the eternal paradox of human life that we realise at every moment. (*CW*, 997)

Ruminating on the restrictions imposed on his own free movement, and the role Douglas played in his incarceration, Wilde considers how an apparently artificial form might challenge external modes of authority. Describing Douglas as the submissive prop of others, Wilde also acknowledges the puppet's ability to undermine dominant structures of power through its own 'passions'; its assertions of creative agency. In this sense, Wilde describes a paradox that Kleist also recognised in the dancing marionette: while it lacks the disruptive force of human consciousness – the damaging ingredient of self-awareness – it possesses the ability to move 'freely', its 'limbs' acting like a 'pendulum' that moves in its 'own fashion without anyone's aid'.[68] Writing near the close of the nineteenth century, Wilde's understanding of the risks of autonomous machines was perhaps more developed than Kleist's, although their theorising of marionette behaviour is strikingly similar.

These philosophical reflections on the figure of the marionette speak to a widespread and somewhat surprising interest in the mechanical body as a potential source of freedom and grace in movement. Turn-of-the-century changes in dance technique – in both modern dance and ballet – reflected this mechanical orientation in various ways, as dancer-choreographers from Duncan to Nijinsky pursued, in Mark Franko's terms, 'primitive, mechanical, or futuristic sources of movement innovation', moving towards an achievement of 'expression' rather than 'emotion' in performance.[69] This split represented modernism's broader concern with 'theatrical impersonality', which can be clearly traced through the approaches of Wilde, Yeats, Beckett, Edward Gordon Craig and even Antonin Artaud, all of whom sought, in different ways, to draw out the mechanical qualities of their actors. Yet the creative spirit of the performer need not be fully erased in this turn to depersonalisation, since, as Franko shows, dancers themselves cultivated an aesthetics of mechanisation. Whereas 'emotion' allowed the personality of the dancer or actor to interfere with the body's gestures, 'expression' replaced subjectivity with 'presence', thereby privileging the moving body as an object in itself, rather than an emotive vessel.[70] Working in this vein, Ballets Russes dancers found themselves wrestling with Nijinsky's demanding choreographies, which presented the dancer as 'the medium of an abstract, formal aesthetic'.[71] Kleist's graceful machine clearly loomed large in the new movement vocabularies of dance during this period and in ballets such as *Petrouchka* (1911), which explicitly allowed the modernist marionette to take centre stage.

Following Kleist, who conceptualised the dancing marionette as an embodiment of grace, dancers and theatre practitioners found new possibilities in moving machines. Wilde, too, was part of this shifting landscape of choreographic and dramaturgic theories, and his commentaries on puppetry – in both 'The Harlot's House' and his letters – show how attuned he was to the paradoxical qualities of this figure and the deeper imbrication of modernist performance cultures with unstable notions of selfhood and changing conceptions of grace. His writing on the nature of the performer's integrity, with its attending constraints, aligns with this range of nineteenth- and twentieth-century theories of corporeality and subjectivity, as the 1890s saw him develop more sophisticated political considerations of the place of performance in a world that, to him, appeared increasingly shaped by an overarching 'script' or system of power.[72] Such formulations of the body-in-movement are central to *Salomé*, which has been read as a work populated by 'puppets moved by forces outside themselves', and, conversely, as a play demonstrating 'a rebellious commitment to human agency'.[73] As this discussion of modernist marionettes suggests, a combination of these seemingly oppositional readings opens up new avenues for reading Wilde's complex approach to the bodies of dancing women.

'Serpent of old Nile': Wilde, *The Woman's World* and Sarah Bernhardt

During one of their many meetings in Paris, Wilde reportedly told the Guatemalan critic Gomez Carrillo (later the biographer of the dancer Mata Hari) that he '[could not] conceive of a Salome who is unconscious of what she does, a Salome who is but a silent and passive instrument'.[74] The feminist overtones of this statement are undermined by Wilde's insistence that his Salome must dance 'utterly naked', save for jewels that render 'the utter shamelessness of that warm flesh even more shocking'. Emphasising his dancer's 'limitless cruelty', Wilde slips back into the coarse judgements of sexual transgression and monstrous womanhood previously espoused by the Symbolists in their portraits of feminine degeneracy.[75] Yet Carrillo goes on to note the inconsistency of Wilde's position: 'on other occasions his Salomé was almost chaste [. . .] there were ten, no, a hundred Salomés that he imagined'.[76] Emerging from this account is a sense of Salome's multiplicity; her composite nature, taken from a wide range of sources, and her openness to interpretation.

Salomé's complex sexual politics have long been a source of critical debate: scholars have often focused on the homoeroticism of Wilde's language and design, the ambiguities of Beardsley's Art Nouveau illustrations, and the complex feminist authority of Salome herself.[77] Kerry Powell is one of a number of scholars who reads the decapitated figure of Iokanaan as a castrated body, signalling Wilde's 'homosexual horror' at the deformed masculine characteristics embodied by the New Woman.[78] Yet this interpretation does not fully align with Wilde's attitudes towards feminist reconfigurations of womanhood in the late nineteenth century, which provide an important context for reading *Salomé*. Sos Eltis has done much to revise critical understandings of Wilde's engagement with early feminist politics, showing that he was in fact deeply immersed in the conversations surrounding women's rights, including debates on issues such as women's education and dress reform, which doubtless shaped his own reinvention of Salome and his other dramatic projects in the 1890s.[79] During a crucial period in his artistic development, Wilde took over the editorship of the Victorian women's magazine *The Lady's World*, immediately renaming it *The Woman's World* and dramatically adjusting the content in order to attract a better-educated and more artistically inclined female readership. His work for this publication suggests an active involvement in contemporary women's issues, contrary to some characterisations of Wilde as a writer more interested in critiquing and parodying female characters than engaging with women in sincere terms.

During Wilde's two-year editorship (1887–89), *Woman's World* declared its ambition to 'include the more elevated regions of women's thought and effort', soliciting contributions from prominent female writers and leading suffragists including Margaret Sandhurst and Millicent Fawcett.[80] Though *Woman's World* did not depart from its earlier attachment to fashion, dress and design, Wilde wanted the magazine's contributors to approach these subjects in a more self-consciously intellectual way, in line with movements such as Pre-Raphaelitism, Symbolism and Art Nouveau, which also informed his own aesthetic values. It is important to note that the content of the magazine during this period aligned with the views Wilde had espoused in essays such as 'Woman's Dress' (1884) and 'The Philosophy of Dress' (1885), where he argued in favour of a liberal approach to female fashion based on classical models that allowed women to move more freely. Without a corset, Wilde declared, 'the body is left free and unconfined for respiration and motion, there is more health and consequently more beauty' (*CW*, 945). He went on to note that 'the laws of Greek dress may be perfectly realised' in hanging dresses from the shoulders rather than the hips, allowing 'the exquisite play of light and line that one gets from rich and rippling folds' (*CW*, 946). In advocating for the revival of Hellenism in fashion, Wilde was working to restore and reimagine ancient images of gender for modern Victorian women, for whom the study of classics was beginning to open up at universities such as Oxford and Cambridge. Yopie Prins has shown that progressive students of classics such as Jane Ellen Harrison, who contributed to *Woman's World* during Wilde's tenure, held an 'imaginative identification' with the figure of the Greek maenad, who provided an exciting alternative to the more conventional singularity of unmarried spinsterhood.[81] During this time, Greek models of movement and gesture also began to suffuse the sphere of performance, as classicists such as Harrison moved away from philology towards the realm of archaeology, promoting the study of classical ruins, objects and material culture.[82] In her essay 'The Picture of Sappho', published in *Woman's World* in 1888, Harrison examines depictions of Sappho on ancient illustrated vases, tracing the 'measured gestures' of 'the Lesbian muse' and her community of women to reveal the social and aesthetic significance of particular poses and actions.[83] This work illuminated the fertile iconography that Warburg would later mine for his repertory of ancient images, in which the Greek maenad – as Nympha – occupies a central place.

In *Woman's World*, female readers found an accessible – though challenging – collection of texts and images that proposed subtle connections between the Hellenic leanings of Wilde's aestheticism and the pressing social and political issues facing late Victorian women. The magazine's illustrations often sat in uneasy relation to the content of the articles: Lady Juliet Pollock's wide-ranging article on 'The Drama in Relation to Art', for instance, is accompanied by a small drawing of a woman's severed head, open-mouthed like the Greek mask of Tragedy and crowned with flowers and dark protruding feathers. Here, Pollock's critique of 'truth' and spiritual seriousness in art is placed in striking juxtaposition with this grotesque and primitive object, signalling a very different visual register of Bacchic violence and pagan worship. The title pages between 1888 and 1890 also hint at a dormant register of feminine wildness underpinning the magazine's more respectable highbrow content, suggested by its logo of a maenad-like female hunter holding a longbow, captioned 'La Belle Sauvage'.[84] Wilde's editorial principles, Petra Clark explains, were not merely designed to turn the magazine into a 'vehicle for aesthetic pleasure', but rather to ensure that its female readers could 'actively work towards greater artistic sophistication'.[85] Importantly, this was achieved through a combination of Wilde's oversight and the vision of individual contributors, from Jane Harrison, Olive Schreiner and Amy Levy to prominent male artists such as Charles Ricketts and Gustave Fraipont. Wilde's wife, Constance, and his mother, Lady Wilde, also contributed articles on topics ranging from 'Children's Dress' and 'Muffs' to 'Irish Peasant Tales'. Published in 1888, Lady Wilde's poem 'Historic Women' celebrated formidable figures drawn from a wealth of historical and religious sources, including Cleopatra, 'self-slain, in all her splendour like a Queen', and Judith, 'gorgeous in her painted tire', who 'freed her people by one mighty stroke'.[86] Although he evidently lost interest in the magazine at the end of the decade, Wilde's editorship at *Woman's World* shows his commitment to a different sort of artistic vision for progressive Victorian readers, revolving around the emancipation of women's bodies through their affiliation with both ancient and modern aesthetic models.

Wilde's involvement with *Woman's World* shows that he held a more complex set of opinions on the 'gender question' than a mere dandyish unease towards the New Woman. This context is important for understanding his approach to *Salomé*'s female protagonist and her controversial dance, two aspects of the play that were doubtless shaped by Wilde's concern for the restrictions placed on women's bodies, as well as his soliciting of contributions from suffragists and women's rights activists. Much scholarship on the play, however, has tended to read its gender politics through the lens of Wilde's own sexuality and his engagement with the aesthetics of Decadence and Symbolism. Regenia Gagnier, for instance, reads the text's Symbolist idiom together with Beardsley's illustrations as coded expressions of same-sex desire, attempting to 'seduce a broader audience into an awareness of its suppressed longings'.[87] Energised by Wilde's biography, other have pursued this notion of suppressed and subtextual desire in relation to *Salomé*.[88] Elaine Showalter uses the famous photograph of 'Wilde in costume as Salome' (initially reproduced in Ellmann's biography) to unveil the play's 'buried and coded messages', conflating 'female corrosive desire and male homosexual love'.[89] The figure dressed as Salome in this photograph was later identified as the Hungarian opera singer Alice Guszalewicz, showing how a critical eagerness to discern the author among Salome's veils risks entirely ignoring the historical presence of a real woman's body. Despite producing fruitful and thoughtful readings, these approaches to *Salomé* tend to privilege the position of Wilde at the expense of the women who performed the dance on stage, as suggested by Showalter's praise for Lindsay Kemp's all-male *Salomé*, and her contrary disappointment that 'women's performances of Salome have seemed so unsatisfying'.[90] Although the body of Salome is enveloped by Wilde's linguistic style as well as by her costume, it is possible to trace the emergence of a subtle form of female creative self-assertion in this liminal textual space.

In *Salomé*, solid accounts of embodiment are evaded by streams of mutating similes, tropes of mirroring and spectrality, and elliptical Symbolist descriptions. Salome in particular is consistently abstracted through Wilde's elaborate web of metaphors. The young Syrian Captain expresses his desire for her in language that appears to lose its object at the moment it seeks to represent her: 'Never have I seen her so pale. She is like the shadow of a white rose in a mirror of silver' (*PI*, 707). Wilde's dialogue is rife with allusions to 'pale[ness]', 'shadow[s]' and other indicators of insubstantiality, and here the simile reduces Salome to a reflection, using the image of the mirror that enjoyed such popularity among French Symbolists. In Mallarmé's *Hérodiade*, for instance, the eponymous speaker addresses her mirror in very similar terms: 'I have appeared in you like a distant shadow, / But horror! Evenings, in your severe fountain, / I have known the nudity of my sparse dream'.[91] In both Mallarmé's and Wilde's writing, mirrors act as repositories for fragmented forms of self-knowledge, but ultimately return, in Margaret Stoljar's reading, 'a shadow, a question, perhaps a delusion', in line with a Symbolist figuration of the self as an artificial construct.[92]

Such an anxiously postulated body tests the limits of spectatorship and gives rise to concerns about the effects of watching Salome perform. The Page of Herodias frets that the Syrian Captain is 'always looking at [Salome]. You look at her too much. It is dangerous to look at people in such a fashion' (*PI*, 707). The pair then note the Tetrarch's 'sombre look', and wonder 'at whom is he looking?' (*PI*, 707). Salome finds it 'strange that the husband of [her] mother looks at [her] like that' (*PI*, 710), while Herod admits that he has 'looked at [her] overmuch' (*PI*, 726). Above all the players, the moon, continuously aligned with Salome, appears 'like a dead woman. One might fancy she was looking for dead things' (*PI*, 707). Building a network of suspect gazes, Wilde subtly refutes previous configurations of Salome as a passive muse, whose dangerous lust is reinterpreted as a projection of the male spectator's fantasies. If, as Dierkes-Thrun suggests, Wilde's Herod is modelled on Huysmans's male aesthete, he is an aesthete whose attempts to turn the body of the woman into an artwork consistently fail.[93] Wilde's Salome is envoiced: she challenges the 'strange' gaze of Herod, and, as Armstrong perceptively notes, she rejects his offers of jewels, peacocks and gifts, eschewing the lure of Decadent aesthetics and asserting her own desire in its place; a desire predicated on the destruction of the male body.[94]

Wilde's protagonist resolutely looks back. Her language is explicit, full-bodied and sensuous, and, like the rest of the play's dialogue, it also measures its objects in Symbolist terms, demonstrating what Symons terms a characteristic excess of 'description [. . .] heaping up of detail, [and] passionately patient elaboration'.[95] This account of the Symbolist method certainly applies to Salome's address to Iokanaan, which parodies the fervent effusiveness of the Song of Solomon:

> It is thy mouth that I desire, Iokanaan. Thy mouth is like a band of scarlet on a tower of ivory. It is like a pomegranate cut in twain with a knife of ivory. The pomegranate flowers that blossom in the gardens of Tyre, and are redder than roses, are not so red. The red blasts of trumpets that herald the approach of kings, and make afraid the enemy, are not so red. (*PI*, 714)

These lines are rich in extravagant allusion, but on closer inspection, Iokanaan's body slips further from its analogic counterparts as Salome's description intensifies.⁹⁶ His mouth, initially grounded in the obstinate materiality of an ivory tower, softens into the flesh of a fruit, before thinning into a flower's petals, and finally evaporating into the airy nothing of sound. Symbolist utterances will not grant Salome the body she seeks to possess, but her colonising of the aesthete's idiom powerfully unsettles the gender dynamics of Wilde's play.

Wilde's allusive and metaphor-laden style has been interpreted as a means of disavowing bodily presence. Comparing the dramatic speech of *Salomé* to a sixteenth-century blazon, Chad Bennett argues that the lyrical ornamentation of the play removes the possibility of stable meanings and physical presences, 'transforming what it forms, effacing what it faces, and disfiguring what it figures'.⁹⁷ Moreover, for Bennett, Salome herself is a point of crisis for this poetics of disavowal: 'there is a gap in Wilde's play: the body of Salome is missing'.⁹⁸ Describing Salome as 'the speaking icon of the male gaze', other critics have concurred that to look at Salome is 'to see the eye of the male beholder looking back at itself – to see the blank space of the nameless daughter'.⁹⁹ While these readings identify the veiled nature of Salome's body at the level of language, they miss the clear promise of Wilde's rhetorical strategies: if Salome's body is construed as a 'gap' that cannot be readily apprehended by the male players, a space is created for the dancer to author her own performance. While some modern dancers clearly worked to foreground their corporeal presence on stage and accentuate the contours of their bodies, others – notably Fuller and her imitators – sought to obscure and dematerialise themselves, using the notion of an absent centre, conjured suggestively in Wilde's text, to test new spatial models in performance. The failure of Symbolist language to conjure Salome's body leaves open the possibility that Salome might write her own form into the play through the alternative language of dance, much as Fuller deployed her veils to conceal the work of her moving body and thereby construct her own expansive corporeal art.

In this way, new possibilities for the actor in Salome's role are enabled through the comparative brevity of Wilde's stage direction: 'Salome dances the dance of the seven veils' (*PI*, 725). Unlike the surrounding dialogue, it summons a body to perform, rather than abstracting it through extended metaphors. Although Wilde's lack of specificity surrounding the choreography for the dance has been a source of frustration, his determination that Sarah Bernhardt should play Salome offers an insight into the kind of performance he might have envisaged for the first London production. Wilde's preference for Bernhardt implies that his Salome would not be embodied by a semi-naked ingénue but instead by a singularly powerful actor and producer, whose performances had transformed the nineteenth-century theatre.

Although her rendition of Salome's dance remained an imagined one, Bernhardt's association with this role was important for other interpreters, as Fuller's reflections on the French actor suggested in the previous chapter.

Bernhardt's reputation gave Salome a new seriousness, imbuing the role with her idiosyncratic gender fluidity and affirming its feminist possibilities. Wilde claimed that 'the only person in the world who could act Salomé is Sarah Bernhardt, that "serpent of old Nile," older than the Pyramids'.[100] Alluding to Bernhardt's famous performance in Sardou's *Cléopâtre*, Wilde subtly aligns his Salome with other landmark queens of the ancient world, granting her an important share of the power in a narrative that has often cemented the patriarchal authority of Herod's court at Salome's expense.[101] W. Graham Robertson was to design the production in London featuring Bernhardt, and the costumes from *Cléopâtre* were undergoing modification to be reused in *Salomé*, promising a visual symmetry between the two plays.[102] Despite Wilde's previous claim that an ideal actor would respect the presiding will of the dramatist, it appears that Bernhardt was able to assert her creative authority early on. She declared that her hair would be dyed blue for the role, prompting Wilde to object that Herodias, not Salome, should have blue hair. Not to be deterred, Bernhardt simply replied, 'I *will* have blue hair.'[103] The 'divine Sarah' had the artistic capital to shape the course of the production, suggesting that it was to be a collaborative effort between actor, playwright and director, rather than a mere vessel for the writer's dramatic intentions.

Bernhardt's body also denoted a particular range of possibilities for the role of Salome. Articles published in *Woman's World* in the late 1880s celebrated Bernhardt's style and physical comportment, even offering a history of her 'tea-gown' and praising her appearance in historical dress for a production of *La Tosca*. Another piece by Sophie de Maucroix on 'First Nights in Paris' detailed the French actor's specific physical qualities onstage: 'the languid, serpentine grace, the far-off wandering look, the slumberous, drawling, but so melodious voice, the *voix d'or* [. . .] the enchanting restfulness and repos [sic] of the whole'.[104] Discussing the failed London production of *Salomé*, Riquelme points out that Bernhardt, who was nearly fifty in 1892, 'could have been no sylph', rendering it unlikely that Salome's dance would be staged as a 'provocative spectacle'.[105] Rather than anything erotically inflammatory, however, the term 'sylph' in this period would have conjured images of the romantic ballerinas of *La Sylphide*, whose structured costumes and fastidiously executed pointe-work seem quite unlike anything Wilde would have imagined for his *Salomé*. Bernhardt was viewed as a performer with an unusually effective control over her physical gestures, displaying what critics have termed a 'contained mobility, a coiled vitality even when at rest'.[106] Notably, she refused to wear a corset, which allowed her body to 'twist and spiral' across the stage without restriction. In her memoirs, Bernhardt declared that her 'peculiar way of dressing, [her] scorn of fashion, [her] general freedom in all respects, made [her] a being quite apart from all others', alluding to an underlying connection between her physical self-fashioning and her sense of personal liberation.[107]

Distancing herself from the tightly structured costume of the ballerina, or the corseted form of the upper-class woman, Bernhardt grounded her feminist authority onstage in the free movements of her body.

Reflecting her own self-assessment, Bernhardt's contemporaries also wrote about her singular presence and grace. Ellen Terry, a successful actor in her own right (and mother of Edward Gordon Craig), recalled Bernhardt's disregard for social or theatrical convention, as well as her curious ease of movement:

> I noticed that she hardly ever moved, yet all the time she gave the impression of swift, butterfly movement. While talking to Henry [Irving] she took some red stuff out of her bag and rubbed it on her lips! This frank 'making-up' in public was a far more astonishing thing in the 'eighties than it would be now. But I liked Miss Sarah for it, as I liked her for everything.
>
> How wonderful she looked in those days! She was as transparent as an azalea, only more so; like a cloud, only not so thick. Smoke from a burning paper describes her more nearly! She was hollow-eyed, thin, almost consumptive-looking. Her body was not the prison of her soul, but its shadow.
>
> On the stage she has always seemed to me more a symbol, an ideal, an epitome than a woman. It is this quality which makes her so easy in lofty parts such as Phèdre. She is always a miracle.[108]

Such a description highlights the contained nature of Bernhardt's body and her ability to convey an impression of stillness, even when moving across the stage. It is also interesting that Terry should note the near transparency of her peer, whose physical presence seems highly unstable, shifting between various descriptors that stress her lightness and fragile grace. This passage invites comparison with the reviews of Fuller's early serpentine dance performances, which rely on a similar vocabulary of nebulous and delicate forms: butterflies, clouds, waves, smoke. In a similar manner to Fuller, Bernhardt's body seems to exist as a kind of vanishing point beneath the layers of images and ideas she is able to project, leading Terry to call her a 'miraculous' symbol, rather than a real woman. At an earlier point in her memoirs, Terry recalled the words of her childhood dance-master Oscar Byrn, who told her that 'an actress was no actress unless she learned to dance early'.[109] Bernhardt's particular qualities of movement seemed to convey a perfect physical equilibrium, and she was able to conceal and dematerialise her body in a manner that would prove influential for modern dancers, for whom she often functioned as a kind of muse. According to her contemporary Bram Stoker, Bernhardt's 'incarnate grace' was perfectly captured in Bastien Lepage's famous painting, exhibited at the Grosvenor Gallery in 1879, which depicts her 'as a serpent with all a serpent's grace'.[110] Such metaphors, used frequently in accounts of the actor, correspond with Hogarth's 'line of grace' and its conspicuous revival in the movement aesthetics of modern dance, as well as the kinaesthetics of modernist performance more widely.

Reports and reviews during the period reflected this perception of Bernhardt's transformative qualities, highlighting her ability to shift between typical configurations of gender. Commenting on a production of de Musset's *Lorenzaccio* at the Adelphi Theatre in 1897, the *Manchester Guardian* reviewer admitted that 'though a woman in a man's part is seldom altogether pleasing, it must be owned that Madame Bernhardt makes an effective figure in her black Hamlet-like costume'.[111] These acknowledgements of Bernhardt's ambiguous womanhood anticipated her most famous role in *Hamlet*, which played in Paris and London in 1899. The *New York Tribune* expressed incredulity at Bernhardt's ready embodiment of the male figure, praising her 'graceful, boyish' appearance, and concluding that 'every move and gesture is that of a man'.[112] Bernhardt's vocabulary of physical motions, rather than the sonorous tones of her famous voice, equipped her to adopt the guise of a man. Preparing for the lead in *Salomé*, Bernhardt probably grasped, according to Garelick, the 'camp appeal of a middle-aged woman portraying [. . .] a nubile princess'.[113] Such an interpretation of the role importantly deviates from the conventional treatment of Salome's body as a site of passive sexual spectacle, instead allowing an authoritative Salome to resist the petrifying gaze of the aesthete and assert control over the play's gender dynamics, along with its Symbolist register.

Cruel Incarnations: Beardsley's Naughty Scribbles

Since Bernhardt's production of *Salomé* was cancelled before it could be staged, her plans for the dance of the seven veils remain in the realm of speculation. Certainly, she was determined to perform the dance herself. When asked if she would have a trained dancer step in at the necessary moment, as often happened in subsequent productions of Strauss's *Salome* opera, Bernhardt replied firmly that she would be undertaking the dance on her own.[114] Asking for details of the choreography, Robertson was told: 'Never you mind.'[115] Echoing Wilde's sly avoidance of visual clarity – his allusions to an 'invisible' dance – Bernhardt gave little away regarding her intentions, retaining a sense of the dance's mysterious resistance to articulation, its continuous evasion of language. Bernhardt did reveal that she felt that the play was 'heraldic, fresco-like', and required 'no rapidity of movement but stylised hieratic gestures'.[116] Whether or not such slow, precise and religious poses would have extended to her dance is uncertain, but they do suggest an alternative way of interpreting Salome's movements, standing at a distance from the belly-dances and stripteases of other versions, and demonstrating Bernhardt's ability to read the bodily rhetoric of the play on her own terms.

Although the 'dance of the seven veils' is a frustratingly cryptic stage direction, it nonetheless operates as a focal point for the dramatic action; as Donohue asserts, 'Salome as dancer, and Salome's dance, together set the keynote for understanding the play'.[117] Of course, Bernhardt was merely one imagined Salome, and Wilde refuted claims that he had written the play specifically with her in mind. In a letter of March 1893 to the editor of *The Times*, Wilde explained that while it was 'a source of pride and pleasure to [him]' that 'the greatest tragic actress of any stage now living' should accept the part of Salome, he had 'in no sense of the words written [it] for this great actress'.[118] Furthermore, he confided to Adolphe Retté, who read and corrected an early version of the play in French, that he 'would like to see the role of Salome played by an actress who was also a first-class dancer'. Retté recalls that Wilde then 'imagined all the possibilities of this idea and held [him] spell-bound'.[119] The choreography of the dance was clearly a source of multiple creative possibilities as far as Wilde was concerned, and it is important to note that he emphasised the choreographic abilities of the dancer to Retté, signalling the importance of the dance to the form and dramatic efficacy of the play, despite Ross's scepticism about this particular element.

Given the prohibition of the English stage version of *Salomé*, the first visual account of this dance was provided through Aubrey Beardsley's illustrations, which originally accompanied the 1894 English translation and were reprinted in uncensored form in the 1907 reissue of *Salomé*. Wilde apparently had a vexed relationship with these drawings: he called them 'cruel and evil [. . .] like naughty scribbles a precocious schoolboy makes in the margins of his copybook'.[120] Perhaps he was offended by Beardsley's wry insertion of him into one of the images: in 'The Woman in the Moon', Wilde's recognisable features are etched on to the moon, looking longingly at the naked form of a feminised man. This may have come a little close to the bone after the success of *The Poet and the Puppets*, a play by Charles Brookfield and J. M. Glover that premiered in 1892 and was, in Wilde's words, 'a burlesque of Lady Windermere's Fan in which an actor dressed up as me and imitated my voice and manner!!!'[121] That the censor should license such a work in London and refuse *Salomé* a stage was of particular outrage to Wilde, and in the wake of such a humiliation, Beardsley's sly caricatures seemed to demote him from presiding artist to mere prop, alluding uncomfortably to his sexual proclivities.

Yet Beardsley's illustrations have become inseparable from Salome's legacy, and Wilde clearly felt that Beardsley understood his vision for the play, since he declared him the only other individual who could see Salome's 'invisible dance'. The dance itself is portrayed in an image titled 'The Stomach Dance', which, far from 'invisible', explicitly emphasises the erotic charge of the performance (Fig. 2.2). Salome is shown dancing on a dark floor, which reflects Ricketts's original plans to stage the play on a black surface in contrast

2.2 'The Stomach Dance'. From a portfolio of Aubrey Beardsley's drawings illustrating *Salomé* by Oscar Wilde.
© The British Library

to Salome's luminous feet, described by the Syrian Captain as 'little white doves'.[122] In 'The Stomach Dance', one of these delicate white feet is scaled and clawed, revealing the animalistic potential of Salome's body, which was often connected to Medusan metaphors of petrification and unveiling.[123] Salome is shown with her breasts and stomach fully exposed, rendering the dance a titillating display for the wretched minstrel lurking in the corner of the frame, nursing a fairly obvious erection that was surprisingly missed by the play's publisher, John Lane. Beardsley's Salome is staring back at her viewers, her gaze fixed resolutely ahead, confronting any voyeuristic spectator peering at the illustration. Furthermore, the outlandish creature in the corner can be interpreted as a satirical take on the aesthetes who lingered over Salome's image for their own enjoyment, writ large on his contorted face and leering expression. Although Beardsley's image proved influential for the course of the Salome dance in popular culture after the *fin de siècle*, encouraging its performance as a striptease, it also critiques the function of the dance as erotic spectacle, foregrounding the imposing authority of the female performer and reducing the role of the voyeur to that of masturbatory grotesque.

Despite its essential place in Wilde's dramatic imagination, Salome's dance retained a sense of impossibility, or, at least, unfathomable multiplicity. Recalling Wilde's long meditations on the nature of Salome's movements and appearance, Carrillo described the numerous transformations undergone by Wilde's princess, as the dramatist consulted the many paintings and texts dedicated to her enigmatic dance:

> The curves of her long, pale body, he said to me, are like those of a lily. Her beauty has nothing of this world about it ... Thin veils woven by the angels wrap round her slender figure. The golden waves of her hair conceal the delights of her neck. Her eyes shine and sparkle, and are the very stars of hope or faith.
> [...]
> Yet these priestess-like visions quickly gave way to weird sexual fantasies, to cruel incarnations of Beauty the Prophetess, to hallucinatory and mythic portrayals of Woman's omnipotence.[124]

At one moment, Wilde imagined his dancer as a vision of unearthly grace, enveloped and protected by her sacred veils, yet soon after, these same veils were deployed to accentuate her nakedness, emphasising the eroticism and spectacular excess of her performance. According to Carrillo, whose voluptuous account must be treated with a degree of caution, Wilde's speculative conversations about the choreography were framed by such a wide variety of sources – from Titian, Stanzioni and Veronese, to Bernardo-Luigi, Dürer, Regnault and Huysmans – that his own scope for invention was paradoxically tightened: 'The great English poet was always looking for, but never finding, the real Salomé who remains lost in the mist of ages.'[125] Carrillo's phrasing, however, suggests that he may have misconstrued Wilde's intentions. It is unlikely that the author of 'The Decay of Lying' would be overly preoccupied with discovering the 'real' Salome; rather, as that essay suggests, the best art, in Salomean fashion, must 'kiss [the] false, beautiful lips' of invention in the knowledge that 'Truth is entirely and absolutely a matter of style' (*CW*, 1081). The 'dizzying chain of collapsing paradoxes' Hugh Haughton identifies in this essay reflects Wilde's ambivalent approach to the concepts of truth, reality and authenticity, which were so often circumscribed by his dedication to style and performance.[126] In this context, Wilde's dance of the seven veils can be read as a site of stylistic innovation and individual authorship, controlled by each adapter and performer of the myth as they dance in the wake of a long line of Salomes, each as true and beautifully false as the last.

For many critics and interpreters of the performance, Salome remains a consummate undresser, whose dance is primarily a means of seduction. Although Wilde's elliptical directions do not specify that Salome's veils should be discarded at any point, the veil itself has been read as a marker of erotic revelation, loosely concealing a body that dances continually on the brink of exposure. This is not, however, the veil's only or ultimate purpose, as we have seen. When modern dance pioneers began to experiment with costume and technology, they consciously divested the veil of its specific sexual meaning and proposed new methods of construing the relationship between the veil and the female body. Defending her choice of a 'filmy scarf' as her preferred costume, for example, Isadora Duncan described herself as 'a perfect pagan to all, fighting the Philistines', reminding her readers 'how beautiful and innocent the naked human body was when inspired by beautiful thoughts'.[127] As Richard Allen Cave has observed, the lack of evidence relating to the performance of Salome's dance in other early productions, such as the 1906 *Salomé* featuring Florence Darragh, has made it difficult to write with certainty about the nature of the choreography.[128] It is clear, however, that the historical entanglements of Wilde, Bernhardt and Beardsley at least qualify the traditional narrative of Salome's dance as simply a seductive striptease, since they reveal the ability of the dancer to write her body into the performance, displacing the Herodian spectator from the play's dramatic centre.

Salome's dancing body thus came to operate as a cultural shorthand for a range of (sometimes opposing) erotic interests and experiments in form and dramatic language. For Wilde, Salome's body was a synecdoche for the play itself, and he even personified the published text when he sent copies out to his friends. He wrote to Edmund Gosse that he hoped 'Salome will find her way to that delightful library you have let us know of, and if she be not too Tyrian in her raiment be suffered to abide there for a season', wryly continuing: 'should she try to dance, a stern look from a single tome by an eighteenth century writer will quell her, for common sense she has none'.[129] This rhetorical manoeuvre was echoed by Wilde's correspondents, who similarly described the book as if it were the body of a woman. When his copy of the play failed to materialise, George Bernard Shaw retorted that 'Salome is still wandering in her purple raiment in search of me, and I expect her to arrive a perfect outcast, branded with inky stamps, bruised by flinging from hard hands into red prison vans, stuffed and contaminated.'[130] Passed between these men, Salome's body is treated as chattel, roughly manhandled (in Shaw's case) as her text travels from place to place. Yet this correspondence also shows that her body was figuratively construed as a living, embodied means of stimulating artistic discourse in this creative community. Moreover, as Shaw's letter suggests, the dancer remains unmastered: a body that has been promised but not, in the event, delivered.

'THE ANDROGYNOUS MIME': BALLET AFTERLIVES

Salome's enduring power as a source of collaborative possibility between writers and dancers, which persisted across the twentieth century, can perhaps be traced back to a meeting between Wilde and the young Sergei Diaghilev at the close of the *fin de siècle*. In the summer of 1897, Diaghilev travelled to Dieppe and met Aubrey Beardsley, although the apparent purpose of his journey was to secure an introduction to Wilde, who had recently been released from prison.[131] Missing the author on this occasion, Diaghilev then went to Paris in February 1898, where he met with Wilde, who described the Russian ingénue as 'a great amateur of Aubrey's art'.[132] According to Diaghilev, the two men strolled arm in arm down the Grands Boulevards, while prostitutes 'shouted abuse' at them from the doors of cafés, in scenes redolent of 'The Harlot's House'.[133] Although it is not clear which subjects they discussed, Wilde's mention of Beardsley in conjunction with Diaghilev's artistic interests suggests the illustrations for *Salomé* as a point of contact between the three men. Certainly, Salome was the Wildean figure that apparently lingered longest in Diaghilev's mind. *La Tragédie de Salomé* (indebted partly to Fuller) was just one of many instances of dancers and choreographers reinventing the figure of Salome after Wilde, underlining the growing imaginative proximity between literary and choreographic practitioners, which was fuelled by modernist engagements with dance, performance and theories of movement.

These imaginative overlaps between the work of Wilde and his interpreters also extended to female performers in the years after his death. Ida Rubinstein, who went on to dance with the Ballets Russes between 1909 and 1911, gave one of the more controversial renditions of Wilde's *Salomé* in December 1908 at the St Petersburg Conservatory. In collaboration with the Russian choreographer Michel Fokine and scenographer Léon Bakst, Rubinstein used Alexander Glazunov's music to structure her sensuous, daring interpretation of the dance of the seven veils, for which she donned a long diaphanous tunic decorated with stylised leaves. According to Nicoletta Misler, Rubinstein's appearance and choreographic aesthetic combined the oriental and seductive connotations of the role with the image of the 'nymph – innocent, unsullied, and identified with nature'.[134] Certainly, Rubinstein's rumoured decision to strip naked during the performance has ensured her preservation in the canon of early twentieth-century Salomes, although she shared with Wilde the threats and pressures of censorship: the governing Synod of the Russian Orthodox Church, disturbed by the resurrection of Wilde's most decadent heroine in the hallowed halls of a national institution, cancelled Rubinstein's *Salomé* after just one performance. Intriguingly, however, she navigated the ruling by resorting to one of her more notable talents: mime.[135] The Church prohibited the utterance of Wilde's text – by now fully imbricated with his public prosecution and his death in 1900 – but permitted Rubinstein to interpret the play's dramatic content using silent gestures and movements.

While composing *Salomé*, Wilde himself had been quite taken with the acrobatics of the Romanian dancer Eugenie Petrescue, who achieved fame by dancing on her hands at the Moulin Rouge.[136] Rubinstein's callisthenic abilities and her talent for mime somewhat compensated for her lack of classical training. Her corporeal strategies drew on the less well-known history of Salome as a 'contortionist', memorably preserved in Flaubert's version of the tale.[137] Rubinstein was known for the suppleness of her torso, and 'the plunge of her backbend', recalling the arched or 'hooped' backs of the Salome dancers depicted in medieval illustrations and effigies.[138] Crucially, Rubinstein's silent interaction with Wilde's play (in the second iteration of the production) recast Salome's body as a tool of textual as well as corporeal interpretation, rendering poetic language itself the absent, unuttered centre beneath the dancer's moving body. Wilde's intricate Symbolist dialogue vanishes into the same void from which the modern dancer's body emerges: prohibited by the censor, language becomes the invisible presence concealed and yet communicated by Rubinstein's veils.

Rubinstein's fascination with Wilde's tragic muse seemed to persist throughout her career. After *Salomé*, she deepened her association with loosely 'oriental' choreographies through her role in a Ballets Russes production of *Cléopâtre* (1909), for which she 'gradually discarded all her veils and gave herself up to the ecstasy of love [. . .] disclosing the divine body omnipotent in its beauty'.[139] Then in 1911, Rubinstein took the lead in a ballet based on Gabriele D'Annunzio's *Le Martyre de Saint Sébastien*, with music by Claude Debussy and costumes again designed by Bakst. Perhaps unsurprisingly, Rubinstein's controversial affiliation with Wilde was resurrected in reviews of this production:

The venom is stealthy and subtle. It is undoubtedly the poison of performances such as 'Salome' which has led us to this. What we have vaguely dreaded throughout the evening – nay, throughout the past years in which dancing-women, in the name of Art, have whirled with tinted feet over hallowed ground, and have thrust their white hands and pink nails into the locks of a beheaded saint – here reaches its culmination. *Explicit sacrilegium.*

'Je danserai, je danserai,' says the androgynous mime. [. . .]

And the adolescent saint, under the lusting eyes of the Emperor, *dances the Passion of the Christ!*[140]

The similarities between this review and early responses to Wilde's *Salomé* are arresting. Moving like an externally controlled automaton, 'as if unseen hands were hoisting her upwards', and 'bowed as under some mysterious weight', Rubinstein performed her dance in the manner of a Kleistian marionette left to dangle on its strings, unnerving her audience with 'the sudden droop of the inert head, the lifeless dropping of the bloodless arms, the sinking knees, and final fall of the frail, shattered form'.[141] Here, she combines the puppet's apparent submissiveness with its eerie self-determination, pinning the other aspects of the production to her 'stiff and motionless' body, 'Debussy's mystic music raging around her like a storm'.[142] Rubinstein's 'androgynous' St Sebastian collapsed the boundaries, not only between genders, but also between the different iconographies that vividly defined her performance: the wounded body of the saint; the passion of the Christ; the dance of the seven veils. In *Saint Sébastien*, Rubinstein incorporated two central aspects of the choreographic imaginary previously traced by Wilde, embodying both the damaged figure of the male saint and the dancer who desires him. In this way, the martyr's queer and feminised body delineates the homoerotic possibilities of Wilde's 'invisible dance', but now it is a female performer who conjures and controls the spectacle. The multiple religious sources collated in Rubinstein's performance were absorbed into a larger modernist paradigm of 'dancing-women' who, like the Greek maenads, 'whirl' over 'hallowed ground', upsetting the orthodoxies of sex and power 'in the name of Art'. As we shall see in the next chapter, such complex negotiations with the 'dance of veils' can be found frequently in the work of female silent film pioneers, who took inspiration from Wilde's landmark play and from the aesthetics of modern dance.

Notes

1. Oscar Wilde, *The Letters of Oscar Wilde*, ed. Rupert Hart-Davis (London: Hart-Davis, 1962), 348.
2. For a textual history of the play, see Rodney Shewan, 'Oscar Wilde's *Salomé*: A Critical Variorum Edition from Three Extant Manuscripts – Proofsheets and Two

Early Printed Texts Transcribed in Parallel', 2 vols, PhD dissertation, University of Reading, 1982.
3. Elliot L. Gilbert, '"Tumult of Images": Wilde, Beardsley and *Salome*', *Victorian Studies* 26.2 (1983): 133–59; Jason Boyd, 'Staging the Page: Visibility and Invisibility in Oscar Wilde's *Salome*', *Nineteenth Century Theatre & Film* 35.1 (2008): 17–47.
4. Garber, *Vested Interests*, 338–46.
5. Ibid., 341–2.
6. For further context and discussion of Wilde's trials, see Michael Foldy, *The Trials of Oscar Wilde: Deviance, Morality, and Late Victorian Society* (New Haven, CT: Yale University Press, 1997); see also Merlin Holland, ed., *The Real Trial of Oscar Wilde: The First Uncensored Transcript of the Trial of Oscar Wilde vs. John Douglas Marquess of Queensbury, 1895* (New York: Fourth Estate, 2003).
7. Oscar Wilde to Alfred Douglas, (?) 2 June [1897], *Letters*, 588.
8. Katharine Worth, *The Irish Drama of Europe from Yeats to Beckett* (London: Athlone Press, 1978), 99.
9. McCarren contemplates the cinematic responses to dance in *Dancing Machines*, 43–61.
10. Flaubert, 'Herodias', 102.
11. Tydeman and Price, *Salome*, 93. For a comprehensive history of censorship laws and practices during this period, see John Russell Stephens, *The Censorship of English Drama, 1824–1901* (Cambridge: Cambridge University Press, 1980).
12. Pigott quoted in Stephens, *Censorship*, 112.
13. W. B. Yeats, *The Trembling of the Veil*, in *Autobiographies*, ed. William O' Donnell and Douglas N. Archibald, vol. 3 of *The Collected Works of W. B. Yeats* (New York: Scribner, 1999), 255.
14. Arthur Symons, 'The Decadent Movement in Literature' [1893], in *The Symbolist Movement in Literature*, ed. Matthew Creasy (Manchester: Carcanet, 2014), 170.
15. Symons, *The Symbolist Movement in Literature*, 7.
16. Sherry claims that the relationship between Symons's 1893 and 1899 essays is 'fraught with second thoughts' and exposes a crucial 'set of tensions in the developing conceptions of the origins of modernist poetry'. See *Modernism and the Reinvention of Decadence*, 4–6.
17. Ibid., 8.
18. Ibid., 8.
19. Patrick McGuinness draws this distinction in his introduction to *Symbolism, Decadence, and the Fin de Siècle: French and European Perspectives*, ed. Patrick McGuinness (Exeter: University of Exeter Press, 2000), 1–3. See also Charles Bernheimer, *Decadent Subjects: The Idea of Decadence in Art, Literature, Philosophy, and Culture of the Fin-de-Siècle in Europe* (Baltimore, MD: Johns Hopkins University Press, 2002).
20. Adolphe Retté claims that, in Paris, 'not a single one of [Wilde's] friends disowned him'. See 'Salomé', in *Oscar Wilde: Interviews and Recollections*, vol. 1, ed. E. H. Mikhail (London: Macmillan, 1979), 191.
21. 'We Noticed Mr. Oscar Wilde's "Salome"', *The Times*, 8 March 1894.
22. Regenia Gagnier, *Idylls of the Marketplace: Oscar Wilde and the Victorian Public* (Aldershot: Scolar Press, 1987), 146.
23. Dijkstra, *Idols of Perversity*, 382.
24. Joris-Karl Huysmans, *Against Nature*, trans. Nicholas White (Oxford: Oxford University Press, 2009), 46.
25. Symons, 'The Decadent Movement in Literature', 180.

26. Wilde, *The Picture of Dorian Gray*, 107.
27. Pigott, quoted in Stephens, *Censorship*, 112.
28. Michel Foucault, *The History of Sexuality Volume One*, trans. Robert Hurley (New York: Random House, 1978), 55–6.
29. Janet Beizer connects Charcot's practice to a scene in Rachilde's novel *Monsieur Vénus* (1899), in which the artist Raoule creates a wax effigy of her (ambiguously gendered) lover Jacques; see *Ventriloquised Bodies: Narratives of Hysteria in Nineteenth-Century France* (Ithaca, NY: Cornell University Press, 1994), 254. In a Salomean act of necrophilia, Raoule kisses the model's lips at night.
30. Meltzer, *Salome and the Dance of Writing*, 24.
31. Yeats, *The Trembling of the Veil*, 247.
32. Ibid., 247.
33. Ibid., 246.
34. Jane Marcus, 'Salomé: The Jewish Princess was a New Woman', *Bulletin of the New York Public Library* 78.1 (1974): 99, 96.
35. Martin Puchner, *Stagefright: Modernism, Anti-Theatricality and Drama* (Baltimore, MD: Johns Hopkins University Press, 2002), 21.
36. Joseph Donohue, 'Salomé: Drame en un Acte: Introduction', in *PI*, 391.
37. Charles Ricketts, *Recollections of Oscar Wilde* (London: Pallas Athene Arts, 2011), 53.
38. Tydeman and Price, *Wilde: Salome*, 26.
39. Maeterlinck elaborated on his concept of the 'static theatre' in his essay 'The Tragic in Daily Life' (1896). See *The Treasure of the Humble*, trans. Alfred Sutro (London: George Allen, 1903), 95–121.
40. Patrick McGuinness, *Maurice Maeterlinck and the Making of Modern Theatre* (Oxford: Oxford University Press, 2000), 113.
41. Tydeman and Price, *Wilde: Salome*, 26.
42. Ibid., 29. The line 'He was my brother, and nearer to me than a brother' (*PI*, 715) has been read as the clearest suggestion of a homosexual desire between the Page and the Syrian Captain.
43. Jean de Tinan, quoted in Tydeman and Price, *Wilde: Salome*, 30.
44. Yeats, *The Trembling of the Veil*, 265–6.
45. Ibid., 264.
46. Thomas Postlewait, 'Cultural Histories: The Case of Alfred Jarry's *Ubu Roi*', in *The Cambridge Introduction to Theatre Historiography* (Cambridge: Cambridge University Press, 2009), 60–86.
47. See Günter Berghaus's account of *Ubu Roi* in *Theatre, Performance, and the Historical Avant-Garde* (New York: Palgrave Macmillan, 2005), 46–50, 48.
48. Ibid., 48.
49. Yeats, *The Trembling of the Veil*, 266.
50. Taxidou, *Modernism and Performance*, 2.
51. Jill Fell, 'Dancing Under their own Gaze: Mallarmé, Jarry, and Valéry', *Journal of European Studies* 24 (1999): 133–55.
52. Jones, *Literature, Modernism and Dance*, 8.
53. See Emilie Morin, 'Theatres and Pathologies of Silence: Symbolism and Irish Drama from Maeterlinck to Beckett', in *Silence in Modern Irish Literature*, ed. Michael McAteer (Leiden: Brill-Rodopi, 2017), 35–48; Anthony Paraskeva, 'Beckett, Biomechanics, and Eisenstein's Reading of Kleist's Marionettes', *Journal of Beckett Studies* 22 (2013): 161–79.
54. Heinrich von Kleist, 'On the Marionette Theatre', trans. Thomas G. Neumiller, *TDR* 16.3 (1972): 26.
55. Ibid., 23.

56. Lucia Ruprecht, *Dances of the Self in Heinrich von Kleist, E. T. A. Hoffmann and Heinrich Heine* (Aldershot: Ashgate, 2006), 22.
57. Ibid., 36.
58. Ibid., 37.
59. Carrie J. Preston, 'Modernism's Dancing Marionettes: Oskar Schlemmer, Michel Fokine, and Ito Michio', *Modernist Cultures* 9 (2014): 116. See also John Bell, 'Puppets, Masks and Performing Objects at the End of the Century', *The Drama Review* 43.3 (1999): 15–27.
60. Taxidou, *Modernism and Performance*, 17.
61. Ellmann, *Oscar Wilde*, 349.
62. Harold B. Segel discusses the *ombres chinoises* and modernist responses to puppetry in *Pinocchio's Progeny: Puppets, Marionettes, Automatons, and Robots in Modernist and Avant-Garde Drama* (Baltimore, MD: Johns Hopkins University Press, 1995).
63. Nancy Forgione, '"The Shadow Only": Shadow and Silhouette in Late Nineteenth-Century Paris', *The Art Bulletin* 81.3 (1999): 490–512.
64. Warburg, 'The Theatrical Costumes for the Intermedi of 1589', in *The Renewal of Pagan Antiquity*, 381.
65. Dierkes-Thrun, *Salomé's Modernity*, 48.
66. Wilde to the Editor of the *Daily Telegraph*, 19 February [1892], *Letters*, 311.
67. Oskar Schlemmer, quoted in Julian Olf, 'The Man/Marionette Debate in Modern Theatre', *Educational Theatre Journal* 26.4 (1974): 491.
68. Kleist, *On the Marionette Theatre*, 22.
69. Franko, *Dancing Modernism/Performing Politics*, x.
70. Ibid., x–xi.
71. Jones, *Literature, Modernism, and Dance*, 10.
72. Kerry Powell, *Acting Wilde: Victorian Sexuality, Theatre, and Oscar Wilde* (Cambridge: Cambridge University Press, 2011), 3–4.
73. Worth, *Irish Drama*, 101; Dierkes-Thrun, *Salomé's Modernity*, 2.
74. Gomez Carrillo, 'How Oscar Wilde Dreamed of Salomé', in Mikhail, ed., *Interviews*, vol. 1, 193.
75. Ibid., 193.
76. Ibid., 194.
77. Critical efforts to address Wilde's gender and sexual politics in *Salomé* include Garber, *Vested Interests*, 338–46; Rhonda K. Garelick, *Rising Star: Dandyism, Gender and Performance in the Fin de Siècle* (Princeton, NJ: Princeton University Press, 1998), 128–53; Helen Davies, 'The Trouble with Gender in *Salomé*', in *Refiguring Oscar Wilde's Salome*, ed. Michael Y. Bennett (Amsterdam: Rodopi, 2011), 55–69.
78. Powell, *Acting Wilde*, 64; Armstrong also reads Iokanaan's body as an emblematic of castration anxieties in *Modernism, Technology and the Body*, 161.
79. Sos Eltis, *Revising Wilde: Society and Subversion in the Plays of Oscar Wilde* (Oxford: Clarendon Press, 1996).
80. 'Announcement', *Woman's World* 1 (1888), 3.
81. Yopie Prins, 'Greek Maenads, Victorian Spinsters', in *Victorian Sexual Dissidence*, ed. Richard Dellamora (Chicago: University of Chicago Press, 1999), 46.
82. Ibid., 62.
83. *Woman's World* 1, 274–6.
84. The London offices of the magazine at Cassel & Co. were named 'La Belle Sauvage', a mutation of the Bell Savage inn that had stood there since the fifteenth century.

85. Petra Clark, '"Cleverly Drawn": Oscar Wilde, Charles Ricketts, and the Art of *The Woman's World*', *Journal of Victorian Culture* 20.3 (2015): 398.
86. *Woman's World* 2, 96.
87. Gagnier, *Idylls of the Marketplace*, 140.
88. For example, Gail Finney argues that 'Wilde's *Salomé* emerges less as a misogynistic denunciation of the femme fatale than as a masked depiction of one man's longing for another'. See *Women in Modern Drama: Freud, Feminism, and European Theater at the Turn of the Century* (Ithaca, NY: Cornell University Press, 1989), 65.
89. Elaine Showalter, *Sexual Anarchy: Gender and Culture at the Fin-de-siècle* (New York: Virago, 1992), 156. See Ellmann, *Oscar Wilde*, 402–3.
90. Showalter, *Sexual Anarchy*, 167, 164.
91. Mallarmé, 'Herodiade', 583.
92. Margaret Stoljar, 'Mirror and Self in Symbolist and Post-Symbolist Poetry', *The Modern Language Review* 85 (1990): 364.
93. Dierkes-Thrun, *Salome's Modernity*, 39.
94. Armstrong, *Modernism, Technology and the Body*, 160–1.
95. Symons, *The Symbolist Movement in Literature*, 76.
96. See Song of Solomon 1:1–12 and 7:1–10 in particular. Powell notes the similarity between the Song of Solomon and Salome's speech to Iokanaan in *Acting Wilde*, 60–1.
97. Chad Bennett, 'Oscar Wilde's *Salome*: Décor, Des Corps, Desire', *ELH* 77 (2010): 309.
98. Ibid., 317.
99. Brad Bucknell, 'On "Seeing" Salome', *ELH* 60.2 (1993): 523.
100. Wilde to Leonard Smithers, 2 September [1900], *Letters*, 834. Wilde also uses this line from *Antony and Cleopatra* in his poem for the actor Ellen Terry, 'Camma': 'And yet – methinks I'd rather see thee play / That serpent of old Nile, whose witchery / Made Emperors drunk, – come great Egypt [. . .]'; see CW, 861.
101. For discussion of Wilde, Salome and orientalism, see Yeeyon Im, 'Oscar Wilde's *Salomé*: Disorienting Orientalism', *Comparative Drama* 45.4 (2011): 361–80; Ian Christopher Fletcher, 'The Soul of Man under Imperialism: Oscar Wilde, Race, and Empire', *Journal of Victorian Culture* 5.2 (2000): 334n41.
102. Tydeman and Price, *Wilde: Salome*, 20–3.
103. Ellmann, *Oscar Wilde*, 351.
104. *Woman's World* 1, 207.
105. John Paul Riquelme, 'Shalom/Solomon/*Salomé*: Modernism and Wilde's Aesthetic Politics', *The Centennial Review* 39 (Fall 1995): 583.
106. Sharon Marcus, 'Salomé!! Sarah Bernhardt, Oscar Wilde, and the Drama of Celebrity', *PMLA* 126.4 (2011): 1004, 1005.
107. Sarah Bernhardt, *My Double Life: Memoirs of Sarah Bernhardt* (London: William Heinemann, 1907), 288.
108. Ellen Terry, *Story of My Life: Recollections and Reflections* (New York: Doubleday, 1908), 237.
109. Ibid., 23.
110. Bram Stoker, *Personal Reminiscences of Henry Irving* (London: William Heinemann, 1907), 344.
111. 'Madame Sarah Bernhardt in London', *Manchester Guardian*, 18 June 1897.
112. 'Bernhardt's Hamlet', *New York Tribune*, 11 June 1899.
113. Garelick, *Rising Star*, 149.
114. In the first performances of Strauss's *Salome* in Dresden and New York, the opera

singer Olive Fremstad was replaced with the ballerina Bianca Froehlich. See Tydeman and Price, *Wilde: Salome*, 128.
115. Ellmann, *Oscar Wilde*, 351.
116. Tydeman and Price, *Wilde: Salome*, 20.
117. Joseph Donohue, 'Distance, Death and Desire in *Salomé*', in *The Cambridge Companion to Oscar Wilde*, ed. Peter Raby (Cambridge: Cambridge University Press, 1997), 121.
118. Wilde to the Editor of *The Times*, 1 March [1893], *Letters*, 335–6.
119. Retté, 'Salomé', in Mikhail, ed., *Interviews*, vol. 1, 191.
120. Wilde, quoted in Robert Tanitch, *Oscar Wilde on Stage and Screen* (London: Methuen, 1999), 138–9.
121. Wilde to William Rothenstein, July [1892], *Letters*, 316.
122. Ricketts, *Recollections*, 53. See also Tydeman and Price, *Wilde: Salome*, 46.
123. Showalter reads Salome and Medusa as signs of a castration complex using Freud's short essay on 'Medusa's Head' (1922). See *Sexual Anarchy*, 145–6.
124. Carrillo, 'Salomé', in Mikhail, ed., *Interviews*, vol. 1, 193.
125. Ibid., 195.
126. Hugh Haughton, 'Oscar Wilde: Thinking Style', in *Thinking Through Style*, ed. Michael D. Hurley and Marcus Waithe (Oxford: Oxford University Press, 2018), 267.
127. Duncan, *My Life*, 136.
128. Richard Allen Cave, 'Staging Salome's Dance in Wilde's Play and Strauss's Opera', in Bennett, ed., *Refiguring Oscar Wilde's Salome*, 149.
129. Wilde to Edmund Gosse, 23 February [1893], *Letters*, 331.
130. George Bernard Shaw to Wilde, 28 February [1893], *Letters*, 332.
131. This meeting is described by Diaghilev's friend Alexandre Benois in his *Memoirs*, trans. Moura Budberg (London: Chatto and Windus, 1964), 103. For a full account, see Annabel Rutherford, 'The Triumph of the Veiled Dance: The Influence of Oscar Wilde and Aubrey Beardsley on Serge Diaghilev's Creation of the Ballets Russes', *Dance Research* 27 (2009): 93–107.
132. Wilde to Leonard Smithers, c. 4 May [1898], *Letters*, 734.
133. Richard Buckle, *Diaghilev* (London: Hamish Hamilton, 1979), 38. See Rutherford, 'The Triumph of the Veiled Dance', 94.
134. Nicoletta Misler, 'Seven Steps, Seven Veils: Salomé in Russia', *Experiment* 17 (2011): 158.
135. Michael de Cossart, 'Ida Rubinstein and Diaghilev: A One-Sided Rivalry', *Dance Research Journal* 1.2 (1983): 4.
136. Ellmann, *Oscar Wilde*, 324. John Stokes identified Petrescue as the acrobat; see *In the Nineties* (Chicago: University of Chicago Press, 1989), 191.
137. Misler, 'Seven Steps, Seven Veils', 163.
138. Lynn Garafola, 'Soloists Abroad: The Prewar Careers of Natalia Trouhanowa and Ida Rubinstein', *Experiment* 2 (1996), 29.
139. Benois, *Memoirs*, 296.
140. A. Vivanti Chartres, 'D'Annunzio's New Play *St. Sebastian*', *The English Review* 8 (July 1911), 696.
141. Ibid., 697.
142. Ibid., 697.

3

'HARMONIES OF LIGHT': CINÉ-DANCES AND WOMEN'S SILENT FILM

In her essay 'Three Encounters with Loïe Fuller' (1928), the French film director Germaine Dulac identified an important connection between Fuller's choreographic creations and her own approach to film-making. 'Loïe Fuller created her first harmonies of light at the moment when the Lumière brothers gave us the cinema', Dulac wrote. 'Strange coincidence at the dawn of an epoch, which is and will be that of visual music; the work of Loïe Fuller aligns with our own, and that is why *cinéastes* here owe her a profound and ultimate homage.'[1] For Dulac, the creator of avant-garde films including *La Coquille et le clergyman (The Seashell and the Clergyman*, 1928) and *La Souriante Madame Beudet (The Smiling Mme. Beudet*, 1923), Fuller's serpentine dance provided a luminous kinetic ideal for her cinematographic method, demonstrating the same powerful synthesis of light and the moving image that would prove central to the 'grammar of cinema' emerging during this period.[2] The abundance of musical analogies in Dulac's criticism speaks to her conscious dissolution of the boundaries between distinct art forms, manifesting again as an intensely rhythmical sensibility – apparent both formally and in terms of subject matter – in her own creative work. While she believed cinema to be a distinct art form that demanded a new type of sensory engagement, Dulac nonetheless pursued, in Tom Gunning's words, an 'art of motion' indebted to Fuller, with whom she shared a belief in 'the redeeming effect of the rhythms of art'.[3] Her memories of watching Fuller perform as a child suggest that modern dance offered a vital blueprint for her theoretical and practical engagements with film, as it did for many of her *cinéaste* peers.

This intermedial overlap had been present, as Dulac suggests, since the invention of the *cinématographe*, and persisted well into the twentieth century. Laura Marcus has shown that the effects of cinema on modernist aesthetics and literary form were both specific and diffuse, encouraging broader considerations of the 'interplay between stasis and mobility' and the 'mechanical [. . .] and the organic', shaping 'new understandings of vision and identity in a moving world'.[4] Much as they were enthralled by the imaginative possibilities afforded by dance, writers and performers were also intrigued by, and often involved in, early film-making. New vocabularies of movement were emerging across different facets of the avant-garde: in Germany, the 'expressionist' *Ausdruckstanz* pioneered by Mary Wigman and Rudolf von Laban paralleled the evolution of Expressionism in cinema, while in Paris, the Ballets Russes collaborated on their ballet *Parade* (1917) with visual artists including Picasso and Jean Cocteau, who would become a prominent avant-garde film-maker in the 1930s and 1940s.[5] The creative opportunities represented by the cinema were recognised too by dancers such as Fuller, who was highly attuned to the kinaesthetic 'harmonies' shared between her creative method and the other arts. Beyond incorporating magic lanterns and luminescent technologies into her stage performances, Fuller collaborated with her partner Gab Sorère on three silent films: *Le Lys de la vie* (1921), *Visions des rêves* (1924) and *Les Incertitudes de Coppelius* (1927), of which only the first survives. Stars of the silent screen who began their careers as dancers included Louise Brooks, trained by Ted Shawn and Ruth St Denis at the Denishawn School, and Pola Negri, who danced with Warsaw's Imperial Ballet Academy. More than just a 'strange coincidence' then, the close alignment of film and dance is borne out in disciplinary historiographies and might be read as a telling sign of modernism's fixation with technologies of movement and the types of bodily performance they facilitated.

As this chapter demonstrates, Dulac's celebration of Fuller's career as a precursor to her own also speaks to the importance of feminist lineages in these developing spheres of modernist production. The 'women's modernity' traced by film scholars Rosanna Maule and Catherine Russell emerged at the intersections between the peripheral new force of avant-garde cinema and the more 'dominant' movements of Symbolism and Art Nouveau, which, as previous chapters have shown, took dancers such as Fuller as potent symbols of the modern.[6] If Dulac saw Fuller's 'harmonies of light' as a model for her own ambitions in film, she was also keenly drawn to the pre-eminent female actors of the period, much as Fuller and Maud Allan idolised Sarah Bernhardt and sought to emulate her dramatic methods. After watching the Russian actor Alla Nazimova in Albert Capellani's *La Lanterne rouge* (1919), Dulac wrote to the producer Louis Nalpas:

> I saw Nazimova again, yesterday in *La Lanterne rouge*. And I am enthused. Her slightest gesture is the synthesis of an entire state of mind. She is beautiful, powerful and true, and she knows how to express her spirit without false means. She is great among the greats.[7]

Once the highest paid actress in Hollywood and a famed interpreter of Henrik Ibsen's New Woman protagonists, Nazimova courted notoriety with her acting and directorial work on *Salomé: An Historical Phantasy by Oscar Wilde* (1922), a self-consciously camp adaptation of Wilde's Symbolist play that layered visual styles derived from a range of theatrical, choreographic and cinematographic sources. As a trained dancer, Nazimova treated her body as a powerful instrument by 'synthesising' meaning through carefully worked gestures and poses, facilitating the kinaesthetic cinephilia that feminist film historians have viewed as central to the experiences of early female filmgoers. This sensory engagement was predicated on a 'bodily incorporation' perhaps most clearly encoded in 'the swirling scarves of Loïe Fuller's serpentine dances', which became, as we have seen, both Fuller's individual moniker and an important modernist movement aesthetic, replicated in Nazimova's 'dance of the seven veils' in her *Salomé*.[8]

Indeed, Maule and Russell claim that the 'cinephilic discourse of the 1920s' provides an apt mechanism for drawing Fuller, an emblem of *fin-de-siècle* visual culture, 'into line with a modernist aesthetic distinctly marked as feminine'.[9] Despite working in very different filmic contexts, Nazimova and Dulac were similarly steeped in the late nineteenth-century performance traditions that included artists as varied as Wilde and Fuller, and both women notably drew on the conventions of dance as a model for their cinematic praxis. Jennifer Bean reminds us that a critical cartography of women's early film-making must account for 'the range of sites in which women produced, consumed and performed in the growing industry', while also making use of the interdisciplinary tools that enable a fuller exploration of the interlocking aesthetic and cultural discourses that historically constituted early cinema culture, which itself can be understood as 'a constellation of radically heterogenous film forms and styles'.[10] Women's silent films do not 'simply reflect or reproduce already constituted or given definitions of woman', as Sandy Flitterman-Lewis reminds us; cinema 'is itself a process of production – of woman as a category and of femininity within a signifying discourse', consistently 'activated by the conjunction of "woman and the cinema"'.[11] Nazimova and Dulac are brought together in this chapter through an emphasis on the palimpsestic nature of their creative output; both women negotiated the early film industries of Hollywood and France via their rich engagement with the aesthetic and formal contours of European symbolist theatre, as well as the modernist visual styles popularised through Art Nouveau, modern dance and the synthesised artistic productions of the Ballets Russes.

Arriving in New York as a Russian migrant in 1905, Nazimova carved a space for herself in an America culturally inflamed by Salomania and soon to fashion new cinematic categories of modern, mobile femininity between which she seamlessly moved: boyish androgyne, Jazz Age flapper girl and, perhaps most notably, predatory 'vamp', a racially fraught shorthand for stars of the silent screen, including Marlene Dietrich and Theda Bara, whose seductive charisma was coded in complex ethnic and sexual terms. This chapter examines how the construction of these categories intersected with modernist literary forms via the work of Djuna Barnes, whose interviews with Salome dancers, including Nazimova and Mimi Aguglia, reveal her dedicated interest in deconstructing popular conceptions of female performers within an ironic, self-referential journalistic framework, further developed in her satirical short story about Salome, 'What Do You See, Madam?' (1915), inspired by these interviews. This chapter is attentive to the ways in which such ambiguously constructed gender delineators, playfully critiqued by Barnes, permeated both contemporary responses to Nazimova and to women's early cinematic discourse more broadly. Throughout their careers, and especially in the films considered here, both Nazimova and Dulac prioritised partnerships with other female creatives – including Natacha Rambova, Irène Hillel-Erlanger and Stasia Napierkowska – which often crossed over into private intimacy, thus marking their cinematographic experiments as distinctly queer collaborations, focused on the moving female body as a source of visual and kinaesthetic pleasure. In this respect, Fuller is again an important precursor: as Susan Potter has recently argued, Fuller's performance archive in itself signals how 'same-sex erotic spectatorial relations may have been subtly inflected and reorganised via moving image practices and technologies that preceded [. . .] early films'.[12] Such an imbrication of aesthetic forms and queer erotics has underwritten many of the case studies examined in this book, revealing the range of ways in which modernism's choreographic imagination constellated around a queering of the veiled dance and its associated iconography and techniques.

The richly varied collection of images, textual coordinates and movement vocabularies that this book has assembled around the dance of Salome thus includes and intersects with the work of Nazimova and Dulac in ways that are both readily apparent (through direct adaptation) and more oblique. This chapter extends the latter category to consider Dulac's studied interest in Salome's choreographic interpreters – Fuller, Napierkowska, Rubinstein – and her persistent return to visual metaphors of veiling, dancing and severance in her narrative and abstract films. Crucially, Dulac was one of the first to appreciate Fuller's contribution to the formation of cinema, and her own oeuvre – especially her short abstract works – pays 'homage' to this dancer's rewriting of a new cinematographic language, drawing on the properties of the serpentine line and the interplay between light and surface. The idea of a 'visual language' might, as Tom Gunning observes, 'pose a rather awkward oxymoron', but there nonetheless 'exists a rhetoric of vision' in film and other performance cultures of the period that 'plays with (rather than simply assumes the power of) sight'.[13] By the turn of the century, Jonathan Crary argues, moving image technologies were underpinned by an attention to the embodied, physiological conditions of spectatorship, in which 'the very possibility and value of a sustained looking, of a "fixed" vision, became inseparable from the effects of dynamic, kinetic, and rhythmic modalities of experience and form'.[14] This chapter considers how the literary and choreographic genealogies formed around the 'dance of veils' map on to the realm of silent film, revealing the sustained influence of Symbolist constructions of the feminine on the work of *cinéastes* such as Dulac and Nazimova and on other modernist engagements with the so-called seventh art.

SERPENTINE WEAVINGS: ALLA NAZIMOVA, MIMI AGUGLIA, DJUNA BARNES

'When was it that I first saw Alla Nazimova?' This is Djuna Barnes's opening question in her interview with the Russian actor, published in *Theatre Guild Magazine* in June 1930, by which time Nazimova's extraordinary celebrity had considerably waned. Barnes's rhetorical manoeuvre seems to allude, however subtly, to the mystique of her subject, suggesting, as it does, this modernist writer's attempt to locate some initial, transformational encounter in her memory: a moment when the singularity of the 'star' was recognised and understood. It was not, Barnes recalls, in any of the 'Ibsen plays she made glorious' but in one of her more 'emotional' melodramas; 'She wore ten good yards of that slinky material which, when molded about the hips, spells a woman bent on the destruction of the soul.'[15] Barnes's recollection conjures an image of Nazimova as a quintessential 'vamp', a type of alluring yet perilous femininity that had its literary roots, of course, in the sexually transgressive vampirism of Sheridan Le Fanu's *Carmilla* (1872) and the three 'weird sisters' in Bram Stoker's *Dracula* (1897). Although her moral intentions were undoubtedly coded as destructive, the female vamp offered a prominent incarnation of what Lori Landay reads as the 'kinetic powers and pleasures – a new kinaesthetic – of the modern body in motion'.[16] One of the first cinematic depictions of this feminine type, *The Vampire* (1913), tellingly structures its moment of bloodletting around a dance performance: the titular vamp, played by Alice Eis, executes a modern scarf dance before descending to bite her hapless spectator in the manner of a parasitic Isadora Duncan.

Perceived as 'utterly foreign' by contemporary commentators, Nazimova was seen to embody both the transnational kinetic mobility of the modern subject and the unfixable errancy of the oriental other, paradoxical qualities that were rendered in filmic iterations of vampish women more widely.[17] Indeed, film became the ideal medium for the sinuous movements of the vamp; gestures we might align with the kinaesthetic of 'torsion' that Schwartz has identified as an integral component of modernist performance. Cinema 'demanded a reading of the body in motion and an appreciation of the full impulse of that motion', Schwartz argues; 'the glamour of the stars came to be equated with a dynamism that drew on the new kinaesthetic', captured by the 'dynamic balance' of Charlie Chaplin, the 'menacing torque of villains' and the 'seductive spirals of vamps'.[18] With her costume forming a 'slinky' 'mould' around her natural contours, Nazimova too created a mobile interplay between material surface and serpentine movement, her body itself becoming almost textual; the script that 'spells' out psychological intent.

Though Barnes's profile veers in places towards physiognomic cliché – noting Nazimova's 'winged nostrils and an upper lip to match, made doubly dangerous by a lower' – she seems cognisant of the limiting effect of the dramatic stereotypes she describes: '[Nazimova's] managers had forbidden her to display any of her other myriad abilities [. . .] they obliged her to feed her great talents to a public which had appetite for nothing more than the conventional stage vampire'.[19] In Barnes's account, the audience, rather than the actor, becomes the vampiric force, 'feeding' on the female performer who is obliged, through economic demand, to reproduce the images of the popular theatre. In these eccentric and self-conscious interviews with female actors, Barnes may be attempting, as Daniela Caselli puts it, 'to chip away at the performing image of tragic femininity'.[20] There is certainly a reductive aspect to the predictable motions of the roles that Nazimova and her contemporaries were compelled to inhabit; the varied kinaesthetic register that loosely interlinks vampish 'spirals' and the 'serpentine' torsion of Fuller's modern dance does not, it should be noted, permit a flattening equation of these varied techniques. Yet some of these performers successfully bridged this apparent gap between melodrama and high art: Barnes writes that 'Nazimova's artistry was so extraordinarily flexible and persuasive that she could make a common vampire of melodrama seem, for the moment, as great a creation as Hedda [Gabler]'.[21] There is a continuity, then, between Nazimova's early stage creations and her later experiments in avant-garde film-making, culminating in her homage to Wilde's *Salomé*, whose theme, as Barnes acknowledges, clearly dismantles distinctions between 'high' and 'low' art in its status as 'common property'.[22]

Nazimova was not the only Salome who lingered in Barnes's imagination or ghosted the pages of her journalism, which featured interviews with other dancers including Valentine de Saint-Point, Flo Ziegfeld and Ballets Russes choreographer Adolf Bolm. Years earlier, in December 1913, Barnes had interviewed the Italian performer Mimi Aguglia for the *New York Press*, one week after Aguglia performed the lead role in an abridged version of Wilde's *Salomé*, translated into Italian, at the Comedy Theatre. According to one impressed critic, Aguglia 'out Salomed all other Salomes', using dance to communicate with those audience members who did not understand the Italian language: 'From then on, there was no one in the theatre who did not understand the remainder of the entertainment [. . .] Mme. Aguglia writhed over [the head] on stage as no other Salome has ever writhed before.'[23] Barnes too was impressed, if characteristically sardonic, about Aguglia's formidable presence, describing her as 'some hundred pounds of passionate flesh' who danced in 'lunge[s]' and 'spasms' on stage, and coddled her pet monkeys in private.[24]

Barnes's encounter with Aguglia became the basis of a short story, 'What Do You See, Madam?', published in the *All-Story Cavalier Weekly* in March 1915. In this tale, Barnes constructs a satirical take on the craze for Salome dancers and broader censorious responses to Wilde's legacy, perhaps in light of the Boston mayor's decision to ban Aguglia's performance of *Salomé*. This brief text follows a thinly veiled Aguglia – the dancer Mamie Saloam – who, 'at the age of ten [. . .] had learned to interpret Oscar Wilde, when Oscar Wilde had gone in, rather extensively, for passion and the platter'.[25] Barnes borrows something of Wilde's epigrammatic wit in this text, narrating an exchange between Mamie Saloam and her stage manager, Billy, who laments that 'the Prevention of Impurities upon the Boards' committee, the P.I.B., has demanded a purely 'impartial rendering' of the title role in *Salomé*. Unsurprised by their prudish demands, Saloam knowingly situates her own performance in the context of American popular dance and previous depictions of Salome:

> 'Of course they have [prejudices],' said Mamie calmly; 'they have seen Mme. Aguglia, Mary Garden, Gertrude Hoffman, and Trixie Friganza do the stunt; they have all seen what they wanted to see because the aforesaid showed them what they wanted to see. I'll admit that John hasn't been properly loved since the original gurgle ceased; I'll admit that as we have gotten further and further away from the real head, we have dealt with rather papier-mâché passions.'[26]

It is little surprise that Barnes should be struck by the endless reproducibility of the Salome dance, which had, in her words, transitioned away from 'real' bodies to 'papier-mâché passions'. The latter metaphor could refer to the morbid, synthetic forms that populate Barnes's own modernist works, from her Beardsley-inspired monochrome illustrations to the 'ersatz decadence' of *The Book of Repulsive Women* (1915), which articulates, according to Alex Goody, 'both a corporeal repulsion of the grotesque female body and an antipathy to fixed meaning or origin', singling out the very idea of the 'originary' as 'itself ersatz'.[27] Equally, in 'What Do You See, Madam?', the final replacement of the false head of John the Baptist with the living head of Billy does not signal the return of the 'real', as Barnes playfully fractures and dismantles the bodily language of performance by stressing its grotesque machinery.

Performing the dance, Mamie Saloam's movements are jerky, 'halting' and difficult to visualise: she approaches the head with crab-like circuity, 'sideways, forward', before breaking into 'a semi-circle of half-steps', reaching out with her 'plastic hands' and making 'gurgling, throaty little noises' in a fusion of the primal and the artificial. Her surreal choreography is an ironic success with the ladies of the P.I.B, who admire her 'perfect impartiality' and 'control' before 'pass[ing] out', prompting a wink from the single stage item that ought to be inanimate: 'John the Baptist batted his right eye.'[28] If, as Goody argues, Barnes uses images of dance to 'parody the functional machine body of American modernity by exposing its chthonian grotesque', her satirical text critiques moralising responses to decadent literature while also exposing the fiction of 'origins' that has always underwritten Salome's narrative, disrupting the line between real body and prop and ironically reproducing the sensuous vampish dance as a performance of machine-like 'impartiality'.[29] The superhuman grace of the Kleistian marionette is turned on its head in this story, as Barnes reveals the grinning automaton beneath the seemingly human veneer.

Women like Mamie Saloam appear throughout Barnes's work. As her profiles of Nazimova, Aguglia and others show, Barnes 'took the cinema vamp quite seriously', despite occasionally mocking her 'mythical aura'.[30] Critics have even read *Nightwood*'s (1936) Robin Vote, modelled on Barnes's lover Thelma Wood, as coming 'perilously close to the classic cinema vamp' in her chilly promiscuity and nocturnal wanderings.[31] Described by Barnes as 'the infected carrier of the past', Robin is 'flesh that will become myth'; like Nazimova, she projects a parasitic air but is herself consumable: 'we feel that we could eat her, she who is eaten death returning'.[32] Robin wears down the distinction between the human and other categories of matter, construed, in Barnes's amorphous neo-decadent descriptors, as a hybrid of the animal and the botanical: 'The perfume that her body exhaled was of the quality of that earth-flesh, fungi [. . .] her flesh was the texture of plant life, and beneath it one sensed a frame, broad, porous and sleep-worn'.[33] Terming Robin 'the splinter in the skin of the text', Teresa de Lauretis identifies a register in *Nightwood* that is 'highly charged with affect' but wholly 'sensory', encoded in Robin's non-verbal, gestural and kinetic exchanges with animals, ultimately marking a queer collapsing of the sex drive and the death drive.[34]

While using less self-consciously experimental prose, journalistic accounts of cinema vamps, and Nazimova especially, drew on a similar linguistic register to Barnes. Of Nazimova, a *New York Tribune* article proclaimed, 'the almost inevitable word [. . .] is "exotic." [Nazimova] is a strange plant, a night blooming marvel, that may have strange poisons in its flowers or leaves.'[35] Romantic metaphors are here corrupted, absorbing the decaying quality of Baudelaire's *fleurs du mal* but also containing a hint of Barnes's neo-decadent images with their fungal 'bloom'. Solita Solano, Barnes's friend and a member of the same Parisian lesbian network, found Nazimova 'admirably fitted physically to portray an entire gallery of predatory females', of which Salome was one of the more notable examples.[36] In her summary of Nazimova's stage roles, Solano suggested that the actor's performances were characterised by a perverse 'intensity; their eyes burned with unquenchable desires; their mouths were blood red'.[37]

Late nineteenth-century pseudo-science and degeneration theory had provided the diagnostic tools for such a range of racial and sexual forms of alterity, which saturated the language of decadence on which modernists such as Barnes drew. Clearly, the mystique of vampish dancers, especially those who harked back to the *fin-de-siècle*'s emblematic *femme fatale*, were also calculated in highly racialised terms. Like Salome herself, Nazimova was of Jewish heritage, and many of these sources repeated familiar antisemitic stereotypes, alluding to innate connections between Nazimova's 'dark' countenance and the threatening feminine allure she was believed to project.[38] In this way, Nazimova fell victim to the competing racial myths often imposed upon Jewish bodies, which were portrayed, in Maren Tova Linett's words, as 'exotic or romantic or eerily powerful [...] weighted with pathos and laden with history'.[39] In *Nightwood*, the Jewish Felix, and his father Guido, are described as 'heavy with impermissible blood', though Barnes seems intent on critiquing such racial mystification, later writing that 'the Christian traffic in retribution has made the Jew's history a commodity'.[40] Salome dancers such as Nazimova reflected fantasies about the figure of the sensuous 'Jewess' and concomitant anxieties about the feminisation of modern men, wryly alluded to in Barnes's depiction of Guido as 'a gourmet and a dandy, never appearing in public without the ribbon of some quite unknown distinction'.[41] In some ways like the dandy, the real and imagined figure of the Jew was often seen to embody the cultures of modernity – mobility, rootlessness, the metropolis – but was at the same time an excluded or marginalised subject.[42]

Throughout her career, Nazimova was associated with either the sensationalism of the stage vamp or Ibsen's New Woman, and, as a queer Russian Jew, her body was interpreted as a site of plural signification in performance, working through 'the veil of a barbarous tongue' by 'play of feature and of body'.[43] The following review of *Hedda Gabler*, for instance, stresses the kinaesthetic dimension of Nazimova's moving form:

> It was in her face that the spectator read the creeping and calculated cruelties of her Hedda Gabler, princess of the Orient. In her body he saw the perverse and morbid languors with which she chose to clothe her. Serpentine were her coilings about Lövborg's spirit, and serpentine were equally her weavings and her hisses about Brack. Her Hedda was conceived out of her own imagination and nowhere else. All the allurements of her personality could not beguile Ibsen's play to it; but granted that

> conception, it was by feature, gesture and body that she most suggested and defined it. In her body again was Nora's grace, and in her face, above all, Nora's fear and illumination.⁴⁴

Through Nazimova's studied movements, Ibsen's Nordic protagonist is reimagined as a 'princess of the Orient', sharing something of Salome's rebellious agency and serpentine body language.⁴⁵ This review crucially locates Nazimova's unique artistry in her body, suggesting that audience members were invited to 'read' and decipher her character through her corporeal syntax of gestures and poses, rather than in the spoken text. While Nazimova's biographer Gavin Lambert points out that 'almost every critic evoked the serpent or the cobra to describe [her]', it seems that these metaphors were not merely aesthetic judgements imposed upon her body, but qualities that Nazimova herself cultivated onstage.⁴⁶

In a profile for American *Vogue*, Nazimova described her preparations for the role of Hedda Gabler, repeatedly stressing her intention to create spiralling motions with her body:

> Hedda seems to me a snake-like woman, and when she appears for the first time, between the curtains, I try to give the impression of a snake, slowly uncoiling, slowly raising, then advancing her head. In my opinion she was a decadent, an unconscious poser.⁴⁷

Anticipating her critics, Nazimova describes her movements in terms of slow, serpentine unwinding, transcribing Hedda's inscrutable and elusive personality through a bodily language grounded in twisting, curling lines; as Schwartz might have it, 'a model of motion as a spiral at whose radiant centre was a mystical solar plexus'.⁴⁸ Nazimova's terminology may differ from that of Isadora Duncan and Ruth St Denis, but her stagecraft reflects the wider shift towards this movement register in the work of dancers who sought to liberate and engage the torso. This transition was not merely characteristic of modern dance: while Diaghilev's Ballets Russes has been largely associated with the reinvention of the athletic male ballet dancer and a disregard for the ballerina's pointe-work, dance historian Lynn Garafola has shown how the choreographer Michel Fokine 'used arms and a newly pliant, uncorseted torso to create a more "natural" female body, one that moved freely and expansively, arching, stretching, twisting, bending, in a way that enhanced its plasticity and three-dimensionality'.⁴⁹

Fokine's movement philosophy, which shaped the careers of dancers such as Tamara Karsavina, engaged a sensorial dimension that we might compare to that of early cinema and the techniques of film actors such as Nazimova. Scholars of silent film have argued for the strong connections between the sensory effects of dance and the emergence of film as 'a dispenser of automorphic images that began informing the very processes of our visual imaginings'.[50] If the movements of dancers had physiological effects on their spectators – Mallarmé, for one, found himself enthralled, dizzy and intoxicated by Loïe Fuller – then the effects of cinematic spectacle also went beyond mere optics.[51] Returning to Mallarmé's accounts of dance, Christophe Wall-Romana claims that the body of the dancer prompted in the poet 'a sensorial uncoiling experienced as both inner body feeling and outer visual movement', shaping his perception of the kinaesthetic links between dance and poetry, as well as the development of cinematographic motion – forms of aesthetic experience that Mallarmé later sought to combine in his unfinished intermedial project, *Livre*.[52] The creative symmetries between these arts were further demonstrated by silent films such as Fernand Léger's *Ballet Mécanique* (1924) and Man Ray's rhythmic *cinépoème Emak Bakia* (1926). Certainly, the interconnected kinaesthetics of dance and silent film shaped both literary forms and modes of perception, instituting a new kind of sensory communion between spectators and these twin arts of movement.

Nazimova's description of Hedda as a 'decadent [...] poser' reveals where her artistic interests lie, and her subsequent account of Ibsen's protagonist '[contemplating] a single flower with a look of rapt ecstasy' recalls a decadent mode of aesthetic contemplation.[53] Although Nazimova claimed elsewhere that she did 'not know what pose really means', her use of the term in this passage is conscious and deliberate.[54] In this sense, she was part of a broader discourse concerning the aesthetic and somatic value of posing, stimulated by the popularity of Delsartism among actors, dancers and women's health movements in the US and Europe. Previous chapters have noted the importance of this movement for modern dance and stage performance, but it was also an important source of training for film actors: advocates of Delsartism looked to the classical proportions of Ancient Greek and Roman sculpture for their models, promoting recitation and solo posing based on mythic imagery in order to ground this new art form in accepted models of grace. Preston has shown how 'Delsartism developed mythic posing into a central modernist kinesthetic: a philosophy and technique of movement emphasising a tension between stasis and motion, poses of classical beauty, framed cinematic compositions, and speeding bodies'.[55] In this sense, the language of 'posing' that spread among theatre and film performers was deeply connected to the technological cultures of modernity, while expressing a sense of nostalgia for antique forms that might be newly imagined in modernist performance.

The popularity of Delsartism among middle- and upper-class women also reflected, Preston argues, a desire for 'self-cultivation', which paralleled early feminist efforts to grant women more freedom in civic and domestic life.[56] This widespread interest in the liberating effects of physical activity, posing and performance might further, in part, explain the extraordinary popularity of

Salome dancers, both in Europe and America, in the early twentieth century. Embodying both a visceral feminine corporeality and an astuteness in political exchange, Salome offered the radical promise of female self-realisation through the art of dance, which was an important component of new body techniques. The interconnected discourses around dance and Delsartean posing provided women with a modernised classical language that might subvert patriarchal meaning: 'Striking a statue pose and performing a desired identity', Preston suggests, 'would gradually achieve that self; "personality" was a malleable project rather than a static identity.'[57] Nazimova's 'serpentine weavings' and 'decadent' posing thus constituted an attempt to navigate the familiar judgements pronounced upon the bodies of female actors, as she developed a powerful syntax of physical expression that emphasised her dynamism and strength on stage but also her ultimately unfixable personality.

It is no surprise, therefore, that Nazimova was eventually drawn to the dance of Salome. Nazimova believed that choreography was intimately connected to other types of performance, and she spoke about her own background in dance as an important part of her professional training. In a 1910 interview, she claimed that ballet was the best means of achieving precision in bodily expression, declaring, 'there is nothing which puts the body into such perfect control as dancing. Every muscle is taught to respond to every command of the brain.'[58] For Nazimova, the division between bodily matter and the intellect was not a stable one; she continues, 'Instinctively the body gets to harmonize with one's thoughts, and quite unconsciously a sad thought makes me assume a gesture of despair [. . .] What little grace I have I imagine is due to my ballet training.'[59] While dance training, for Nazimova, ensured the body's total and immediate harmony with the intellect, it also created a non-hierarchical equivalence between gesture and thought that resulted in a form of physical intelligence. In this way, Nazimova's techniques and understanding of her own body were aligned with the new kinaesthetic that 'insists upon rhythm, wholeness, fullness, fluidity and a durable connection between the bodiliness of the inner core and the outer expressions of the physical self'.[60]

The strong connections that Nazimova built between posing, dance and self-fashioning were informed by wider choreographic practices that bore a particular relevance to women's body cultures in the early twentieth century. A fascination with particular forms of movement, derived from the serpentine line and the spiralling motion of torsion, emphasised the continuities between technological rhythms, revitalised by silent film, and the powerfully liberated bodies of modern dancers. This reflected a growing appreciation of dance, and the language of the body more generally, as a critical aspect of performance. Reviews of Nazimova in a 1907 production of *A Doll's House* celebrated her expert rendering of Nora's tarantella, and lamented, 'The inability to trip the light fantastic toe has likewise proven of inestimable trouble to those actresses who, although they could act with their minds, faces, voices, and hearts, could not act with their feet.'[61] In a suggestive juxtaposition, the same critic goes on to invoke another dance that had caught the attention of American audiences: the dance of Salome, performed by Julia Marlowe, in a production of Hermann Sudermann's *John the Baptist*, which was described as incomparable and 'tumultuous'.[62] This enticing pairing implies that, as in her many other reviews and profiles, Nazimova's singular stage presence was defined in terms of her corporeal techniques; furthermore, it confirms that in early twentieth-century New York, the figure of Salome was still a vehicle for startling inventiveness among actors and dancers.

Salomé (1922) and Ballet Modernism

Nazimova herself was the force behind one such startling invention. On New Year's Eve 1922, when her *Salomé* had its opening midnight screening at the Criterion Theatre, critics dubbed it 'a striking and bizarre photoplay of unusual artistic beauty'.[63] Although the film would go on to spell financial disaster for its star-producer, it signalled Nazimova's strong intention to meld her wider cinematic appeal – even her somewhat undesirable status as a seductive 'vamp' – with avant-garde ambitions, positioning her artistically in relation to the traditions of European theatre. Dierkes-Thrun describes the film's style as 'popular avant-gardism, the combination of highbrow theatrical aesthetics with fashionable themes and styles of the times'.[64] By 1922, Salome was one such 'fashionable theme', having already danced her way from stage to screen in a range of other films, many of which are now lost or exist only in partial form in archives. Though the Lumière brothers had recorded Fuller's serpentine dance as early as 1896, the British-American director James Stuart Blackton, founder of Vitagraph Studios, seems to have been the first to make a film about Salome specifically. Surviving sections of his *Salome* (1908) suggest that, unlike Nazimova, his sources were the Gospels rather than Wilde's play, since early parts of the film stress the Baptist's role as messiah, as opposed to focusing on the decadence of Herod's palace or Salome's errant sexual power. The following year saw the release of *Salome Mad* (1909), a satirical take on 'Salomania' that follows its comic protagonist George as he chases a poster of Salome, his 'ideal woman', across the town. When the poster ends up submerged in the harbour, he dives in after it, only to find himself swimming in a surreal underwater scene in which mermaid-like women dance for him until Salome herself arrives to perform. Before George can watch the dance of the seven veils, a fisherman hooks him back up, and Salome remains in the realm of fantasy, submerged in her aqueous underworld. Instead of focusing on the original narrative, this short piece offers a light-hearted critique of the biblical dancer's unbridled popularity, commenting on the obsessive quality of the cultural phenomenon itself, rather than offering yet another reproduction of a familiar theme.

It was, however, Theda Bara's role in James Gordon Edward's lavish *Salomé* (1918) that probably encouraged Nazimova to see the cinematic possibilities inherent in this particular dramatic source. As Salome, Bara donned 'twenty-five costumes' with 'more than one hundred thousand pearl beads used for the trimmings'. The dance of the seven veils allegedly required 'thirty-five yards of varicoloured crape', suggesting that the use of a substantial volume of material was seen as integral to the aesthetic effect of the choreography, rather than being a flimsy addition that could be easily discarded.[65] It is difficult to get a sense of how the dance itself was performed, though the reviewers noted that 'someone does a dance, discarding her veils in the approved fashion. If it was really Miss Bara then Miss Bara can dance as well as emote.'[66] If Fatty Arbuckle and Buster Keaton's parody of Bara's dancing in *The Cook* (1918) is anything to go by, the sequence revolved largely around a series of loose grapevine steps and an expressive, pseudo-Egyptian use of hand gestures. Bara herself stressed her desire to approach the role with artistic integrity, writing that she 'tried to absorb the poetic impulse of Oscar Wilde [. . .] The lines of Oscar Wilde's drama of *Salome* are vivid paintings of human demoralization.' She protested at her popular reputation as a vamp, arguing that prominent stage actors such as Eleanora Duse and Sarah Bernhardt, associated with some of her own roles – Cleopatra, Salome – had 'not been accused of being vampires' and that 'the word vampire has become a stench in my cinematograph nostrils'.[67] Bara's lamentations were, it seems, in vain: the year after her *Salome*'s release, the *New York Tribune* printed an illustration of 'Vamps and Near-Vamps' that strategically juxtaposed an image of Salome, 'queen of historic vamps', with that of Nita Naldi, a Theda Bara impersonator, who was apparently delivering a 'realistic' impression of 'filmdom's greatest vamp' at the Century Theatre.[68] Like Salome, Bara had herself become paradigmatic; a quintessential 'type' to be reproduced by willing interpreters.

It is striking that Bara, like Nazimova, should use Wilde's name to signal the authenticity of her creative intentions, invoking a late nineteenth-century theatrical tradition that, while controversial, permitted her to claim some form of aesthetic autonomy within the sometimes crushing economic matrix of film production – what Bara called 'the crude mechanics of this vast industry [. . .] that violate the instincts of good taste'.[69] The choice of *Salomé* as a subject for adaptation, according to Patricia White, similarly allowed Nazimova to '[affiliate] herself with Oscar Wilde – with his *author*ity as with his notoriety', though it seems likely that Nazimova was also influenced by the example of other Salome interpreters, including Maud Allan, Gertrude Hoffmann, Bara herself, and the dancers of the Ballets Russes.[70] Nazimova's own designation as a 'vamp' had been assured through roles in films such as *Revelation* (1918), in which she played the part of a cabaret singer who consents to sit for a painter in a variety of antique poses: as Sappho, Cleopatra, the Virgin Mary and, fittingly,

Salome. In a familiar doubling of the roles of actor and sex worker, this film frames Nazimova's body as a site of masculine objectification and exchange, consigning her to the role of painterly muse. Her subsequent independent film projects – *Salomé* and *A Doll's House* – would reverse this dynamic, foregrounding her feminist interpretations of Wilde and Ibsen's protagonists. During this period, Nazimova's contract with Metro made her the highest-paid actress in Hollywood, and her biographer even claims that she was seen to fill the 'sexual gap' left by Bara, whose popularity was already beginning to ebb.[71] Nazimova's creative authority can therefore be understood in both imaginative and material terms: her extraordinary earnings as an actor enabled her to found her own company, Nazimova Productions, which financed the making of *Salomé*.[72] Although the name of her husband, Charles Bryant, appears as director in the credits, film scholars have shown that Nazimova pioneered the venture from its inception, and that this was 'a twentieth-century, decadent, American, cinematic, woman-made Salome'.[73]

Nazimova's dual position as the creative force behind this film and as its star and primary commercial draw makes *Salomé* a rare example of a silent film almost wholly developed around the artistic vision of a single female performer. Stylistically, the set of *Salomé* recalls a theatre stage, complete with a proscenium arch, aligning the film with earlier avant-garde productions such as Max Reinhardt's famous 1903 *Salomé* in Berlin.[74] In early cinema, as Kristin Thompson notes, 'the camera usually remained at a distance from the action, framing it in a way that suggested a stage seen by a spectator in a theatre seat'.[75] Nazimova, however, both embraces and subverts these conventions throughout; for instance, she makes innovative use of close-up technique in several shots of Salome's eyes, framing her direct gaze against a black screen in a manner that visually reiterates Wilde's own emphasis on unnatural gazes. The film's extravagant Art Nouveau costume and set design were undertaken in collaboration with Natacha Rambova, the wife of silent film star Rudolph Valentino and formerly a trained dancer, who had studied with the Russian ballet master Theodore Kosloff. While there are clear aesthetic similarities between Rambova's designs for *Salomé* and Aubrey Beardsley's 1894 illustrations, Rambova may also have been influenced by previous choreographic iterations of this theme. As a young woman, she was educated in England and spent her summers at the Paris Opera House under the instruction of the dancer Rosita Mauri. Here, Rambova saw the Ballets Russes production of *Swan Lake* with Anna Pavlova, and it seems likely that she also saw *La Tragédie de Salomé*, danced by Tamara Karsavina to the Florent Schmitt score used by Loïe Fuller in 1907.[76] This piece was performed at the Théâtre des Champs-Elysées and then at Drury Lane's Theatre Royal during the Ballets Russes' 1913 season, the same year the company premiered Nijinsky's more famous creations, *Le Sacre du Printemps* and *Jeux*.[77]

La *Tragédie de Salomé* constituted an interesting sidestep for Diaghilev's company during this period, which is more closely associated with Nijinsky's controversial artistic contributions to *Sacre*, *Jeux* and *L'Après-midi d'un Faune*. Hanna Järvinen has shown that *Faune*, Nijinsky's debut as choreographer, was seen as disconcertingly unorthodox in its self-conscious artifice, use of two-dimensional 'bas-relief' spatiality that harked back to the stage 'tableau', and the suppression of Nijinsky's celebrated virtuosity in favour of 'hieratic poses' and moments of choreographed stasis, punctuated by sensuous, even obscene gestures.[78] *Salomé*, on the other hand, appears to have been framed as a 'sufficiently minor' work, designed to reward Tamara Karsavina for her loyalty to Diaghilev while ensuring that there was little to distract from Nijinsky's modernist innovations.[79] The ballet was choreographed by the dancer Boris Romanov, whose only other credit in this capacity for the Ballets Russes is Stravinsky's *Le Rossignol* (1914), and the original programme note by poet Robert d'Humières suggests that it was very much a vehicle for the *prima ballerina*, with the *corps de ballet* taking the roles of slaves and *bourreaux* (executioners) enraptured by Salome's *pas de deux* with the severed head.[80] There are no roles for Iokanaan, Herod or Herodias: unusually for a Ballets Russes production of this period, the sole choreographic focus is on the capabilities of Karsavina, otherwise 'rarely called upon to make full use of her powers as a classicist'.[81]

The *Observer* was less than glowing in its review of the production at Drury Lane, writing that while the entrance of Salome in 'Aubrey Beardsley costume' was 'highly effective', the 'exaggerated and meaningless remainder' was choreographically 'disastrous'.[82] While this ballet was not resurrected after the 1913 season – with other performances in Berlin, Rio de Janeiro and Monaco – the production does seem to have pleased some critics who were ambivalent about Nijinsky's formal daring. Jacques Debey described *Salomé* as a return to the original style of the Ballets Russes, praising Romanov as '*un jeune danseur qui se signale comme maître de ballet de valeur*' [a young dancer who stands out as a valuable choreographer].[83] On stage, the slaves moved as three independent groups in a dance that was 'sometimes wild, sometimes serious', with the 'giant head of Iokanaan' forming the centrepiece until the appearance of Salome 'at the very back of the stage, glittering like a comet, a marvellous and distant flower'. Karsavina's dancing is described as '*frénétique*', with Debey expressing reservations about a level of dissonance between Schmitt's 'melodious and rhythmic' score and Romanov's 'varied choreographic steps'.[84] This was perhaps more typical of Diaghilev's 'exotic' and antique ballets, which tended to divest the dances of any restrained classicism, and certainly did away with pointe-work.[85] Serge Soudeïkine's set and costume design obviously stressed the decadent orientalism of Herod's palace, with the slaves costumed in white wigs and ostrich feathers, some of them holding sabres and belts bejewelled with snakes. When she entered as Salome, Karsavina also wore a substantial white cape, embossed with an ornate rose design in black, 'the heavy train unfold[ing] as it descend[ed] [. . .] the gold and black staircase' (Fig. 3.1).[86]

While Beardsley's illustrations were certainly an important influence on Rambova – as they were on Soudeïkine – the visual composition of *La Tragédie de Salomé* forms another important, and thus far largely unexplored, precursor to Nazimova's avant-garde film. Indeed, Nazimova herself claimed that she imagined the film 'in the style of the Russian ballet', suggesting that she had seen productions by Diaghilev's company.[87] Extant photographs of Karsavina in costume reveal striking similarities with the monochrome cape Nazimova wears as she awaits Iokanaan's execution, while her eccentric 'bubble' wig – worn in the early part of the film – is intriguingly close to the bulbous white headwear donned by Romanov's dancing slaves. Indeed, these characters also play an important role in Nazimova's film more broadly: Salome's assistants participate in the opening steps of the dance of the seven veils, and, as in the Ballets Russes production, there is a troubling use of blackface to designate the slaves in the background of Herod's political assembly, including the scantily clad executioner (Frederick Peters Tuite). This is one respect in which the film design departs from Beardsley, whose highly stylised figures and objects disclose a *fin-de-siècle* vogue for *Japonisme*: the racial politics of Nazimova's *Salomé*, with its uncomfortable interweaving of flamboyant eroticism and primitivist cliché, are closer to Diaghilev's 1913 ballet.

The aesthetics of ballet modernism thus constitute a crucial touchstone for discussions of Nazimova's *Salomé* and its layered visual composition. While Rambova's costumes and set design bear the obvious traces of an Art Nouveau style that predates Diaghilev's company, *La Tragédie de Salomé*, positioned chronologically between the original illustrations and the silent film, exists in vital intertextual dialogue with both sources, providing a framework for harmonising Beardsley's imagery with the unique demands of choreographic spectacle. Romanov's arrangement of the *corps de ballet* into distinct groups on stage may well have carried over into the film's movement design, in which the slow harmonised steps of the soldiers and attendants form an important kinetic refrain. Throughout the film, however, Nazimova also stresses moments of stillness, arranging her actors in deliberately orchestrated poses that comprise an almost sculptural grammar of performance. The 'semiotics of gesture' developed through Delsartean posing may be one of Nazimova's models here, since it was taken up enthusiastically by other film-makers including Lev Kuleshov, who saw cinematic montage as a 'rhythmic succession of motionless shots', and D. W. Griffith, who had his actors trained in Delsartean technique at the Denishawn School.[88] Again, however, Nazimova's conspicuous use of static poses, with the actors stationed in a seemingly two-dimensional bas-relief, resonates with both the theatrical *tableau vivant* and the five still

3.1 'In the Beardsley Manner: The Salomé of the Russian Ballet'. *The Illustrated London News*, 28 June 1913.
National Library of Scotland.
Reproduced under Creative Commons License CC-BY 4.0

'positions' that constitute the foundation of classical ballet. Moments of exaggerated or artificial stillness were certainly a significant component of modern ballet, just as they were in the Symbolist drama of writers such as Maeterlinck. The 'short freezings' of movement choreographed by Nijinsky in *L'Après-midi d'un Faune* may have frustrated some critics, but, as Jarvinen argues, their 'pictorial effect' chimed with the core principles of the balletic pose while also reflecting the use of stillness as a 'heightening device' in modernist theatre and film.[89]

This language of posing is also an integral aspect of *Salomé*'s homoerotic register, to which much attention has been devoted in queer readings of the film. White, for instance, uses the metaphor of the veil, with its 'specifically feminine and orientalist connotations', to read the film's 'homosexual secret' as a subtext veiled by the 'public sexualization of the female body'.[90] Her interpretation is energised by the oft-repeated notion that the film was shot with an entirely gay and bisexual cast, along with rumours of an affair between Nazimova and Rambova, which would imply that their collaboration underwrote film aesthetics with private intimacy. Barnes, another queer female modernist, perhaps alludes to these covert histories in her interview with Nazimova, where she writes of stories 'too incredible to be false'.[91] The stylised interplays between the film's design and the actors' use of gesture are crucial to the film's camp aesthetic. Art Nouveau, according to Susan Sontag in her 'Notes on "Camp"', is 'the most typical and fully developed camp style', with its constant translation of 'one thing into something else'.[92] Sontag gives the example of the 1890s Paris Métro entrances designed in the shape of 'cast-iron orchid stalks', which are closely replicated in the stylised iron flowers that appear behind Iokanaan's cistern in *Salomé*. It is also no surprise to find that Beardsley, Loïe Fuller, *Salomé* and the ballet *Swan Lake* all appear in Sontag's 'Notes', as do 'Tiffany lamps', one of which, after being used in Nazimova's *Salomé*, was exhibited as part of a Beardsley retrospective at New York's Gallery of Modern Art.[93] However, it is not just the presence of particular objects and visual styles that signal *Salomé*'s queer aesthetic, but also the highly choreographed poses of the bodies on screen (Fig. 3.2).

Early in the film, such poses are adopted most conspicuously for the roles of the Syrian Captain and the Page of Herodias. The first shot of the pair shows them facing in opposite directions: the Syrian Captain's bolder physical presence is heightened by his crossed arms; the Page, dancer-like, is in a more graceful effeminate repose, his arms lightly splayed and his leg crooked. The actors hold their positions as the camera lingers on their bodies, suggesting that their detachment, rendered emphatic in their stances, is fixed and unmoving, possibly even policed by the executioner visible in the background, though he too is part of the film's queer aesthetic. A subsequent medium shot invites the audience to take a closer look and here, the distance between the Page and the

MODERNISM AND THE CHOREOGRAPHIC IMAGINATION

3.2 'Salome'. *The Picturegoer* 4 (August 1922). National Library of Scotland. Reproduced under Creative Commons License CC-BY 4.0

Captain has been discernibly reduced. The heightened proximity between the men implies that the camera's movement has unveiled a conflicted desire that strains towards both intimacy and estrangement, despite the static poses of the performers. The queer dynamic between Narraboth and the Page, frequently cited as the clearest vessel for the play's homoeroticism, is thus made legible through a carefully orchestrated sequence of poses that translate Wilde's veiled language – 'he was [...] nearer to me than a brother' (*PI*, 715) – into a heightened corporeal syntax, generating meaning through the interplay between static *tableau* and cinematographic movement.

This dynamic between the Captain and the Page is made more explicit in later shots where they are seen facing the same direction: their bodies touch but this contact is mediated by deliberate poses that again suggest a desire that cannot be directly confronted. Particular significance is granted to these moments of carefully measured contact, creating a strained relationship between the two men that hinges on tactile meaning. In this way, the kinesis of the cinematic medium plays with the ambiguities of sensory engagement, probing into the inconsistencies of sight and appealing to other senses through an emphasis on bare skin, set against the coldness of over-sized jewels, and a heightened attention to touch. The kinaesthetic impulses concentrated around the language of posing and touch in *Salomé* align with what Vivian Sobchack has called the 'carnal foundations of cinematic intelligibility'.[94] While the mechanisms of the gaze in *Salomé* have been described as 'virtual, mediated, distanced, and safe, enabling unrestrained voyeurism',[95] an attention to the physiological conditions of spectatorship, as well as visual effects, underlines the sensory dimensions of Nazimova's directorial vision: the resistant, slowly formulated exchange between the Page and the Syrian Captain is able to get under the spectator's skin, proposing a sensory relationship between this unsanctioned touch and the responsive bodies in the audience.

In this vein, Sobchack has shown that viewers in the film auditorium can undergo 'a phenomenological experience structured on ambivalence and diffusion, on an interest and investment in being *both* "here" *and* "there," in being able *both* to sense *and* to be sensible, *both* the subject *and* the object of tactile desire'.[96] Although *Salomé*'s use of theatrical convention seems to indicate a stable separation between audience and diegesis, the film's spatial principles place a keen stress on the prospect of slowly forged bodily contact, delineated through a highly self-conscious use of posing that entreats the haptic and kinaesthetic senses. This multi-sensory appeal is evident too in the relationship between Salome and Iokanaan, which unfolds in a tense choreography of erotic intimacy, characterised by moments of both proximity and angry denial. Appearing in abridged form in the intertitles, Salome's blazonic refrains, poetically intensified through Wilde's accumulating and repetitive similes, are encoded in Nazimova's movements as she appraises Iokanaan from various angles, using her hands and her shifting posture to merge a sense of aesthetic contemplation with mounting sexual desire. Iokanaan, initially entirely static as Salome approaches, is presented in sculptural terms, his face turned heavenwards in an implicit rejection of Salome's earthly carnality that is also a form of self-effacement, transforming his own body into a faceless, impersonal surface to be read iconographically. His subsequent engagement with Salome – his caressing of her neck and shoulders – culminates in an almost ecstatic merging of the two figures as Iokanaan pushes Salome back, creating a highly charged image that is both a denial and a consummation. Here and elsewhere, the deferral of tactile intimacy serves to heighten the effect of physical contact when it does occur, appealing again to the audience's kinaesthetic sensitivity.

These intricately choreographed sequences anticipate the film's dramatic apex: Salome's dance of the seven veils. The dance begins with Salome emerging from a chrysalis of radiant material, with her veils held by a row of retreating attendants. Nazimova is dressed in a tightly fitted costume that emphasises her slight, androgynous figure. The dance movements comprise a series of *chaîné* turns on demi-pointe, with the arms raised in fifth position to keep the veils aloft and conceal Nazimova's face, creating the visual impression of a closed flower head. As Salome lowers her veils, the dance becomes more erratic and seemingly spontaneous, demanding an expressive use of the arms to twist and float the white material, as Nazimova combines sequences of rapid circling steps with moments of stasis, raising her chin and holding stark poses. Lambert describes this as Nazimova 'falling back on her interpretive Isadora-style routine',[97] but Nazimova seems more intent on creating a sense of disruptive angularity than philhellenic grace, perhaps edging closer to the '*frénétique*' rhythms of Karsavina in *La Tragédie de Salomé*. Midway through the dance, however, Nazimova crucially retreats beneath a large translucent veil, held at four points by her attendants, which she manipulates with her hands to produce a stream of rippling shapes (Fig. 3.3). The resonances with Fuller's serpentine dance, and later her fire dance, are clear. Stressing the centrality of the veil to the development of the choreography, Nazimova similarly eschews the primacy of her own body in favour of a more ambiguous, genderless kind of corporeality, allowing her billowing materials to construct and suggest forms as she moves.

Critics at the time were disappointed and even perplexed by this scene. The reviewer for the *New York Times* declared it 'an exceedingly tame and not remarkably graceful performance', and was perturbed by the dissonance

3.3 Still from *Salomé: An Historical Phantasy by Oscar Wilde* (dir. Charles Bryant, 1922)

between the dance itself and the reaction it precipitated in Herod (Mitchell Lewis) and the other observers:

> Yet on the faces of Herod and the other onlookers you see expressions intended to indicate that such a dance as you have been led to imagine is being performed. It shows you part of it and in what you see there is nothing to account for the gross eagerness on the faces of the men.[98]

For this reviewer, there is 'nothing' at the core of the dance, implying that this particular Salome has failed to deliver the erotic revelation promised by her reputation. Yet it is precisely this asymmetry between the real spectators and their fictitious counterparts on screen that underlines the subversive quality of Nazimova's performance. Those reviewers who anticipate the dance with 'gross eagerness' find their voyeuristic impulses reflected in the grotesque figure of Herod, a lascivious patriarch finally undone by Salome's creative bartering. Salome's body, however, disrupts expectation by resisting a final unveiling, instead orchestrating her dance from a position of relative visual obscurity. Using the techniques of Fuller, Nazimova makes her bodily vanishing point the site of her creative power, recasting the veils as luminous surfaces complicit in her image-making system rather than accessories to her imagined nakedness. Far from reducing her body to its bare essentials, the veils enhance and expand her bodily presence, destabilising the gaze that seeks only a naked form and appealing instead to a subject attentive to the implications of her choreographic project, which prioritises female creative individuality in its reclaiming of the veiled dance.

By developing this conception of the veiled dance as an ideal vessel for her ambitions in film-making and performance, Nazimova placed herself alongside those other female artists who used Salome to fashion new forms of bodily expression, recalibrating the modes of desire so often associated with this dance. The genealogy of choreographic modernisms formed around her *Salomé*, encompassing the traditions of Symbolist theatre and the very different models of Fuller and the Ballets Russes, works to unsettle the voyeuristic expectations attached to this woman and her unveiling. *Salomé*'s grammar of poses and gestures invites aesthetic contemplation only to undercut an approach to the body as a fixed image, using the cinema's promise of motion to engage the audience's perception of their own moving, feeling, sensorial bodies. '[I]n every image there is always a kind of *ligatio* at work', writes Agamben; 'a power that paralyses, whose spell needs to be broken; it is as if, from the whole history of art, a mute invocation were raised towards the freeing of the image in the gesture.'[99] Nazimova presents her dancing body as a force of alterity and visual effacement, disrupting desires with her serpentine motions and using Salome's veils to create a site of female resistance.

'Dances yet unknown': Dulac's Visual Rhythms

Along with direct adaptations of Salome's story, of which Nazimova's was the most influential and sophisticated, film practitioners in both America and Europe were influenced in myriad ways by the work of dancers. Dance was not merely incorporated into silent films as a theme or dramatic device but also as an underlying compositional principle: the forms and aesthetics of dance offered film-makers new technical and visual vocabularies for the art of the moving image. In *Salomé*, Nazimova strategically presented herself as the inheritor of both Wilde's *fin-de-siècle* text and a developing cinematic avant-garde, thereby creating transatlantic dialogues between the currents of European symbolism, new modes of dance and a burgeoning American modernism. Elsewhere, other female directors looking to produce experimental or artistic films – rather than stagey melodramas – were making dedicated use of a similar set of aesthetic coordinates. Germaine Dulac's theoretical writings on cinema, alongside her incorporation of choreographic forms into her films, show how dance was worked into the very fabric of French film-making in the 1920s. In her essay 'From Sentiment to Line', published in the only issue of her film journal *Schémas* (1927), Dulac articulated a theory of cinematic composition that drew explicitly on the imagery and methods of dance:

> I conjure up a dancer! A woman? No. A leaping line of harmonious rhythms. I conjure up a luminous projection on a voile. Precise matter? No. Fluid rhythms. Why deny the screen pleasures that movement procures at the theatre. Harmony of line; harmony of light.[100]

Dulac's suggestion that the art of the cinema should take the image of the dancing line as its elemental form is part of a broader philosophy of movement that she espouses throughout the essay, and, indeed, practised in her own work. It was her belief that the first duty of cinema was to capture movement, and she asserts in the same article that 'Movement and rhythm remain in any case – even in the more material and significant embodiment – the intimate and unique essence of cineographic expression.'[101] Her understanding of movement as the fundamental and determining basis of the cinema draws on Henri Bergson's concept of vitalism, as articulated in *Creative Evolution*: 'In reality the body is changing form at every moment', Bergson writes; 'or rather, there is no form, since form is immobile and reality is movement.'[102] Bergson's aesthetic philosophy would prove foundational to much French film criticism during this period: French film-maker Jean Epstein almost exactly echoed this formulation when he declared that 'the cinematograph shows us that form is only one unsettled state of an essentially mobile condition'.[103] Dulac's appreciation of motion – specifically of motion designed to replicate the structures of a musical harmony – is couched in a certainty that the real purpose of movement is to enable 'evolution and transformation'.[104]

Dulac's interest in dance as a blueprint for the 'harmonious' unity she pursued in her cinematographic compositions seems quite unlike the sense of jarring dissonance and affect of 'shock' sought by surrealists such as Antonin Artaud, with whom Dulac collaborated on *The Seashell and the Clergyman*. Although critical discussions of Dulac's career frequently centre on this fraught partnership, Donia Mounsef has argued that Dulac's 'concerns with rhythm, structure, and movement contradicted Surrealism's notion of a primitive and violent cinema', suggesting that Surrealism might not offer the only conceptual lens through which to explore her practice.[105] Recent scholarship has focused particularly on Dulac's importance as a theorist of early cinema and her place within a nascent feminist avant-garde.[106] Her conceptualisation of 'cineographic expression' as a filmic language indebted to modern dance importantly existed within wider debates about film aesthetics and narrative form, which preoccupied writers and artists in early twentieth-century France. Other filmmakers, including the music and dance critic Émile Vuillermoz, felt Bergson's theories to be 'a perfect apologia for cinégraphie', underpinning a conception of film as a representational rather than a narrative or action-based medium, closely related to music.[107] Like Dulac, Vuillermoz was influenced by the aesthetics of Symbolism, which led him to advocate for 'cinégraphie' as a 'new symbolist mode of subjective expression' in which actors were seen as 'astral bodies', beautiful but depersonalised signs arranged by the director, whose role in creating the film becomes heavily poeticised.[108] For Dulac, however, the ideal cinematographic artist was represented not by the poet but by the modern dancer.

As this emphasis on rhythmic unity suggests, early film theorists were drawn to the lexicons of music and choreography in their efforts to explain the representational functions of cinematic movement, which seemed to reflect dance's ability to unify form and content in the motions of the body through space. Arguing that cinema required 'a new sense' to accompany the other artistic senses, Dulac expressed her dismay that few cinemagoers, or creators of narrative films, had grasped the medium's 'aesthetic truth', which she saw as resting on the fact that 'a shifting of lines can arouse one's feelings'.[109] Criticising the art form's early tendency to mimic the conventions of theatrical naturalism, Dulac proposed that 'the evolution and transformation of a form, or of a volume, or of a line' ought to be taken as the basis of cinematic enquiry, rather than the pantomimic development of character.[110] In this sense, Dulac was in broad agreement with other French film theoreticians who were seeking to dissolve the conventions of narrative cinema, including Vuillermoz, who believed that true cinematic images should be 'symphonies of light' and admired D. W. Griffith for his ability to 'harmonize his plastic phrases'.[111]

Louis Delluc, Dulac's frequent collaborator and editor-in-chief of the magazine *Le Film*, developed Vuillermoz's principles by promoting a 'lyrical' style of film-making, whose central idea should be 'articulated symbolically or connotatively through the photogenic becoming cinematic'.[112] Delluc's influential concept of *'photogénie'*, taken up in the later writings of André Bazin, stressed the singularity of the cinematic image, imbued with transformative potential by the interventions of the camera and the medium's other technical elements. *'Photogénie'*, according to Richard Abel, 'de-familiarized the familiar', taking 'ordinary things' as the basis for cinematic representation but stressing the film-maker's capacity to make them 'radically new'.[113] It was partly via such an understanding of film's aesthetic properties that commentators came to treat cinema as a central modernist art form.

Fuller's ability to harness the projections of magic lanterns and electric lights to the undulating surface of her veils left Dulac enthused about the possibilities afforded by a performance that took the movement of light as its basis: 'Could light, like words, sounds, gestures, provoke emotion? Touch our sensibilities?'[114] As the terms 'emotion' and 'sensibilities' suggest, Dulac was intrigued by the range of sensory responses that cinema could precipitate beyond its optical effects, reaching towards the modern kinaesthetic embodied by various dancers and film performers, such as Nazimova, whom she admired. For Dulac, the body of the silent performer was imbued with a magnetic significance, aligned with broader modernist understandings of what Marcus terms the 'speaking' body – of a non-textual language of corporeal expression – which 'further intersected [...] with the ideals of the "elemental" gesture and physical expressiveness developed and developing in symbolist, expressionist and avant-garde theatre'.[115] Dulac was deeply interested in Symbolist theatre, particularly the work of Maeterlinck, whose emphasis on deliberate symbolic motion in performance bears a close relevance not only to Dulac's own understanding of cinematic language, but also to the sculptural grammar of performance elaborated in Nazimova's *Salomé*.[116] Dulac's appreciation of Symbolist aesthetics was developed in part through her friendships with the 'mystic' director Aurelien Marie Lugné-Poë, who first produced Wilde's *Salomé* in 1896, and his wife, the actor Suzanne Després, who also acted in this production.[117] Després, like Nazimova, built her career through notable performances in productions of Ibsen, and she brought her reputation for 'subtlety and simplicity' to the broader 'symbolist framework' of Dulac's first film, *Les Soeurs enemies* (1916), scripted by Irène Hillel-Erlanger, author of the strange esoteric novel *Voyages en kaléidoscope* (1919).[118]

These social and collaborative networks played a formative role in shaping the interplays between literary, cinematic and choreographic spheres during this period. Dulac's own personal relationships with her collaborators form another thread in this history. While she also had romantic partnerships with her screenwriter Hillel-Erlanger and, later, with the film programmer Marie-Anne Colson-Malleville, her interests in Salome and the rhythmic movements of the feminine body began to emerge as a result of her relationship with the Russian dancer Stasia Napierkowska (Fig. 3.4).[119] In late 1911, Napierkowska had gained a colourful reputation in London by performing *The Dance of the Bee* at the Palace Theatre, which, according to Brandstetter, combined a variety of styles and movement techniques, recalling 'nineteenth-century ballet versions of the bee dance; movement forms taken from *freir Tanz*; and eclectic components of "exotic" dance'.[120] The symbolic and political parallels between Napierkowska's *Dance of the Bee* and Salome's dance are implicit in the narrative setup: Napierkowska plays the role of a Moroccan princess who, under the orders of the chief holding her captive, performs the 'dance of the bee', removing her clothes at his pleasure before she collapses, and finally performs a dance of self-sacrifice, 'la Danse du Feu'.[121] As the *Pall Mall Magazine* reported in an article entitled 'The Invasion of the Dancers', Napierkowska moved in 'a paroxysm of excitement and pain caused by the bee in the folds of her garments'. She removed items of clothing 'one after the other' in a sequence of unveiling familiar to audiences who had seen versions of Salome's dance, which had achieved its most recent surge in popularity in England through Maud Allan's *Vision*.[122] Indeed, *The Dance of the Bee* incited similar moral anxieties for the writer of the article, H. M. Walbrook, who called it 'a daring performance [. . .] symptomatic of a certain broadening of public taste'.[123] The article's rhetoric of invasions and paroxysms suggests that the violent ecstasies of Wilde's princess had not been forgotten, even if Napierkowska's dance appeared to transmute them into a darkly comic setting that belied a sinister tale of female imprisonment and supplication.

Intriguingly, however, the terms used to delineate Napierkowska's dancing reflected with uncanny exactitude the lexical choices exercised by reviewers of Nazimova's stage performances and Fuller's earlier experiments with serpentine movement: as one critic put it, 'the serpentine Mlle Napierkowska continues to wriggle herself out of her clothes [. . .] Her strong point is [. . .] serpentine coilings of the body.'[124] While the reiteration of such serpentine descriptors may seem incidental or merely semantic, the proliferation of this vocabulary in early twentieth-century critiques of dance nonetheless points towards a 'model of motion as a spiral' that characterised modern dance, as variously demonstrated in the 'sensuous pulsing' of Ruth St Denis, Isadora Duncan's 'earthward stamping, spinning gestures', and the dynamics of contraction and release privileged by Martha Graham.[125] The particular forms of bodily imagery that this chapter has read in relation to the broader kinaesthetics of modernist performance illustrate, in Irina Sirotkina and Roger Smith's terms, that early twentieth-century artists existed in 'a cultural world deeply

3.4 Stasia Napierkowska (c. 1910). Library of Congress

informed by the metaphors of touch, movement and life, that is, by metaphors of bodily sensing thought to transcend social and artistic conventions'.[126]

Such metaphors frequently crystallised around modernism's paradigmatic veiled dancer. Napierkowska's *Dance of the Bee* offered an oblique play on the theme of unveiling, but she addressed this connection more explicitly in her two screen performances as Salome: in Albert Capellani's *Salomé* (1908) and Ugo Falena's *La Figlia de Herodiade* (1916), both distributed by Pathé.[127] According to enthusiastic critics, the second of these films saw Napierkowska, 'the great Russian danseuse', perform 'the chief part with distinction', reminding audiences of the 'stir' caused by her *Dance of the Bee*.[128] Unfortunately, both of these silent films appear to have been lost, although surviving images from Falena's *La Figlia de Herodiade*, his second film adaptation of Wilde's *Salomé*, show Napierkowska in scant oriental costume wielding a large translucent veil. It is almost certain that Dulac was intimately familiar with this work, since she accompanied Napierkowska on her film shoots in Rome while the dancer was working with Falena.[129] Moreover, after seeing Napierkowska take the lead role in a production of Strauss's *Salome*, and also a private performance of Ida Rubinstein's *Salomé* choreographed by Fokine in 1912, Dulac made plans to collaborate on a new version of Wilde's *Salomé*, drawing sketches for a production to be directed by Maurice Maeterlinck.[130] Evidence of Dulac's interest in dance and in Salome particularly can be traced through films such as *Vénus Victrix* (1917), which stars Napierkowska as Djali, a bewitching Hindu dancer who 'danced dances yet unknown'. This film reformulates, at least on the surface, many of the orientalist tropes and attitudes common in earlier interpretations of Salome's story, playing on popular imaginings of the East as a topography of sexual excess.[131] Ida Rubinstein's performances as Salome and Scheherazade provided apt models for the gestural vocabulary of Napierkowska in *Vénus Victrix*, confirming the influence of Salome's dance on the film's visual register, as well as the expansive kinaesthetic community of women focused around this compelling figure.[132]

Vénus Victrix concerns a theatre owner who intends to desert his wife for the dancer Djali, a plot that reflects historical fears – expressed in various news sources – that 'dancers [were] natural disturbers of the family peace'.[133] As one *Washington Post* journalist put it, 'the light toe creates more trouble in the household than the light purse', citing 'the justly famous Salome' as prime example.[134] However, in *Vénus Victrix*, as Williams has argued, Dulac's visual configuration of dance imagery goes beyond the simple exoticisation of Napierkowska's body, suggesting a somewhat problematic but conceptually powerful adoption of the Orient as a space of feminist emancipation, sinuously emerging from a broadly conceived model of patriarchal control.[135] In this vein, Gaylyn Studlar has observed that 'the spectacle of orientalised identities [was] associated with ambiguous feminine power', and dancers themselves drew connections between modern conceptions of womanhood and rhythmic sensuality.[136] Other early twentieth-century sources reveal a similar impulse: in Kate Chopin's short story 'An Egyptian Cigarette' (1902), the experience of smoking a foreign cigarette precipitates a galvanising bodily transformation in the New Woman narrator, sending 'a subtle, disturbing current [. . .] through [her] whole body' and transporting her to an Egyptian dreamscape, which becomes, in this fragmented proto-modernist narrative, a space of poetic possibility and corporeal passion, characterised by the narrator's sense of kinaesthetic disorientation: 'Why must I drag myself thus like a wounded serpent, twisting and writhing?'[137] Despite reproducing an uneasy equivalence between women's bodies and colonised or foreign territories, these literary and cinematic interventions nonetheless sought to find an alternative mode of engagement with images of 'eastern' sensuality; one that might dislodge these versions of the feminine from the iconography of masculine imperial power.

While it is possible to retrospectively read the symmetries between Dulac's cinematic philosophy and her interest in particular dancers, Dulac herself articulated similar connections, declaring, 'It's alongside this beautiful artist Napierkowska, and thanks to her, that I learned the secrets of the cinegraphic art.'[138] Formulating the mechanisms of film as a 'secret', Dulac implies a potential association between her practice as a film-maker and the clandestine nature of her queer relationships, as well as the ambivalence surrounding queer women's bodies. Williams notes that Napierkowska used to send Dulac sketches of 'curved and spiral-like poses and movements (laying down, knees up, floating), provocatively labelled "tendrils," "trembling," and "spinning"'.[139] Curves and spirals suggest the female form, and the description of floating, tendril-like objects reflects the spectral qualities so often attached to sex between women, while also gesturing to the 'leaping' and 'fluid' lines that Dulac admired in Fuller's performances.[140] Both appear to be based on an internal harmony that resists, or at least supersedes, the conventions of narrative logic: while the queer woman has often been positioned theoretically against existing categories of gender and representation,[141] Dulac's understanding of '*cinégraphie*' emphasised the construction of a poetic symbolism opposed to linear narrative forms.

The theoretical positions that formed around the development of the seventh art in the early twentieth century echoed earlier responses to the emergence of modern dance, similarly drawing on the rhetorical tropes of other arts to formulate new aesthetic categories and interpretative tools. As these critiques suggest, the play of light on a moving screen, so critical to the development of modern dance, also underpinned a range of approaches to the status of the cinematic image. For Rancière, the production of specific artistic scenes and the responses they engender in turn reinscribe these moments into 'a moving constellation in which modes of perception and affect, and forms of interpretations defining a paradigm of art, take shape'.[142] Dulac's reflections on *'cinégraphie'* constellated around images of dance, illustrating the continuous reciprocity of choreographic and cinematographic forms of movement in the early twentieth century.

ARABESQUES AND CINÉ-DANCES

Dulac's interest in combining dance aesthetics with 'exotic' eastern settings persisted across a number of her narrative films after *Vénus Victrix*, including *Malencontre* (1920), which starred the Franco-Indonesian dancer Djemil Anik. Apparently directly inspired by the performance style of Nazimova, Anik's syntax of gestures and poses defined the film's field of movement, described by the critic Jean Morizot as 'a science of postures and eurhythmy pushed to perfection'.[143] Surviving stills from *Malencontre* show Anik dressed in studded veils and an ornate jewelled headpiece, posing seductively in the manner of a Salome dancer. However, by the late 1920s, Dulac's cinematographic vision had become somewhat more abstract, leading her to produce a series of three short films in which the female body is displaced from its previous position at the centre of the screen's visual register, but in which dance nonetheless remains the critical kinaesthetic force threading the images together. In this way, Dulac crafted a filmic logic that departed from her earlier presentation of the female body as the primary object of visual attention, instead foregrounding movement and transformation as the foundation of cineographic expression.

In this respect, Dulac was working to achieve the vision laid out in her theoretical texts, which corresponded with broader modernist aspirations for the cinematic medium. In her well-known essay 'The Cinema' (1926), Virginia Woolf claimed that film might do better if it paid less heed to the conventions of literature and theatre; if it were able to discover 'something abstract, something moving, something calling only for the very slightest help from words or from music to make itself intelligible'.[144] Perhaps Woolf had the language of dance in mind – she was interested in ballet, and images of human movement in her own novels often hover, as Jones has argued, 'on the borderlands between quite ordinary gestures and a more formalized, ritualized activity'.[145] Eager to defend the novel against the stultifying effects of adaptation, Woolf alluded to a 'new mode of symbolization [...] capable of conveying the emotions in visual terms'.[146] Her ideas about the cinema's representational capacities, although couched in sceptical prose, chimed with Dulac's writing and the theories advanced by Vuillermoz and Delluc. Dulac similarly criticised straightforward adaptations of novels in her essay 'The Music of Silence' (1928), arguing for the cinema's role as an expressive medium, in which 'the clarity of its images should suggest rather than specify, creating, like music, through particular chords, that which is imperceptible'.[147] Developing her concept of *'the silence of the eye'*, Dulac argued that 'although cinema may, in its technique, be solely visual [. . .] it disdains the purely visual', appealing to the spectator's richer sensory and emotional life through the dynamic rhythms that instil vital meaning in its images.[148] She had previously explained in 'Photographie – Cinégraphie' (1926) that she felt 'hostile towards the photographic effect that removes from the art of the screen the spontaneity in movement'.[149] By rejecting the formal constraints of linear narrative, both Woolf and Dulac participated in a feminist 'lyrical' avant-garde, 'encouraging audiences to venture further in exploring experience and sense beyond the habitual'.[150] It was, moreover, dance that provided Dulac with the closest model for her cinematographic vision, which evolved into the kind of moving abstractions from which Woolf imagined the cinema might devise its new language.

Forms of organic evolution, as well as the automatic movements of machines, underpin much of Dulac's work. She frequently illustrated her lectures with scientific films of germinating wheat grains, attempting to give the 'spirit a sensation, which through movements is rhythmed by forms, whose undefinable structures vary incessantly following a given rhythm'.[151] Dulac puts this principle of formal variation within a consistent rhythm into practice in her short film *Thèmes et Variations* (1929). This abstract work disregards narrative realism in favour of a coherence based on imagistic and rhythmic repetition and development. Dulac intercuts shots of a ballerina, Lilian Constantini, dancing gracefully with images of machines spinning and unreeling along the same lines of movement (Fig. 3.5 and 3.6). 'Each movement of the animated dance is developed by a variation, drawn from life and sometimes extended by simple abstract lines', wrote Dulac in her screenplay for this short work.[152] This sequence also includes a brief, time-lapsed shot of a germinating plant, referred to by Dulac as a 'ciné-dance'.[153] This blossoming life form is juxtaposed with an image of the dancer's hands, as they twist and unfurl to create an impression of swan-like movement. The plant's tendrils suggestively imitate the coiling gestures of the hands, allowing for a mirroring between the two forms that defines the film's broader scheme of visual metaphor. Presenting the plant's evolution in a compressed timeframe, the cinematic apparatus exceeds human perceptual limits, rapidly accelerating a lengthy process in order to satisfy the film's compositional framework.

For Dulac, these techniques, like slow motion, '[augment] the number of recorded images, allow[ing] us to analyse the logic of a movement's beauty', which she describes as 'the invisible, the materially existent that lies beyond our visual perception'.[154] In this sense, the 'ciné-dance' in *Thèmes et Variations* exemplifies the film-maker's own play on the concept of the invisible dance, whose long history this book has traced through Wilde and Fuller to women's film-making in the 1920s. For Dulac, Fuller's body was *'un corps invisible'*; 'An invisible body melted into the diaphanous materials', which offered a vital

'HARMONIES OF LIGHT'

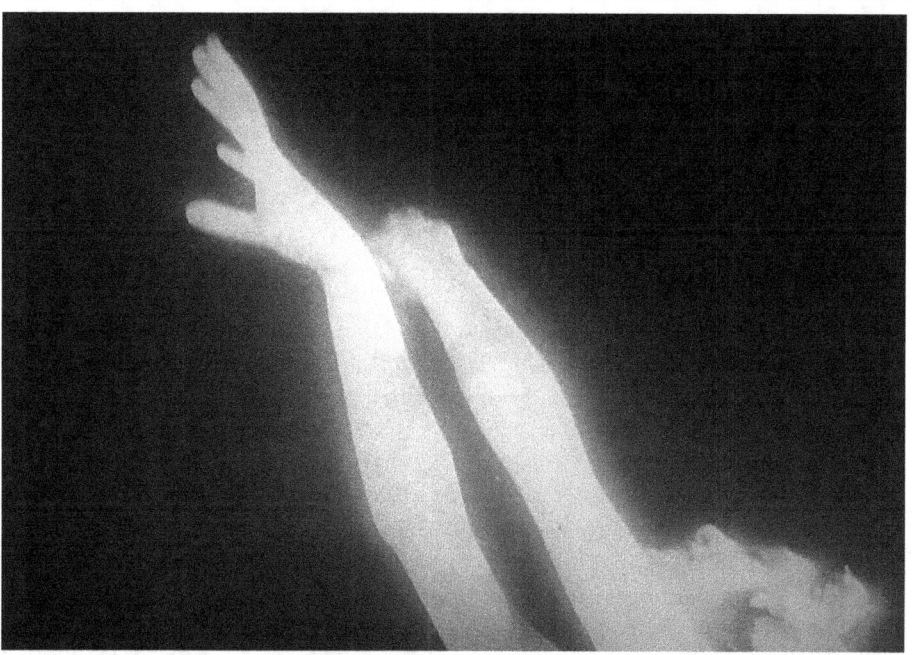

3.5 Still from *Thèmes et Variations* (dir. Germaine Dulac, 1929)

3.6 Still from *Thèmes et Variations* (dir. Germaine Dulac, 1929)

precedent for the cinema's incorporation of light and action into a mobile screen.[155] The 'ciné-dance' of *Thèmes et Variations* suggests symmetries between the gestures of the dancer and the blossoming of a minuscule life form, as well as the torsion of the machinery. In this way, the mechanisms of the film, created and edited by Dulac, make the 'invisible' dance of and *between* these forms perceptible, occluding and yet expanding the body of the dancer (who is only shot in part) and also, of course, the woman film-maker who choreographs the images. For Dulac, this work was 'un véritable ballet' [a real ballet].[156]

Fuller's techniques, in Gunning's opinion, encouraged Dulac to 'discover in nature new forms of motion [. . .] the pulsating, intricate, even dissonant rhythms of the arabesque and the serpentine, expanding and recoiling simultaneously'.[157] The complex sensory effects of Fuller's particular movement vocabulary are implicit in Dulac's recollection of Fuller's dance, which she describes as 'another music, this time a visual one [. . .] revealed to me almost stealthily'.[158] The mobile torsion of the serpentine and the arabesque, distinct but not entirely dissimilar lines, recur in Dulac's own short films, particularly *Étude cinégraphique sur une Arabesque* (1929). Often associated with Islamic art but common through European aesthetic traditions, the arabesque is defined as a 'decorative scroll-work and other ornament loosely derived from branches, leaves, tendrils, and vegetation [. . .] arranged in imaginatively intertwined symmetrical geometrical patterns'.[159] Perhaps the spinning 'tendrils' that Napierkowska sent to Dulac emerge again in her fascination with this form. Importantly, the arabesque is 'usually defined as free from human or animal figures',[160] suggesting that its intertwining lines offered Dulac a prototype for the kind of abstract forms she sought to represent in her films of the late 1920s, recalling the concealed body of Fuller in her serpentine dances.

The arabesque is also a florid, decorative piece of music and a position in classical ballet, in which the dancer stands on one leg with the other raised at an angle or extended behind.[161] Dulac's *Arabesque* therefore codified a range of stylistic connections across the arts of music, dance and architecture. Indeed, Dulac described *Arabesque* and her other short film *Disque 957* (1928) as '*illustrations de disques*', or 'illustrated records', standing as visual counterparts to the music they invoke (Debussy's *Arabesques* 1 and 2, and Chopin's *Préludes* 5 and 6).[162] In *Arabesque*, Dulac's camera lingers on the motions of objects and life forms – the interaction between rain and the rippling surface of water, and the play of light in a kaleidoscope. Movement itself is the film's subject, and it connects the series of apparently disparate images: a delicate flower in bloom, a veiled woman on a rocking chair, the fluttering of sheets in the wind. The woman who briefly appears in *Arabesque*, largely draped in white materials and obscured by the rapid cuts of the director, is 'veiled' by both her costume and the workings of the camera, allowing the cinematic apparatus to engage in the transformation of this particular female body – a figure Gunning reads as an allusion to the veiled Loïe Fuller.[163] Dulac's theories of cinematic composition have been described as 'a Symbolist aesthetic of fusion and synthesis', which, for Mallarmé, Dulac and others, took on its elemental shape in Fuller's veiled choreographies of light.[164] Although the dancers of *Vénus Victrix* and *Malencontre* might appear to reformulate the myth of Salome more directly, the mechanism of the veiled dance resurfaces in Dulac's *Arabesque*, another 'ciné-dance' that uses both the image and the function of the veil to explore the conditions of visibility on screen.

Severed and Whole: A Sublime Dancer

Even where Salome appears to have vanished, then, she leaves her kinaesthetic imprint. The serpentine lines and arabesques that work as Dulac's organising principles appear across early twentieth-century films and live performances, following in the wake of Fuller's luminous choreographies, and the spiralling torsion embodied by Nazimova, Napierkowska, Rubinstein and the dancers of the Ballets Russes. The reciprocity between choreographic forms and cinema culture during this period is clear. Oskar Fischinger's short film *Spirals* (1926), for instance, is far more visually disorienting than Dulac's *Arabesque*, but it too offers a pictorial representation of the effects of continuous motion and its variations, presenting a kaleidoscope of moving spirals on black or luminous centres. Film-makers of this period continually turned to the whirling cogs, spinning discs and crunching levers of machines for inspiration; to 'the swing, tramp, and trudge [. . .] the carriages, motor cars, omnibuses, cans, sandwich men shuffling and swinging' that Woolf found everywhere in the rush and clamour of the modern world.[165] In these same phenomena, however, writers and artists also sensed a rhythmic principle; 'the sound of wheels chime and chatter in queer harmony'.[166]

What is striking is the sheer extent of Salome's imaginative reach during this period, and the manner in which Nazimova, Dulac and other women modified her image to suit their creative agendas in silent films of the 1920s. Moreover, this chapter has by no means exhausted the rich history of Salome on screen. Besides the direct adaptations made by James Blackton and William Fox, the dance of the seven veils recurred as a motif in a range of cinematic contexts, from Van Dyke Brooke's *Sawdust and Salome* (1914) to Léonce Perret's *A Modern Salome* (1920). In Tod Browning's *The Show* (1927), the dance is one of the many acts performed to entertain a hypnotised crowd at a variety show. As Salome (Renée Adorée) dances, the camera cuts to the audience and there is a moment of suggestive contrast posed between the leering gaze of the men and the astonished, transfixed stare of the women. The prospect of a different kind of spectatorship, what Sandy Flitterman-Lewis calls a 'different desire, desire in difference', arises momentarily in this view of a divided crowd.[167]

What re-emerges as a source of anxiety in Browning's film, however, is the severed head, fully concealed in Nazimova's *Salomé* beneath the skirts of the dancer, and all but lost in Dulac's screen choreographies, which prioritise rhythmic harmony over the shock of psychic juxtaposition favoured by her one-time collaborator Antonin Artaud.[168] The act of decapitation, one of the illusions performed by the troupe in *The Show*, turns into a real threat when Salome's spurned lover (Lionel Barrymore) replaces the false sword with a real one. In an inversion of the original myth, Salome recognises the difference and manages to save the life of the actor playing John (John Gilbert), ironically preserving the wholeness of the Baptist's body while confronting the possibility of its severance. With this, audiences are reminded of the enduring connection between the veiled dance and the act of violence it precipitates. Writing about the decollation of John the Baptist in *The Severed Head: Capital Visions*, Julia Kristeva proposes that these images and their theme 'mark the first crossroads in modern figuration [. . .] [W]e must be prepared to *experience* the figure, severed *and* whole, in its severing *and* its dance: to inhabit it, rigid *and* fleeting, violent *and* happy, blood *and* spirit, horror *and* promise.'[169] For Kristeva, Salome is 'the sublime woman' who embodies the 'horror of the feminine', without which horror would have no power at all.[170] The uncanny image of the severed head, with its attendant fears about female hostility, makes a conspicuous return in the 1930s: in the work of Artaud and the Surrealists, but perhaps most conspicuously, in the dance-dramas of W. B. Yeats.

Notes

1. Germaine Dulac, 'Trois Rencontres avec Loïe Fuller', in *Écrits sur le cinema: 1919–1937*, ed. Prosper Hillairet (Paris: Éditions Paris Experimental, 1994), 110. Translations from this work are my own unless otherwise specified.
2. Jean Epstein, 'The Photogenic Element', trans. Tom Milne, in *Jean Epstein: Critical Essays and New Translations*, ed. Sarah Keller and Jason N. Paul (Amsterdam: Amsterdam University Press, 2012), 301.
3. Tom Gunning, 'Light, Motion, Cinema! The Heritage of Loïe Fuller and Germaine Dulac', *Framework* 46.1 (2005): 111.
4. Laura Marcus, *The Tenth Muse: Writing about Cinema in the Modernist Period* (Oxford: Oxford University Press, 2007), 3, 5.
5. For a full discussion of the various collaborations underwriting *Parade*, see Gay Morris, 'Massine/Picasso/*Parade*', *Modernist Cultures* 9.1 (2014): 46–61.
6. Rosanna Maule and Catherine Russell, 'Another Cinephilia: Women's Cinema in the 1920s', *Framework* 46.1 (2005): 52
7. Letter from Germaine Dulac to Louis Nalpas, 25 November 1919. Tami Williams cites this letter in her study *Germaine Dulac: A Cinema of Sensations* (Urbana, IL: University of Illinois Press, 2014), 110.
8. Maule and Russell, 'Another Cinephilia', 52.
9. Ibid., 52.
10. Jennifer Bean, 'Introduction: Towards a Feminist Historiography of Early Cinema', in *A Feminist Reader in Early Cinema*, ed. Dianne Negra and Jennifer Bean (Durham, NC: Duke University Press, 2002), 3, 6.

11. Sandy Flitterman-Lewis, *To Desire Differently: Feminism and the French Cinema* (New York: Columbia University Press, 1996), 11.
12. Susan Potter, *Queer Timing: The Emergence of Lesbian Sexuality in Early Cinema* (Urbana, IL: University of Illinois Press, 2019).
13. Tom Gunning, '"We are Here and Not Here": Late Nineteenth-Century Stage Magic and the Roots of Cinema in the Appearance (and Disappearance) of the Virtual Image', in *A Companion to Early Cinema*, ed. André Gaudreault, Nicolas Dulac and Santiago Hidalgo (London: Wiley-Blackwell, 2012), 53.
14. Jonathan Crary, *Suspensions of Perception* (Cambridge, MA: MIT Press, 1999), 282. Laura Marks and Giuliana Bruno have also done much to revise critical approaches to film as a predominantly visual medium, since they emphasise the haptic and kinaesthetic dimensions of cinematic experience, which resonate particularly with the art of dance. See Laura Marks, *The Skin of the Film: Intercultural Cinema, Embodiment and the Senses* (Durham, NC: Duke University Press, 2000); Giuliana Bruno, *Atlas of Emotion: Journeys in Art, Architecture and Film* (New York: Verso, 2002).
15. Djuna Barnes, 'Alla Nazimova, One of the Greatest Living Actresses, Talks of her Art', in *Djuna Barnes: Interviews*, ed. Alice Barry (College Park, MD: Sun and Moon Press, 1985), 354.
16. Lori Landay, 'The Flapper Film: Comedy, Dance, and Jazz Age Kinaesthetics', in Negra and Bean, eds, *A Feminist Reader in Early Cinema*, 224.
17. 'At Close Range with Alla Nazimova the Russo-English Actress', *New York Times*, 18 November 1906.
18. Schwartz, 'Torque', 101.
19. Barnes, 'Alla Nazimova', 354.
20. Daniela Caselli, *Improper Modernism: Djuna Barnes's Bewildering Corpus* (Aldershot: Ashgate, 2009), 21.
21. Barnes, 'Alla Nazimova', 356.
22. Ibid., 357.
23. 'Out-Salomes all Salomes: Mimi Aguglia Gives Surprise Italian Version of Wilde's Tragedy', *New York Times*, 23 December 1913.
24. Barnes, 'The Wild Aguglia and Her Monkeys', in *Djuna Barnes: Interviews*, 22.
25. Djuna Barnes, 'What Do You See, Madam?', in *Smoke and Other Early Stories*, ed. Douglas Messerli (Los Angeles: Sun and Moon Press, 1993), 47.
26. Ibid., 50.
27. Alex Goody, *Modernist Poetry, Gender and Leisure Technologies: Machine Amusements* (Basingstoke: Palgrave Macmillan, 2019), 171.
28. Barnes, 'What Do You See, Madam?', 52–3.
29. Goody, *Machine Amusements*, 170.
30. Nancy J. Levine, '"I've always suffered from sirens": The Cinema Vamp and Djuna Barnes' *Nightwood*', *Women's Studies* 16 (1989): 274.
31. Ibid., 278.
32. Djuna Barnes, *Nightwood* (London: Faber and Faber, 2007), 41.
33. Ibid., 38.
34. Teresa de Lauretis, '*Nightwood* and the "Terror of Uncertain Signs"', *Critical Enquiry* 34.S2 (2008): 124.
35. 'Art and Alla Nazimova: Russian Actress Sought out as Model and Inspiration', *New York Tribune*, 17 December 1911.
36. Solita Solano, 'Ibsen Reforms a Vampire', *New York Tribune*, 19 May 1918.
37. Ibid.
38. See Ritchie Robertson, 'Historicizing Weininger: The Nineteenth-Century

German Image of the Feminized Jew', in *Modernity, Culture and 'The Jew'*, ed. Bryan Cheyette and Laura Marcus (Cambridge: Polity, 1998), 23–39. Robertson identifies Heine's Herodias in *Atta Troll* as a transformation of the feminine Jewish stereotype into the *femme fatale* (26). See also Jonathan Freedman, 'Transformations of a Jewish Princess: Salome and the Remaking of the Jewish Female Body from Sarah Bernhardt to Betty Boop', *Philological Quarterly* 92 (2013): 89–114.
39. Maren Tova Linett, *Modernism, Feminism and Jewishness* (Cambridge: Cambridge University Press, 2007), 2.
40. Barnes, *Nightwood*, 5, 13.
41. Ibid., 4.
42. Bryan Cheyette and Laura Marcus, 'Introduction', in *Modernity, Culture and 'the Jew'*, 3.
43. 'The Transformation of Nazimova', *Current Literature* XLIII, December 1907.
44. Ibid.
45. Jane Marcus describes Salome as a 'biblical Hedda Gabler'. See 'The Jewish Princess was a New Woman', 105. For further discussion of Nazimova's performances in Ibsen's plays, see Thomas Arthur, 'Female Interpreters of Ibsen on Broadway, 1896–1947: Minnie Maddern Fiske, Alla Nazimova & Eva Le Gallienne', *Ibsen Studies* 1 (2000): 54–67.
46. Gavin Lambert, *Nazimova: A Biography* (New York: Alfred A. Knopf, 1997), 164.
47. Alla Nazimova in Elise Lathrop, 'Profile: Alla Nazimova', *Vogue* 28, 1906.
48. Schwartz, 'Torque', 75.
49. Lynn Garafola, 'Reconfiguring the Sexes', in *The Ballets Russes and its World*, ed. Lynn Garafola and Nancy Van Norman Baer (New Haven, CT: Yale University Press, 1999), 252.
50. Christophe Wall-Romana, *Cinepoetry: Imaginary Cinemas in French Poetry* (New York: Fordham University Press, 2013), 23.
51. Mallarmé, 'Another Study of Dance', 135.
52. Christophe Wall-Romana, 'Mallarmé's Cinepoetics: The Poem Uncoiled by the Cinématographe, 1893–98', *PMLA* 120.1 (2005): 136.
53. Lathrop, 'Profile: Alla Nazimova'.
54. 'At Close Range with Alla Nazimova: Absorbs Her Parts', *New York Times*, 24 April 1910.
55. Preston, *Modernism's Mythic Pose*, 5–6.
56. Ibid., 69.
57. Ibid., 12.
58. 'At Close Range with Alla Nazimova'.
59. Ibid.
60. Schwartz, 'Torque', 104.
61. 'Dancing Wins Actresses Applause', *Chicago Daily Tribune*, 7 April 1907. Jane Marcus compares Nora's tarantella to Salome's dance in 'The Jewish Princess was a New Woman', 105.
62. Ibid.
63. 'Nazimova's Salome Opens Tonight at Criterion Theatre', *New York Tribune*, 31 December 1922.
64. Dierkes-Thrun, *Salome's Modernity*, 126.
65. Valentia Steer, *The Secrets of the Cinema: Your Favourite Amusement from Within* (London: Pearson, 1920), 80.
66. 'On the Screen: Theda Bara Brings a Celluloid Salome to Enliven Broadway', *New York Tribune*, 8 October 1918, 13.

67. Theda Bara, 'The Curse on the Moving Picture Actress: Describing the Conflict in Her Artistic Experiences of the Moving-Picture Art', *Forum*, July 1919, 83.
68. 'Vamps and Near-Vamps', *New York Tribune*, 11 May 1919, E6.
69. Bara, 'The Curse on the Moving Picture Actress'.
70. Patricia White, 'Nazimova's Veils: "Salome" at the Intersection of Film Histories', in Negra and Bean, eds, *A Feminist Reader in Early Cinema*, 61.
71. Lambert, *Nazimova: A Biography*, 190.
72. Ibid., 190.
73. White, 'Nazimova's Veils', 61.
74. For a history of this production, see Tydeman and Price, *Wilde: Salome*, 35–40.
75. Kristin Thompson, 'Classical Narrative Space and the Spectator's Attention', in David Bordwell, Janet Staiger and Kristin Thompson, *The Classical Hollywood Cinema: Film Style and Mode of Production to 1960* (London: Routledge, 1988), 310.
76. Lambert, *Nazimova: A Biography*, 234.
77. Jane Pritchard, 'Serge Diaghilev's Ballets Russes – An Itinerary. Part 1: 1909–1921', *Dance Research* 27.1 (2009): 109–98.
78. Hanna Järvinen, 'Dancing without Space – On Nijinsky's *L'Après-Midi d'un Faune* (1912)', *Dance Research* 27.1 (2009): 28–64.
79. Garafola, 'Reconfiguring the Sexes', 251.
80. Robert d'Humières, 'La Tragédie de Salomé', *Théâtre des Champs-Élysées: saison russe* [programme, 13 juin 1913], 248–9, BnF Gallica.
81. Garafola, 'Reconfiguring the Sexes', 258.
82. 'The Russian Ballet: Florent Schmitt's *La Tragédie de Salome*', *The Observer*, 6 July 1913.
83. Jacques Debey, 'La Tragédie de Salomé', *Comœdia Illustré* [5 July 1913], 906–7. Translation my own.
84. Ibid., 906–7.
85. Garafola, 'Reconfiguring the Sexes', 252. Describing the shift towards orientalism in the Ballets Russes's productions of *Cléopâtre* and *Schéhérazade*, Deborah Jowitt observes this change in style: 'Denizens of the East didn't wear pointe shoes, and their torsos were as mobile as could be wished [. . .] Even a virtuous maiden [. . .] displayed a sensuous plasticity'; see *Time and the Dancing Image* (Berkeley, CA: University of California Press, 1988), 114–15.
86. Debey, 'La Tragédie de Salomé', 906–7.
87. Lambert, *Nazimova: A Biography*, 260.
88. Preston, *Modernism's Mythic Pose*, 94.
89. Järvinen, 'Dancing without Space', 46.
90. White, 'Nazimova's Veils', 67.
91. Barnes, 'Alla Nazimova', 357.
92. Susan Sontag, *Notes on 'Camp'* (London: Penguin, 2018), 8.
93. Ibid., 5–6.
94. Vivian Sobchack, *Carnal Thoughts: Embodiment and Moving Image Culture* (Berkeley, CA: University of California Press, 2004), 59.
95. Dierkes-Thrun, *Salome's Modernity*, 155.
96. Sobchack, *Carnal Thoughts*, 66.
97. Lambert, *Nazimova: A Biography*, 261.
98. 'The Screen: A New Salome', *New York Times*, 1 January 1923.
99. Agamben, 'Notes on Gesture', 139.
100. Germaine Dulac, 'From Sentiment to Line', in *Red Velvet Seat: Women's Writing on the First Fifty Years of Cinema*, ed. Antonia Lant (London: Verso, 2006), 190.
101. Ibid., 190.

102. Henri Bergson, *Creative Evolution*, trans. Arthur Mitchell (London: Macmillan, 1922), 319.
103. Jean Epstein, 'To a Second Reality, a Second Reason' [1947], trans. Sarah Keller, in *Critical Essays and New Translations*, 322.
104. Dulac, 'From Sentiment to Line', 190.
105. Donia Mounsef, 'Women Filmmakers and the Avant-Garde: From Dulac to Duras', in *Women Filmmakers: Refocusing*, ed. Jacqueline Levitin, Judith Plessis and Valerie Raoul (London: Routledge, 2003), 44–5.
106. See Tami Williams, 'Toward the Development of a Modern "Impressionist" Cinema: Germaine Dulac's *La Belle Dame sans Merci* (1921) and the Deconstruction of the Femme Fatale Archetype', *Framework* 51.2 (2010): 404–19; E. Ann Kaplan, 'The Avant-Gardes in Europe and the USA', in *Women & Film: Both Sides of the Camera* (New York: Routledge, 1988), 85–90; Sandy Flitterman-Lewis, 'The Image and the Spark: Dulac and Artaud Reviewed', *Dada/Surrealism* 15 (1986): 110–27.
107. Émile Vuillermoz, quoted in Richard Abel, 'On the Threshold of French Film Theory and Criticism: 1915–1919', *Cinema Journal* 25.1 (1985): 22.
108. Ibid., 20–1.
109. Germaine Dulac, 'The Aesthetics, the Obstacles, Internal Cinégraphie', *Framework* 19 (1982): 6.
110. Ibid., 7.
111. Vuillermoz, quoted in Abel, 'On the Threshold of French Film Theory', 25.
112. Ibid., 25.
113. Ibid., 23.
114. Dulac, 'Trois Rencontres avec Loïe Fuller', in *Écrits*, 109.
115. Marcus, *The Tenth Muse*, 10.
116. Williams, *Germaine Dulac: A Cinema of Sensations*, 41–2.
117. Ibid., 35.
118. Ibid., 68.
119. Ibid., 51–2.
120. Brandstetter, *Poetics of Dance*, 172–3.
121. Ibid., 174.
122. H. M. Walbrook, 'The Invasion of the Dancers', *Pall Mall Magazine*, January 1912, 26.
123. Ibid., 26.
124. 'The Censor Again: "Hardy Plays" At Dorchester', *The Times of India*, 12 December 1911.
125. Schwartz, 'Torque', 75.
126. Irina Sirotkina and Roger Smith, *The Sixth Sense of the Avant-Garde: Dance, Kinaesthesia and the Arts in Revolutionary Russia* (London: Bloomsbury, 2017), 5.
127. David J. Shepherd, *The Bible on Silent Film: Spectacle, Story and Scripture in the Early Cinema* (Cambridge: Cambridge University Press, 2013), 199.
128. 'Dancing on Screen: Napierkowska's Masterpiece', *The Times of India*, 20 July 1916.
129. Williams, *Germaine Dulac: A Cinema of Sensations*, 52.
130. Ibid., 52.
131. Ibid., 70.
132. Ibid., 69.
133. 'Science Explains their Fascination', *Washington Post*, 15 March 1914.
134. Ibid.
135. Williams, *Germaine Dulac: A Cinema of Sensations*, 70.

136. Gaylyn Studlar, '"Out-Salomeing Salome": Dance, the New Woman, and Fan Magazine Orientalism', *Michigan Quarterly Review* 34.4 (1995): 491.
137. Kate Chopin, 'An Egyptian Cigarette', in *Daughters of Decadence: Women Writers of the Fin de Siècle*, ed. Elaine Showalter (London: Virago, 1993), 4.
138. Germaine Dulac, quoted in Williams, *Germaine Dulac: A Cinema of Sensations*, 53.
139. Ibid., 52.
140. Drawing on Terry Castle's work, Elizabeth English examines the metaphor of the 'spectral lesbian body' in *Lesbian Modernism: Censorship, Sexuality and Genre Fiction* (Edinburgh: Edinburgh University Press, 2015), 60–1.
141. As Monique Wittig writes, 'Thus a lesbian *has* to be something else, a not-woman, a not-man, a product of society, not a product of nature, for there is no nature in society'. See 'One is not Born a Woman', in *The Norton Anthology of Theory and Criticism*, ed. Vincent B. Leitch et al. (New York: W. W. Norton, 2010), 1908.
142. Rancière, *Aisthesis*, xi.
143. Jean Morizot, quoted in Williams, *Germaine Dulac: A Cinema of Sensations*, 109.
144. Virginia Woolf, 'The Cinema', in *Selected Essays*, ed. David Bradshaw (Oxford: Oxford University Press, 2008), 175.
145. Jones, *Literature, Modernism and Dance*, 129.
146. Marcus, *The Tenth Muse*, 117.
147. Germaine Dulac, 'The Music of Silence', in Lant, ed., *Red Velvet Seat*, 218.
148. Ibid., 218.
149. Germaine Dulac, 'Photographie – Cinégraphie', in *Écrits*, 80.
150. Cheryl Hindrichs, 'Feminist Optics and Avant-Garde Cinema: Germaine Dulac's "The Smiling Madame Beudet" and Virginia Woolf's "Street Haunting"', *Feminist Studies* 35.2 (2009): 307, 317.
151. Marcel Zahar and Daniel Burret, 'Une heure chez Mme. Germaine Dulac', *Cinéa-Ciné pour Tous*, 63 (June 1926): 13–14. Translated and cited by Williams, *Germaine Dulac: A Cinema of Sensations*, 154.
152. Germaine Dulac, 'Thème visuel et variation cinégraphique' [typescript], Fonds Germaine Dulac, Paris, Cinémathèque française, 80-B8. My translation.
153. Williams, *Germaine Dulac: A Cinema of Sensations*, 154.
154. Dulac, 'The Music of Silence', 217.
155. Dulac, 'Trois Rencontres avec Loïe Fuller', in *Écrits*, 109.
156. Dulac, 'Thème visuel', 80-B8.
157. Gunning, 'Light, Motion, Cinema!', 115.
158. Dulac, 'Trois Rencontres avec Loïe Fuller', in *Écrits*, 109.
159. James Stevens Curl, 'Arabesque', in *A Dictionary of Architecture and Landscape Architecture*, 2nd edn (Oxford: Oxford University Press, 2006), Oxford Reference Online.
160. Ibid.
161. 'Arabesque', in *The Oxford Companion to Music*, Oxford Music Online; Debra Craine and Judith Mackrell, 'Arabesque', in *The Oxford Dictionary of Dance* (Oxford: Oxford University Press, 2010), 19.
162. Germaine Dulac, 'La nouvelle évolution', in *Écrits*, 136.
163. Gunning, 'Light, Motion, Cinema!', 120.
164. Flitterman-Lewis, 'The Image and the Spark', 114–15.
165. Virginia Woolf, *Mrs Dalloway*, ed. David Bradshaw (Oxford: Oxford University Press, 2009), 4.
166. Ibid., 58.
167. Flitterman-Lewis, *To Desire Differently*, 2.

168. For Flitterman-Lewis, Artaud's conceptual 'allegiance to Surrealism required a degree of violence in the work of art powerful enough to achieve that psychic directness of the Freudian dream-work'; see 'The Image and the Spark', 114.
169. Julia Kristeva, *The Severed Head: Capital Visions* (New York: Columbia University Press, 2014), 65–6.
170. Ibid., 110.

4

'HERODIAS' DAUGHTERS HAVE RETURNED AGAIN': W. B. YEATS AND THE IDEAL BODY

In May 1905, W. B. Yeats wrote to the American lawyer and art collector John Quinn to express his distaste for a performance he had just seen in London. The play was the first production in England of Wilde's *Salomé*, performed privately at the Bijou Theatre without much critical success.[1] In his letter, Yeats suggests that the play's author was better suited to the demands of comedy, and that his talents were lost on this 'unactable literary drama', which possessed 'every sort of fault'.[2] Yeats felt as if he had been denied the imagined 'thrill' of Salome's dance – he could not understand the 'great outcry against its repulsiveness' as he had 'felt nothing', and emerged from the theatre disappointed.[3] In much the same vein, he later described *Salomé* to T. Sturge Moore as 'thoroughly bad', 'empty, sluggish & pretentious': a harsh verdict indeed.[4] In the early years of the new century, and with Wilde's recent death still hanging over the surviving members of the 'tragic generation', the notorious *fin-de-siècle* dancer might not have seemed the most fruitful or appropriate theme for the modern stage. After opening the doors of the Abbey Theatre with Lady Gregory the previous year and laying out their plans for the rejuvenation of Irish drama, Yeats may have been keen to distance himself from the artistic controversies of the preceding decade, especially those attached to his late compatriot.

When he came to write *A Vision* (1925), however, it was to the aesthetic and intellectual contexts of decadence that Yeats returned, according Salome a privileged position in his complex historical system:

> When I think of the moment before revelation I think of Salome – she too, delicately tinted or maybe mahogany dark – dancing before Herod and receiving the Prophet's head in her indifferent hands, and wonder if what seems to us decadence was not in reality the exultation of the muscular flesh and of civilization perfectly achieved.[5]

Although it is the literature of decadence that Yeats cites, this Salome is not, Frank Kermode observes, quite the same figure that Yeats received from Wilde. Here, her dance encapsulates a definitive 'moment of cultural equilibrium [. . .] the great "antithetical" phase of Christian dominance, the end of the full heroic life'.[6] She represents, too, the unification of the intellect and the ideal body, echoing Yeats's earlier contention in Book III, 'Dove or Swan', that 'when revelation comes athlete and sage are merged'.[7] Perhaps surprisingly, it is to the 'athletic' body that Yeats devotes a curious level of attention in this passage. He is preoccupied with the hue of the dancer's skin, with her 'muscular' stature and, subsequently, with the gratuitous specifics of her bodily rituals: 'I see her anoint her bare limbs [. . .] with lion's fat'.[8] While venerated for her 'indifference', the dancer's ecstatic, muscle-bound form is nonetheless foregrounded as a source of expressive power. Portrayed as a counterpart to the struggling Leda, whose image is inextricable from the founding of Greek civilisation, Salome's body is conceptualised as not merely a symbol in *A Vision* but a crucial historical touchstone. As Yeats puts it at the close of this section in Book III, she is 'myth' become 'biography'; her violent destruction of the prophetic male body is perhaps figured as a form of vengeance following Leda's rape at the hands of a divine sovereign.[9]

A Vision therefore speaks to the underlying importance of the Salomean dancer to Yeats's highly singular and evolving aesthetic philosophy. For Kermode, the figure of Salome is intrinsic to any reading of Yeatsian aesthetics: 'whenever Yeats refers back to the historical concept of unity of being, or to the aesthetic one of beauty as a perfectly proportioned human body, the image of Salome is likely to occur to him'.[10] As the letter to Quinn suggests, Yeats often masked the considerable impact that Wilde's *Salomé* had on his vision for the theatre, to which he hoped to bring 'a remote, spiritual and ideal' drama, divorced from the 'stupefying' theatre of commerce.[11] In her important study *The Plays of W. B. Yeats: Yeats and the Dancer*, Sylvia Ellis demonstrates how the 'ideal' dancer, for Yeats, was, crucially, an impersonal force: in Loïe Fuller's case, 'pure abstraction as the flesh and blood of the living woman became subsumed into the flowing illuminated draperies'.[12] As a practice contingent on the performer's compliance with exacting technique, leaving varying degrees of room for expressive style, dance offered Yeats a very productive model for the kind of performance conditions he sought to facilitate. While Yeats often sought to quash subjective expression in his performers and demanded control over most aspects of his dramatic productions, his writing on dance, and on Salome in particular, produces unresolved tensions between the playwright's authority and the dancers whose technical interventions would shape his dramatic texts. Throughout his career, dancers and choreographers played central creative roles in Yeats's work, not merely as abstract presences who yielded to the dramatist's totalising vision, but also as embodied artists who brought a fresh kinaesthetic dimension to his literary compositions.

Despite Yeats's reservations about the quality of Wilde's *Salomé* as a piece of dramatic theatre, the emblem of the dancer aligned with his developing approach to the moving body as part of a broader dramatic and symbolic programme. Salome, for Yeats, was not an easily assimilated image, but was rather associated with uncontrollable forms – with the ambiguous feminine power of the *Sidhe*, and with the creeds of the *fin-de-siècle* aesthetic movements that continued to exert a hold on his work in the 1920s and 1930s. Yeats might, as Ellis argues, offer 'dance as a transfiguration of words into another medium' and prioritise 'the dancer as abstraction', as the unification of form and content that eclipses the (often female) body producing it.[13] Yet, as she also observes, the 'plays for dancers' were, crucially, *for* dancers – for performers trained not only to execute dance movement but also to engage actively in the process of choreographic interpretation. Both Michio Ito, a Japanese dancer trained in Kabuki, and Ninette de Valois, a pupil of Enrico Cecchetti and later founder of the Royal Ballet, made extensive contributions to the evolution of Yeats's theatre, influencing the form of the dramatic texts and their live productions. Their efforts filled an important gap in Yeats's aspirations for these plays: as he acknowledged in his Preface to *Four Plays for Dancers* (1921), 'the dancing will give me the most trouble, for I know but vaguely what I want'.[14] This chapter contends that Yeats came to understand dance as part of an aesthetic system that largely drew its tenets from authors indebted to European Symbolism, including Wilde, Arthur Symons and Edward Gordon Craig, but that he depended on professional dancers to clarify what could only ever present itself to him in 'vague' terms.

Although he possessed little knowledge of dance as a craft, Yeats was determined to incorporate it into his dramatic productions, and it also came to occupy an increasingly important place in his poetry and prose works. The oft-quoted final couplet of 'Among School Children' seems to underline a tension between the choreographed artwork and its bodily means of production, which would continue to dominate Yeats's ruminations on dance: 'O body swayed to music, O brightening glance, / How can we know the dancer from the dance?' (*VP*, 446). It is worth noting that, as in *A Vision*, it is a 'Ledaean body' (*VP*, 443) that the speaker dreams of in an earlier stanza of this poem, suggesting a continuing imbrication of the Greek myth with the figure of the dancer in Yeats's aesthetic system, and signalling a Hellenic return of the sort that Warburg found in Renaissance art. Formulating a Ledaean genealogy, Yeats seems to be thinking almost uncannily along the same lines as Warburg, visualising the 'daughters of the swan' (*VP*, 444) as figures in a fifteenth-century painting: 'Her present image floats into the mind – / Did Quattrocento finger fashion it?' (*VP*, 444). Yeats's instinctive coupling of these metamorphic images of femininity with the resurgence of classical forms was in line with the dance cultures of the period. In the first year of the new century, Yeats had seen Isadora Duncan's *Dance Idylls* with T. Sturge Moore and Philip Comyns Carr, and he also joined George Bernard Shaw in sponsoring Ruth St Denis's first London tour.[15] He was similarly enthused by the Ballets Russes and may have found inspiration for his own theatrical ideals in Diaghilev's unified modern spectacle.[16] Indeed, Yeats's engagement with dance must be understood, Mary Fleischer contends, as one that permeated every aspect of his theatrical work, 'connected to his experiments with stage space, differing levels of reality and abstraction, and the role of the moving actor'.[17] Placing a number of Yeats's poems and essays in dialogue with two important dance-dramas – *At the Hawk's Well* (1916) and *The King of the Great Clock Tower* (1934) – this chapter argues that the work of dancers was central to Yeats's theatrical corpus, shaping his understanding of the relationship between text and movement and underpinning his various negotiations with the dancing figures he discovered in Wilde, Symons and other artists of the 1890s.

REVISING *SALOMÉ*: YEATS, WILDE AND SYMBOLISM

Wilde occupies a contradictory status in Yeats's reflections on the literature of the late nineteenth century: in a letter of 1906, Yeats described him as merely 'a wit and a critic [who] could not endure his limitations', yet in *The Trembling of the Veil* he would muse at length on his memories of Wilde, engaging in a more conscious and carefully crafted memorialising of the older Irishman, perhaps to secure his own reputation through proximity to the luminaries of past decades.[18] Recalling his 'astonishment' at meeting a man who was capable of 'talking with perfect sentences, as if he had written them all overnight with labour and yet all spontaneous', Yeats seems captivated by the memory of Wilde's wit and rhetorical skill, which here appears as a form of constrained spontaneity, a quality he also found in dance.[19] When Wilde experienced his crippling public decline during his trials in 1895, Yeats was much moved, telling his friend, the Irish poet Edward Dowden, 'I went to try and see Wilde today to tell him how much I sympathised with him in his trouble.'[20] Furthermore, he speculated that the actor Florence Darragh, whom he first saw in the lead role in Wilde's *Salomé*, might be 'the finest tragedian on the English stage'.[21] Yeats's shifting positions on both the quality of Wilde's one-act drama and the legacy of its controversial author speak to his somewhat fraught attempts to accommodate strains of Wildean aestheticism in his own work. Although he criticised many aspects of the *Salomé* he saw performed, the play's recourse to an antique and austere symbolism couched in incantatory declamations resonated powerfully with his own ambitions for the stage. In his essay 'The Theatre', Yeats stressed the necessity of rediscovering 'grave and decorative gestures such as delighted Rossetti and Madox Brown', encouraging dramatists to restore the place of 'ritual' and bardic chanting in performance, thereby 'recalling words to their ancient sovereignty'.[22]

Other critics have traced Wilde's influence on the development of Yeats's work as a playwright, including Charles Armstrong, who observes rich parallels between Wilde's *Salomé* and Yeats's *The Resurrection* (1931), especially in their treatment of religious and sacrificial themes.[23] Noreen Doody has also argued for the singular importance of *Salomé* as a precursor to Yeats's dance-dramas: following recurring symbols in his work such as 'the gaze, the moon, the kiss, dance, and severed head', she claims that Yeats reworked plays such as *At the Hawk's Well* and *The King of the Great Clock Tower* to give prominence to these motifs, suggesting that his 'metaphysical and poetic aesthetic was directed in its initial stages by the thought of Oscar Wilde'.[24] Drawing on Harold Bloom's account of influence as the poet's 'swerve' from the precursor, she concludes that Yeats transcends Wilde's legacy by creating a more symbolically rich and cohesive dramatic system, thus rendering Wilde's original work 'an echo of someone else's music'.[25] Based on an almost filial conception of the literary canon, Bloom's model of influence privileges the individuality of the male poetic spirit in a manner that does not leave much space for the kinds of interventions that this book considers: the lingering traces of women's dance performances betrayed in poetic allusions and dramaturgic choices, or the practical contributions of trained choreographers to the staging of modernist play-texts.[26]

Yeats's wariness of acknowledging his debts to Wilde's *Salomé* has led some critics to term his response to Wilde 'indirect', alleging that he 'named neither Salome nor Herodias in his work'.[27] Yeats does, however, make specific references to both of these figures in a number of creative works and letters, revealing their elasticity as recurring metaphors. Along with the previously cited passage describing Salome in *A Vision*, Yeats accords this figure a central place in his post-war poem 'Nineteen Hundred and Nineteen' (1921), a work that marks a revival of the *fin-de-siècle*'s cultural emblems, conjuring something of that decade's conflicted spirit of pessimism and apocalyptic renewal. The dance images that permeate this text speak to Yeats's memories of the theatres and music halls he visited with his friend Arthur Symons, whose own poetry probably played a part in nursing his preoccupation with dynamic motifs of women-in-motion. In one of these works, 'The Dance of the Daughters of Herodias' (1897), Symons draws on the images and qualities of movement that Warburg identified as characteristic of the Nympha, that 'pagan stormy petrel' who interrupts the 'slow moving respectability of subdued Christianity'.[28] Symons even merges the images of fruit-bearer and head-hunter:

> And, in the cloudy darkness, I can see
> The thin white feet of many women dancing,
> And in their hands . . . I see it is the dance
> Of the daughters of Herodias; each of them
> Carries a beautiful platter in her hand,
> Smiling, because she holds against her heart
> The secret lips and the unresting brow
> Some John the Baptist's head makes lamentable;
> Smiling as innocently as if she carried
> A wet red quartered melon on a dish.[29]

The slippage between the severed head and the 'wet red quartered melon' signals a subtle melding of the grotesque and the quotidian, attesting to the difficulty of reading this figure and deciphering her insidious intent as the colour seamlessly bleeds from head to fruit, the stability of the spectacle jeopardised by the dancer's movements. As the ellipsis in the third line indicates, Symons's speaker struggles to make the image settle. This poem reflects too the broader mingling of profane and comic registers that haunts the Baptist's decollated forms, especially as they appear on stage. Ellen Crowell has recently observed that 'symbolism and naturalism are left spectacularly unreconciled' in *Salomé*, creating an 'affective dissonance' centred on Salome's blazonic appeals to the severed head.[30] For Yeats, the severed head would become a similarly equivocal prop in his dance-dramas, and Symons too senses an incongruity underpinning the image of the veiled dancer and her capital prize: it is an alternative iconography built around the continuous interpolation of ancient forms through their modern surfaces; in this case, the philhellenic fruit-bearer ghosting the nineteenth-century *femme fatale*, thus inscribing the Nympha's dual symbolism into the dancers' 'shadowy and invisible presences'.[31]

Offering a continuation of Wilde's 'invisible dance', these spectral forces elicit a crisis of perception that also troubled Yeats. In 'Nineteen Hundred and Nineteen', the movements of dancers are described as symptomatic of the broader historical cycles that he would systematise most clearly in *A Vision*, initiating a 'whirling' circuitous motion that prefigures the helix of the gyre:

> When Loïe Fuller's Chinese dancers enwound
> A shining web, a floating ribbon of cloth,
> It seemed that a dragon of air
> Had fallen among dancers, had whirled them round
> Or hurried them off on its own furious path (*VP*, 430)

Mistakenly characterising Fuller as the leader of a Chinese dance company, Yeats may be misremembering her tour with the Japanese dancer Sada Yacco, or possibly thinking of the Javanese dance troupe that Symons found so entrancing at the 1889 Exposition Universelle.[32] Nonetheless, he identifies Fuller as the source of this 'whirling' line of motion that repeats and expands: the neologism 'enwound' commences a pattern of verbal winding that continues in 'web' and 'whirled', repeated later in the stanza as 'the Platonic Year / Whirls out new right and wrong, / Whirls in the old instead' (*VP*, 430). The metaphor of the luminous web not only suggests that Yeats recalled Fuller's use of light technologies to create shimmering effects through her 'floating' veils, but also that he was struck by the movement patterns she prioritised: the 'whirling' torque that emanated from her twisting torso and circling arms, rippling through her fabrics to draw larger rotations in the air. Fuller's labouring body, possessed by the 'dragon of air', thus becomes the central animating force in a larger scheme of movement, offering an apt model for the recursive antitheses of Yeats's own historical system, signalled in this stanza by the return of the 'old' in the 'Platonic Year'.

The repetition of 'whirl' in 'Nineteen Hundred and Nineteen' thus enables and in fact dynamically registers a shift from the single image to the overarching historical paradigm; dance movement signals a spiralling temporal process, realised through an almost Nietzschean mode of eternal recurrence that also formed an influential philosophical bedrock for Warburg's *Pathosformel*. This reiterative mode is affirmed in the final stanza, where the image of the Fulleresque modern dancer is overlaid with her mythical counterpart:

> Herodias' daughters have returned again,
> A sudden blast of dusty wind and after
> Thunder of feet, tumult of images
> Their purpose in the labyrinth of the wind (*VP*, 433)

Yeats was probably thinking here of the 'pale and windy multitude' of dancers in Symons's 'Dance of the Daughters of Herodias', which he cited in a note to *The Wind Among the Reeds*.[33] The Salome conjured in these lines is not a source of equilibrium and balance; rather, she casts images into disorder with the force of her movements, providing the kind of destructive, even apocalyptic energy most famously associated with the 'slouching' beast of 'The Second Coming' (*VP*, 402). For Yeats, however, this dancer was not reducible to the tenets of Christian orthodoxy but instead allied with the metamorphic figures of Irish legend, as he explicitly articulated in a 1907 letter to Nancy Maude, comparing Salome to the *Sidhe*:

> The Sidhe move in dust storms & in all whirling winds. There is some connection between them & whirling movement hard to fathom. When

the country people see bits of straw or dust whirling on the road they say it is 'the Sidhe'. In the middle ages it was said to be the dance of the daughters of Herodias – an attempt to Christianize something which was pre-christian. The Sidhe are also associated with mist & a dust storm is a kind of mist.[34]

This importantly dislodges the veiled dancer, in Yeats's mind, from both a purely biblical framework and the alternative Hellenic paradigm suggested by the maenads, as well as from the array of sexually destructive figures produced by Decadence and Symbolism. Though she combines all these varied contexts, the veiled 'daughter of Herodias' is here also connected to the *Sidhe*, the feminine spirits of Irish mythology who, like the other 'conscious beings' chronicled in *Fairy and Folktales of the Irish Peasantry* (1888), 'have no inherent form but change according to their whim, or the mind that sees them'.[35] Yeats's description renders the 'whirling' dancer an agent of transformation, both as a consequence of her self-directed 'whims' and, crucially, through the aesthetic inclinations of her perceiver, for whom her motions stabilise into visible forms in brief moments.

Yeats declared in 'The Celtic Element in Literature' (1897) that 'the symbolical movement [. . .] is certainly the only movement that is saying new things', though it was his hope that the 'new beauty' of the 'Irish legends' would give 'the opening century its most memorable symbols'.[36] Given his Protestant Ascendancy background and his very limited knowledge of the Irish language, Yeats's co-option of these native myths is somewhat disquieting, and seems based on a determination to re-read Irish cultural forms in relation to the external aesthetic movements he found most productive. Yeats's ruminations on the *Sidhe* and their connections to Christian and pre-Christian narratives indicate his attempts to cleave the visual index of the European symbolist movement, closely tied to the 'dance of the daughters of Herodias', to his own project to revitalise Irish national mythology.

Scholars have examined the ways in which Yeats sought to combine these traditions in his early dramatic works, including *Deirdre* (1907), which absorbs something of the spatial abstraction and deliberate sense of lethargy he gleaned from Symbolist theatre. As one of the principal heroines of Irish myth, Deirdre appealed to Yeats as a choice for dramatic adaptation: she shared certain qualities with the other 'romantic and mysterious' muses he admired in the work of the Symbolists, though he feared that this abstracted, purified version of femininity was threatened by the materialism of the modern age. In his version of *Deirdre*, he sought the essence of the idealised feminine figures found in the paintings of D. G. Rossetti and the Pre-Raphaelites, in which 'Woman herself' was still symbolic; 'the priestess of her shrine'.[37] The staging requirements of his play, however, seem most clearly beholden to the 'static theatre' valorised by Maurice Maeterlinck: according to Michael McAteer, Yeats shares Maeterlinck's interest in depicting states of alienation and dislocation, 'a quality of estrangement that was unsettling in its time'.[38] In this vein, the house in *Deirdre* forms the locus of the play's action and is described as a place of 'silence and loneliness', with unseen 'curtained off' areas, the sense of blindness and exclusion compounded by the fact that 'the curtains are drawn' (*CP*, 171). Yeats's play-text feeds on the disturbing otherness conjured by Maeterlinck's descriptions of strange and estranged domestic spaces, where communication fails and proximity is a threat.[39] Katherine Worth agrees that Yeats's highly developed 'visual tastes' were European, reflecting his sensitivity to the power of 'stage pictures' that might be 'enhanced' through careful groupings, precise gestures and a conscious use of silence and stillness that had been perfected by French actors such as Sarah Bernhardt.[40] Appropriately, it was at a performance of another Symbolist play that he found an actress who he believed could play his Deirdre effectively, in line with these ambitions.

While writing *Deirdre* in June 1906, Yeats attended the King's Theatre in Covent Garden to see a production of Wilde's *Salomé*, directed by his friend Charles Ricketts, with Florence Darragh in the lead role. He was greatly taken with Ricketts's use of lighting and was so impressed by Darragh that he immediately hired her for his *Deirdre*, writing to W. G. Fay that as soon as he 'thought of [Darragh] for Deirdre [he] began to write better, [he] thought of moments of her Salome, and ventured and discovered subtleties of emotion [. . .] never attempted before'.[41] Deirdre, in Yeats's play, is aligned with Salome's dangerous femininity, suggested by her own appraisal of her precarious womanhood: 'although we are so delicately made, / There's something brutal in us, and we are won / By those who can shed blood' (*CP*, 199). As it is for Wilde, female desire is here inevitably tangled with bloodshed, suggesting that the violence staked in the name of women reflects their own inner 'brutality'. Yeats's Deirdre might therefore be read as a composite of various influences, grounded, of course, in the national legend that his compatriot Æ (George William Russell) had adapted for the stage in his *Deirdre* of 1902, but reconceived, in Yeats's mind, as a figure in line with the images of womanhood that he took from the Pre-Raphaelite and Symbolist painters, imbued with the darker elements of Wilde and Beardsley. For McAteer, *Deirdre* is 'poignant and spartan', in contrast to the 'lascivious and decadent' *Salomé*.[42] Yet Yeats shares with Wilde a Symbolist preoccupation with the defamiliarising qualities of ornament and artifice: Deirdre, wearing her murderous husband's rubies, is like a 'glittering dragon' (*CP*, 178), foreshadowing the 'dragon-ridden' days of 'Nineteen Hundred and Nineteen' that herald the return of the daughters of Herodias. As we will see, this was a 'return' that would leave its traces across Yeats's work in the decades after he saw these influential, if sceptically received, productions of *Salomé*.

'ALL THINGS SPRING FROM MOVEMENT': YEATS, EDWARD GORDON CRAIG AND STAGE CHOREOGRAPHIES

Yeats's conflicted attitude towards Wilde's *Salomé* recalls the tone of his horrified fascination at the sight of Jarry's overgrown puppet-actors in *Ubu Roi*, a work he eventually drew on for his own 'heroic farce' *The Green Helmet* (1910).[43] With their ties to the experimental French stage of the 1890s, writers such as Wilde, Jarry and Maeterlinck might seem unlikely models for Yeats's professed efforts to transform Ireland's national literary culture, an ambition grounded in the regeneration of loosely collated 'Celtic' peasant vernacular traditions and myths. Nevertheless, even Yeats's most self-consciously revivalist works of this period exist in curious proximity to the strains of European Decadence: the poems 'A Cradle Song' and 'The Valley of the Black Pig', for instance, appeared together under the heading 'Two Poems Concerning Peasant Visionaries' in Symons and Beardsley's audacious little magazine *The Savoy* (1896), published by the late Victorian pornographer Leonard Smithers as a kind of successor to *The Yellow Book*. Such a publication, illustrated with Beardsley's art, certainly made an unusual home for poetic evocations of 'faery children' and peasants 'labouring by the cromlech on the shore', but, for Yeats, the nostalgic romance of the Literary Revival was not wholly irreconcilable with the Decadent movement's moral and aesthetic provocations.[44]

Indeed, the theories of experimental dramatists also bled into his work in unexpected ways; for some critics, Yeats's drama even anticipated the radical abstraction of later twentieth-century playwrights such as Samuel Beckett, with its 'self-referentiality, its scepticism about language, its modernist turn to the body'.[45] For many, Yeats was at the centre, rather than on the peripheries, of modernism's networks; as T. S. Eliot put it, Yeats 'was one of those few whose history is the history of their own time, who are part of the consciousness of an age that cannot be understood without them'.[46] Like Eliot, who felt that 'poetic drama' would be best served by following the example of modern ballet, Yeats found dance an especially productive sphere for expressing these modernising inclinations. In particular, his approach to marrying choreography with acting techniques and the use of stage space was shaped by the English writer and set designer Edward Gordon Craig, who had a crucial and lasting influence on Yeats's development of a unique form of modernist theatre.

Yeats first became familiar with Craig's work when he attended a matinée performance of *Dido and Aeneas* by the Purcell Society in March 1901.[47] He was greatly taken with the design for the production, which he described as 'the only good scenery [he] ever saw', declaring in a letter to Craig that he had 'created a new art'.[48] The son of the eminent Victorian actress Ellen Terry, Craig had begun his career as an actor at the Lyceum Theatre under the tutelage of Henry Irving, before turning his attention to design. Craig sought to synthesise all elements of the theatre under the director's guiding vision and, like Yeats, the body of the actor posed a problem to the fulfilment of his dramatic philosophy. Craig's essay 'The Actor and the Über-Marionette' (1907), published in his theatre journal *The Mask*, articulated a desire to have actors freed from the 'bondage' of personality and somehow replaced by automata.[49] The marionette seemed an attractive prospect to Craig, as it was for Wilde, because it could be manipulated to perform without the interruption of personal feeling. Yeats sympathised with this position, famously suggesting that his actors should be placed in barrels so that he could 'shove them about with a pole when the action required it'.[50] Aside from its mere pliability, Craig also conceived of his ideal marionette as a relic from the theatre's origins in ritual: 'a descendant of the stone images of the old temples – he is today a rather degenerate form of a god [...] The marionette appears to me to be the last echo of some noble and beautiful art of a past civilization.'[51] Clearly, Craig also had a strong sense of drama's ritualistic qualities, which fed into his collaborations with Yeats and their shared co-option of the Japanese Nō theatre, with its celebration of masks and dances.[52]

At the root of Craig's long-standing fascination with dance was his relationship with Isadora Duncan, whom he met in 1904. It has been suggested that Craig gave Duncan 'the theoretic basis for her dancing', while he found in her performances 'the substantiation of his ideas and dreams regarding human movement'.[53] Falling into familiar claims about the gendered division of mind and body, this reading does not fully account for the sophisticated theories that Duncan herself developed about her practice. Her philhellenistic movement vocabulary, apparently derived from the poses emblazoned on Greek vases at the British Museum, affiliated her with related movement philosophies that had gained a purchase in American and European body cultures, including Delsartism, pioneered by Genevieve Stebbins in the US. Scholars have shown that Duncan both conceptualised and performed a relationship between dance and her personal feminist politics, departing from the ideology of the suffragettes but positing an alternative construction of creative individualism that married her apparently 'antimodern spiritualism' with dances 'so fluid and continuous that they appeared to be the spontaneous movements of a body propelled by a motor'.[54] Yeats shared Duncan's sense of dance and dancer as 'an indivisible unit of form and signification', and Duncan's performances may also have provided him with a suggestive visual embodiment of woman as an autonomous machine.[55]

Although Duncan saw performances of Wilde's *Salomé*, she was one of the few modern dancers who did not dance specifically as Salome; indeed, in her autobiography, she explicitly distanced herself from the reputation of this figure:

> But at least I was not Salome. I wanted the head of no one: I was never a Vampire, but always an Inspirational. If you refused me 'your lips, Johannes', and your love, I had the intelligent grace of 'Young America' to wish you Godspeed on your journey of virtue.[56]

Duncan was eager to differentiate her own metaphysical and classical conceptions of dance from the vampiric decadence she associated with Salome, as her paraphrasing of Wilde suggests. Following this passage in her autobiography, she also proceeds to define her own 'American' values against what she perceives to be Salome's libidinous orientalism. Nevertheless, Duncan's dedicated excavation of Greek imagery, drawn from both museum artefacts and the Renaissance paintings and sculpture she contemplated on her trips to Italy, speaks to her creative absorption of a pathos formula of 'ecstatic movement' centred on the expressive female body – captured, for Duncan, in the Dionysian energy of the maenad, but taking on a related form in the exoticism of Salome.[57] As we have seen, these two movement registers are intertwined, not antithetical; the Greek head-hunter whose destructive potential is encoded in her free-flowing garments and ecstatic poses readily crosses over into the veiled Salome in the dance cultures of the period, as demonstrated by Maud Allan, who integrated 'Greek' dances into the programme for her *Vision of Salome*.[58] 'Entranced by the rhythm and the flowing lines of the dancing graces', Allan also found her creative aspirations 'crystallised into a distinct idea' before Botticelli's *Primavera*, a painting that provided her with the model of grace she sought.[59] This revival of classical forms in modern dance cultures, which Taxidou links to 'a type of modernist primitivism', appealed to dramaturgs such as Craig, who set aside much of his own theatrical work during his relationship with Duncan in order to better understand her methods.[60] Indeed, there was even a dispute about which of them bore responsibility for the sparse, blue-curtained stage that was to become Craig's signature theatrical space.[61]

Recalling the first time he watched Duncan perform, Craig wrote: 'she was speaking in her own language, not echoing any ballet master, and so she came to move as no one had ever seen anyone move before'.[62] Craig would come to draw on the language of movement he had observed in Duncan's dances to articulate his vision for a revived English theatre. In his essay 'The Artists of the Theatre of the Future' (1908), he imagined an ideal artist who would bring to the theatre 'noble artificiality' and 'beauty', which he described as 'something which has the most balance about it, the *justest* thing'.[63] For Craig, beauty was dynamic and embodied, figured in terms of how it might display 'balance', which accords with his sense that movement is the underlying principle of the stage: 'all things spring from movement, even music [. . .] it is our supreme honour to be the ministers to the supreme force . . . Movement'.[64]

Reformulating Pater's dictum that 'all art constantly aspires towards the condition of music', Craig announces 'movement' as the physical, spiritual force from which all things emerge.[65] Moreover, he declares it the mission of the theatrical artist to understand and demonstrate the capacities of this energy. His concept of a mobile, dynamic theatre space, choreographed by an ideal dramaturg, translates to the sphere of drama the principles of (spontaneous yet lucid) motion that he saw in Duncan's dancing.

Real dancers, however, sometimes fell short of Craig's idealised vision of the performer. He penned a series of articles attacking the Ballets Russes in *The Mask*, including an article titled 'Kleptomania, or the Russian Ballet'. Under the pseudonym John Balance, Craig accused Diaghilev of '[stealing] an idea or two from the only original dancer of the age, the American, and another idea or two from the most advanced scene designers of Europe'.[66] He clearly considered himself one of the victims of this plagiarism, and was equally outraged by what he saw as the Russian Ballet's shameless co-option of Isadora Duncan's success. This was, however, symptomatic of the uneasiness Craig often experienced in personal relationships with dancers. Despite his effusive response to Duncan's dancing, he suggested at points during their relationship that she should give it up to support him in his own career.[67] His relationships with Diaghilev and Nijinsky also tell of personal awkwardness and missed opportunities. Although his essays declare otherwise, Craig was undeniably intrigued by the Ballets Russes, and there were even plans for him to collaborate with the group on a ballet of *Cupid and Psyche*, with Craig in charge of staging and Vaughan Williams as composer.[68] Quite why this ballet fell apart is unclear, although Roger Savage has suggested that perhaps Craig assumed responsibilities as choreographer as well, and the plans he showed Diaghilev were deemed 'too daring' even for the Ballets Russes.[69]

Yeats, on the other hand, was fascinated by the Ballets Russes performances he witnessed in May 1911, which inspired him to compose a lyric for his *Countess Cathleen*. He saw them again with Charles Ricketts in March 1913 and once more found them 'exquisite'.[70] It was through working with Craig's screens, however, that he first discovered a means of incorporating such choreographic forms into his work for the stage. Yeats felt that Craig's work in stage design was 'a perfect fulfilment of the ideal [he] had always had', and the two worked closely together on designs for future plays.[71] Yeats's plans for a reformation of the theatre in Ireland were guided, according to Mary Fleischer, by his 'interest in experimenting with patterns and rhythms inherent in the theatre's constituent media', which brought drama back to its 'origins in ritual and spiritual experience'.[72] Like Craig, Yeats published regularly on this subject in *The Mask*, writing about the value of Craig's screens to his own dramatic method in his essay 'The Tragic Theatre' (1910):

> All summer I have been playing with a little model, where there is a scene capable of endless transformation, of the expression of every mood that does not require a photographic reality. Mr. Craig, who has invented all this, has permitted me to set up upon the stage of the Abbey another scene that corresponds in the scale of a foot for an inch [...] He has banished a whole world that wearied me and was undignified and given me forms and lights upon which I can play as upon a stringed instrument.[73]

Echoing Craig's comparison of music and movement, Yeats describes the screens in terms that emphasise their malleability, an advantage he repeated in a letter to Lady Gregory: 'rapidity of change is one of [the invention's] chief merits'.[74]

Disregarding the conventional limits of the static backdrop, these screens became part of the rhetoric of movement that Craig and Yeats believed to be essential to a modern theatre, partly derived from the grammar of motion elaborated by Isadora Duncan before their eyes. In this vein, James Flannery has argued that Craig's screens offered a material realisation of the corporeal plasticity he glimpsed in Duncan's performances: 'By becoming three-dimensional, as flexible, and as interesting in itself as the body of a trained dancer, and by changing shape before the eyes of the audience, [the scenery] would provide a new kind of theatrical experience.'[75] Craig's designs thus complemented Yeats's sense of the theatre as a noble ritualistic medium, providing a means of synthesising the stage-space itself with the formalised actions and gestures of the performers. His contributions not only influenced Yeats's ideas about the staging of his plays, but also encouraged him to rethink his approach to dramatic language. Yeats revised *The Land of Heart's Desire*, *The Countess Cathleen* and *The Hour Glass* in light of his work with Craig, staging them with the new scenery in 1911 and then rewriting his texts, in Karen Dorn's words, through 'a language that not only acts with the stage space, but grows from the movement within it'.[76]

Craig's screens allowed Yeats to experiment first-hand with the physical space of the theatre – a role that might otherwise have been left to set designers. In 1910, Yeats repeated to Lady Gregory how 'exciting and exhausting' he found the work: 'a couple of hours work with it getting lighting & forms so that the picture is beautiful leave me worn out'.[77] Working with the screens encouraged Yeats to think seriously about the role of light in the theatre, and how it might fit into the themes of his drama. He became convinced that the key to discovering 'the beauty of the moving figure' was in the dance of light in space, and declared, 'we should begin our reform by [...] clearing from round the stage and above the stage everything that prevents the free playing of light'.[78] Interestingly, by late 1911 his work with the screens had evolved to incorporate other technologies. As he detailed in another letter:

'Monday I spent in the Theatre [...] showing the Craig screens. We had a man with a magic lantern & made all sorts of experiments.'[79] Magic lanterns had long been used in all kinds of entertainment forms, and, as discussed in previous chapters, Fuller was one of a number of dancers to use them in her performances. Yeats's enthusiasm for the lanterns and their ability to make 'beautiful little landscapes on the screens' shows how his thinking about stagecraft evolved from the static to the mobile, fuelled by Craig's theories of dramatic representation and action.[80] Yet Craig's input, essential as it proved, was just one aspect of Yeats's evolving choreographic imagination during this period. Real dancers, who so often collided with the 'ideal' image held by artists of the period, gave Yeats a concrete sense of how he might integrate dance movement into his plays, balancing the spare poeticism of his texts with carefully delineated gestures and physical routines. As we will see, first Michio Ito, and later Ninette de Valois, did as much as Craig, perhaps more, to shape Yeats's ideas about how the human body might become an integral part of his theatrical aesthetic and, moreover, how poetic drama might even emerge from the principles of movement.

'From behind a veil': Michio Ito and *At the Hawk's Well*

In the introduction that he wrote for Ezra Pound's *Certain Noble Plays of Japan* (1916), published by his sister Elizabeth's Cuala Press, Yeats took the opportunity to announce that he himself had 'written a little play that can be played in a room for so little money that forty or fifty readers of poetry can pay the price'.[81] The play in question was *At the Hawk's Well*, the first of Yeats's 'plays for dancers', which was performed to a select audience in Lady Cunard's drawing room on 2 April 1916. The connection with Pound's translation of Ernest Fenollosa's Nō manuscripts was an important one; for Yeats, the Nō texts were relics of an austere and sacred theatre – from them, he created his own 'form of drama, distinguished, indirect and symbolic'.[82] While some criticism has been directed at Pound and Yeats for their error-laden interpretations of the Nō sources and dramatic conventions, others have suggested that this site of cultural exchange nonetheless had a 'generative function', producing fascinating points of contact between the type of symbolic modernist drama that Yeats and Pound sought to create and what they took to be the Nō theatre's non-mimetic characteristics.[83] Their much mythologised collaborations at Stone Cottage in Sussex, where Pound intermittently worked as Yeats's secretary between 1913 and 1916, encouraged each writer's appetite for incorporating elements of this remote Japanese art form into their own work; in Yeats's case, he felt he could use the Nō's pedagogical and nationalist functions to create something similar for Dublin audiences. Rather than attempting to reconstruct an 'authentic' version of the Nō theatre, then, Yeats was eager to convey something of its 'aristocratic' spirit and 'distance from life' in his own work for the 'Irish dramatic movement'.[84] As his introduction to *Certain Noble Plays of Japan* makes clear, the role of dance in the Nō texts was one of the qualities that most interested Yeats, although in the Pound drafts he read, this dance remained, of course, merely abstract.

It was upon encountering a real dancer, Michio Ito, that *At the Hawk's Well* began to take shape as dramatic material. Through Pound, Yeats met Ito in 1915 and saw him perform a group Nō recital, along with a second dance performance in a drawing room, possibly in the home of Ito's patron, Lady Ottoline Morrell. Although Yeats came to associate Ito with the Nō tradition, Ito's background in performance was mixed: he was probably trained in Kabuki, a form of Japanese drama that blends music and dance and borrows some elements from the Nō.[85] He also studied Japanese classical dance (*nihon buyō*) and Western opera, before spending two years at Dalcroze's school of eurhythmics in Hellerau, where he was exposed to the ideas and designs of the theatre practitioner Adolphe Appia and began to devise his own choreographic techniques, which drew on these varied educations.[86] While Preston has shown that *nihon buyō* and Kabuki shared with the Nō 'similar pedagogical formats and performance philosophies' based on 'direct, teacher-to-student transmission' and the 'parrot-repetition method', Dalcroze eurhythmics probably encouraged Ito's improvisatory abilities, allowing him to combine his Japanese training and bodily practices with a European movement style based on the principle of self-expression rather than strict technique.[87] Yeats wrote of Ito:

> My play is made possible by a Japanese dancer whom I have seen dance in a studio and in a drawing-room and on a very small stage lit by an excellent stage-light. In the studio and in the drawing-room alone where the lighting was the light we are most accustomed to, did I see him as the tragic image that has stirred my imagination. There where no studied lighting, no stage picture made an artificial world, he was able, as he rose from the floor, where he had been sitting cross-legged or as he threw out an arm, to recede from us into some more powerful life.[88]

The power of Ito's effect, it is suggested here, lies in the way he 'recedes' from the spectator – a quality of estrangement that takes the dancer, paradoxically, into 'the deeps of the mind'. Yeats was enthused to discover that this form of 'separating . . . intimacy' was enhanced, even enabled by the minimalist setting – the natural light and the familiar interior – to which he was accustomed, but which became newly strange as Ito's dance commenced. Divorced from the conventions of theatrical realism, this performance in a dance studio provided Yeats with an example of what his own private form of theatre, created for a small audience in a drawing room, might achieve, confounding viewers' expectations by making them conscious of the spectacle's symbolic potency, outside the theatre's studied artifice. For Yeats, this art of the imagination retained its distance from worldly things, and all aspects of the performance 'help in keeping the door'. In Ito, Yeats believed that he had discovered a performer capable of embodying the portentous tragic symbolism of *At the Hawk's Well*, which melded narrative themes and acting methods taken from the Nō with Irish legendary sources, focused around the hero Cuchulain.

Intriguingly, Yeats describes his experience of the modern theatre up until this point as reaching him 'from behind a veil', suggesting that Ito's performance had clarified previously obscure images and sensations.[89] For Yeats, the veil was an influential metaphor for the sometimes opaque relation between the world and the vision of the artist; as he wrote in a letter to Horace Reynolds: 'All one's life one struggles towards reality, finding always but new veils.'[90] Ito's dance thus had a Salomean function: his body, for Yeats, marked the exposure of the 'tragic image' he had been seeking, perhaps because Ito was uniquely able to combine the 'ancient salt' of the Nō with the European performance styles that Yeats had already encountered through his work with Craig and his interest in Symbolist theatre.[91] Ito himself drew links between these theatrical modes in his autobiography, recalling how working with Pound opened his eyes to the curious modernity of the Nō: 'I was wondering how anything that good could come out of Japan! . . . I have been thinking that the ideas of European stage-artists of that time such as Gordon Craig and Max Reinhardt were really nothing but Noh.'[92] Yeats may have been attempting to unify these diverse forms as early as the writing of *Deirdre* in 1907, when the poet Yone Noguchi seems to have first introduced him to the Nō.[93] It was Ito, however, who made this fusion possible, encouraging Yeats to construct *At the Hawk's Well* around the language of dance.[94]

A heightened attention to gesture and rhythmical bodily movement is evident from the opening action of the play. The First Musician carries 'a folded black cloth' on to the stage with him, and when the three musicians begin to sing the first lines of the verse, they perform a ritual with the cloth:

> As they unfold the cloth, they go backward a little so that the stretched cloth and the wall make a triangle with the First Musician at the apex supporting the centre of the cloth. On the black cloth is a gold pattern suggesting a hawk. The Second and Third Musicians now slowly fold up the cloth again, pacing with a rhythmic movement of the arms towards the First Musician and singing. (*CP*, 208)

This cloth is an idea imported from the Nō, and Liam Miller interprets it as a device Yeats appropriated from his Japanese model in order to '[create] a ritual uniquely suited to his own form of drama'.[95] Like Craig's mobile screens, however, this cloth performs its metaphoric purpose choreographically. The actors' repeated gestures of folding and unfolding transform the cloth from a prop into a symbol, revealing the avian image and foregrounding the later dance of the Guardian, performed in the manner of a hawk, in the drama's visual register. In this way, Yeats creates a theatrical counterpart to Fuller's 'shining web', similarly highlighting the function of the cloth or the veil as a manipulable surface that reveals its symbols through the art of motion. Importantly, the actors' bodies are part of this ritualistic performance: they pace the stage 'with a rhythmic movement' approaching the conditions of dance.

The rhetoric of movement that Yeats develops in *At the Hawk's Well* emphasises a mechanical style of motion. According to Yeats, the Nō plays were written for 'those movements of the body copied from the marionette shows of the 14th century', which naturally bore a new relevance to his vision of the modern theatre in light of Craig's treatise on the über-marionette.[96] The Old Man who lingers by the site of a dry well treads the stage with precisely this gait: 'His movements, like those of the other persons of the play, suggest a marionette' (*CP*, 210). While audiences accustomed to naturalistic theatre might interpret the Old Man's physical bearing as indicating an absence of agency, this figure, who also appears in *The Death of Cuchulain* (1939), seems to represent a pedagogue or instructive example for the young hero Cuchulain, reflecting Yeats's interest in dynamics of learning and submission, which Preston links to the hierarchical methods of the Nō.[97] Dance also underpins the play's mythical narrative, which revolves around the hollow well, attended by a Guardian, and 'the holy shades / That dance upon the desolate mountain' (*CP*, 213), who are closely aligned with the *Sidhe* and, by association, with the dancing daughters of Herodias. At the mercy of the *Sidhe*, who control this strange and sacred region, the Old Man has spent a lifetime waiting for the well to fill with its fabled 'miraculous water'. He tells the Young Man: 'This place / Belongs to me, that girl there, and those others, / Deceivers of men' (*CP*, 213). When Cuchulain asks why he 'rail[s] / Upon those dancers that all others bless', the Old Man replies that he is 'one whom the dancers cheat' (*CP*, 213). The *Sidhe* are formless, linked to the spectral dancers of the Nō, with their leader emerging as 'the unappeasable shadow', who is 'always flitting upon this mountain side / To allure or to destroy' (*CP*, 214–15).

The action of 'flitting' conveys a ghostly lightness secured by the fact that the *Sidhe* never appear on the stage, instead transmitting their strange energies through the (female) body of the Guardian of the Well, played by Ito in 1916 and by Ninette de Valois in the 1933 revival at the Abbey. The Old Man recognises the Guardian's possession, pointing to her 'shivering' limbs as a sign that 'the terrible life / Is slipping through her veins' (*CP*, 215). He admonishes Cuchulain for looking at her: 'She has felt your gaze and turned her eyes on us; / I cannot bear her eyes, they are not of this world' (*CP*, 216). In these lines, the threatening allure of the Guardian's eyes and the dangerous spectacle she produces seem to echo Wilde's emphasis on the dangers of the gaze in *Salomé*, with the Guardian also cementing her power over the men in the play through a hypnotic dance that lulls the Old Man into sleep and causes Cuchulain to turn 'pale and stagger to his feet' (*CP*, 217), led offstage 'as if in a dream' (*CP*, 217). 'Moving like a hawk' (*CP*, 216), the Guardian's body is figured as a source of grotesque, inhuman energy; 'a horrible deathless body' (*CP*, 217) that captures something of the harsh, bestial imagery Iokanaan uses to describe Salome's visible demonstrations of bodily pleasure. Possessed by the *Sidhe*, the dancing Guardian is aligned with an idiom of corporeal ecstasy that Yeats may well have gleaned from the modern dance performances he saw, as much as from Wilde's *Salomé* or from various Irish myths of metamorphic spirits, such as the Pooka, a 'wild staring phantom' that 'has many shapes' and is 'only half in the world of form'.[98] It seems likely that Ito's choreography for this climactic dance sequence would have elaborated on the marionette movement style that Yeats required of the Old Man and the Musicians: Ito subsequently became famous, particularly in the US, for his 'marionette dance', performed to Léo Delibes's well-known 'Pizzicati' from the ballet *Sylvia*, and his students recalled how he taught them to move as if strings were attached to their fingers.[99] Preston describes Ito's dance in *Hawk's Well* as 'a hybrid of noh-like movement and *nihon buyō* with modern dance movement', with particular importance placed on the dancer's manipulation of his sleeves to represent the hawk's wings, recalling Fuller's similar use of sticks to control her veils (Fig. 4.1).[100] Indeed, when Ito performed his 'marionette dance' at the Rose Bowl in 1929, he had his body illuminated from below so that his shadow loomed behind him on a large screen, 'emphasis[ing] the dancer's body as manipulable stage material' and giving the live performance the kind of cinematic textures created by Fuller with her luminous veils decades earlier.[101]

Whether or not Ito had his work with Yeats in mind at this point, his shadow screen performance harks back to the modernist experiments with space and design, influenced by Craig, that defined the first production of *At the Hawk's Well*, a play Ito himself revived for New York's Greenwich Theatre in 1918. He would subsequently stage the play elsewhere in the US and then in Tokyo in 1940, just one year before he was arrested – and later deported – as a result of American hostility towards Japanese migrants in the wake of Pearl Harbor. Yet the performance archive concentrated around *Hawk's Well*, Preston argues, ought to 'serve as an exemplary case study in modernist transnational circuits', both in terms of its collaborative histories and networks of exchange, and its thematic complexities.[102] The play is an amalgamation of mythical-cultural imagery, from the 'noble half-Greek, half-Asiatic' design of Edmund Dulac's masks and the exotic notes of the score, to the Japanese and European influences in Ito's choreography.[103] The Irish legendary setting appears to venerate the patient toil of the Old Man and the heroism of Cuchulain, while at the same time offering a possible critique of the very myths it reproduces:

4.1 Michio Ito as 'the Hawk' in W. B. Yeats's play *At the Hawk's Well* (1916). Photograph by Alvin Langdon Coburn. George Eastman Museum

the *Sidhe* are not a redemptive or unifying force for the Irish nation, but rather a kind of spectral menace, enacting their own insidious form of occupation in the 'deathless' possession of the Guardian's body. Much like the daughter of Herodias – with whom they are closely aligned in Yeats's mind – the dancing *Sidhe* carry a disruptive and often conflicted political energy, revealing both the seductiveness and the dangers of collective violence, soon to be signalled by the 'barbarous clangour of a gong' that spurs on the dancers in 'Nineteen Hundred and Nineteen' (*VP*, 430). After Ito left for the United States in December 1916, Yeats had to wait for another performer to realise his very particular vision of a national dramatic form, which increasingly saw him return to the fraught but familiar symbols of the ambiguously dancing woman and the severed head she craves.

'Dance, woman, dance!': Ninette de Valois at the Abbey Theatre

The performer who helped Yeats to achieve these theatrical ambitions was the Irish dancer Ninette de Valois. Yeats met her at Cambridge's Festival Theatre in May 1927.[104] They spoke over breakfast on a Sunday morning; Yeats had seen her the previous evening in a production of *The Player Queen* and was struck by her 'inventive genius'.[105] He held her interest with talk of his dance-dramas and proposed that de Valois come to the Abbey Theatre in order to establish a school of ballet, promising her practical experience in managing an artistic company. As de Valois records of the meeting:

> I would visit Dublin every three months and produce his Plays for Dancers and perform in them myself; thus, he said the poetic drama of Ireland would live again and take its rightful place in the Nation's own Theatre, and the oblivion imposed on it by the popularity of peasant drama would become a thing of the past.[106]

For de Valois, who would go on to found the Royal Ballet, the prospect of working with the creative contingent at the Abbey Theatre was exhilarating: 'I would work among those people whose efforts to establish the Irish Theatre were in progress at the time that I struggled with an Irish jig in a farmhouse at the foot of the Wicklow Hills.'[107] If a nostalgic de Valois was invigorated by the opportunity to align her expertise with the vision of Ireland's national theatre, Yeats was eager to find a dancer who, like Michio Ito, could help him to hone and develop the choreographic elements of his plays. He had been dissatisfied with the amateur dancing in the 1926 double bill of *The Only Jealousy of Emer* and *The Cat and the Moon*, and he understood the credibility that a trained professional such as de Valois could bring to the realisation of his dramatic concepts.[108] De Valois had received her classical education from the ballet masters Enrico Cecchetti and Nicholas Legat, but she was also in the unusual position – for an Irish dancer – of having joined Diaghilev's Ballets Russes in 1923, gaining valuable experience of working with innovative designers and modern ballet choreographers including Bronislava Nijinska and Georges Balanchine. Under Diaghilev's guidance, de Valois claimed, she 'became aware of a new world, a world that held the secrets of that aesthetic knowledge that [she] sought', based on the principle of 'perfect unity in a creative work'.[109] De Valois's appreciation of the connections between ballet and the other stage arts chimed with Yeats's outlook: in 1926, she wrote in *The Dancing Times* that 'the true aim of modern ballet' was to build on 'the authentic methods of the classical ballet' while also expanding 'the art of dancing in harmony with the other arts of the theatre'.[110]

As de Valois's recollections of her move to the Abbey suggest, her decision to work with Yeats was also influenced by her fondness for the familiar rhythms of Irish theatre and culture, perhaps a consequence of those years spent touring with Diaghilev's company – a period of revelation but also rootless mobility. 'The Irish', de Valois writes in her autobiography, 'are natural actors', with a wonderful 'sense of timing and interplay', and an intuitive understanding of the musicality of language: 'they can all intone; with them the "keen" becomes a strange chant'.[111] Betraying hints of an exoticising Celticism that reflects Michio Ito's willingness to play on orientalist stereotypes for both his London patrons and his wider audiences, de Valois's descriptions of Irish performance nonetheless resonate with Yeats's own desire to resurrect the bardic arts, an ambition grounded in his vision of a culturally authentic theatre that would, as Ronald Schuchard puts it, see 'the living voices of a chanting tradition that had retreated into solitary walkways and private quarters [brought] back into the public realm'.[112] Yeats's long-standing interest in bardic chanting was connected to his appreciation for dance, notably through the activities of his collaborator Florence Farr. Inspired by Nietzsche's celebration of dance in *Thus Spoke Zarathustra*, Farr established a company called 'The Dancers' in order to support poetic drama: the troupe performed in Yeats's *Cathleen Ni Houlihan* and provided the Dionysian chorus for a production of Euripides' *Hippolytus*.[113] De Valois too was intrigued by the embedding of dance in the dramatic action of Greek tragedy, a tradition in which she had become immersed at the Festival Theatre under the directorship of her cousin Terence Gray.

A disciple of German Expressionism, Gray had turned the Festival Theatre into a hive of avant-garde innovation, moving firmly away from the tenets of realism and naturalism. Indeed, the stage at the Festival Theatre, devoid of a proscenium arch and characterised by a large central staircase that connected the audience to the actors, was 'so designed that conventional realistic production was almost impossible'.[114] De Valois called the arrangement of the theatrical space 'the last thing in modernity', remembering her time there as an 'exhilarating' opportunity to marry her technical knowledge of dance with the other creative elements of stage performance.[115] Gray engaged de Valois in the movement design for his productions: her work included choreographing the Greek chorus for a 1926 staging of the *Oresteia*, and the lead role in Yeats's *The Player Queen*. She also contributed choreographies to a number of productions of Wilde's *Salomé*, which Gray produced in 1929 and 1931. In Gray's opinion, the 'dramatic value' of Wilde's play was realised through an emphasis on 'stylisation, artifice, rhythmic structure, musical repetition and "expressionist" methods', aligning Wilde's Symbolist text with the forms of the 'Greek chorus [. . .] unsullied by Realism or Romanticism'.[116] The design for this production brilliantly conferred these artificial effects: a 'massive, stylised [. . .] staircase' topped with three irregular thrones, and 'huge cylindrical columns' created an imposing display of 'abstract power' not confined to any particular historical setting.[117] This abstract design, with its elaborate variety of lines, angles and shapes, made the stage itself a site in which objects and space were carefully choreographed, echoing Craig's belief that dramatic movement was best realised within a dynamic stage setting. Indeed, the daunting columns that featured in Gray's production of *Salomé* reflect the starkly rendered pillars that dominate the stage in Craig's model for a 1912 production of *Hamlet* and many of his other sketches that similarly played with height and proportion through such structures.[118]

De Valois returned to Salome's dance on a number of occasions during this period of her career. Along with choreographing the dances for Vivienne Bennett and Beatrix Lehmann in the two Festival Theatre productions of *Salomé*, de Valois also performed the dance herself in *The Dancer's Reward* and devised a dance of the seven veils for Margaret Rawlings, who played the lead role in Peter Godfrey's 1931 staging of Wilde's play at the Gate Theatre Studio in London.[119] Intriguingly, the veils in this production were not wrapped around the dancer's body but arranged across the stage, 'withdrawn one by one to discover the rhythmically moving limbs of Salome', integrating the stage space into the choreography in a manner most recently seen in Yaël Farber's *Salome* (2017).[120] One bewildered commentator, while commending Rawlings's spirit, was unconvinced by the dance's erotic promise, suggesting that the performance 'seemed of a nature to warm a professor of calisthenics rather than to convulse an unholy hedonist'.[121] It seems that de Valois's interpretation of the role did not align with the more explicitly sexualised depictions of Salome, perhaps favouring instead a style indebted to the expressive individualism of rhythmic gymnastics or calisthenics, part of Dalcroze's programme of eurhythmics at Hellerau. De Valois's collaborations with these Salome dancers certainly left their mark: many years later, she recalled Margaret Rawlings's impressive choreographic instincts during their work on *Salomé*, writing: 'I know no actress with a greater sense of natural movement than hers.'[122] Vivienne Bennett, whose dance of the seven veils de Valois arranged, was also a colleague at the Abbey Theatre and oversaw the opening of the ballet school.[123]

As Yeats had intended, de Valois's broader activities at the Abbey School of Ballet had a profound effect on the development of dance in Ireland. Many of the Abbey Theatre programmes between 1928 and 1934 list ballet school performances alongside the main theatrical productions. A performance of Lennox Robinson's *The White Blackbird* in April 1928 was followed by de Valois and her pupils dancing to music by Chopin and Glière, as well as a Mexican solo dance by de Valois, drawing together elements from diverse international dance traditions in a single evening.[124] In November 1929, Lady Gregory's *Spreading the News* and Yeats's *Oedipus the King* were produced alongside a 'Turkish Ballet', a solo by de Valois called 'A Daughter of Eve', and four other short dance pieces.[125] Victoria O'Brien claims that the school probably 'produced the first generation of classically trained dancers, teachers, choreographers and artistic directors that had been trained in Ireland'.[126] Carrying the imprint of her training under Cecchetti and Legat, along with the pioneering choreographers of the Ballets Russes, de Valois influenced the technique of her Irish pupils and exposed audiences in Dublin to modern ballets in their national theatre space. This major shift in the landscape of Irish performance culture stemmed from a conversation between Yeats and de Valois in 1927. By this point, Yeats's vision of a national literary theatre had clearly expanded to include dance as a discipline in its own right, which could be showcased alongside the output of Ireland's foremost playwrights and integrated into their dramatic works. Moreover, following de Valois's work on three separate productions of *Salomé* between 1929 and 1931, Yeats's plays for dancers began to demonstrate an even deeper preoccupation with the Wildean drama that had left its traces in his poetic idiolect for decades.

The Abbey Theatre programme for 30 July 1934 lists the first performances of Yeats's *The King of the Great Clock Tower*, the play that bears perhaps the strongest comparison to Wilde's *Salomé* in Yeats's body of work.[127] In the short preface Yeats wrote for the first performances of *Clock Tower* at the Abbey, he accepted Wilde's influence to a degree, acknowledging that he had adopted 'the symbol used by Wilde in his *Salome*'.[128] On a cultural and historical level, however, Yeats separated his play from Wilde's, claiming he had adapted the Salome theme to the framework of a related Irish myth: 'In an Irish form of perhaps the same symbol there is no dance, but the head of a slain lover singing to his mistress. I have combined dance and song.'[129] Wilde's source material, according to Yeats, was Jewish, filtered through the German writer Heinrich Heine's long poem *Atta Troll*. Yeats's mythical drama, on the other hand, apparently derived from an old Irish narrative – a narrative omitting the dance that becomes such a crucial device in *Clock Tower*. Despite the cagy tone of Yeats's commentaries, his play bears the traces of his profound engagement with previous representations of this figure, including those he found in Wilde and Symons, and in the modern dance cultures with which he was clearly well acquainted. It is also significant that Yeats began to consciously engage with this complex literary material in the wake of his leading dancer's choreographic work on a number of *Salomé* productions.

Yeats's distancing of his own play from Wilde's 'Jewish' material is troubling in the context of his political activities during this period. It is well known that in 1933, Yeats spent a number of months in the company of the Irish Blueshirt General Eoin O'Duffy and composed a selection of marching songs for the Blueshirts, believing the paramilitary group to be a tool against chaos and social disorder.[130] Although he later disavowed this period of fascist sympathy – as he often disavowed his overtly political statements – it sits very uneasily alongside his rejection of Wilde's Jewish source in favour of an Irish myth, suggesting some form of attempt to cleanse the theme of any racial and religious elements that did not reflect his particular version of Irish culture.[131] Yeats had betrayed his anti-Jewish feeling in a letter of 1931 to Olivia Shakespear, in which he wrote about his admiration for the 'generation of Bergson', but added that he 'hate[d] the Jewish element in Bergson, the deification of the moment, that for minds less hard & masculine than [Henri Gaudier-Brzeska's] turned the world into fruit-salad'.[132] Antisemitism is here compounded with homophobia, with the 'Jewish element', for Yeats, representing something corrosive and feminine, almost queer, and certainly not masculine. Read alongside Yeats's denial of Wilde's influence – which is also a denial of a queer author's hand – his recreation of the Salome narrative becomes a political as well as a literary act, emerging from a particularly unsavoury period of right-wing collusion.

Without attempting to sanitise Yeats's political leanings or flatten the complexities of his refashioning of the Salome theme, it is possible to hold the paradoxes of his work in view, acknowledging moments of productive ambivalence in his engagement with dance as a vital element of Irish national drama. In his introduction for the Cuala edition of *The King of the Great Clock Tower*, he again confronts the spectre of Wilde, arguing that the older Irishman 'had not made this legend his property' and suggesting that his own play 'might give it a different setting':

> In the first edition of The Secret
> Rose there is a story bassed on so some old Gaelic legend
> A certain man swears to sing the praise of a certain
> Woman, his head is cut off & the head sings.
> A poem of mine ~~beg~~ called 'He gives his Beloved Certain
> Rhymes' was the song of the head. In attempting to
> Put this story into a dance play I found that I had
> Recreated ~~the S this~~ Salome's dance.[133]

The deletions in the last line are perhaps a telling indicator of Yeats's uncertainty about the true extent of his 'recreation'. The themes of *Clock Tower* certainly bear striking similarities to Wilde's *Salomé*, despite Yeats's attempt to link the play to his own poetry, and his insistence that the 'different setting' puts distance between the two works. These moments of doubt, inscribed in the manuscripts, foreground the intertextuality of *The King of the Great Clock Tower*, suggesting that previous iterations of Yeats's theme press through the surface of the text even as he attempts to wrestle the subject into a design of his own making.

In any case, commentators at the time were evidently conscious of the play's relevant precursors. Reflecting the pensive mysticism of *At the Hawk's Well*,

Yeats's *Clock Tower* is a drama of a remote place and time, described by a *Sunday Times* critic as 'an adaptation to an Irish legendary setting of the theme of Salome'.[134] The eponymous King is frustrated by the enduring silence of his Queen, who has been mute ever since she arrived at the Clock Tower one year previously. Unnerved, the King questions; 'Why sit you there / Dumb as an image made of wood or metal, / A screen between the living and the dead?' (*CP*, 634). Yeats's language calls attention to the play's design elements, particularly the Queen's 'beautiful impassive mask' (*CP*, 633), which quite literally renders her face 'an image made of wood', perhaps securing the impersonality Yeats sought in his performers. From the outset, the Queen is presented as a curious extension of this stage; her form is material, inarticulate and not quite human, much like the blue Craig screens that frame the fictive world. Richard Allen Cave suggests that it would take 'the discipline of a trained dancer' to 'achieve the palpably live but marmoreal stillness that is required here'.[135] As such, the Queen comes close to embodying the kind of actor Craig celebrated in his essay on the über-marionette: a manipulable symbol, wrought from the same stuff as the theatre's other controllable elements. The tableau itself, Cave notes, is strikingly similar to the stage design for both Charles Ricketts's *Salomé*, which Yeats saw in 1906, and Terence Gray's production, replicating both 'the encompassing curves of the cyclorama' and 'the dominant background colouring in shades of blue'.[136] Moreover, much as *Salomé* is framed by historical contexts of occupation and displacement, Yeats's anxious King seems to view his Queen as a kind of interloper: 'I put you on that throne [. . .] / I ask your country, name and family, / And not for the first time' (*CP*, 634). Like Salome, whose actions might be read as a seditious attempt to claim political agency, Yeats's Queen seems to pose a silent threat to the stability of monarchic rule, representing an unknown foreign influence within the King's state.

This royal stalemate is disrupted by the arrival of a Stroller, who announces that he has come to see the renowned beauty of the Queen for himself. To the King's horror he brazenly declares that the Queen shall dance for him, and in return he will sing for her and receive a kiss: 'Your Queen, my mouth, the Queen shall kiss my mouth' (*CP*, 637). As Doody and others have noted, the familiar images of the dance, the head and the kiss are all in evidence.[137] Once more, the dance performance becomes the play's critical nexus, focusing the opposing desires and acquisitive energies of the male characters. Unlike Wilde's Salome, however, the Queen does not encourage and divide her pursuers through speech, but remains silent, expressing herself only through a vocabulary of gestures, supported by the ventriloquism of others. At one point, the Second Attendant is possessed by the Queen's distant voice, singing her song of strange violence and sexual conquest: 'He longs to kill / My body, until / That sudden shudder / And limbs lie still' (*CP*, 638). The shudder of sexual ecstasy is framed as a climax of violence that recalls both the prostrations of

Wilde's Salome before her bloody prize and 'the sudden blow' and 'shudder' of the female body in 'Leda and the Swan' (*VP*, 441), further intertextual traces that connect the figures of Leda and Salome. This song precedes the Queen's dance, and although Yeats does not explicitly describe the performance in the stage directions, the tempo of the language suggests a building intensity and speed to the Queen's movements, with the King repeating his command: 'Dance, woman, dance!' (*CP*, 639). Reviewers were captivated by de Valois's performance in this role, with the *Irish Times* theatre correspondent writing that 'those of us who had not seen Miss Ninette de Valois before were amazed by the beauty of her dancing'.[138]

If the possessed body of the Guardian in *At the Hawk's Well* seemed to locate the dancer's energy in some external source, the ventriloquism in *The King of the Great Clock Tower* achieves a different effect. Transmitting her song through the other players on the stage, the dancing Queen is able to inhabit bodies that are not her own. Her muteness, ostensibly a sign of feminine passivity in the face of royal male authority, belies the extent of her bodily presence, which allows her vocal power to be uncannily redistributed. The Queen's silently dancing form therefore marks a rupture in the corporeal economy of the play, as she emerges as the author, not only of her own bodily language, but of the voices pressed through the mouths of the musicians. Crucially, her movements also enliven the morbid object she carries in her hands: the severed head of the Stroller (represented by a mask). 'His eyelids tremble, his lips begin to move' (*CP*, 639), frets the anxious King, as the decollated face vibrates, and begins to sing. The ghost of an all too real body lingers behind this motif, if, as Kimberly Myers argues, the severed head constitutes Yeats's attempt to work through the issue of sexual impotence and the regeneration he experienced after his Steinach operation in April 1934.[139] Previously described as a 'screen between the living and the dead', the dancing Queen lifts the veil separating inert and animated matter, restoring vitality to the limp object she carries.

Myers's psychoanalytic reading of the severed head certainly aligns with similar interpretations of Salome as a figure encoded with repressive anxieties – the 'horror of virginity' in Mallarmé's terms. In his essay 'The Taboo of Virginity' (1917), Freud uses the myth of Judith and Holofernes, another decapitation narrative, to theorise the female instinct to 'take vengeance for her defloration', which, in Judith's case, is both sexual (as a symbolic act of castration) and political: killing Holofernes, she becomes 'the liberator of her people'.[140] A similar principle applies to Salome, who also seeks revenge after what might be considered a sexual rite of passage, although she is finally punished, in Wilde's version at least, by the restoration of monarchic power. However, in *The King of the Great Clock Tower*, Yeats, unlike Wilde, does not encode the final retaliation of patriarchal authority into the play's structure. The King, having 'risen and drawn his sword' to mirror Herod's violence, 'appears about to strike [the Queen], but kneels, laying the sword at her feet' (*CP*, 640). This symbolic show of deference to female rule recasts the Queen's dance as an act, not of amatory seduction, but of political self-determination. Her mute choreography thus redirects the source of meaning in the play from speech to gesture, and from words to bodies, turning her dancing form into the drama's central dispenser of authorial signification.

In the role of the Queen, then, Ninette de Valois emerges as a decisive creative force within the work. She carefully choreographed the dance, drawing on her training in mime as well as her experience of working for Terence Gray on his expressionist productions of Greek tragedies.[141] In her autobiography, she describes the extent of her own influence on the dance-dramas, recalling that Yeats 're-wrote *The King of the Great Clock Tower* and *The Only Jealousy of Emer* so that the "Queen" in the former and the "Woman of the Sidhe" in the latter could be interpreted by me in dance mime, wearing masks for both roles'.[142] Cave has persuasively shown that 'what is remarkable about the sequence of manuscript materials for *The King of the Great Clock Tower* [...] is that they allow one to watch a *performance text* steadily come into being'.[143] The revisions Yeats made in 1934 were responsive to the demands of real performance; for instance, he restructured the text around the dance to allow de Valois 'moments of repose', showing 'a finer awareness of the need for pacing'.[144] In the Cuala edition, he also acknowledged the centrality of de Valois's technical abilities to the unity of the play, describing it as 'a romantic setting for a dance by Miss Nanette [*sic*] de Valois', designed to showcase her 'skilful, charming, muscular body'.[145] While it is difficult to determine exactly how de Valois arranged the choreography for the Queen's dance – described by Yeats as an 'expression of horror and fascination' – it is clear that it was performed as a *pas de deux* between the Queen and the severed head, with the Stroller's mask operating as a focal point for the dancer's attention as she raises it in her hands and, at one point, places it on her shoulder.[146] Cave suggests that these directions render Yeats's Queen 'a wholly original creation' since she is 'engaged not in solo-work but in a *pas de deux*, where *she* is the supporting partner', a role usually taken by the male dancer in classical ballet.[147] While this choreographic arrangement certainly differs from Wilde's dance of the seven veils – performed by Salome prior to Iokanaan's execution – it does echo the structure of the Ballets Russes' *La Tragédie de Salomé*, which similarly focused the audience's attention on the dynamic between the frenetically dancing Karsavina and the prop of the severed head. Much as Diaghilev framed that ballet as an opportunity for his leading female soloist to demonstrate her abilities, Yeats conceived of *The King of the Great Clock Tower* in part as a declaration of gratitude to de Valois for her commitment to the Abbey School of Ballet; the play was deemed an appropriate vessel for the dancer's talents in what would be her final performance at the Abbey Theatre.

'There must be severed heads': Yeats's Departed Dancers

Yeats's numerous defences and clarifications on the subject of Wilde's influence have led scholars to look closely at the precedent that *Salomé* set for the dance-dramas. Certainly, there are comparisons to be made at the level of symbolism: fateful gazes, violent dancers and severed heads recur in Yeats's work, particularly from *At the Hawk's Well* onwards. Yeats's collaborations with dancers, however, set him apart from Wilde, who did not have the opportunity to work closely with a performer to determine how the choreography would shape the realisation of *Salomé*. Indeed, in his thinking about physical performance, Yeats was conscious of the need for real dancers to bring life to the visual promise of language. He wrote to his father: 'Rhythm implies a living body a breast to rise & fall or limbs that dance while the abstract [is] incompatible with life.'[148] It is this 'living body' that he summons in his final play, *The Death of Cuchulain*, which opens with an Old Man's impassioned call for a real dancer:

> I promise a dance. I wanted a dance because where there are no words there is less to spoil. Emer must dance, there must be severed heads – I am old, I belong to mythology – severed heads for her to dance before. I had thought to have had those heads carved, but no, if the dancer can dance properly no wood-carving can look as well as a parallelogram of painted wood. But I was at my wit's end to find a good dancer; I could have got such a dancer once, but she has gone; the tragi-comedian dancer, the tragic dancer, upon the same neck love and loathing, life and death. I spit three times. I spit upon the dancers painted by Degas. I spit upon their short bodies, their stiff stays, their toes whereon they spin like peg-tops, above all upon that chambermaid face. (*CP*, 694)

As in *At the Hawk's Well*, the Old Man, though enfeebled by age, is figured as an instructive presence for both the play's other characters and the audience he addresses. In this soliloquy, Yeats uses the Old Man's voice to explicate the relationship between text and performance, articulating the very difficulties that he himself faced throughout his career writing plays for dancers. This Old Man too is at his 'wit's end to find a good dancer', following the departure of 'the tragic dancer' who could have done the performance justice, perhaps Michio Ito or Ninette de Valois, both long 'gone' from the Abbey. The violence with which the Old Man rejects the romantic ballerinas painted in a famous series by Edgar Degas is telling: Yeats decries the 'stiffness' of their bodies, suggesting that his own choreographic preferences lie elsewhere, in the freer movement forms practised by modern dancers such as Isadora Duncan and Loïe Fuller, or the strains of expressionism and mime that shaped the dances of even a classically trained performer such as de Valois. Yeats's ruminations on dance in *The Death of Cuchulain* importantly suggest that he placed a high value on the performer who danced with a sense of creative intent and individualism, rather than strictly adhering to predetermined attitudes or external directions.

Once again, it is a familiar figure who dances, veiled, at the heart of these plays. 'There must be severed heads', insists the Old Man. The 'parallelogram of painted wood' that signifies the hero's head in *The Death of Cuchulain* is a curious prop, stationed somewhere between the mask and the screen in the complex material world of Yeats's stage. For some critics, this parallelogram indicates that Yeats was finally able to 'rely on the unsettled and irreconcilable nature of the material', a difficulty that he had consistently encountered in his dealings with the severed head as an object and its communicative power, as demonstrated by the singing mask in *The King of the Great Clock Tower*.[149] An object inscribed with violent and erotic potentiality, the severed head is used to signal liveliness and renewal, in spite of its suggestion of execution: its muteness, its stillness. Indeed, the moment of Cuchulain's decapitation in this play marks the beginning of Emer's dance, directed by the Morrigu, 'a woman with a crow's head' holding 'a black parallelogram', with 'six other parallelograms near the backcloth' (*CP*, 703). For the Morrigu, these objects represent the heads of those who inflicted Cuchulain's 'six mortal wounds'; seven in total, the parallelograms symbolically denote a Yeatsian dance of the seven veils, charging the artificial space of the stage with a transformative energy, mirrored by the actors as 'Emer runs in and begins to dance' (*CP*, 703). An earlier moment in the play has already established the close relationship between the wounded body and the veil: when Aoife, the mother of Cuchulain's son, uses her veil to bind him to a pillar, she tells him 'I wind my veil about this ancient stone / And fasten you to it' (*CP*, 700), causing him to regret that she has 'spoil[ed] her veil' (*CP*, 700) with his blood. The woman's veil and the injured male form are thus conjoined in the powerful image of Cuchulain as an almost sacrificial figure, feminised by Aoife's drapery; the tableau recalls similar religious emblems of Christ and Saint Sebastian.

As in Yeats's earlier plays, there is no easy reconciliation between the performance's various cultural and aesthetic registers: between the figurative and the embodied, the abstract and the historically specific, the national and the global. At the end of her dance, Emer, hearing the music of a contemporary 'Irish fair', 'stands motionless' between 'the head [of Cuchulain] and what she hears' (*CP*, 704): a dancer doubtfully positioned in the gap between the ancient mythical deed and the intrusion of twentieth-century Irish culture. The stage darkens and when the lights come up, Emer and the head have vanished, though the singer who closes the play hauntingly comments on the use of Oliver Sheppard's Cuchulain statue as a memorial to Patrick Pearse and James Connolly, leaders in the Easter Rising:

> What stood in the Post Office
> With Pearse and Connolly?
> What comes out of the mountain
> Where men first shed their blood?
> Who thought Cuchulain till it seemed
> He stood where they had stood? (CP, 704–5)

While the statue, installed in the General Post Office by Eamon de Valera in 1935, troublingly entwines national mythology with the violence of the uprising, it was crucially, for Yeats, the dancer who paused in the face of such memorialisation: though the actress playing Emer 'moves as if in adoration or triumph' (CP, 703) towards the 'pedestal' venerating Cuchulain's head, she 'seems to hesitate' (CP, 704) at the sound of the music, her body forming a subtle challenge to the interlinking of the legendary execution and the modern political forces that would aim to co-opt such imagery. It seems significant that it should be the body of the female dancer that transcribes Yeats's own hesitations and contradictory views regarding Ireland's national literary movement, especially in the climate of the late 1930s. For Eliot, it was through the 'gradual purging out of poetic ornament' in the later plays for dancers that Yeats discovered 'his right and final dramatic form'.[150] Yeats's admission, in the Old Man's speech, that he 'wanted a dance because where there are no words there is less to spoil' taps into a particular anxiety around the capacity of words to speak truly, a scepticism about language that reaches its pause-laden apex in Samuel Beckett's tightly choreographed dramas.

Notes

1. Tydeman and Price, *Wilde: Salome*, 40.
2. WBY to John Quinn, 29 May [1905], *CL InteLex* 160.
3. Ibid.
4. WBY to T. Sturge Moore, 6 May [1906], *CL InteLex* 401.
5. W. B. Yeats, *A Vision: The Original 1925 Version*, ed. Catherine E. Paul and Margaret Mills Harper, vol. 13 of *The Collected Works of W. B. Yeats* (New York: Scribner, 2008), 154.
6. Kermode, *Romantic Image*, 75.
7. Yeats, *A Vision*, 154.
8. Ibid., 154.
9. Ibid., 154. The poem 'Leda and the Swan' opens Book III, with Yeats outlining the centrality of this myth to his understanding of historical cycles: 'I imagine the annunciation that founded Greece as made to Leda' (151).
10. Kermode, *Romantic Image*, 76.
11. W. B. Yeats, 'The Theatre', in *The Major Works*, ed. Edward Larrissy (Oxford: Oxford University Press, 2001), 366.
12. Sylvia Ellis, *The Plays of W. B. Yeats: Yeats and the Dancer* (Basingstoke: Palgrave Macmillan, 1995), 162.
13. Ibid., 355.
14. W. B. Yeats, 'Preface', in *Four Plays for Dancers* (London: Macmillan, 1921), v.

15. John Kelly records Yeats's attendance at Duncan's performance in *A W. B. Yeats Chronology* (Basingstoke: Palgrave Macmillan, 2003), 65. Teri A. Mester offers the detail about Ruth St Denis in *Movement and Modernism*, 10.
16. Kelly, *Yeats Chronology*, 149, 162.
17. Mary Fleischer, *Embodied Texts: Symbolist Playwright–Dancer Collaborations* (Amsterdam: Rodopi, 2007), 159.
18. WBY to T. Sturge Moore, 6 May [1906], *CL InteLex* 401.
19. Yeats, *The Trembling of the Veil*, 124.
20. WBY to Edward Dowden, 6 January [1895], *CL InteLex* 18.
21. WBY to J. B. Yeats, 21 July [1906], *CL InteLex* 435.
22. Yeats, 'The Theatre', 368.
23. Charles I. Armstrong, *Reframing Yeats: Genre, Allusion, and History* (London: Bloomsbury, 2013), 63–76.
24. Noreen Doody, '"An Echo of Someone Else's Music": The Influence of Oscar Wilde on W. B. Yeats', in *The Importance of Reinventing Oscar: Versions of Wilde During the Last 100 Years*, ed. Uwe Böker et. al (New York: Rodopi, 2002), 178. See also Noreen Doody, *The Influence of Oscar Wilde on W. B. Yeats: 'An Echo of Someone Else's Music'* (Basingstoke: Palgrave Macmillan, 2018); Marilyn Gaddis Rose, 'The Daughters of Herodias in *Hérodiade*, *Salomé*, and *A Full Moon in March*', *Comparative Drama* 1.3 (1967): 172–81.
25. Doody, 'An Echo of Someone Else's Music', 178.
26. Harold Bloom, *The Anxiety of Influence* (Oxford: Oxford University Press, 1997).
27. Jones, *Literature, Modernism and Dance*, 36.
28. Warburg, quoted in Gombrich, *Aby Warburg*, 113.
29. Arthur Symons, 'The Dance of the Daughters of Herodias', in *Poems by Arthur Symons*, vol. 2 (London: William Heinemann, 1902), 103.
30. Ellen Crowell, 'The Ugly Things of *Salome*', in *Decadence in the Age of Modernism*, ed. Kate Hext and Alex Murray (Baltimore, MD: Johns Hopkins University Press, 2019), 48.
31. Symons, 'The Dance of the Daughters of Herodias', 103.
32. Jones makes this observation about Sada Yacco. See *Literature, Modernism and Dance*, 30n54.
33. Roy Foster, *W. B. Yeats: A Life: Vol. II, The Arch Poet, 1915–39* (Oxford: Oxford University Press, 2003), 197.
34. WBY to Nancy Maude, 20 November [1907], *CL InteLex* 701.
35. W. B. Yeats, 'Introduction and headnotes to *Fairy and Folktales of the Irish Peasantry*, ed. by W. B. Yeats (1888)', in *Prefaces and Introductions*, ed. William H. O'Donnell, vol. 6 of *The Collected Works of W. B. Yeats* (New York: Macmillan, 1989), 11.
36. W. B. Yeats, 'The Celtic Element in Literature', in *The Major Works*, 378.
37. Yeats, *The Trembling of the Veil*, 234.
38. Michael McAteer, *Yeats and European Drama* (Cambridge: Cambridge University Press, 2010), 39.
39. McAteer has also recently compared the way Maeterlinck and Yeats use 'gesture and vocal delivery for the sake of spiritual or psychic movement'. See 'Music, Setting, Voice: Maeterlinck's *Pelléas et Mélisande* and Yeats's *The Countess Cathleen*', *International Yeats Studies* 2.1 (2017): Article 2.
40. Worth, *The Irish Drama of Europe*, 24, 37.
41. WBY to W.G. Fay, 13 August [1906], *CL InteLex* 453.
42. McAteer, *Yeats and European Drama*, 50.
43. Ibid., 6.

44. W. B. Yeats, 'Two Poems Concerning Peasant Visionaries', *The Savoy: An Illustrated Monthly*, April 1896, 109. Yeats substantially revised both 'A Cradle Song' (retitled 'The Unappeasable Host') and 'The Valley of the Black Pig': see *VP*, 146, 161.
45. Jones, *Literature, Modernism and Dance*, 39.
46. T. S. Eliot, 'Yeats', in *The Complete Prose of T. S. Eliot: The Critical Edition*, vol. 6, *The War Years: 1940–1946*, ed. David E. Chinitz and Ronald Schuchard (Baltimore, MD: Johns Hopkins University Press, 2017), 87.
47. Kelly, *Yeats Chronology*, 74.
48. WBY to Edward Gordon Craig, 2 April [1901], *CL InteLex* 32.
49. Edward Gordon Craig, 'The Actor and the Über-Marionette', in *Craig on Theatre*, ed. Michael J. Walton (London: Methuen Drama, 1983), 84.
50. Yeats, quoted in Taxidou, *Modernism and Performance*, 82.
51. Craig, *Craig on Theatre*, 86.
52. Taxidou, *Modernism and Performance*, 22–33.
53. Arnold Rood, introduction to *Craig on Movement and Dance*, by Edward Gordon Craig (New York: Dance Horizons, 1977), xiii–xiv.
54. Preston, *Modernism's Mythic Pose*, 188, 190. See also Roger Copeland, 'Dance, Feminism and the Critique of the Visual', in *Dance, Gender and Culture*, ed. Helen Thomas (London: Macmillan, 1993), 139–50; Ann Daly, 'Dance History and Feminist Theory: Reconsidering Isadora Duncan and the Male Gaze', in *Gender in Performance: The Presentation of Difference in the Performing Arts*, ed. Laurence Senelick (Hanover, NH: University Press of New England, 1993), 239–59.
55. Ellis, *The Plays of W. B. Yeats*, 196.
56. Duncan, *My Life*, 192.
57. Brandstetter, *Poetics of Dance*, 153–4.
58. Felix Cherniavsky, 'Maud Allan Part II: First Steps to a Dancing Career, 1904–1907', *Dance Chronicle* 6.3 (1982), 207.
59. Allan, *My Life and Dancing*, 53.
60. Olga Taxidou, '"Do not call me a dancer": Dance and Modernist Experimentation', in Bradshaw, Marcus and Roach, eds, *Moving Modernisms*, 110.
61. Brandstetter, *Poetics of Dance*, 155.
62. Edward Gordon Craig, quoted in *Craig on Movement*, xiv.
63. Craig, 'The Artists of the Theatre of the Future', in *Craig on Movement*, 28.
64. Ibid., 33.
65. Walter Pater, *Studies in the History of the Renaissance*, ed. Matthew Beaumont (Oxford: Oxford University Press, 2010), 124.
66. Craig, 'Kleptomania, or the Russian Ballet', in *Craig on Movement*, 81.
67. Renée Vincent, 'The Influences of Isadora Duncan on the Designs of Edward Gordon Craig', *Theatre Design and Technology* 34.1 (1998): 37–48.
68. Craig issued a cryptic denial of the project in 1913: see Craig, 'Editorial Note. The Russian Ballet', in *Craig on Movement*, 102.
69. Roger Savage, *Masques, Mayings, and Music-Dramas* (Woodbridge: Boydell and Brewer, 2014), 211. See also Karen Dorn, 'Dialogue into Movement: W. B. Yeats's Theatre Collaboration with Gordon Craig', in *Yeats and the Theatre*, ed. Robert O'Driscoll and Lorna Reynolds (Toronto: Macmillan of Canada, 1975), 109–36.
70. Kelly, *Yeats Chronology*, 149, 162.
71. WBY to Lady Gregory, 3 April [1901], *CL InteLex* 32.
72. Fleischer, *Embodied Texts*, 152.
73. Yeats, 'Appendix G: Conclusion to "The Tragic Theatre" in *Plays for an Irish*

Theatre (1911)', in *Early Essays*, ed. George Bornstein and Richard J. Finneran, vol. 4 of *The Collected Works of W. B. Yeats* (New York: Scribner, 2007), 315.
74. WBY to Lady Gregory, 31 December [1909], *CL InteLex* 1255.
75. James Flannery, 'W. B. Yeats, Gordon Craig, and the Visual Art of the Theatre', in O'Driscoll and Reynolds, eds, *Yeats and the Theatre*, 94.
76. Karen Dorn, *Players and Painted Stage: The Theatre of W. B. Yeats* (Brighton: Harvester Press, 1984), 20.
77. WBY to Lady Gregory, 4 and 6 February [1910], *CL InteLex* 1288, 1290.
78. WBY to unidentified correspondent, 8 June [1910], *CL InteLex* 1366.
79. WBY to Lady Gregory, 20 December [1911], *CL InteLex* 1786.
80. Ibid.
81. Yeats, *Certain Noble Plays of Japan*, in *Essays and Introductions*, 221.
82. Ibid.
83. Carrie J. Preston, *Learning to Kneel: Noh, Modernism, and Journeys in Teaching* (New York: Columbia University Press, 2016), 24.
84. Yeats, *Certain Noble Plays of Japan*, 221.
85. Preston, *Learning to Kneel*, 75.
86. Fleischer, *Embodied Texts*, 169.
87. Preston, *Learning to Kneel*, 75.
88. Yeats, *Certain Noble Plays of Japan*, 224.
89. Ibid., 222, 224.
90. WBY to Horace Reynolds, 24 December [1932], *CL InteLex* 5799.
91. Yeats used this metaphor to delineate his poetics in relation to traditional forms: 'Ancient salt is best packing'; W. B. Yeats, 'A General Introduction for My Work', in *The Major Works*, 387.
92. Ito, quoted in Preston, *Learning to Kneel*, 109.
93. Edward Marx, 'No Dancing: Yone Noguchi in Yeats's Japan', *Yeats Annual* 17 (2007): 51–94.
94. Curtis Bradford has shown how the revisions of *At the Hawk's Well* reveal the emerging centrality of the dance to the performance, since Yeats cut portions of text that he felt Ito's body already expressed perfectly well; see *Yeats at Work* (Carbondale, IL: Southern Illinois University Press, 1965), 174–216.
95. Liam Miller, *The Noble Drama of W. B. Yeats* (Dublin: Dolmen Press, 1977), 220.
96. Yeats, *Certain Noble Plays of Japan*, vii.
97. Preston, *Learning to Kneel*, 63.
98. W. B. Yeats, 'Introduction and Headnotes to *Fairy and Folktales of the Irish Peasantry*', in *Prefaces and Introductions*, 15–16.
99. Preston, 'Modernism's Dancing Marionettes', 127.
100. Preston, *Learning to Kneel*, 88.
101. Preston, 'Modernism's Dancing Marionettes', 129.
102. Preston, *Learning to Kneel*, 104.
103. Yeats, *Certain Noble Plays of Japan*, 221.
104. Richard Allen Cave, *Collaborations: Ninette de Valois and William Butler Yeats* (Alton: Dance Books, 2011), 5.
105. WBY to George Yeats, 23 May [1927], *CL InteLex* 4999.
106. Ninette de Valois, *Come Dance With Me: A Memoir, 1898–1956* (Dublin: Lilliput Press, 1992), 88.
107. Ibid., 88.
108. Cave, *Collaborations*, 4–5.
109. De Valois, *Come Dance With Me*, 58.

110. Ninette de Valois, quoted in Kathrine Sorley-Walker, 'The Festival and the Abbey: Ninette de Valois' Early Choreography, 1925–1934, Part One', *Dance Chronicle* 7.4 (1983): 385.
111. De Valois, *Come Dance With Me*, 89.
112. Ronald Schuchard, *The Last Minstrels: Yeats and the Revival of the Bardic Arts* (Oxford: Oxford University Press, 2008), xxi.
113. Ibid., 151–6.
114. Norman Marshall, *The Other Theatre* (London: John Lehmann, 1947), 54.
115. De Valois, *Come Dance With Me*, 87.
116. Terence Gray, quoted in Tydeman and Price, *Wilde: Salome*, 88–9.
117. Ibid., 89.
118. Janet Leeper, *Edward Gordon Craig: Designs for the Theatre* (London: Penguin, 1948), 25. See also the 3D digital reconstructions of Yeats and Craig's designs for productions at the Abbey, produced by researchers at Trinity College Dublin, available at <http://craigscreens.blog.oldabbeytheatre.net/?page_id=298> (accessed 22 October 2020).
119. Tydeman and Price, *Wilde: Salome*, 91.
120. Reviewer, quoted in ibid., 92.
121. H.H. 'Gale. Salome', *The Observer*, 31 May 1931.
122. De Valois, *Come Dance with Me*, 98.
123. Victoria O'Brien, *A History of Irish Ballet: 1927–1963* (Oxford: Peter Lang, 2011), 11. See also Deirdre Mulrooney, *Irish Moves: An Illustrated History of Dance and Physical Theatre in Ireland* (Dublin: Liffey Press, 2006).
124. 'Programme: April 16 [1928]', Atlanta, GA, Stuart A. Rose Library, Emory University, Abbey Theatre Collection: Series 2, Box 2, Folder 58.
125. 'Programme: November [1929]', Stuart A. Rose Library, Abbey Theatre Collection: Series 2, 2: 91.
126. O'Brien, *A History of Irish Ballet*, 32.
127. 'Programme: July 30 [1934]', Stuart A. Rose Library, Abbey Theatre Collection: Series 2, 4: 64.
128. Ibid.
129. Ibid.
130. See Conor Cruise O'Brien, 'Passion and Cunning: An Essay on the Politics of W. B. Yeats', in *In Excited Reverie: Centenary Tribute to W. B. Yeats*, ed. A. Norman Jeffares and K. G. W. Cross (London: Macmillan, 1965), 207–78; Elizabeth Cullingford, *Yeats, Ireland and Fascism* (Basingstoke: Palgrave Macmillan, 1981).
131. Yeats later called his entanglement with the Blueshirts 'our political comedy'. WBY to Olivia Shakespear, 20 September [1933], *CL InteLex* 5942.
132. WBY to Olivia Shakespear, 2 August [1931], *CL InteLex* 5497.
133. W. B. Yeats, *The King of the Great Clock Tower and A Full Moon in March: Manuscript Materials*, ed. Richard Allen Cave (Ithaca, NY: Cornell University Press, 2007), 333.
134. Anonymous critic, quoted in Yeats, *King of the Great Clock Tower*, lxviii.
135. Cave, *Collaborations*, 100.
136. Ibid., 98.
137. Doody, 'An Echo of Someone Else's Music', 180.
138. 'The Dublin Theatres: Abbey Players again on Tour; Winter Season Opens', *Irish Times*, 3 October 1934.
139. Kimberly R. Myers, 'W. B. Yeats's Steinach Operation, Hinduism, and the Severed-Head Plays of 1934–35', *Literature and Medicine* 28 (2009): 102–37.
140. Sigmund Freud, 'The Taboo of Virginity' [1917], in *The Standard Edition of*

the Complete Psychological Works of Sigmund Freud, Vol. 11: Five Lectures on Psycho-Analysis, Leonardo da Vinci and Other Works, trans. Angela Richards (London: Hogarth Press, 1957), 207.
141. Yeats, *King of the Great Clock Tower*, xliv.
142. De Valois, *Come Dance with Me*, 89.
143. Yeats, *King of the Great Clock Tower*, xl.
144. Ibid., xlv.
145. Ibid., 319.
146. WBY to Olivia Shakespear, 7 August [1934], *CL InteLex* 6080.
147. Cave, *Collaborations*, 107.
148. WBY to J. B. Yeats, 14 March [1916], *CL InteLex* 2902.
149. Paige Reynolds, '"A Theatre of the Head": Material Culture, Severed Heads, and the Late Drama of W. B. Yeats', *Modern Drama* 58.4 (2015): 453.
150. Eliot, 'Yeats', 85.

EPILOGUE
'DANCED THROUGH ITS SEVEN PHASES': SAMUEL BECKETT AND THE LATE MODERNIST SALOME

Charting the various lines of influence, collaborative partnerships and transnational networks of exchange that brought these dancers, film-makers and dramatists into creative proximity has revealed the ways in which modernist performance was deeply imbricated in a range of late nineteenth- and twentieth-century dance forms, devoted, in many instances, to redefining the powerful image of the veiled woman-in-movement whom Warburg termed the 'Nympha' and who achieved her most potent incarnation during this period as Salome. The aesthetics of ballet, taken in new directions by Diaghilev and his choreographers, and modern dance – from the seemingly disembodied abstraction of a veiled Loïe Fuller to the expressive philhellenism of Isadora Duncan and Maud Allan – offered fruitful models for playwrights looking to develop new kinds of stage pictures predicated on the embodied gestural power of the human performer, as well as for *cinéastes* pursuing a nascent art form. Salome certainly reached the height of her popularity as a choreographic theme in the early years of the twentieth century, and exerted, as we have seen, a kind of spectral pressure on the plays of Yeats in the 1920s and 1930s, although, by this point, she was already associated with the *fin de siècle*'s spirit of decline, and her appearances in the interwar years were largely (though not completely) relegated to new stagings of Wilde's play.

In 1944, at the Coolidge Auditorium in Washington's Library of Congress, the American modern dancer Martha Graham premiered her *Herodiade*, a work for two female dancers based on Mallarmé's poem and set to music by Paul Hindemith. The dynamic, angular solos of the two dancers – in the role of 'Woman' and 'attendant' – are interspersed with moments of fraught stasis, when the dancers freeze in poses alternately triumphant and supplicating, framed by the skeletal mirror designs of Isamu Noguchi. As Henrietta Bannerman notes, this form of 'danced conversation' between the two women has a shifting tonal register, transitioning from phrases of frenetic uncertainty – signalled by steps that are twisting, jerky and asynchronous – to dance passages of fluid lyricism and slow profundity; images of consonance and intimacy between the figures as they shadow and respond to one another's movements.[1] Graham's choreography exists too in conversation with the literary antecedents of her theme, drawing on the portentous fragments of Mallarmé's dramatic poem – with its anguished metaphors of mirroring and reflection – to create an intriguing dialogue between these French Symbolist texts and her own brand of choreographic modernism.

Graham's *Herodiade* transforms the Symbolist myth into a performance that is spare and abstract, reconfiguring the elements of alienation and chilling sublimity found in Mallarmé's poem through the movement design and arrangements of the stage space, delimited by Noguchi's three gaunt sculptures. This dance piece provides evidence of Salome's continued purchase on the imaginations of modern dancers, although the exhaustive decadent details of her narrative have faded from view: like Mallarmé, Graham omits the lurid fantasy of Herod's feast and the dance of the seven veils, with Salome's 'unveiling' restricted to a moment of slow, tender exchange between the dancers, as the attendant helps the Woman to remove her outer garments. Wearing only her nightgown, the Woman holds her rigid pose for nearly a minute, her arms fully outstretched and her face turned upwards in a gesture of almost Christ-like piety, carrying, perhaps unknowingly, the ghost of Ida Rubinstein's sacrificial dance as Saint Sebastian several decades previously.

As Graham's sparse staging suggests, after the fever of 'Salomania' had waned, signs of the veiled modernist dancers ubiquitous in the early years of the twentieth century became suddenly phantasmal, elusive and difficult to spot. Two films in the 1950s returned to the well-worn trope: Billy Wilder's Hollywood satire *Sunset Boulevard* (1950) alludes to the legendary status of Wilde's dancer throughout, while William Dieterle's *Salome* (1953), starring Rita Hayworth, offers a loose take on the Gospel sources, revising Salome's narrative as one of Christian conversion. In later years, however, Salome would become increasingly indistinguishable from the figure of Wilde himself, resurrected in concert with burgeoning LGBT and feminist movements, along with a new-found appreciation for Wilde's own progressive modernity. In this respect, *Salome's Last Dance* (1988), directed by Ken Russell, offers the clearest homage to the author of *Salomé*, producing what Dierkes-Thrun describes as a 'gleefully ironic historical fable' that 'politicises Wilde by making him a sexual and aesthetic martyr'.² Russell frames the theatrical staging of *Salomé* with a narrative centring on Wilde's relationship with Lord Alfred Douglas, setting the play itself in a brothel and substituting Salome's body for that of a man at the dance's climactic moment of revelation. In a similar vein, Owen Horsley's more recent version of *Salomé* at the RSC in Stratford-upon-Avon (2017) commemorated fifty years since the partial decriminalisation of homosexuality, casting a young male actor (Matthew Tennyson) in the lead role and creating a visceral, modern soundscape with music by the queer artist Perfume Genius. This production coincided with a curious revival of the theme in other contexts: in the same year, the Royal Opera House offered a new staging of Strauss's *Salome*, while the South African playwright Yaël Farber reclaimed the text as a parable of colonial brutality and occupation in her one-act play at the National Theatre.

The figure of Salome, as dancer, thus unspools along multiple trajectories as modernism itself is subjected to new fractures and forms of dismantling. In *Sunset Boulevard*, for instance, Salome's story specifically becomes a shorthand for a lost age, aligned with the decline of silent cinema and its faded female star, Norma Desmond (Gloria Swanson), who seeks to revitalise her career by scripting and performing in a new version of this notorious role. Like Desmond herself, the Salomean myth is figured as a belated anachronism, fruitlessly resuscitated beyond its natural lifespan, out-of-step with the desires and technologies of a new era. And yet, as Desmond explicitly articulates to her incredulous script editor Gillis (William Holden), she is making a 'return', not a 'comeback'. Such 'returns', Yeats reminds us in 'Nineteen Hundred and Nineteen', are seldom benevolent, but rather fraught with a violent energy that unsettles pre-existing aesthetic categories and modes of perception: 'Herodias' daughters have returned again, / A sudden blast of dusty wind and after / Thunder of feet, tumult of images' (*VP*, 433). In *Sunset Boulevard*, these destructive instincts, and Salome's capacity for aesthetic renewal, remain unchecked: after shooting the male protagonist who ridiculed her creative efforts, Desmond once again, in the final frame of Wilder's picture, takes control of the terms on which her body becomes spectacle, embodying the role of Wilde's heroine and demanding her infamous close-up. What is decadent, feminine and out of time – at once premature and overdue – moves slowly towards the camera and into a state of beguiling murkiness, promising 'those wonderful people out there in the dark' that there will be 'another picture and another picture'.

Holding these varied and ambiguous 'returns' in view for the remainder of this epilogue, I want to examine one final case study in Salome's intricate genealogy by considering her veiled and opaque presence in late modernism, focusing on the work of Samuel Beckett. Despite the spectral nature of Salome's returns in Beckett's work, traces of her particular mode of body imagery persist, albeit radically transformed, in texts as distinct as *Dream of Fair to Middling Women* and the intensely rhythmical late plays *Not I* and *Quad I + II*, consolidated by Beckett's lifelong interest in dance and his desire to accommodate the language of the body in his writing.[3] Daniel Albright points out that Beckett owes much to writers of the late nineteenth century, though he crucially remains 'a symbolist without symbols', his reconfiguration of these sources one of forms and movements rather than allegorical images.[4] To reflect the tenor of his engagement with the choreographic imagination examined in this book, the types of evidence this epilogue collates are, like Salome herself, disparate and unsettled in nature, revealing traces of Beckett's moorings in older sources and aesthetic movements, but always reformulating his influences in new and unreconciled ways. The method outlined at the beginning of this study permits and, indeed, encourages such an understanding of this dancer's phantasmic function, since she is always already invested with the remnants of previous iterations of the same gestural impulse; as Warburg famously said of his *Mnemosyne Atlas*, history is 'a ghost story for the fully grown-up': a means of recovering spectres rather than fixed forms.[5]

Not only did Beckett enjoy dance, as his attendance at various ballets in the 1930s indicates, but he also owed much to the dramatic theorists and practitioners who incorporated elements of dance into their work, including Kleist, Yeats, Maeterlinck and Craig.[6] Beckett shared with these writers a sustained desire to work through the conceptual and practical difficulties presented by the body; these issues were especially pertinent to dramatists, such as Beckett, who were seeking absolute precision and clarity in their stage imagery and increasingly engaged with forms of modernist abstraction. While his drama has frequently been interpreted as a testament to forms of inertia, diagnosed as 'exhaustion' by Gilles Deleuze, Beckett often embraced polarities of corporeal experience within single texts, attending, in the vein of Maeterlinck and Yeats, to conditions of stasis and decay as well as vital energy, positioning them as crucially interlinked on the plane of physical gesture.[7] Challenging the 'critical myths' that have long stipulated the inevitability of 'disembodiment, silence and stasis' in Beckett's work, Ulrika Maude has recuperated the status of the physical body in Beckett, insisting upon its centrality as a site of sensory experience and meaningful possibility, even in its most severed and abject states.[8] The body is not, she emphasises, merely a diminished vessel for the incisive operations of thought, but a crucial marker of knowledge and feeling in the very physically oriented sphere of Beckett's work. Beckett's is a literary corpus that presents an 'astonishing gallery of postures, gaits, and positions', to use Deleuze's words.[9] The later plays in particular develop, according to Jones, 'a new formalist aesthetics of movement' that leaves the body 'unencumbered by visual display or narrative complexity'.[10] While Beckett's abstract formalism might signal a new direction for choreographic modernism after the Second

World War, his reduced, ahistorical stage spaces, carefully delineated gestures and mimes, ventriloquised body parts and emphasis on rhythm (in language and in movement) as the source of the dramatic might be traced back to the Salome-themed plays of Yeats and the broader properties of Symbolism. 'Many lines of the European imagination meet in Beckett', acknowledges Katherine Worth, but 'as a playwright he is above all the heir of Yeats and the Irish/French drama' of the late nineteenth century.[11] By reading Beckett through Salome's dance – and Salome's dance through Beckett – this epilogue suggests ways of extending accounts of modernism's choreographic fixations into the late twentieth century, lighting upon unexpected reformulations of Symbolist and Decadent themes in Beckett's texts and proposing connections between his abstract stage choreographies and the methods of much earlier dancers.

'Bovril into Salome': Vuillard, Moreau and the *Dream*

In February 1954, Beckett published a little-known essay in an issue of the American journal *ARTnews*, a popular visual arts magazine based in New York. The essay in question, titled 'Vuillard and the Poets of Decadence', was Beckett's English translation of a piece by his friend, the French art critic Georges Duthuit. Published to accompany a retrospective on the French painter Édouard Vuillard at the Museum of Modern Art, the essay suggestively associates Vuillard's oeuvre with the methods and principles of the Symbolist movement, ruminating on the aesthetic tastes and commitments of an epoch now long past. Covering four pages, the piece is illustrated with colourful reproductions of Vuillard's work, including his *Woman with Bowl* (1897) and *View of Switzerland* (1900), along with a small painting of Mallarmé's house at Valvins, which Vuillard created in 1895 after attending one of the poet's afternoon teas. Set alongside these images are monochrome reproductions of some of Gustave Moreau's best-known works: his paintings of Jupiter and Semele, Helen of Troy and, of course, *Salomé dansant devant Hérode*, described in the explanatory caption as a 'conversation-piece' at the 1876 Salon and 'a favourite' of Huysmans's 'decadent heroes', a reference to Des Esseintes in *À Rebours*.[12] Framing the essay, the pages are also crowded with advertisements for exhibitions on Matisse, Cézanne, Picasso, Chagall and Braque, as well as a new full-length book on Fernand Léger, marketed as the first of its kind. Clearly, by 1954, these harbingers of European modernism (and modernists proper) had become the object of dedicated reflective study, canonised for their contributions to a thriving transatlantic avant-garde and absorbed into the cultural discourse of the forward-looking New York art scene. They are modern, still, but not contemporary, the luminaries of a recent history now hanging on the walls of the city's most fashionable galleries and museums.

The Symbolists, however, have an awkward place in this history. In his translation of Duthuit's essay, Beckett lingers on the 'esoteric reek of decay' suffusing the works of Vuillard and his contemporaries, identifying the 'cold, untouchable' figure of Mallarmé's *Hérodiade* as the inspiration for Moreau's *Salomé dansant devant Hérode*, in which 'sadistic' womanhood is 'hypostasized as the divinity of all the malignant forces of nature'.[13] Beckett himself had already expressed reservations about the 'Jesuitical' elements of Mallarmé's *Hérodiade*, although it was clearly, as he noted in a letter to his friend Thomas MacGreevy, a work that bore re-reading.[14] While identifying the common root of these three artists' imaginative outlooks, 'Vuillard and the Poets of Decadence' praises Mallarmé and Vuillard for transforming their 'intense intellectual ascesis' into a 'profound [. . .] personal experience', whereas Moreau is treated more sceptically for attempting to harness his 'literary' instincts to the 'technical exigencies of painting'.[15] Like the 'creeping paralysis' that consumes the mansion in *Sunset Boulevard*, the Moreau Museum on the Rue de la Rochefoucauld in Paris – the artist's former residence – is dismissed as an 'unworshipped necropolis' of 'mouldering halls', home to paintings that, according to Duthuit, show Moreau's failure to 'digest' fully the 'doctrines' of Symbolism, leaving them 'extraneous, figuring on the surface of his canvases in the form of *themes*'.[16] Whether or not Beckett agreed with Duthuit's diagnosis of Moreau's pseudo-literary style, this piece certainly prompted him to reflect on the extent to which the movement succeeded (or failed) in transcending the boundaries between different art forms – literature, painting and even dance – in its search for essential symbols. Salome, unsurprisingly, is placed at the centre of these cross-disciplinary endeavours: describing the image of 'Herodias' dancing before the head of the Baptist, the essay argues that it is 'to her, finally, that offering is always made of these sanguinary sacrifices which not only constitute the subject of so many of the master's pictures, but even command their construction'.[17] By grounding the concept of 'a supreme and ineffable Ideal' in these various representations of Salome, this essay sketches out a vital relationship between her veiled dance and Symbolist aesthetics, showing that Beckett, through Duthuit, was ruminating on the choreographic predilections of early modernism in his own translation work.[18]

The essay's language and tone, however, convey the fate of Symbolism and its offshoots in much twentieth-century critical discourse, since what Duthuit and Beckett condemn in Moreau's paintings of Salome is grounded in the artist's perceived propensity towards the decadent: all that is 'mouldering' and 'decay[ing]' in his aesthetic world is also taken as evidence of 'impotence', 'sterility' and, in the article's emphatic final word, '*impurity*'. A moral weakness, rooted in not-so-subtle insinuations of queerness and effeminacy, is detected here: Moreau's method and daily habits are detailed at length, portraying the artist as a kind of nineteenth-century Norman Bates, enamoured of all that is lifeless and fossilised, carefully curating his own gothic interior world:

> Moreau paints with the blinds down, his only subject being the still-life of certified lifelessness (the stuffed aviary of his aged mother). He shudders away from every form of raw immediacy, accumulates the curtains between himself and reality: thus he prefers to work from pictures or, better still, from reproductions of pictures. He lived like a hermit for the greater part of his life, with only the company of his mother, seldom going out and assuaging with books his hunger for knowledge. The atmosphere of dusty stuffiness appears only too clearly in the subject of his paintings, of which it is almost superfluous to say that they are literary to the point of asphyxiation [. . .]
>
> This almost total rejection of the world, common to a Mallarmé and a Moreau, so far from being necessarily the sign of superior greatness of the soul, points rather to impotence.[19]

A shuddering, impotent figure enclosed in his own tightly delimited interior sphere: readers of Beckett will now surely be drawing connections with the Irish author's own representations of immobility and incapacity, even if it is the 'raw immediacy' of such conditions that drives Beckett's literary project. Vincent Sherry had recently made precisely this claim, arguing that, far from being entirely removed from these nineteenth-century aesthetic movements, the 'self-enclosed chamber of writing' presented in Beckett's texts is strikingly indebted to Decadence's typical *mise-en-scène*, captured so clearly in the above description of Moreau's working method.[20] The narrator of *The Unnamable*, for instance, recalls how he or she 'simply stayed in' and found themselves 'powerless ever to do anything again', save for the necessary demands of language and the almost taxonomic process through which this voice catalogues their inner thoughts and sensations.[21] Salome, as she appears in the Symbolist works described above, might seem to represent the apotheosis of an outdated aesthetic programme with which Beckett has little in common, yet, as his translation of Duthuit suggests, she is a figure still worthy of critical attention in mid-twentieth-century art writing, despite the shifting literary dialogues and discourses of the intervening decades.

Beyond this important engagement with Symbolism, the shifts in Beckett's own choreographic imagination can be traced across his body of writing. Dance has an important purchase on his earliest novel *Dream of Fair to Middling Women*, written in the summer of 1932 and finally published sixty years later. The 'fair to middling women' of whom the indolent protagonist Belacqua Shuah 'dreams' are largely drawn from Beckett's own relationships with dancers; his cousin Peggy Sinclair is loosely reformulated as the 'Smeraldina-Rima', cruelly introduced as 'a slob of a girl' near the beginning of the novel, while James Joyce's daughter, the dancer Lucia Joyce, appears as the 'Syra-Cusa', 'her body more perfect than dream creek, amaranth lagoon'.[22]

Sinclair, with whom Beckett had his first serious relationship, introduced him to modern methods of exercise and rhythmical intuition when she enrolled at Dalcroze's Schule Hellerau-Laxenburg, located nine miles south of Vienna. As we have seen in relation to Michio Ito, Dalcroze's techniques of eurhythmics, improvisation and soflège, designed to complement and enhance the body's musical sensibilities, had a profound influence on the dancers who visited and trained at his schools, including Marie Rambert, Nijinsky and Diaghilev.[23] Dalcroze wrote in *Rhythm, Music and Education* (1921) that he wanted his pupils to develop 'an intimate understanding of the synergies and conflicting forces of [their] bodies', accompanied by a knowledge of 'the many processes of counterpointing, phrasing, and shading musical rhythms with a view to their plastic expression'.[24]

When Beckett visited Sinclair at the school in October 1928, he absorbed enough of this Dalcrozean programme to satirise its essentials with biting accuracy in the *Dream* as 'the very vanguardful Schule Dunkelbrau', home to classes on 'Harmonie, Anatomie, Psychologie, Improvisation, with a powerful ictus on the last syllable in each case'.[25] The Smeraldina is described as 'everybody's darling' who has 'a curious talent for improvisation', stimulating her instructor Herr Arschlochweh 'to certain velleities of desire' with her 'bending and stretching'.[26] Her corporeal talents are strikingly reflected in her way with language: when in 'form', she possesses 'a strange feverish eloquence, the words flooding and streaming out like a conjuror's coloured paper', keeping her listeners 'convulsed with the ropes and ropes of logorrhoea streaming out in a gush'.[27] Beckett's florid descriptors point to an important connection between bodily and linguistic contortions, sardonically portraying the Smeraldina's excitable verbal performances as an extension of her Dalcrozean training. Dalcroze primarily sought to instil in his students an understanding of musical rhythms and structure, often asking them to improvise movement either to harmonise with or provide a counterpoint to a piece of music. By satirising the Smeraldina's 'talent' for this particular activity – and her tendency towards logorrhoea – Beckett indicates a continuity between the choreographic techniques associated with eurhythmics and the rhythms of spoken language, perhaps suggesting that both are generated by an underlying musicality, though, in the Smeraldina's case, the melody quickly descends into disorder.

It is Peggy Sinclair's body, grounded in metaphors of feminine softness, that becomes a source of acerbic study in the *Dream*. The Smeraldina appears thus: 'Poppata, big breech, Botticelli thighs, knock-knees, ankles all fat nodules, wobbly, mamose, slobbery-blubbery, bubbub-bubbub, a real button-bursting Weib, ripe.'[28] In such passages, language collapses into senselessness, producing an unstructured body that is all flesh and no thought. Sinclair's efforts to fashion her own bodily aesthetic through choreographic discipline at Hellerau-

Laxenburg are scrutinised and subtly overwritten in this text, as Belacqua surveys her 'Botticelli thighs' and 'Primavera buttocks', mocking the philhellenistic focus of many of the period's physical cultures rather than recognising the result of this dancer's careful self-cultivation.[29]

As a former pupil at the Dalcroze Institute on the Rue de l'Annonciation in Paris, Lucia Joyce had a similar background to Sinclair, though she had undergone much more intensive choreographic training, first with the flamboyant pedagogue Raymond Duncan – who promoted a return to classical Greek living and dance forms – and then with the English dancer Margaret Morris.[30] Beckett met Lucia while working in an informal capacity as a research assistant for James Joyce in 1929, when the writing of the *Work in Progress* (published as *Finnegans Wake* in 1939) was underway. Lucia Joyce's cipher in the *Dream*, the Syra-Cusa, is subjected to similar critique, though her capacity for grace is foregrounded: Belacqua compares her body to Constantin Brancusi's abstract modernist sculptures and notes that her 'blue arch of veins and small bones, rose like a Lied to the firm wrist of the reins'.[31] She too, however, is somewhat ungenerously imagined in terms of a corporeality divorced from intellect: 'her neck was scraggy and her head was null'.[32] Yet Beckett's apparent readiness to undermine the creative integrity of these female performers belies important debts: it is surely no coincidence that at the same moment that he was developing his own ideas about the connections between language, gesture and rhythm, he was forging important creative relationships with two women – Sinclair and Joyce – who were fully immersed in Europe's newest dance forms and body cultures.

Indeed, it is in this early novel that Salome, as dancer, first appears in Beckett's work.[33] Walking past Trinity College Dublin, where Beckett himself was a student, Belacqua encounters the sight of Dublin's famous illuminated Bovril sign on the corner of College Green. This spectacle horrified Yeats, who bemoaned the 'discordant architecture' of O'Connell Street: 'all those electric signs, where modern heterogeneity has taken physical form'.[34] Yet for Beckett – and for the inebriated Belacqua, emerging 'happy body from the hot bowels of McLoughlin's' – the sign is not so much 'discordant' as rhythmically generative, reactivating the traces of other texts and literary sources:

> Bright and cheery above the strom of the College Green, as though coached by the star of Bethlehem, the Bovril sign danced and danced through its seven phases.
>
> The lemon of faith jaundiced, annunciating the series, was in a fungus of hopeless green reduced to shingles and abolished. Next, in reverence for the slain, the light went out. A sly ooze of gules, carmine of solicitation, lifting the skirts of green that the prophecy might be fulfilled, shocking Gabriel into cherry, annexed the sign. But the long skirts

> rattled down, darkness covered their shame, the cycle was at an end. Da Capo.
> Bovril into Salome, thought Belacqua, and Tommy Moore there with his head on his shoulders.[35]

Reimagined as a dancer, the static material of the Bovril sign, enlivened by its electric illumination, approaches the conditions of embodiment, albeit in amorphous and incomplete form: it is fungal; it oozes and floods; its 'long skirts' reconstitute the draperies of the modern dancer. Beckett may have had Arthur Rimbaud's synaesthetic sonnet 'Voyelles' ('Vowels', 1883) in mind for this symphony of colour, which revels in sensory confusion, 'jaundiced' like a sickly human body.[36] Other critics have picked up on the rich intertextuality of this passage: there are subtle allusions to the three Irish Graces of Joyce's 'The Dead' (1914), as well as Dante's *Purgatorio*, which allegorises the Virtues of Faith, Hope and Love as dancing women clothed in red, white and green.[37] In recycling both Rimbaud's colour sequence and Dante's veiled figures, Beckett creates an intriguingly layered image of dance that he would obliquely return to in his late play *Quad I + II*, whose dancers are more often read as versions of Dante's Hypocrites, solidly pacing in their leaden robes.[38] Yet it is the Salome metaphor in the final line that reveals Beckett's interest in repurposing the literary and choreographic motifs of his Symbolist precursors, with the 'seven phases' of the sign's dance offering the clearest nod to the dance of the seven veils coined by Wilde, coalescing here with the image of Dante's seven dancing virtues.

This passage shows Beckett responding to the vogue for Salome dancers that preoccupied modernist writers in the early years of the twentieth century, even if this is an image he appropriates here for the sake of parody.[39] Belacqua's attention to the sensual properties of colour in this passage echoes Huysmans's appraisal of Moreau's *L'Apparition* in *À Rebours*: Des Esseintes, standing before the painting, admires 'the incandescent contours of the body of the woman; catching her at the neck, the legs, the arms, with sparks of fire, bright red like glowing coals, violet like jets of vapour, blue like flaming alcohol, white like starlight'.[40] Displacing these properties from Moreau's watercolour to a lurid advertising display, Beckett subtly mocks the ornate sensuality of the aesthete's idiom, while perhaps also noting the corruption of Symbolism's ideals in the age of commercial advertising. A drunken Belacqua, entranced by the Bovril sign, undergoes a synaesthetic delirium comparable to Des Esseintes' raptures before his *fin-de-siècle* artwork. Here, there are echoes too of Loïe Fuller's bewitching illuminated spectacles, which had, of course, married technological innovation with a Symbolist visual poetics long before Beckett created this image, suggesting a way of harnessing the seductive effects of Salome's dance to the interplay between the performer's veils and colourful electric lights.

While Beckett is certainly alert to the loftier antecedents of his Salomean metaphor (antecedents that are crucial to the image's ironic function), he deftly shifts this trope into a local setting, diffusing the symbolic weight of his allusion through the lowbrow associations of the Bovril sign. After performing Salome's game of exposure and concealment, the sign begins again, directed by Beckett's musical instruction: 'Da Capo'. The literal translation of this term ('from the head') not only implies that the dance reiterates – as Salome's dance always does in its various reproductions – but also gestures towards the 'head' severed from the body of the Baptist, the second motif in the biblical narrative. Again, there is a humorous subtext at play: the nearby statue of the Irish poet Thomas Moore, Beckett's John the Baptist figure, might have 'his head on his shoulders' for now, but the statue was apparently decapitated when placed on its pedestal in 1857. It is little surprise, therefore, that it becomes a source of mockery for Belacqua, as it had done for Stephen Dedalus, who also comes across the 'droll statue' with its 'servile head' in Joyce's *A Portrait of the Artist as a Young Man* (1916).[41] 'It was a Firbolg in the borrowed cloak of a Milesian', writes Joyce, subtly merging primitivist tropes of the indigenous Irish 'Firbolgs' with that of the legendary Milesian invaders and thus alluding to the uncritical sentimentalising of Moore's status as 'national poet', as well as the somewhat shoddy execution of the statue itself.[42] Much as Oliver Sheppard's Cuchulain bronze becomes a source of anxiety for Yeats in *The Death of Cuchulain*, the statue of Thomas Moore is wittily deconstructed by Joyce, and later by Beckett, as evidence of a confusedly nostalgic expression of national culture, a kind of poetic patriotism that makes people 'lose their heads'. Set beside the Bovril sign, coyly flashing in a kind of striptease, this monument to the nation's literary memory is pointedly aligned with the seductive effects of twentieth-century consumerism.

As a novel that alludes to Joyce above any of Beckett's contemporaries, the *Dream* shows Beckett recalibrating his Symbolist influences in concert with the work of his Irish modernist peers. In this respect, he was mirroring Joyce, who similarly imports the tale of Salome and John the Baptist into a quotidian setting in *Portrait*, with Stephen Dedalus repeatedly imagining his friend Cranly as a Baptist figure: a product of 'the exhausted loins [. . .] of Elizabeth and Zachary', the aged parents of the Baptist.[43] When he thinks of Cranly, Dedalus sees 'always a stern severed head or deathmask as if outlined on a grey curtain or veronica [. . .] What do I see? A decollated precursor trying to pick the lock.'[44] Attempting to visualise Cranly, Dedalus is never able to 'raise before his mind the entire image of his body but only the image of the head and face'.[45] The slippage between the pronoun and the definite article, from 'his body' to 'the head', marks a subtle change in property: the Baptist's severed head, for Joyce, is a body part dispossessed.

Joyce's complex distilling of the religious sources into a satirical recurring trope – of Cranly's 'deathmask' – reflects the bleak humour that Beckett himself favoured in his images of bodily severance, which became increasingly central to the visual register of his drama. Such figures haunt Beckett's stage, and those detached faces imagined by Joyce return in the partial bodies of works such as *Play* (1964) and *That Time* (1975), forms 'shadowed by remembered or imagined incarnations', according to Anna McMullan.[46] In *That Time*, the lone face situated '10 feet above stage level' (*CDW*, 388), luminous and pale against the black set, gleams uncannily like the Baptist's incandescent head in Moreau's *L'Apparition*. In this resolutely static play, the movements of an absent dancer are suggested by the disembodied voices, rhythmically 'modulat[ing] back and forth without any break in the general flow except where silence indicated' (*CDW*, 388), achieving the kind of rhythmical abstraction that Beckett often sought in his uses of dance. By following these allusions to Salome and her capital prize, it becomes clear how the symbolic vernacular of much late nineteenth-century art is reactivated in both Joycean and Beckettian contexts, playfully set to the rhythms of technological synaesthesia in the *Dream*, and later finding new forms in Beckett's work for the theatre. When it came to the question of integrating choreographic elements into his dramatic texts, Beckett would look again to the images of dance and dismemberment that characterised so many of the sources this book has examined.

'Whole body like gone': *Not I* to *Quad*

When he took a trip to Malta in October 1971, Beckett visited St John's Cathedral in Valletta, where he spent over an hour contemplating Caravaggio's *Decollation of St John the Baptist* (1608). In letters to his biographer James Knowlson and the artist Avigdor Arikha, he revealed the significant impression left by this painting, extracting from its stark and gruesome tableau the kernel of an idea for a play of his own.[47] The old woman standing next to Salome in Caravaggio's scene, holding her face in her hands as she watches the execution of the Baptist, became the model for the figure of the Auditor in *Not I*.[48] A veiled and anonymous presence concealed beneath a djellaba, the Auditor repeats the old woman's 'gesture of helpless compassion', punctuating the fervent and hypnotic utterances of another severed body part: Mouth (*CDW*, 375). Mouth is a decollated object with her own cranial obsessions: snatches of text telling of a 'dull roar in the skull' (*CDW*, 378) and 'the whole body like gone' (*CDW*, 382) contrive an image of a human figure in pieces, yet she also performs what might be considered a frantic verbal dance, structured by what the actor Billie Whitelaw, Beckett's frequent collaborator, calls 'the dynamic rhythms of Beckett's word-music'.[49]

The image of the Baptist's execution certainly lingered with Beckett until late in his life. In a letter of March 1986, composed many years after his initial encounter with Caravaggio's *Decollation*, Beckett described his response to the painting to Edith Kern: '[It] shows, outside & beyond the main area, at a safe distance from it, a group of watchers intent on the happening. Before the painting, from another outsidededness, I behold both the horror & its being beheld.'[50] These bystanders – the old woman, probably Herodias, and the two prisoners watching from their cell – certainly accord with the waiting, listening, often arrested figures that populate Beckett's stage world. Emilie Morin has suggested that that the *Decollation* may have offered Beckett 'a formal precedent for his own distribution of zones of light and darkness on stage', with the dramatic illumination of the beheading, and the barely lit figures observing from the gloom.[51] The painting's proportion of dark and apparently empty space, enfolding the central figures in a framing blackness, also reflects Beckett's own use of negative space, and his deliberate, sparing deployment of props and lighting. The stage in *Not I*, for instance, is 'in darkness but for MOUTH [. . .] faintly lit from close-up and below' (*CDW*, 376). Unlike other paintings depicting this biblical scene, such as Caravaggio's earlier treatment of the subject, *Salome with the Head of John the Baptist* (c. 1607), the *Decollation* does not foreground the severed head, bloody and inanimate, at the centre of the work. Rather, Caravaggio shows the *act* of decapitation, relegating the figure of the Baptist to the bottom of the frame in a state somewhere between life and death – wholeness and division – as the executioner bears down on him, and Salome readies her platter. It is this immediate negotiation with the boundaries of liveliness that bears a key relevance to late modernist engagements with the motif of the severed body part, especially in a play such as *Not I*, which generates its dramatic affect through Mouth's uncanny volubility. The singing severed heads that Beckett encountered through Yeats's dance-dramas shadow Mouth's rapid articulations and find further echoes in the talking heads of *Play*. An early prototype for Mouth might even be discerned in the 'feverish eloquence' of the Smeraldina-Rima, whose words come 'streaming out in gush' in the *Dream*. The Smeraldina's ability to 'convulse' her listeners with the effect of her 'logorrhoea' – connected to her abilities in rhythmic movement – reflects Beckett's own desire to produce a physiological response in his spectators: he told the director Alan Schneider that he imagined *Not I* as 'breathless, urgent, feverish, rhythmic, panting along [. . .] addressed less to the understanding than to the nerves of the audience'.[52]

Taking Beckett at his word and reading *Not I* as a dramatic meditation on the biblical scene depicted by Caravaggio produces these kinds of suggestive comparisons in which a language of the body is paramount, despite the sense of physical constraint and claustrophobia that defined Whitelaw's experience in this role. This combination of corporeal control and 'rhythmic' urgency is repeated elsewhere in Beckett's oeuvre, including in his late televisual dance play *Quad I + II*, first transmitted by the German network Süddeutscher Rundfunk in 1981 and by the BBC the following year. *Quad* involves four hooded dancers pacing a square area along their own 'particular course' (*CDW*, 451), moving along the peripheries and towards the centre, a 'danger zone' (*CDW*, 453) from which they all sharply deviate. Around this quincunx, they walk alone and in combinations: once the first player has completed his or her circuit, the next player joins and does the same, and so on. Beckett composed the piece for the Stuttgart Preparatory Ballet School and stipulated in his directions that at least 'some ballet training [was] desirable' (*CDW*, 453). With their 'gowns reaching to the ground, [and] cowls hiding [their] faces' (*CDW*, 452), these dancers closely resemble the djellaba-clad Auditor of *Not I*, suggesting that Beckett had long been ruminating on how to incorporate this figure into a stage performance, though the Auditor's 'gesture of helpless compassion' is here transformed into a stark choreography wholly resistant to the possibility of human connection. Entirely veiled, the bodies of the dancers themselves are points of physical indeterminacy: *Quad*'s players, their faces hidden by cowls, were to be 'as alike in build as possible' (*CDW*, 453), though their 'sex' was 'indifferent' (*CDW*, 453). Each player enters and exits at a different point, walking along his or her own course and, according to the published text, *Quad I* presents them in different-coloured gowns – white, yellow, blue and red – illuminated by a tinted light. Such coloured intermingling of material and light, structured by the rhythms of this grave *pas de quatre*, reproduces the luminous choreographies of the Bovril sign in the *Dream*, moving, in this earlier text, from yellow to green to red. Although the colours associated with the players in *Quad* alter the palette of Belacqua's electric sign, they show how Beckett's vision of a dance of veils developed and persisted across his work.

Quad II offers a bleaker realisation of the same theme, with the four figures progressing at a greatly reduced pace, their once brightly coloured gowns now merely white. This modification suggests that Beckett was attuned to the shifting interactions between veil and body, with the costume alterations mirroring the reduced nature of the choreographed movement. Where a percussive accompaniment lent some musical liveliness to *Quad I*, the second iteration is accompanied merely by a metronome and the sound of shuffling feet. *Quad*'s intensely repetitive movement – perhaps especially in this second version – 'catalyzes', in Hannah Simpson's words, 'a similar embodied recoil by the *spectator* from the performing bodies', mirroring, to a degree, the dynamics of attraction and retreat that defines the dancers' movements around the 'danger zone' at the centre of the stage.[53] This focal point for the dancers' energies provides an intriguing gap in the material world of the stage. As the central point of the quincunx – a point that prompts each dancer to swerve – it operates as a site of tension that crystallises the anxieties of both the performers and the audience, who view it as the likeliest source of error or bodily collision between the dancers.[54] It is also, therefore, the source of what we might cautiously call the play's effectiveness as choreographic spectacle, functioning as the primary generator of dramatic meaning.

The visual premise of *Quad* can be found, McMullan suggests, in the incomplete 'J. M. Mime' (1963), a play written for the actor Jack MacGowran that was directly conceived around the image of Thomas Browne's quincunx, which appears as a symbol of God's wisdom in his work *The Garden of Cyrus* (1658).[55] Browne describes the quincunx as 'the emphatical decussation, or fundamental figure', an image reproduced throughout art and the natural world as evidence of the elaborately conceived but perfectly repeated design of an intelligent creator.[56] It is a symbol that appears elsewhere in Beckett's work, for instance in the short prose piece 'The Lost Ones' (1970), where a group of unfortunate souls are condemned, like *Quad*'s dancers, to a life of continuous movement: they must pace a vast and placeless cylinder, organised around a network of chambers 'disposed in irregular quincunxes roughly ten metres in diameter and cunningly out of line'.[57] Intriguingly, the quincunx also has an important symbolic function in the French modernist poet Guillaume Apollinaire's 'Salomé' (1905), a text Beckett specifically highlighted in his copy of Robert de la Vaissière's *Anthologie poétique du XX siècle* (1923).[58] In this poem, which reinvents Salome as a French princess in the throes of a terrible grief, Salome's dance takes place beneath a quincunx, as she cradles the head of the Baptist:[59]

> Venez tous avec moi là-bas sous les quinconces
> Ne pleure pas ô joli fou du roi
> Prends cette tête au lieu de ta marotte et danse
> N'y touchez pas son front ma mère est déjà froid
>
> [Under the quincunx everyone come with me
> Weep not charming jester
> Take this head in your hands for a bauble and dance
> Touch it not mother the brow is cold][60]

The severed head of the Baptist becomes a peculiar kind of object in Apollinaire's poem: the translator offers 'bauble' for 'marotte', but this word can also mean a 'false head', such as the plaster head that might be used in performances of *Salomé*, or, indeed, those Yeatsian dance plays in which severed heads were represented using masks or wooden parallelograms. Yeats certainly shifted towards abstraction in his dealings with the severed head as part of the theatrical image, finally favouring a blank geometric shape as his ideal prop. In its coldly mathematical arrangements and steady resistance to allegorical readings, *Quad* appears to mark a break with the vivid symbolism or complex design of some earlier modernist drama, focusing the audience's attention solely on the relentless presence of the moving actors. Yet we can see the seeds of this late Beckettian mode in many of the texts that precede it, in which the severed head that accompanies the dance becomes a point of translation, unreality or absence. It is in their performative function rather than in their status as objects that the severed heads of Wilde's and Yeats's dance plays might be read as providing comparable dramatic mechanisms to *Quad*'s 'danger zone': the point around which the veiled dance revolves but which repels and attracts in equal measure.

Dancing through Phantasmata

Through both their aesthetic qualities and underlying formal structures, Beckett's texts solicit choreographic interpretation, and the testimonies of his actors confirm the importance of dance as a model for performing his work. Discussing the process of rehearsing with Beckett in her autobiography, Billie Whitelaw stresses the importance of rhythm and posture, describing how, during rehearsals for *Footfalls* (1976), the playwright 'would endlessly move [her] arms and [her] head in a certain way [. . .] If it didn't feel right he would correct the pose.'[61] Although she did not feel 'restricted' by his meticulous direction or by her character's intensely repetitive pacing, she did feel that '[her] movements were being choreographed' and that these motions 'started to feel like a dance'.[62] Beckett's entire body of work for the theatre engages with such forms of movement: the actor Lisa Dwan has recently said that she 'now approach[es] all [Beckett's] work predominantly as a dancer, first allowing all the elements of the poetry to play itself out, the visuals, the rhythmics, the sensor stimulus – this is vast holistic work that simply will not be served from the neck up'.[63] Subtly blending the roles of actor and dancer, Dwan is attentive to the corporeal vocabulary permeating Beckett's work on the levels of both dialogue and stage directions, an approach that positions her body as an interpretative instrument at the centre of Beckett's dramatic system, rather than a mere vessel.

In its profound conception of a language of movement, Beckett's late modernist theatre can therefore be seen as a radical elaboration of a choreographic model that we have read back through the movement register of modern dance and its adoption by writers at the turn of the century in their varied reconstitutions of the Salome myth. Mallarmé's desire to create a new form of dance-like inscription, comparable to Fuller's ingenious bodily writing, was underpinned by a longing for silence and blankness that Beckett also sought to render in his work. As Brandstetter writes:

> Against the backdrop and at the crossroads of the language crisis and the excesses of discourse, the wordless art of dance appears to offer more than simply an alternative solution to issues of legitimate authorship and work in its focus on body imagery and figurations in space. In an age that

fundamentally calls into question the productive efficiency of language for the investigation and reflection of the changing constellations of twentieth-century awareness [...] free dance embodied, for poets such as Mallarmé and Valéry, Hofmannsthal and Rilke, the idea of a sophisticated form of poetics that aimed at the eloquent elimination of all signs, the staging of absolute silence.[64]

In a letter of 1937 to Axel Kaun, Beckett famously expressed a similar wish to distil his language to its essence: 'more and more my language appears to me like a veil which one has to tear apart in order to get to those things (or the nothingness) lying behind it'.[65] It was 'the whispering of the end-music or of the silence underlying all' that Beckett sought, which found its closest counterpart in the rhythmic Logographs of Gertrude Stein.[66] In the same breath, he lamented the verbiage of Symbolism and its appeal for critical elucidation: 'For in the forest of symbols that are no symbols, the birds of interpretation, that is no interpretation, are never silent.'[67] In attempting to fulfil this anti-Symbolist vision, however, Beckett managed to reconstitute the aesthetics of dematerialisation and absence that his precursors had perceived in modern dance; indeed, his choice of metaphor in this letter is telling: the 'veil' of a language concealing a central 'nothingness' precisely reflects Mallarmé's reading of Fuller's choreographies, illustrating the symmetries between early modernist configurations of dance and Beckett's own literary project. As Albright says of Beckett's writing, he sought 'to refine the procedures through which a text can reflect its lack of content, the central absence'.[68] Such processes are active across modernist theatre and they are particularly visible in a dance play such as *Quad*, a work that gives physical form to this absence via the danger zone at the centre of the stage. This zone is not merely a space of negativity but also one of kinetic regeneration, prompting the dancers to pause, turn and move on. Their rhythmic circumnavigating of this space therefore enacts the pure volition that Mallarmé discerned beneath Fuller's veils – cultivated by Fuller herself – thus repurposing Symbolism's model of corporeal writing to create an abstract choreography of mathematical reiterations: a wordless dance that allows bodies to speak.

The veiled dancer whom Warburg followed back through antiquity and the art of the Quattrocento – who found herself reinvented in many guises in the age of modernism – becomes something else in this type of theatre, her flowing, diaphanous garments now heavy robes, her whirling movements suddenly stiff and repetitive. The platter she once carried is gone, her energies now focused around a blank space that remains emphatic in its resistance to any single symbolic reading. The severed heads are elsewhere, scattered through other texts, illuminated on other stages, performing their verbal dances. Beckett offers a revealing final case study in the transformation of an obsessive myth, showing how the dynamic forces carried by this figure – the draperies, the urgent gestures, the very notion of the dancer as signalling a type of rupture or uncanny return – persisted in some way even after her distinguishing traits had been almost entirely eroded. Salome's dance therefore tells us something about the way that certain myths become recursive touchstones for the concerns of their age; forms that are porous and malleable enough to act as dynamic containers for a range of aesthetic, intellectual, ethical and political ideas, while carrying the traces of their previous incarnations. This is how Agamben understands the function of the Nympha as she appears in Warburg's *Mnemosyne Atlas*:

> [T]he nymph is neither passional matter to which the artist must give new form, nor a mould into which he must press his emotional materials. The nymph is an indiscernible blend of originariness and repetition, of form and matter. But a being whose form punctually coincides with its matter and whose origin in indissoluble from its becoming is what we call time, and which Immanuel Kant, on the same basis, defined in terms of self-affection. *Pathosformeln* are made of time – they are crystals of historical memory, crystals which are 'phantasmatized' (in Domenico's sense) and round which time writes its choreography.[69]

Agamben takes the term 'phantasmatized' from the fifteenth-century Italian dance master Domenico da Piacenza's essay 'On the Art of Dancing and Choreography' (c. 1455), in which he insists that one must 'dance through phantasmata [...] at each *tempo* you appear as if you had seen Medusa's head'.[70] Phantasmata mark, according to Agamben, a 'sudden arrest between two movements', marrying movement and stillness in an 'internal tension' that holds 'the measure and the memory of the entire choreographic series'.[71]

We have seen these freezings of dance movement throughout this book: in the fleeting images conjured by Fuller's veils and crystallised in poetic evocations of her moving form; in the shifts between studied posing and sinuous mobility embodied by Bernhardt, Nazimova, Rubinstein and many other performers. Yeats believed the 'nobleness of art' to be in precisely this 'mingling of contraries [...] overflowing turbulent energy and marmorean stillness'.[72] The modern Salomes examined in the preceding chapters have provided us with 'crystals of historical memory', moments when ancient images perforated modernist forms, bringing the serpentine energy of the dancer into contact with the stillness of the written text, only to reveal the mobile nature of both dance and language. It is neither possible nor desirable to fasten on to any single reading of Salome's dance or to attempt to petrify her image in a final judgement. It is in their reinventions of this dancing figure that so many of these authors – Wilde, Yeats, Mallarmé, Rodenbach, Barnes and Beckett – are at their most mercurial and unsettled, shaping their texts around an image without an origin and opening their literary projects to the influence of dancers whose ephemeral art left them grasping for the right words. The veil that has been such an important visual and conceptual device throughout this study remains suspended at its close, bringing the dancer into view even as it obscures her. 'What poet [. . .] would venture to separate [a beautiful woman] from her costume?' asks Baudelaire in *The Painter of Modern Life*, declaring woman to be 'a general harmony, not only in her bearing and the way in which she moves and walks, but also in the muslins, the gauzes, the vast, iridescent clouds of stuff in which she envelops herself'.[73] It was in these veils, silks and gauzes – keepers of woman's artifice – that Loïe Fuller discovered her capacity for image-making, using her body to alter the symbolic functions of her materials and expand the limits of her corporeal presence. It was the intelligent body of the dancing woman that often bewildered writers in their invocations of Salome, and it is this body that my book has sought to foreground on alternative terms, showing how her veils bridged and demarcated the space between textual and bodily forms, and enabled the creative work of dancers across a range of disciplines and aesthetic contexts.

Notes

1. Henrietta Bannerman, 'A Dance of Transition: Martha Graham's *Herodiade*', *Dance Research* 24.1 (2006): 1–20.
2. Dierkes-Thrun, *Salome's Modernity*, 162.
3. Critical accounts of Beckett, dance and physical movement include Jones, 'Samuel Beckett and Choreography', in *Literature, Modernism and Dance*, 279–306; Josephine Starte, 'Beckett's Dances', *Journal of Beckett Studies* 23.2 (2014): 178–201; Thomas Mansell, 'Describing Arabesques: Beckett and Dance', in *Beckett and Musicality*, ed. Sarah Jane Bailes and Nicholas Till (London: Routledge, 2014), 102–13; Toby Silverman Zinman, 'Lucky's Dance in *Waiting for Godot*', *Modern Drama* 38.3 (1995): 308–23.
4. Daniel Albright, *Beckett and Aesthetics* (Cambridge: Cambridge University Press, 2003), 60.
5. Aby Warburg, quoted in Gombrich, *Aby Warburg*, 287.
6. Beckett attended ballets including *Petrouchka*, which he saw in 1935 in a Polish Ballet production with Léon Woizikowsky in the lead role (Jones, *Literature, Modernism and Dance*, 282). For further discussion of Beckett, dance and marionette movement, see Anthony Uhlmann, 'Expression and Affect in Kleist, Beckett, and Deleuze', in *Deleuze and Performance*, ed. Laura Cull (Edinburgh: Edinburgh University Press, 2009), 54–70; James Knowlson and John Pilling, 'Beckett and Kleist's Essay "On the Marionette Theater"', in *Frescoes of the Skull: The Later Prose and Drama of Samuel Beckett* (New York: Grove Press, 1980), 227–85.
7. Gilles Deleuze, 'The Exhausted', trans. Anthony Uhlmann, *SubStance* 24.3 (1995): 3–28.
8. Ulrika Maude, *Beckett, Technology and the Body* (Cambridge: Cambridge University Press, 2009), 4.
9. Deleuze, 'The Exhausted', 6.
10. Jones, *Literature, Modernism and Dance*, 282–3.
11. Worth, *Irish Drama*, 241.
12. Georges Duthuit, 'Vuillard and the Poets of Decadence', trans. Samuel Beckett, *ARTnews* 53 (1954): 31.

13. Ibid., 29, 31, 62.
14. Beckett to Thomas MacGreevy, 18 October [1932], in *The Letters of Samuel Beckett*, vol. 1: *1929–1940*, ed. Martha Dow Fehsenfeld and Lois More Overbeck (Cambridge: Cambridge University Press, 2009), 134.
15. Duthuit, 'Vuillard and the Poets of Decadence', 63.
16. Ibid., 63.
17. Ibid., 62.
18. Ibid., 62.
19. Ibid., 30.
20. Sherry, *Modernism and the Reinvention of Decadence*, 285.
21. Samuel Beckett, *The Unnamable*, in *Three Novels: Molloy, Malone Dies, The Unnamable* (New York: Grove Press, 1958), 285.
22. Samuel Beckett, *Dream of Fair to Middling Women* (New York: Arcade, 1992), 3, 33.
23. Selma Landen Odom, 'The Dalcroze Method, Marie Rambert, and *Le Sacre du Printemps*', *Modernist Cultures* 9.1 (2014): 9–11.
24. Émile Jaques-Dalcroze, 'Foreword', in *Rhythm, Music and Education*, trans. Harold F. Rubinstein (London: Chatto and Windus, 1921), xi.
25. Beckett, *Dream of Fair to Middling Women*, 13–14. See Jones's discussion of this section of the *Dream* in *Literature, Modernism and Dance*, 72.
26. Beckett, *Dream of Fair to Middling Women*, 14.
27. Ibid., 14.
28. Ibid., 15.
29. Ibid., 50.
30. Carol Loeb Shloss, *Lucia Joyce: To Dance in the Wake* (London: Bloomsbury, 2005), 99–122. Lucia also had a talent for mime and was apparently particularly gifted at delivering impersonations of Charlie Chaplin and Petrouchka (ibid., 87–8), perhaps giving Beckett an early version of the mechanical puppet figure he found so interesting in the Polish Ballet production.
31. Beckett, *Dream of Fair to Middling Women*, 33.
32. Ibid., 33.
33. Salome also appears in the story 'A Wet Night' from the collection *More Pricks than Kicks* (1934), which drew much of its material from the then unpublished *Dream*.
34. W. B. Yeats, 'A General Introduction for my Work', in *The Major Works*, 388–9.
35. Beckett, *Dream of Fair to Middling Women*, 200.
36. Joyce used to recite Rimbaud's 'Voyelles' in French to Beckett while they worked together in the late 1920s. See Knowlson, *Damned to Fame*, 686.
37. Kelly Anspaugh, 'Faith, Hope and – What Was It? Beckett Reading Joyce Reading Dante', *Journal of Beckett Studies* 5.1–2 (1995–96): 18–38.
38. Jones, *Literature, Modernism and Dance*, 299.
39. There are other references to Symbolist authors in the *Dream*. Belacqua's relatives are described as giving him a 'Mallarmean farewell' (*Dream of Fair to Middling Women*, 12) as he leaves for Germany, while elsewhere, 'Mallarmé's complexion' is described as 'high-mettled and viveur' (31).
40. Huysmans, *Against Nature*, 48.
41. James Joyce, *A Portrait of the Artist as a Young Man*, ed. Jeri Johnson (Oxford: Oxford University Press, 2008), 151.
42. Ibid., 151.
43. Ibid., 209.
44. Ibid., 209. Stephen Dedalus confuses St John the Baptist with St John the Evangelist, recalling the story of St John before the Latin Gate with this reference to the lock.

45. Ibid., 149.
46. Anna McMullan, *Performing Embodiment in Samuel Beckett's Drama* (London: Routledge, 2010), 3.
47. Knowlson, *Damned to Fame*, 588.
48. The Auditor was ultimately removed from stage productions of *Not I* as Beckett began to experiment with the play in performance.
49. Billie Whitelaw, *Billie Whitelaw . . . Who He? An Autobiography* (London: Hodder and Stoughton, 1996), 78.
50. Beckett to Edith Kern, 15 March 1986, *Letters*, vol. 4, 671.
51. Emilie Morin, *Samuel Beckett and the Problem of Irishness* (Basingstoke: Palgrave Macmillan, 2009), 150.
52. Beckett to Alan Schneider, 16 October [1972], in *No Author Better Served: The Correspondence of Samuel Beckett and Alan Schneider*, ed. Maurice Harmon (Cambridge, MA: Harvard University Press, 1998), 283.
53. Hannah Simpson, 'Kinaesthetic Empathy, Physical Recoil: The Conflicting Embodied Affects of Samuel Beckett's *Quad*', *Journal of Modern Literature* 42.2 (2019): 143.
54. Ibid., 141.
55. Anna McMullan, 'Samuel Beckett's "J. M. Mime": Generic Mutations of a Dramatic Fragment', *Samuel Beckett Today/Aujourd'hui* 16.1 (2006): 333–45.
56. Thomas Browne, *The Garden of Cyrus* (London, 1736), 4, Gale Eighteenth Century Collections Online.
57. Samuel Beckett, 'The Lost Ones', in *Samuel Beckett: The Complete Short Prose*, ed. S. E. Gontarski (New York: Grove Press, 1995), 204.
58. Dirk Van Hulle and Mark Nixon, *Samuel Beckett's Library* (Cambridge: Cambridge University Press, 2013), 76.
59. See Willard Bohn, 'Apollinaire, Salome and the Dance of Death', *French Studies* 57.4 (2003): 491–500.
60. Guillaume Apollinaire, 'Salomé', in *Alcools*, trans. Anne Hyde Greet (Berkeley, CA: University of California Press, 1965), 91.
61. Whitelaw, *Who He?*, 144.
62. Ibid., 144–5.
63. Lisa Dwan, 'Mouth Almighty – How Billie Whitelaw Helped Me Find Beckett and *Not I*', *American Theatre*, 12 April 2016, available at <http://www.americantheatre.org/2016/04/12/mouth-almighty-how-billie-whitelaw-helped-me-find-beckett-and-not-i/> (accessed 10 July 2017).
64. Brandstetter, *Poetics of Dance*, 23–4.
65. Beckett to Axel Kaun, 9 July [1937], in *Letters*, vol. 1, 518.
66. Ibid., 518.
67. Beckett to Kaun, 9 July [1937], in *Letters*, vol. 1, 519.
68. Albright, *Beckett and Aesthetics*, 13.
69. Agamben, *Nymphs*, 15.
70. Domenico da Piacenza, quoted in ibid., 7.
71. Ibid., 8.
72. Yeats, 'Poetry and Tradition', in *Early Essays*, 186.
73. Charles Baudelaire, *The Painter of Modern Life and Other Essays*, trans. Jonathan Mayne (London: Phaidon, 1964), 30.

BIBLIOGRAPHY

ARCHIVE SOURCES

Abbey Theatre Collection, Stuart A. Rose Library, Emory University, Atlanta, GA
Programme: April 16 [1928], Series 2, Box 2, Folder 58
Programme: November [1929], Series 2, Box 2, Folder 91
Programme: July 30 [1934], Series 2, Box 4, Folder 64
Bibliothèque nationale de France, Gallica
D'Humières, Robert. 'La Tragédie de Salomé'. *Théâtre des Champes-Élysées: saison russe* [programme], 13 June 1913

PUBLISHED WORKS

Abel, Richard, ed. *French Film Theory and Criticism.* Vol. 1, *1907–1939*. Princeton, NJ: Princeton University Press, 1993.
——. 'On the Threshold of French Film Theory and Criticism: 1915–1919'. *Cinema Journal* 25.1 (1985): 12–33.
Adorno, Theodor W., and Max Horkenheimer. *Dialectic of Enlightenment: Philosophical Fragments.* Ed. Gunzelin Schmid Noerr. Trans. Edmund Jephcott. Stanford, CA: Stanford University Press, 2002.
Anger, Kenneth. *Hollywood Babylon.* New York: Dell, 1981.
Agamben, Giorgio. 'Notes on Gesture'. In *Infancy and History: The Destruction of Experience.* Trans. Liz Heron. London: Verso, 1993. 133–40.
——. *Nymphs.* Trans. Amanda Minervini. London: Seagull Books, 2013.
——. *The Signature of All Things: On Method.* Trans. Luca D'Isanto with Kevin Attell. New York: Zone Books, 2009.
Albright, Ann Cooper. *Traces of Light: Absence and Presence in the Work of Loïe Fuller.* Middletown, CT: Wesleyan University Press, 2007.
Albright, Daniel. *Beckett and Aesthetics.* Cambridge: Cambridge University Press, 2003.
——. *Panaesthetics: On the Unity and Diversity of the Arts.* New Haven, CT: Yale University Press, 2014.

——. *Untwisting the Serpent: Modernism in Music, Literature and Other Arts*. Chicago: University of Chicago Press, 2000.
Allan, Maud. *My Life and Dancing*. London: Everett, 1908.
Anspaugh, Kelly. 'Faith, Hope and – What Was It? Beckett Reading Joyce Reading Dante'. *Journal of Beckett Studies* 5.1–2 (1995–96): 18–38.
Apollinaire, Guillaume. *Alcools*. Trans. Anne Hyde Greet. Berkeley, CA: University of California Press, 1965.
Armstrong, Charles. *Reframing Yeats: Genre, Allusion, and History*. London: Bloomsbury, 2013.
Armstrong, Tim. *Modernism, Technology and the Body: A Cultural Study*. Cambridge: Cambridge University Press, 1998.
'Art and Alla Nazimova: Russian Actress Sought Out as Model and Inspiration'. *New York Tribune*, 17 December 1911.
Arthur, Thomas. 'Female Interpreters of Ibsen on Broadway, 1896–1947: Minnie Maddern Fiske, Alla Nazimova & Eva Le Gallienne'. *Ibsen Studies* 1 (2000): 54–67.
'At Close Range with Alla Nazimova the Russo-English Actress'. *New York Times*, 18 November 1906.
'At Close Range with Alla Nazimova: Absorbs her Parts'. *New York Times*, 24 April 1910.
Bach, Alice. *Women, Seduction, and Betrayal in Biblical Narrative*. Cambridge: Cambridge University Press, 1997.
Banes, Sally. *Dancing Women: Female Bodies on Stage*. Abingdon: Routledge, 1998.
Bannerman, Henrietta. 'A Dance of Transition: Martha Graham's *Herodiade*'. *Dance Research* 24.1 (2006): 1–20.
Bara, Theda. 'The Curse on the Moving Picture Actress: Describing the Conflict in Her Artistic Experiences of the Moving-Picture Art'. *Forum*, July 1919, 83.
Barnes, Djuna. *Djuna Barnes: Interviews*. Ed. Alice Barry. College Park, MD: Sun and Moon Press, 1985.
——. *Nightwood*. London: Faber and Faber, 2007.
——. 'What Do You See, Madam?'. In *Smoke and Other Early Stories*. Ed. Douglas Messerli. Los Angeles: Sun and Moon Press, 1993. 47–53.
Barthes, Roland. *Mythologies*. Trans. Annette Lavers. London: Vintage, 2009.
——. *The Pleasure of the Text*. Trans. Richard Miller. New York: Hill and Wang, 1975.
Baudelaire, Charles. *The Painter of Modern Life and Other Essays*. Trans. Jonathan Mayne. London: Phaidon, 1964.
Becker-Leckrone, Megan. 'Salome: The Fetishization of a Textual Corpus'. *New Literary History* 26.2 (1995): 239–60.

Beckett, Samuel. *The Complete Dramatic Works*. London: Faber and Faber, 2006.
——. *The Complete Short Prose*. Ed. S. E. Gontarski. New York: Grove Press, 1995.
——. *Disjecta: Miscellaneous Writings and a Dramatic Fragment*. Ed. Ruby Cohn. London: Grove Press, 1983.
——. *Dream of Fair to Middling Women*. New York: Arcade, 1992.
——. *The Letters of Samuel Beckett*. Ed. George Craig, Martha Dow Fehsenfeld, Dan Gunn and Lois More Overbeck. 4 vols. Cambridge: Cambridge University Press, 2016.
——. *More Pricks than Kicks*. London: Faber and Faber, 2010.
——. *No Author Better Served: The Correspondence of Samuel Beckett and Alan Schneider*. Ed. Maurice Harmon. Cambridge, MA: Harvard University Press, 1998.
——. *The Theatrical Notebooks of Samuel Beckett*. Vol. 5, *The Shorter Plays*. Ed. S. E. Gontarski. London: Faber and Faber, 1999.
——. *Three Novels: Molloy, Malone Dies, The Unnamable*. New York: Grove Press, 2009.
Beizer, Janet L. *Ventriloquised Bodies: Narratives of Hysteria in Nineteenth-Century France*. Ithaca, NY: Cornell University Press, 1994.
Bell, John. 'Puppets, Masks and Performing Objects at the End of the Century'. *The Drama Review* 43.3 (1999): 15–27.
Bellow, Juliet. *Modernism on Stage: The Ballets Russes and the Parisian Avant-Garde*. London: Routledge, 2013.
Bennett, Chad. 'Oscar Wilde's *Salome*: Décor, Des Corps, Desire'. *ELH* 77.2 (2010): 297–324.
Bennett, Michael Y., ed. *Refiguring Oscar Wilde's Salome*. Amsterdam: Rodopi, 2011.
Benois, Alexandre. *Memoirs*. Trans. Moura Budberg. London: Chatto and Windus, 1964.
Bentley, Toni. *Sisters of Salome*. New Haven, CT: Yale University Press, 2002.
Berghaus, Günter. *Theatre, Performance, and the Historical Avant-Garde*. New York: Palgrave Macmillan, 2005.
Bergson, Henri. *Creative Evolution*. Trans. Arthur Mitchell. London: Macmillan, 1922.
——. *Time and Free Will: An Essay on the Immediate Data of Consciousness*. Trans. F. L. Pogson. Mineola, NY: Dover Publications, 2001.
Bernhardt, Sarah. *My Double Life: Memoirs of Sarah Bernhardt*. London: William Heinemann, 1907.
'Bernhardt's Hamlet'. *New York Tribune*, 11 June 1899.
Bernheimer, Charles. *Decadent Subjects: The Idea of Decadence in Art,*

Literature, Philosophy, and Culture of the Fin-de-Siècle in Europe. Baltimore, MD: Johns Hopkins University Press, 2002.

Berryman, John. *The Heart is Strange: New Selected Poems*. New York: Farrar, Straus and Giroux, 2014.

'The Billing Case'. *Manchester Guardian*, 3 June 1918.

Bizot, Richard. 'The Turn-of-the-Century Salome Era: High- and Pop-Culture Variations on the Dance of the Seven Veils'. *Choreography and Dance* 2 (1992): 71–87.

Blanchot, Maurice. *The Gaze of Orpheus and Other Literary Essays*. Trans. Lydia Davis. New York: Station Hill, 1981.

Bland, Lucy. *Modern Women on Trial: Sexual Transgression in the Age of the Flapper*. Manchester: Manchester University Press, 2013.

——. 'Trial by Sexology? Maud Allan, *Salome* and the "Cult of the Clitoris" Case'. In *Sexology in Culture: Labelling Bodies and Desires*. Ed. Lucy Bland and Laura Doan. Chicago: University of Chicago Press, 1998. 183–98.

Bloom, Harold. *The Anxiety of Influence*. Oxford: Oxford University Press, 1997.

Bohn, Willard. 'Apollinaire, Salome and the Dance of Death'. *French Studies* 57.4 (2003): 491–500.

Bordwell, David, Janet Staiger and Kristin Thompson. *The Classical Hollywood Cinema: Film Style and Mode of Production to 1960*. London: Routledge, 1988.

Boyd, Jason. 'Staging the Page: Visibility and Invisibility in Oscar Wilde's *Salome*'. *Nineteenth Century Theatre & Film* 35.1 (2008): 17–47.

Bradford, Curtis. *Yeats at Work*. Carbondale, IL: Southern Illinois University Press, 1965.

Bradshaw, David, Laura Marcus and Rebecca Roach, eds. *Moving Modernisms: Motion, Technology, Modernity*. Oxford: Oxford University Press, 2016.

Braidotti, Rosi. *Patterns of Dissonance: A Study of Women and Contemporary Philosophy*. Cambridge: Polity, 1991.

Brandstetter, Gabriele. *Poetics of Dance: Body, Image, and Space in the Historical Avant-Gardes*. Oxford: Oxford University Press, 2015.

Bristow, Joseph, ed. *Oscar Wilde and Modern Culture: The Making of a Legend*. Athens, OH: Ohio University Press, 2008.

Browne, Thomas. *The Garden of Cyrus*. London, 1736. Gale Eighteenth Century Collections Online.

Bruno, Giuliana. *Atlas of Emotion: Journeys in Art, Architecture and Film*. New York: Verso, 2002.

Buckle, Richard. *Diaghilev*. London: Hamish Hamilton, 1979.

Bucknell, Brad. 'On "Seeing" Salome'. *ELH* 60.2 (1993): 503–26.

Buller, Jeffrey L. 'Looking Backwards: Baroque Opera and the Ending of the Orpheus Myth'. *International Journal of the Classical Tradition* 1.3 (1995): 57–79.

Burke, Edmund. *A Philosophical Enquiry into the Sublime and Beautiful*. Ed. Paul Guyer. Oxford: Oxford University Press, 2015.

Butler, Judith. *Bodies that Matter: On the Discursive Limits of Sex*. London: Routledge, 1993.

——. *Gender Trouble: Feminism and the Subversion of Identity*. 2nd edn. London: Routledge, 1999.

Caddy, Davinia. *The Ballets Russes and Beyond: Music and Dance in Belle-Époque Paris*. Cambridge: Cambridge University Press, 2012.

——. 'Variations on the Dance of the Seven Veils'. *Cambridge Opera Journal* 17.1 (2005): 37–58.

Caselli, Daniela. *Improper Modernism: Djuna Barnes's Bewildering Corpus*. Aldershot: Ashgate, 2009.

Castle, Terry. *The Apparitional Lesbian: Female Homosexuality and Modern Culture*. New York: Columbia University Press, 1993.

Cave, Richard Allen. *Collaborations: Ninette de Valois and William Butler Yeats*. Alton: Dance Books, 2011.

'The Censor Again: "Hardy Plays" at Dorchester'. *The Times of India*, 12 December 1911.

Chartres, A. Vivanti. 'D'Annunzio's New Play *St. Sebastian*'. *The English Review* 8 (July 1911): 697.

Cherniavsky, Felix. 'Maud Allan Part II: First Steps to a Dancing Career, 1904–1907'. *Dance Chronicle* 6.3 (1982): 189–227.

——. *The Salome Dancer: The Life and Times of Maud Allan*. Toronto: McClelland and Stewart, 1991.

Cheyette, Bryan, and Laura Marcus, eds. *Modernity, Culture and 'The Jew'*. Cambridge: Polity, 1998.

Clark, Petra. '"Cleverly Drawn": Oscar Wilde, Charles Ricketts, and the Art of *The Woman's World*'. *Journal of Victorian Culture* 20.3 (2015): 375–400.

Clayton, Michelle. 'Modernism's Moving Bodies'. *Modernist Cultures* 9.1 (2014): 27–45.

'Coming Back to Dance'. *New York Tribune*, 23 February 1896.

Cooke, Peter. 'It Isn't a Dance: Gustave Moreau's *Salome* and *The Apparition*'. *Dance Research* 29 (2011): 214–32.

Copeland, Roger. 'Dance, Feminism and the Critique of the Visual'. In *Dance, Gender and Culture*. Ed. Helen Thomas. London: Macmillan, 1993. 139–50.

Cossart, Michael de. 'Ida Rubinstein and Diaghilev: A One-Sided Rivalry'. *Dance Research Journal* 1.2 (1983): 3–20.

Craig, Edward Gordon. *Craig on Movement and Dance*. Ed. Arnold Rood. New York: Dance Horizons, 1977.

———. *Craig on Theatre*. Ed. J. Michael Walton. London: Methuen Drama, 1983.
Craine, Debra, and Judith Mackrell. *The Oxford Dictionary of Dance*. Oxford: Oxford University Press, 2010.
Crary, Jonathan. *Suspensions of Perception*. Cambridge, MA: MIT Press, 1999.
Crowell, Ellen. 'The Ugly Things of *Salome*'. In *Decadence in the Age of Modernism*. Ed. Kate Hext and Alex Murray. Baltimore, MD: Johns Hopkins University Press, 2019. 47–70.
Cucullu, Lois. 'Wilde and Wilder Salomés: Modernising Wilde's Nubile Princess from Sarah Bernhardt to Norma Desmond'. *Modernism/modernity* 18 (2011): 495–524.
Cullingford, Elizabeth. *Yeats, Ireland and Fascism*. Basingstoke: Palgrave Macmillan, 1981.
Curl, James Stevens. *A Dictionary of Architecture and Landscape Architecture*. 2nd edn. Oxford: Oxford University Press, 2006.
Current, Richard, and Marcia Ewing Current. *Loïe Fuller: Goddess of Light*. Boston, MA: Northeastern University Press, 1997.
Daly, Ann. 'Dance History and Feminist Theory: Reconsidering Isadora Duncan and the Male Gaze'. In *Gender in Performance: The Presentation of Difference in the Performing Arts*. Ed. Laurence Senelick. Hanover, NH: University Press of New England, 1993. 239–59.
'Dancing on Screen: Napierkowska's Masterpiece'. *The Times of India*, 20 July 1916.
'Dancing Wins Actresses Applause'. *Chicago Daily Tribune*, 7 April 1907.
Danius, Sara. *The Senses of Modernism: Technology, Perception, and Aesthetics*. Ithaca, NY: Cornell University Press, 2002.
De Lauretis, Teresa. '*Nightwood* and the "Terror of Uncertain Signs"'. *Critical Enquiry* 34.S2 (2008): S117–S129.
———. *Technologies of Gender: Essays on Theory, Film and Fiction*. Bloomington, IN: Indiana University Press, 1987.
De Valois, Ninette. *Come Dance With Me: A Memoir, 1898–1956*. Dublin: Lilliput Press, 1992.
Debey, Jacques. 'La Tragédie de Salomé'. *Comœdia Illustré*, 5 July 1913.
Delap, Lucy. *The Feminist Avant-Garde: Transatlantic Encounters of the Early Twentieth Century*. Cambridge: Cambridge University Press, 2007.
Deleuze, Gilles. 'The Exhausted'. Trans. Anthony Uhlmann. *SubStance* 24.3 (1995): 3–28.
Didi-Huberman, Georges. *Invention of Hysteria: Charcot and the Photographic Iconography of the Salpêtrière*. Cambridge, MA: MIT Press, 2004.
———. *The Surviving Image: Phantoms of Time and Time of Phantoms: Aby Warburg's History of Art*. Trans. Harvey L. Mendelsohn. Philadelphia: Pennsylvania State University Press, 2017.

Dierkes-Thrun, Petra. '"The Brutal Music and the Delicate Text?": The Aesthetic Relationship between Wilde's and Strauss's *Salome* Reconsidered'. *Modern Language Quarterly* 69.3 (2008): 367–89.

——. *Salome's Modernity: Oscar Wilde and the Aesthetics of Transgression*. Ann Arbor, MI: University of Michigan Press, 2011.

Dijkstra, Bram. *Idols of Perversity: Fantasies of Feminine Evil in Fin-de-Siècle Culture*. Oxford: Oxford University Press, 1989.

Doane, Mary Ann. *Femme Fatales: Feminism, Film Studies, Psychoanalysis*. New York: Routledge, 1991.

Doody, Noreen. '"An Echo of Someone Else's Music": The Influence of Oscar Wilde on W. B. Yeats'. In *The Importance of Reinventing Oscar: Versions of Wilde During the Last 100 Years*. Ed. Uwe Böker et al. New York: Rodopi, 2002. 175–82.

——. *The Influence of Oscar Wilde on W. B. Yeats: 'An Echo of Someone Else's Music'*. Basingstoke: Palgrave Macmillan, 2018.

Doran, Emma. 'Figuring Modern Dance within Fin-de-siècle Visual Culture and Print: The Case of Loïe Fuller'. *Early Popular Visual Culture* 13.1 (2015): 21–40.

Dorn, Karen. *Players and Painted Stage: The Theatre of W. B. Yeats*. Brighton: Harvester Press, 1984.

'The Dublin Theatres: Abbey Players Again on Tour; Winter Season Opens'. *Irish Times*, 3 October 1934.

Dulac, Germaine. 'The Aesthetics, the Obstacles, Internal Cinégraphie'. *Framework* 19 (1982): 6–9.

——. *Écrits sur le cinema: 1919–1937*. Ed. Prosper Hillairet. Paris: Éditions Paris Experimental, 1994.

——. 'From Sentiment to Line'. In *Red Velvet Seat: Women's Writing on the First Fifty Years of Cinema*. Ed. Antonia Lant. London: Verso, 2006. 187–90.

——. 'The Music of Silence'. In *Red Velvet Seat: Women's Writing on the First Fifty Years of Cinema*. Ed. Antonia Lant. London: Verso, 2006. 216–18.

——. 'Thème visuel et variation cinégraphique' [typescript]. Fonds Germaine Dulac. Cinémathèque française, Paris. 80-B8.

Duncan, Isadora. *My Life*. New York: Liveright, 2013.

Duthuit, Georges. 'Vuillard and the Poets of Decadence'. Trans. Samuel Beckett. *ARTnews* 53 (1954): 29–31, 62–3.

Dwan, Lisa. 'Mouth Almighty – How Billie Whitelaw Helped Me Find Beckett and *Not I*'. *American Theatre*, 12 April 2016. http://www.americantheatre.org/2016/04/12/mouth-almighty-how-billie-whitelaw-helped-me-find-beckett-and-not-i/. Accessed 10 July 2017.

Eliot, T. S. *The Complete Prose of T. S. Eliot: The Critical Edition*. Vol. 6, *The*

War Years: 1940–1946, Ed. David E. Chinitz and Ronald Schuchard. Baltimore, MD: Johns Hopkins University Press, 2017.

———. *Selected Essays, 1917–1932*. New York: Harcourt, Brace, 1932.

Ellis, Havelock. *Man and Woman: A Study of Human Secondary Sexual Characters*. London: Walter Scott, 1894.

Ellis, Sylvia. *The Plays of W. B. Yeats: Yeats and the Dancer*. Basingstoke: Palgrave Macmillan, 1995.

Ellmann, Richard. *Oscar Wilde*. London: Hamish Hamilton, 1987.

Eltis, Sos. *Revising Wilde: Society and Subversion in the Plays of Oscar Wilde*. Oxford: Clarendon Press, 1996.

Emmanuel, Maurice. *The Antique Greek Dance, After Sculptured and Painted Figures*. Trans. Harriet Jean Beauley. London: John Lane, 1913.

English, Elizabeth. *Lesbian Modernism: Censorship, Sexuality and Genre Fiction*. Edinburgh: Edinburgh University Press, 2015.

Epstein, Jean. *Critical Essays and New Translations*. Ed. Sarah Keller and Jason N. Paul. Amsterdam: Amsterdam University Press, 2012.

Farfan, Penny. *Performing Queer Modernism*. Oxford: Oxford University Press, 2017.

———. *Women, Modernism, and Performance*. Cambridge: Cambridge University Press, 2004.

Fell, Jill. 'Dancing Under their own Gaze: Mallarmé, Jarry, and Valéry'. *Journal of European Studies* 24 (1999): 133–55.

Felski, Rita. *The Gender of Modernity*. Cambridge, MA: Harvard University Press, 1995.

Finney, Gail. *Women in Modern Drama: Freud, Feminism, and European Theater at the Turn of the Century*. Ithaca, NY: Cornell University Press, 1989.

Flaubert, Gustave. 'Herodias'. In *Three Tales*. Trans. A. J. Krailsheimer. Oxford: Oxford University Press, 1991.

Fleischer, Mary. *Embodied Texts: Symbolist Playwright–Dancer Collaborations*. Amsterdam: Rodopi, 2007.

Fletcher, Ian Christopher. 'The Soul of Man under Imperialism: Oscar Wilde, Race, and Empire'. *Journal of Victorian Culture* 5.2 (2000): 334–41.

Flitterman-Lewis, Sandy. 'The Image and the Spark: Dulac and Artaud Reviewed'. *Dada/Surrealism* 15 (1986): 110–27.

———. *To Desire Differently: Feminism and the French Cinema*. New York: Columbia University Press, 1996.

Foldy, Michael. *The Trials of Oscar Wilde: Deviance, Morality, and Late Victorian Society*. New Haven, CT: Yale University Press, 1997.

Forgione, Nancy. '"The Shadow Only": Shadow and Silhouette in Late Nineteenth-Century Paris'. *The Art Bulletin* 81.3 (1999): 490–512.

Foster, Roy. *W. B. Yeats: A Life*. 2 vols. Oxford: Oxford University Press, 1998.
Foucault, Michel. *The History of Sexuality Volume One*. Trans. Robert Hurley. New York: Random House, 1978.
Franko, Mark. *Dancing Modernism/Performing Politics*. Bloomington, IN: Indiana University Press, 1995.
Freedman, Jonathan. 'Transformations of a Jewish Princess: Salome and the Remaking of the Jewish Female Body from Sarah Bernhardt to Betty Boop'. *Philological Quarterly* 92 (2013): 89–114.
Freud, Sigmund. 'The Taboo of Virginity' [1917]. In *The Standard Edition of the Complete Psychological Works of Sigmund Freud*. Vol. 11: *Five Lectures on Psycho-Analysis, Leonardo da Vinci and Other Works*. Trans. Angela Richards. London: Hogarth Press, 1957. 191–208.
Fuller, Loïe. *Fifteen Years of a Dancer's Life: With Some Account of her Distinguished Friends*. Boston, MA: Maynard, 1913.
Gaëlle-Saliot, Anne. *The Drowned Muse: The Unknown Woman of the Seine's Survivals from Nineteenth-century Modernity to the Present*. Oxford: Oxford University Press, 2015.
Gagnier, Regenia. *Idylls of the Marketplace: Oscar Wilde and the Victorian Public*. Aldershot: Scolar Press, 1987.
Garafola, Lynn. *Legacies of Twentieth-Century Dance*. Middletown, CT: Wesleyan University Press, 2005.
——. *Rethinking the Sylph: New Perspectives on Romantic Ballet*. Middletown, CT: Wesleyan University Press, 1997.
——. 'Soloists Abroad: The Prewar Careers of Natalia Trouhanowa and Ida Rubinstein'. *Experiment* 2 (1996): 9–37.
Garafola, Lynn, and Nancy Van Norman, eds. *The Ballets Russes and its World*. New Haven, CT: Yale University Press, 1999.
Garber, Marjorie. *Vested Interests: Cross-Dressing and Cultural Anxiety*. New York: Routledge, 1992.
Garelick, Rhonda K. 'Electric Salome: Loïe Fuller at the Exposition Universelle of 1900'. In *Imperialism and Theater: Essays on World Theater, Drama, and Performance*. Ed. J. Ellen Gainor. New York: Routledge, 1995. 85–103.
——. *Electric Salome: Loïe Fuller's Performance of Modernism*. Princeton, NJ: Princeton University Press, 2007.
——. *Rising Star: Dandyism, Gender and Performance in the Fin de Siècle*. Princeton, NJ: Princeton University Press, 1998.
Gaudreault, André, Nicolas Dulac and Santiago Hidalgo, eds. *A Companion to Early Cinema*. London: Wiley-Blackwell, 2012.
Gay, Peter. *Education of the Senses: The Bourgeois Experience: Victoria to Freud*. New York: W. W. Norton, 1999.

Gilbert, Elliot L. '"Tumult of Images": Wilde, Beardsley and *Salome*'. *Victorian Studies* 26.2 (1983): 133–59.
Girard, René. 'Scandal and the Dance: Salome in the Gospel of Mark'. *New Literary History* 15.2 (1984): 311–24.
Glenn, Susan A. *Female Spectacle: The Theatrical Roots of Modern Feminism*. Cambridge, MA: Harvard University Press, 2000.
Gombrich, E. H. *Aby Warburg: An Intellectual Biography*. Oxford: Phaidon, 1986.
Goody, Alex. *Modernist Poetry, Gender and Leisure Technologies: Machine Amusements*. Basingstoke: Palgrave Macmillan, 2019.
Gotman, Kélina. 'Mallarmé's "*Livre*": Notes towards a Schizotheatre'. *Textual Practice* 33.1 (2019): 175–94.
Graham, Jorie. *Regions of Unlikeness: Explaining Contemporary Poetry*. Lincoln, NE: University of Nebraska Press, 1999.
Graham, Sheilah. *The Garden of Allah*. New York: Crown Publishers, 1970.
Gunning, Tom. 'Light, Motion, Cinema! The Heritage of Loïe Fuller and Germaine Dulac'. *Framework* 46.1 (2005): 106–29.
——. 'Loïe Fuller and the Art of Motion: Body, Light, Electricity, and the Origins of the Cinema'. In *Camera Obscura, Camera Lucida: Essays in Honour of Annette Michelson*. Ed. Richard Allen and Malcolm Turvey. Amsterdam: Amsterdam University Press, 2003. 75–90.
Hanson, H., and C. O'Rawe, eds. *The Femme Fatale: Images, Histories, Contexts*. Basingstoke: Palgrave Macmillan, 2010.
Haughton, Hugh. 'Oscar Wilde: Thinking Style'. In *Thinking Through Style*. Ed. Michael D. Hurley and Marcus Waithe. Oxford: Oxford University Press, 2018. 264–81.
Heidegger, Martin. *The Question Concerning Technology and Other Essays*. Trans. William Lovitt. New York: Garland, 1977.
Hindrichs, Cheryl. 'Feminist Optics and Avant-Garde Cinema: Germaine Dulac's "The Smiling Madame Beudet" and Virginia Woolf's "Street Haunting"'. *Feminist Studies* 35.2 (2009): 294–322.
Hindson, Catherine. 'The Female Illusionist – Loïe Fuller'. *Early Popular Visual Culture* 4.2 (2006): 161–74.
Hoare, Philip. *Oscar Wilde's Last Stand: Decadence, Conspiracy and the Most Outrageous Trial of the Century*. New York: Arcade, 1998.
Hogarth, William. *The Analysis of Beauty*. London: W. Strahan, 1772.
Holland, Merlin. ed. *The Real Trial of Oscar Wilde: The First Uncensored Transcript of the Trial of Oscar Wilde vs. John Douglas Marquess of Queensbury, 1895*. New York: Fourth Estate, 2003.
Huysmans, Joris-Karl. *Against Nature*. Trans. Nicholas White. Oxford: Oxford University Press, 2009.
Huyssen, Andreas. *After the Great Divide: Modernism, Mass Culture*

and Postmodernism. Bloomington, IN: Indiana University Press, 1986.
Im, Yeeyon. 'Oscar Wilde's *Salomé*: Disorienting Orientalism'. *Comparative Drama* 45.4 (2011): 361–80.
——. '"A Seriousness that Fails": Reconsidering Symbolism in Oscar Wilde's *Salomé*'. *Victorian Literature and Culture* 45.1 (2017): 163–75.
Jacobs, Karen. 'Two Mirrors Facing: Freud, Blanchot, and the Logic of Invisibility'. *Qui Parle* 4.1 (1990): 21–46.
Jaques-Dalcroze, Émile. *Rhythm, Music and Education*. Trans. Harold F. Rubinstein. London: Chatto and Windus, 1921.
Jarry, Alfred. *Ubu Roi*. Ed. Drew Silver. Trans. Beverly Keith and G. Legman. New York: Dover, 2003.
Järvinen, Hanna. 'Dancing without Space – On Nijinsky's *L'Après-Midi d'un Faune* (1912)'. *Dance Research* 27.1 (2009): 28–64.
Jones, Susan. '"At the Still Point": T. S. Eliot, Dance, and Modernism'. *Dance Research Journal* 41.2 (2009): 31–51.
——. *Literature, Modernism and Dance*. Oxford: Oxford University Press, 2013.
——. '"Une écriture corporelle": The Dancer in the Text of Mallarmé and Yeats'. In *The Body and the Arts*. Ed. Corinne Saunders, Ulrika Maude and Jane Macnaughton. Basingstoke: Palgrave Macmillan, 2009. 237–53.
Josephus, Flavius. 'Jewish Antiquities: Book XVIII, Chapter VIII'. In *The Genuine Works of Flavius Josephus*. Birmingham: Christopher Earl, 1770. Gale Eighteenth Century Collections Online.
Jowitt, Deborah. *Time and the Dancing Image*. Berkeley, CA: University of California Press, 1988.
Joyce, James. *A Portrait of the Artist as a Young Man*. Ed. Jeri Johnson. Oxford: Oxford University Press, 2008.
Kalba, Laura Anne. 'Fireworks and Other Profane Illuminations: Color and the Experience of Wonder in Modern Visual Culture'. *Modernism/modernity* 19.4 (2012): 657–76.
Kaplan, E. Ann. *Women & Film: Both Sides of the Camera*. New York: Routledge, 1988.
Kelly, John. *A W. B. Yeats Chronology*. Basingstoke: Palgrave Macmillan, 2003.
Kermode, Frank. 'Poet and Dancer before Diaghilev'. *Salmagundi* 33/34 (1976): 23–47.
——. *Romantic Image*. London: Routledge, 2002.
Kettle, Michael. *Salome's Last Veil: The Libel Case of the Century*. London: Hart-Davis, 1977.
Knowlson, James. *Damned to Fame: The Life of Samuel Beckett*. London: Bloomsbury, 1996.

Knowlson, James, and John Pilling. 'Beckett and Kleist's Essay "On the Marionette Theater"'. In *Frescoes of the Skull: The Later Prose and Drama of Samuel Beckett*. New York: Grove Press, 1980. 227–85.

Komesu, Okifumi. '*At the Hawk's Well* and *Taka No Izumi* in a Creative Circle'. *Yeats Annual* 5 (1987): 103–13.

Koritz, Amy. 'Dancing the Orient for England: Maud Allan's *The Vision of Salome*'. *Theatre Journal* 46 (1994): 63–78.

——. *Gendering Bodies/Performing Art: Dance and Literature in Early Twentieth-Century British Culture*. Ann Arbor, MI: University of Michigan Press, 1995.

Kramer, Lawrence. 'Culture and Musical Hermeneutics: The Salome Complex'. *The Cambridge Opera Journal* 2 (1990): 269–94.

Krasner, David. *A Beautiful Pageant: African American Theatre, Drama and Performance in the Harlem Renaissance, 1910–1927*. Basingstoke: Palgrave Macmillan, 2002.

Kristeva, Julia. *The Severed Head: Capital Visions*. New York: Columbia University Press, 2014.

Kuryluk, Ewa. *Salome and Judas in the Cave of Sex: The Grotesque: Origins, Iconography, Techniques*. Evanston, IL: Northwestern University Press, 1987.

'La Loie in Perihelion'. *Chicago Daily Tribune*, 12 April 1896.

'"La Loie" Talks of Her Art'. *New York Times*, 1 March 1896.

'La National: La Loie Fuller and Her Company'. *Washington Post*, 12 October 1909.

Lambert, Gavin. *Nazimova: A Biography*. New York: Alfred A. Knopf, 1997.

Lant, Antonia, ed. *Red Velvet Seat: Women's Writing on the First Fifty Years of Cinema*. London: Verso, 2006.

Lathrop, Elsie. 'Profile: Alla Nazimova'. *Vogue* 28, 1906.

Latimer, Tirza True. 'Loie Fuller: Butch Femme Fatale'. In *Proceedings of the Society of Dance History Scholars, 22nd Annual Conference*. Albuquerque, NM: University of New Mexico Press, 1999. 83–8.

Leeper, Janet. *Edward Gordon Craig: Designs for the Theatre*. London: Penguin, 1948.

Lejeune, Caroline A. *Cinema*. London: Alexander Maclehose, 1931.

Lepecki, André, ed. *Of the Presence of the Body: Essays on Dance and Performance Theory*. Middletown, CT: Wesleyan University Press, 2004.

Levine, Nancy J. '"I've always suffered from sirens": The Cinema Vamp and Djuna Barnes' *Nightwood*'. *Women's Studies* 16 (1989): 271–81.

Lewsadder, Matthew. 'Removing the Veils: Censorship, Female Sexuality, and Oscar Wilde's Salome'. *Modern Drama* 45 (2002): 519–44.

Linett, Maren Tova. *Modernism, Feminism and Jewishness*. Cambridge: Cambridge University Press, 2007.

Lista, Giovanni. *Loïe Fuller: Danseuse de la Belle Époque*. Paris: Somogy-Stock/La Librairie de la Danse et le Centre de national du livre, 1995.

'Loie Fuller's European Career'. *Chicago Daily Tribune*, 30 July 1893.

Lorrain, Jean. 'Magic Lantern'. In *Late Victorian Gothic Tales*. Ed. Roger Luckhurst. Oxford: Oxford University Press, 2009. 171–6.

'Madame Sarah Bernhardt in London'. *Manchester Guardian*, 18 June 1897.

Maeterlinck, Maurice. *The Treasure of the Humble*. Trans. Alfred Sutro. London: George Allen, 1903.

Mahoney, Kirsten. *Literature and the Politics of Post-Victorian Decadence*. Cambridge: Cambridge University Press, 2015.

Maier, Sarah E. 'Symbolist Salomés and the Dance of Dionysus'. *Nineteenth-Century Contexts* 28.3 (2006): 211–23.

Mallarmé, Stéphane. *Divagations*. Trans. Barbara Johnson. Cambridge, MA: Harvard University Press, 2007.

——. *Igitur, Divagations, Un Coup de dés*. Ed. Bertrand Marchal. Paris: Gallimard, 2003.

——. 'Herodiade'. Trans. David Lenson. *The Massachusetts Review* 30.4 (1989): 573–88.

Manning, Susan. *Ecstasy and the Demon: The Dances of Mary Wigman*. Minneapolis, MN: University of Minnesota Press, 2006.

——. 'The Female Dancer and the Male Gaze: Feminist Critiques of Early Modern Dance'. In *Meaning in Motion: New Cultural Studies of Dance*. Ed. Jane C Desmond. Durham, NC: Duke University Press, 1997. 153–66.

Mansell, Thomas. 'Describing Arabesques: Beckett and Dance'. In *Beckett and Musicality*. Ed. Sarah Jane Bailes and Nicholas Till. London: Routledge, 2014. 102–13.

Mao, Douglas, and Rebecca Walkowitz. 'The New Modernist Studies'. *PMLA* 123.3 (2008): 737–48.

Mao, Douglas, and Rebecca Walkowitz, eds. *Bad Modernisms*. Durham, NC: Duke University Press, 2006.

Marcus, Jane. 'Salomé: The Jewish Princess was a New Woman'. *Bulletin of the New York Public Library* 78.1 (1974): 95–113.

Marcus, Laura. *Dreams of Modernity: Psychoanalysis, Literature, Cinema*. Cambridge: Cambridge University Press, 2014.

——. *The Tenth Muse: Writing about Cinema in the Modernist Period*. Oxford: Oxford University Press, 2007.

Marcus, Laura, Michèle Mendelssohn and Kirsten E. Shepherd-Barr, eds. *Late Victorian into Modern*. Oxford: Oxford University Press, 2016.

Marcus, Sharon. 'Salomé!! Sarah Bernhardt, Oscar Wilde, and the Drama of Celebrity'. *PMLA* 126.4 (2011): 999–1021.

Marks, Laura. *The Skin of the Film: Intercultural Cinema, Embodiment and the Senses*. Durham, NC: Duke University Press, 2000.

Marshall, Norman. *The Other Theatre*. London: John Lehmann, 1947.
Marx, Edward. 'No Dancing: Yone Noguchi in Yeats's Japan'. *Yeats Annual* 17 (2007): 51–94.
Maude, Ulrika. *Beckett, Technology and the Body*. Cambridge: Cambridge University Press, 2009.
Maule, Rosanna. 'The Importance of Being a Film Author: Germaine Dulac and Female Authorship'. *Senses of Cinema* 23 (2002). http://sensesofcinema.com/2002/feature-articles/dulac/. Accessed 21 October 2020.
Maule, Rosanna, and Catherine Russell. 'Another Cinephilia: Women's Cinema in the 1920s'. *Framework* 46.1 (2005): 51–5.
McAteer, Michael. 'Music, Setting, Voice: Maeterlinck's *Pelléas et Mélisande* and Yeats's *The Countess Cathleen*'. *International Yeats Studies* 2.1 (2017): Article 2.
——. *Yeats and European Drama*. Cambridge: Cambridge University Press, 2010.
McCarren, Felicia. *Dancing Machines: Choreographies of the Age of Mechanical Reproduction*. Stanford, CA: Stanford University Press, 2003.
——. 'Stéphane Mallarmé, Loïe Fuller and the Theater of Femininity'. In *Bodies of the Text: Dance as Theory, Literature as Dance*. Ed. Ellen W. Goellner and Jacqueline Shea Murphy. New Brunswick, NJ: Rutgers University Press, 1995. 217–30.
——. 'The "Symptomatic Act" circa 1900: Hysteria, Hypnosis, Electricity, Dance'. *Critical Enquiry* 21 (1995): 748–74.
McGuinness, Patrick. *Maurice Maeterlinck and the Making of Modern Theatre*. Oxford: Oxford University Press, 2000.
——, ed. *Symbolism, Decadence, and the Fin de Siècle: French and European Perspectives*. Exeter: University of Exeter Press, 2000.
McMullan, Anna. *Performing Embodiment in Samuel Beckett's Drama*. London: Routledge, 2010.
——. 'Samuel Beckett's "J. M. Mime": Generic Mutations of a Dramatic Fragment'. *Samuel Beckett Today/Aujourd'hui* 16.1 (2006): 333–45.
Medd, Jodie. '"The Cult of the Clitoris": Anatomy of a National Scandal'. *Modernism/modernity* 9.1 (2002): 21–49.
——. *Lesbian Scandal and the Cultures of Modernism*. Cambridge: Cambridge University Press, 2012.
Meltzer, Françoise. *Salome and the Dance of Writing: Portraits of Mimesis in Literature*. Chicago: University of Chicago Press, 1987.
Mester, Teri A. *Movement and Modernism: Yeats, Eliot, Lawrence, Williams and Early Twentieth-Century Dance*. Fayetteville, AK: University of Arkansas Press, 1997.
Meyerhold, Vsevolod. *Meyerhold on Theatre*. Trans. Edward Braun. London: Methuen, 1969.

Mikhail, E. H., ed. *Oscar Wilde: Interviews and Recollections*. 2 vols. London: Macmillan, 1979.
Miller, Liam. *The Noble Drama of W. B. Yeats*. Dublin: Dolmen Press, 1977.
Mills, Dana. *Dance and Politics*. Manchester: Manchester University Press, 2016.
——. 'The Dancing Woman is the Woman Who Dances into the Future: Rancière, Dance, Politics'. *Philosophy and Rhetoric* 49.4 (2016): 482–99.
Misler, Nicoletta. 'Seven Steps, Seven Veils: Salomé in Russia'. *Experiment* 17 (2011): 155–84.
'Miss Fuller's New Dance'. *New York Times*, 24 January 1896.
Morin, Emilie. *Samuel Beckett and the Problem of Irishness*. Basingstoke: Palgrave Macmillan, 2009.
——. 'Theatres and Pathologies of Silence: Symbolism and Irish Drama from Maeterlinck to Beckett'. In *Silence in Modern Irish Literature*. Ed. Michael McAteer. Leiden: Brill-Rodopi, 2017. 35–48.
Morris, Gay. 'Massine/Picasso/*Parade*'. *Modernist Cultures* 9.1 (2014): 46–61.
Mounsef, Donia. 'Women Filmmakers and the Avant-Garde: From Dulac to Duras'. In *Women Filmmakers: Refocusing*. Ed. Jacqueline Levitin, Judith Plessis and Valerie Raoul. London: Routledge, 2003. 38–50.
'Mr Pemberton Billing and Miss Maud Allan: The Opening'. *Manchester Guardian*, 30 May 1918.
Mulrooney, Deirdre. *Irish Moves: An Illustrated History of Dance and Physical Theatre in Ireland*. Dublin: Liffey Press, 2006.
Myers, Kimberley R. 'W. B. Yeats's Steinach Operation, Hinduism, and the Severed-Head Plays of 1934–35'. *Literature and Medicine* 28 (2009): 102–37.
Negra, Diane, and Jennifer Bean, eds. *A Feminist Reader in Early Cinema*. Durham, NC: Duke University Press, 2002.
Nietzsche, Friedrich. *The Birth of Tragedy: Out of the Spirit of Music*. Trans. Shaun Whiteside. London: Penguin, 1993.
——. *Thus Spoke Zarathustra*. Trans. Graham Parkes. Oxford: Oxford University Press, 2005.
——. *Twilight of the Idols and The Anti-Christ*. Trans. R. J. Hollingdale. London: Penguin, 1990.
Nochlin, Linda. *Women, Art and Power, and Other Essays*. London: Thames and Hudson, 1989.
North, Michael. 'The Ambiguity of Repose: Sculpture and the Public Art of W. B. Yeats'. *ELH* 50.2 (1983): 379–400.
——. *Machine-Age Comedy*. Oxford: Oxford University Press, 2009.
O'Brien, Conor Cruise. 'Passion and Cunning: An Essay on the Politics of W. B. Yeats'. In *In Excited Reverie: Centenary Tribute to W. B. Yeats*.

Ed. A. Norman Jeffares and K. G. W. Cross. London: Macmillan, 1965. 207–78.
O'Brien, Victoria. *A History of Irish Ballet: 1927–1963*. Oxford: Peter Lang, 2011.
O'Driscoll, Robert, and Lorna Reynolds, eds. *Yeats and the Theatre*. Toronto: Macmillan of Canada, 1975.
Odom, Selma Landen. 'The Dalcroze Method, Marie Rambert, and *Le Sacre du Printemps*'. *Modernist Cultures* 9.1 (2014): 7–26.
Okamuro, Minako. 'Alchemical Dances in Beckett and Yeats'. *Samuel Beckett Today/Aujourd'hui* 14 (2004): 87–103.
Olf, Julian. 'The Man/Marionette Debate in Modern Theatre'. *Educational Theatre Journal* 26.4 (1974): 488–94.
'On the Screen: Theda Bara Brings a Celluloid Salome to Enliven Broadway', *New York Tribune*, 8 October 1918.
Ovid. *Metamorphoses*. Trans. A. D. Melville. Oxford: Oxford University Press, 2008.
Paraskeva, Anthony. 'Beckett, Biomechanics, and Eisenstein's Reading of Kleist's Marionettes'. *Journal of Beckett Studies* 22 (2013): 161–79.
——. *The Speech-Gesture Complex: Modernism, Theatre, Cinema*. Edinburgh: Edinburgh University Press, 2013.
Pater, Walter. *Studies in the History of the Renaissance*. Ed. Matthew Beaumont. Oxford: Oxford University Press, 2010.
Pilling, John. *A Samuel Beckett Chronology*. Basingstoke: Palgrave Macmillan, 2006.
Postlewait, Thomas. *The Cambridge Introduction to Theatre Historiography*. Cambridge: Cambridge University Press, 2009.
Potter, Susan. *Queer Timing: The Emergence of Lesbian Sexuality in Early Cinema*. Urbana, IL: University of Illinois Press, 2019.
Powell, Kerry. *Acting Wilde: Victorian Sexuality, Theatre, and Oscar Wilde*. Cambridge: Cambridge University Press, 2011.
——. *Oscar Wilde and the Theatre of the 1890s*. Cambridge: Cambridge University Press, 1990.
Praz, Mario. *The Romantic Agony*. Trans. Angus Davidson. New York: Meridian, 1956.
Preston, Carrie J. *Learning to Kneel: Noh, Modernism, and Journeys in Teaching*. New York: Columbia University Press, 2016.
——. 'Modernism's Dancing Marionettes: Oskar Schlemmer, Michel Fokine, and Ito Michio'. *Modernist Cultures* 9 (2014): 115–33.
——. *Modernism's Mythic Pose: Gender, Genre, Solo Performance*. Oxford: Oxford University Press, 2011.
——. 'The Motor in the Soul: Isadora Duncan and Modernist Performance'. *Modernism/modernity* 12.2 (2005): 273–89.

Prins, Yopie. 'Greek Maenads, Victorian Spinsters'. In *Victorian Sexual Dissidence*. Ed. Richard Dellamora. Chicago: University of Chicago Press, 1999. 43–82.

Pritchard, Jane. 'Serge Diaghilev's Ballets Russes – An Itinerary. Part 1: 1909–1921'. *Dance Research* 27.1 (2009): 109–98.

Puchner, Martin. *Stagefright: Modernism, Anti-Theatricality and Drama*. Baltimore, MD: Johns Hopkins University Press, 2002.

Pym, Anthony. 'The Importance of Salomé: Approaches to a *Fin de Siècle* Theme'. *French Forum* 14.3 (1989): 311–22.

Raby, Peter, ed. *The Cambridge Companion to Oscar Wilde*. Cambridge: Cambridge University Press, 1997.

Rainey, Lawrence, ed. *Modernism: An Anthology*. London: Blackwell, 2005.

Rancière, Jacques. *Aesthetics and its Discontents*. Trans. and ed. Steven Corcoran. Cambridge: Polity, 2009.

———. *Aisthesis: Scènes du régime esthétique de l'art*. Paris: Éditions Galilée, 2011.

———. *Aisthesis: Scenes from the Aesthetic Regime of Art*. Trans. Zakir Paul. London: Verso, 2013.

Reynolds, Dee. 'The Dancer as Woman: Loïe Fuller and Stéphane Mallarmé'. In *Impressions of French Modernity: Art and Literature in France, 1850–1900*. Ed. Richard Hobbs. Manchester: Manchester University Press, 1995. 155–72.

———. *Symbolist Aesthetics and Early Abstract Art: Sites of Imaginary Space*. Cambridge: Cambridge University Press, 1995.

Reynolds, Paige. '"A Theatre of the Head": Material Culture, Severed Heads, and the Late Drama of W. B. Yeats'. *Modern Drama* 58.4 (2015): 437–60.

Rice, David Edgar. 'Why Danger Lurks in Nimble Toes of Dancing Stage Beauties'. *Washington Post*. 15 March 1914.

Ricketts, Charles. *Recollections of Oscar Wilde*. London: Pallas Athene Arts, 2011.

Riordan, Kevin. 'Italic Choreography in the Dance Plays of W. B. Yeats'. *Theatre Annual* 64 (2011): 44–62.

Riquelme, J. P. 'Shalom/Solomon/*Salomé*: Modernism and Wilde's Aesthetic Politics'. *The Centennial Review* 39 (Fall 1995): 575–610.

Rodenbach, Georges. *Bruges-la-Morte*. Trans. Mike Mitchell. Sawtry: Dedalus European Classics, 2005.

Rose, Marilyn Gaddis. 'The Daughters of Herodias in *Hérodiade*, *Salomé*, and *A Full Moon in March*'. *Comparative Drama* 1.3 (1967): 172–81.

Rowden, Clair, ed. *Performing Salome, Revealing Stories*. Farnham: Ashgate, 2013.

Ruprecht, Lucia. *Dances of the Self in Heinrich von Kleist, E. T. A. Hoffmann and Heinrich Heine*. Aldershot: Ashgate, 2006.
'The Russian Ballet: Florent Schmitt's *La Tragédie de Salome*'. *Observer*, 6 July 1917.
Rutherford, Annabel. 'The Triumph of the Veiled Dance: The Influence of Oscar Wilde and Aubrey Beardsley on Serge Diaghilev's Creation of the Ballets Russes'. *Dance Research* 27 (2009): 93–107.
Said, Edward. *Orientalism*. London: Penguin, 2003.
'The Salome Dance Gets into Politics'. *New York Times*, 24 August 1908.
Santini, Daria. 'That Invisible Dance: Reflections on the "Dance of the Seven Veils" in Richard Strauss's *Salome*'. *Dance Research* 29 (2011): 233–45.
Savage, Roger. *Masques, Mayings, and Music Dramas*. Woodbridge: Boydell and Brewer, 2014.
Schmid, Herta. 'Samuel Beckett's Play *Quad*: An Abstract Synthesis of the Theatre'. *Canadian-American Slavic Studies* 22.1–4 (1988): 263–87.
Schuchard, Ronald. *The Last Minstrels: Yeats and the Revival of the Bardic Arts*. Oxford: Oxford University Press, 2008.
Schwartz, Hillel. 'Torque: The New Kinaesthetic of the Twentieth Century'. In *Incorporations*. Ed. Jonathan Crary and Sanford Kwinter. New York: Zone Books, 1992. 71–127.
'Science Explains their Fascination'. *Washington Post*, 15 March 1914.
'The Screen: A New Salome'. *New York Times*, 1 January 1923.
Sedgwick, Eve Kosofsky. *Tendencies*. Durham, NC: Duke University Press, 1993.
Segel, Harold B. *Body Ascendant: Modernism and the Physical Imperative*. Baltimore, MD: Johns Hopkins University Press, 1998.
——. *Pinocchio's Progeny: Puppets, Marionettes, Automatons, and Robots in Modernist and Avant-Garde Drama*. Baltimore, MD: Johns Hopkins University Press, 1995.
Shepherd, David J. *The Bible on Silent Film: Spectacle, Story and Scripture in the Early Cinema*. Cambridge: Cambridge University Press, 2013.
Sherry, Vincent. *Modernism and the Reinvention of Decadence*. Cambridge: Cambridge University Press, 2015.
Shewan, Rodney. 'Oscar Wilde's *Salomé*: A Critical Variorum Edition from Three Extant Manuscripts – Proofsheets and Two Early Printed Texts Transcribed in Parallel'. 2 vols. PhD dissertation, University of Reading, 1982. uk.bl.ethos.403994.
Shloss, Carol Loeb. *Lucia Joyce: To Dance in the Wake*. London: Bloomsbury, 2005.
Showalter, Elaine. *Hystories: Hysterical Epidemics and Modern Media*. New York: Columbia University Press, 1997.

―――. *Sexual Anarchy: Gender and Culture at the Fin-de-siècle*. New York: Virago, 1992.
Shteir, Rachel. *Striptease: The Untold History of the Girlie Show*. New York: Oxford University Press, 2004.
Simonson, Mary. *Body Knowledge: Performance, Intermediality and American Entertainment at the Turn of the Twentieth Century*. Oxford: Oxford University Press, 2013.
Simpson, Hannah. 'Kinaesthetic Empathy, Physical Recoil: The Conflicting Embodied Affects of Samuel Beckett's *Quad*'. *Journal of Modern Literature* 42.2 (2019): 132–48.
―――. '"Now Keep Out of the Way, Whitelaw": Self-Expression, Agency, and Directorial Control in W. B. Yeats's and Samuel Beckett's Theatre'. *Comparative Drama* 49.4 (2015): 399–418.
Sirotkina, Irina, and Roger Smith. *The Sixth Sense of the Avant-Garde: Dance, Kinaesthesia and the Arts in Revolutionary Russia*. London: Bloomsbury, 2017.
Sobchack, Vivian. *Carnal Thoughts: Embodiment and Moving Image Culture*. Berkeley, CA: University of California Press, 2004.
Solano, Solita. 'Ibsen Reforms a Vampire'. *New York Tribune*, 19 May 1918.
Sommer, Sally. 'Loïe Fuller'. *The Drama Review* 19.1 (1975): 53–67.
Sorley-Walker, Kathrine. 'The Festival and the Abbey: Ninette de Valois' Early Choreography, 1925–1934, Part One'. *Dance Chronicle* 7.4 (1983): 379–412.
Spears, Jack. *Hollywood: The Golden Era*. New York: Castle Books, 1971.
Sperling, Jody. 'Book Reviews'. *Dance Films Association: Annual Review* (2008): 14–17.
'The Spread of Bohemianism in English Society'. *New York Times*, 16 August 1908.
Starte, Josephine. 'Beckett's Dances'. *Journal of Beckett Studies* 23.2 (2014): 178–201.
Stebbins, Genevieve. *Dynamic Breathing and Harmonic Gymnastics*. New York: Edgar S. Werner, 1892.
Steer, Valentia. *The Secrets of the Cinema: Your Favourite Amusement from Within*. London: Pearson, 1920.
Stephens, John Russell. *The Censorship of English Drama, 1824–1901*. Cambridge: Cambridge University Press, 1980.
Stoker, Bram, *Personal Reminiscences of Henry Irving*. London: William Heinemann, 1907.
Stokes, John, ed. *Fin de siècle/Fin du globe: Fears and Fantasies of the Late Nineteenth Century*. Basingstoke: Palgrave Macmillan, 1992.
―――. *In the Nineties*. Chicago: University of Chicago Press, 1989.

Stoljar, Margaret. 'Mirror and Self in Symbolist and Post-Symbolist Poetry'. *The Modern Language Review* 85 (1990): 362–72.
Stott, Rebecca. *The Fabrication of the Late-Victorian Femme Fatale: The Kiss of Death*. Basingstoke: Palgrave Macmillan, 1992.
Strauss, Walter A. *Descent and Return: The Orphic Theme in Modern Literature*. Cambridge, MA: Harvard University Press, 1971.
Studlar, Gaylyn. '"Out-Salomeing Salome": Dance, the New Woman, and Fan Magazine Orientalism'. *Michigan Quarterly Review* 34.4 (1995): 487–510.
Sweeney, Bernadette. *Performing the Body in Irish Theatre*. Basingstoke: Palgrave Macmillan, 2008.
Symons, Arthur. *Poems by Arthur Symons*. 2 vols. London: William Heinemann, 1902.
——. *The Symbolist Movement in Literature*. Ed. Matthew Creasy. Manchester: Carcanet, 2014.
Tanitch, Robert. *Oscar Wilde on Stage and Screen*. London: Methuen, 1999.
Taxidou, Olga. *Modernism and Performance: Jarry to Brecht*. Basingstoke: Palgrave Macmillan, 2007.
Taylor, Richard. *The Drama of W. B. Yeats: Irish Myth and the Japanese Nō*. New Haven, CT: Yale University Press, 1976.
Terry, Ellen. *The Story of My Life: Recollections and Reflections*. New York: Doubleday, 1908.
Thurschwell, Pamela. *Literature, Technology and Magical Thinking*. Cambridge: Cambridge University Press, 2001.
Townsend, Julie. 'Alchemic Visions and Technological Advances: Sexual Morphology in Loïe Fuller's Dance'. In *Dancing Desires: Choreographing Sexualities On and Off the Stage*. Ed. Jane C. Desmond. Madison, WI: University of Wisconsin Press, 2001. 73–96.
——. 'Staking Salomé: The Literary Forefathers and Choreographic Daughters of Oscar Wilde's "Hysterical and Perverted Creature"'. In *Oscar Wilde and Modern Culture: The Making of a Legend*. Ed. J. Bristow. Athens, OH: Ohio University Press, 2008. 154–79.
——. 'Synaesthetics: Symbolism, Dance and the Failure of Metaphor'. *The Yale Journal of Criticism* 18 (2005): 126–48.
'The Transformation of Nazimova'. *Current Literature* XLIII (December 1907).
Trotter, David. *Cinema and Modernism*. Oxford: Blackwell, 2007.
Tydeman, William, and Steven Price. *Wilde: Salome*. Cambridge: Cambridge University Press, 1996.
Uhlmann, Anthony. 'Expression and Affect in Kleist, Beckett, and Deleuze'. In *Deleuze and Performance*. Ed. Laura Cull. Edinburgh: Edinburgh University Press, 2009. 54–70

'Vamps and Near-Vamps'. *New York Tribune*, 11 May 1919, E6.
Van Hulle, Dirk, and Mark Nixon. *Samuel Beckett's Library*. Cambridge: Cambridge University Press, 2013.
Veder, Robin. 'The Expressive Efficacies of American Delsarte and Mensendieck Body Culture'. *Modernism/modernity* 17 (2010): 819–38.
Vincent, Renée. 'The Influences of Isadora Duncan on the Designs of Edward Gordon Craig'. *Theatre Design and Technology* 34.1 (1998): 37–48.
Von Kleist, Heinrich. 'On the Marionette Theatre'. Trans. Thomas G. Neumiller. *TDR* 16.3 (1972): 22–6.
Walbrook, H. M. 'The Invasion of the Dancers'. *The Pall Mall Magazine*, January 1912, 19–27.
Walkowitz, Judith R. *Nights Out: Life in Cosmopolitan London*. New Haven, CT: Yale University Press, 2012
———. 'The *Vision of Salome*: Cosmopolitanism and Erotic Dancing in Central London 1908–1918'. *The American Historical Review* 108.2 (2003): 337–76.
Wall-Romana, Christophe. *Cinepoetry: Imaginary Cinemas in French Poetry*. New York: Fordham University Press, 2013.
———. 'Mallarmé's Cinepoetics: The Poem Uncoiled by the Cinématographe, 1893–98'. *PMLA* 120.1 (2005): 128–47.
Warburg, Aby. 'The Absorption of the Expressive Values of the Past (Introduction to the *Mnemosyne Atlas*)'. Trans. Matthew Rampley. *Art in Translation* 1.2 (2009): 273–83.
———. *The Renewal of Pagan Antiquity: Contributions to the Cultural History of the European Renaissance*. Trans. David Britt. Los Angeles: Getty Research Institute, 1999.
'We Noticed Mr. Oscar Wilde's *Salome*'. *The Times*, 8 March 1894.
Weir, David. *Decadence and the Making of Modernism*. Amherst, MA: University of Massachusetts Press, 1995.
Whitelaw, Billie. *Billie Whitelaw … Who He? An Autobiography*. London: Hodder and Stoughton, 1996.
Wilde, Oscar. *The Complete Works of Oscar Wilde*. 5th edn. Ed. Merlin Holland. London: Harper Collins, 1948; reprinted 2003.
———. *The Complete Works of Oscar Wilde*. Vol. 5, Plays I: The Duchess of Padua, Salomé: Drame en un Acte, Salome: Tragedy in One Act. Ed. Joseph Donohue. Oxford: Oxford University Press, 2013.
———. *The Letters of Oscar Wilde*. Ed. Rupert Hart-Davis. London: Hart-Davis, 1962.
———. *The Picture of Dorian Gray*. Ed. Joseph Bristow. Oxford: Oxford World's Classics, 2006.
Williams, Tami. 'Early Cinema and the Archives'. *The Moving Image* 16.1 (2016): ix–xv.

——. *Germaine Dulac: A Cinema of Sensations*. Urbana, IL: University of Illinois Press, 2014.

——. 'Toward the Development of a Modern "Impressionist" Cinema: Germaine Dulac's *La Belle Dame sans Merci* (1921) and the Deconstruction of the Femme Fatale Archetype'. *Framework* 51.2 (2010): 404–19.

Wittig, Monique. 'One is not Born a Woman'. In *The Norton Anthology of Theory and Criticism*. Ed. Vincent B. Leitch et al. New York: W. W. Norton, 2010. 1906–13.

Wollen, Peter. 'Fashion/Orientalism/The Body'. *New Formations* 1 (1987): 5–33.

Woolf, Virginia. 'The Cinema'. In *Selected Essays*. Ed. David Bradshaw. Oxford: Oxford University Press, 2008. 172–6.

——. *Mrs Dalloway*. Ed. David Bradshaw. Oxford: Oxford University Press, 2009.

Worth, Katharine. *The Irish Drama of Europe from Yeats to Beckett*. London: Athlone Press, 1978.

——. *Oscar Wilde*. Basingstoke: Macmillan, 1983.

Yeats, W. B. *Autobiographies*. Ed. William O' Donnell and Douglas N. Archibald. Vol. 3 in *The Collected Works of W. B. Yeats*. Ed. Richard J. Finneran and George Mills Harper. New York: Scribner, 1999.

——. *The Collected Letters of W. B. Yeats* [electronic edition]. Ed. John Kelly, Eric Domville, Warwick Gould, Ronald Schuchard and Deirdre Toomey. 4 vols. Charlottesville, VA: InteLex Corp, 2002.

——. *The Collected Plays of W. B. Yeats*. London: Macmillan, 1960.

——. *Early Essays*. Ed. George Bornstein and Richard J. Finneran. Vol. 4 in *The Collected Works of W. B. Yeats*. Ed. Richard J. Finneran and George Mills Harper. New York: Scribner, 2007

——. *Essays and Introductions*. Ed. William O'Donnell. Vol. 5 in *The Collected Works of W. B. Yeats*. Ed. Richard J. Finneran and George Mills Harper. New York: Scribner, 1994.

——. *Four Plays for Dancers*. London: Macmillan, 1921.

——. *The King of the Great Clock Tower and A Full Moon in March: Manuscript Materials*. Ed. Richard Allen Cave. Ithaca, NY: Cornell University Press, 2007.

——. *The Major Works*. Ed. Edward Larrissy. Oxford: Oxford University Press, 2001.

——. *Prefaces and Introductions*. Ed. William H. O'Donnell. Vol. 6 in *The Collected Works of W. B. Yeats*. Ed. Richard J. Finneran and George Mills Harper. New York: Macmillan, 1989.

——. 'Two Poems Concerning Peasant Visionaries'. *The Savoy: An Illustrated Monthly*, April 1896, 109.

——. *The Variorum Edition of the Poems of W. B. Yeats*. Ed. Peter Allt and Russell K. Alspach. New York: Macmillan, 1957.

———. *A Vision: The Original 1925 Version*. Ed. Catherine E. Paul and Margaret Mills Harper. Vol. 13 in *The Collected Works of W. B. Yeats*. Ed. Richard J. Finneran and George Mills Harper. New York: Scribner, 2008.

Zagona, Helen. *The Legend of Salome and the Principle of Art for Art's Sake*. Geneva: Droz, 1960.

Zatlin, Linda Gertner. 'Wilde, Beardsley, and the Making of Salome'. *Journal of Victorian Culture* 5 (2000): 341–57.

Zinman, Toby Silverman. 'Lucky's Dance in *Waiting for Godot*'. *Modern Drama* 38.3 (1995): 308–23.

Filmography

Disque 957. Directed and produced by Germaine Dulac. France, 1929. Light Cone Film.

Étude cinégraphique sur une Arabesque. Directed and produced by Germaine Dulac. France, 1929. Light Cone Film.

Salome. Directed by J. Stuart Blackton. Vitagraph Company of America, 1908. British Film Institute.

Salomé: An Historical Phantasy by Oscar Wilde. Directed by Charles Bryant. Nazimova Productions, 1922. Alpha Home Entertainment: Lost Silent Classics Collection, 2012.

Salome Mad. Directed by A. E. Coleby. Cricks and Martin, 1909. British Film Institute.

The Show. Directed by Tod Browning. Metro-Goldwyn-Mayer, 1927. Warner Brothers Archive Collection, 2012.

Sunset Boulevard. Directed by Billy Wilder. Paramount 1950. Paramount Collection, 2003.

Thèmes et Variations. Directed and produced by Germaine Dulac. France, 1929. Light Cone Film.

Viva la Dance: The Beginnings of Ciné-dance, 1894–c.1950. Directed by Bruce Posner, David Shephard, Robert A. Haller and Günter Winfried. Anthology Film Archives, 2005.

INDEX

Abbey School of Ballet, 19, 173, 175–6, 180
Abbey Theatre, 19, 26, 153, 166, 170, 173–5, 180–2
Adorno, Theodor, 18, 30n72
aesthetic feeling, 15–16
Aestheticism, 6, 77, 92, 156
Agamben, Giorgio, 13, 15, 21, 133, 206
Aguglia, Mimi, 24, 114, 116–18
Albright, Daniel, 18, 192, 205
Allan, Maud, 5, 6, 16, 20, 22, 23, 26, 35, 57–66, 78, 112, 124, 189
  biography, 58, 65
  Delsartism, 59
  influences, 58–9
  libel trial, 63–6
  natural movement, 59
  queerness, 58, 65
  and suffrage movement, 62–3
  Salomé, 63–6
  The Vision of Salome, 58–60, 137, 164
Allen Cave, Richard, 102, 178, 180
antisemitism, 119, 177
Antipas, Herod, 2, 3, 5, 12, 23, 27, 50, 94, 96, 123, 126, 127, 133, 179, 190
Apollinaire, Guillaume, 26, 203
Apollonian, 8
Appia, Adolphe, 168
arabesque, 86, 144
Arbuckle, Fatty, 124
arc en cercle, 15, 53–4
Arikha, Avigdor, 200
Armstrong, Tim, 19, 42, 94, 108n78
Art Nouveau, 24, 91, 112, 113, 125, 127, 129
Artaud, Antonin, 89, 135, 146
ARTnews, 193
Asquith, Herbert, 58
Asquith, Margot, 58, 65

Ausdruckstanz, 53
Avril, Jane, 41

Bach, Alice, 3
Bakst, Léon, 103, 104
Balanchine, Georges, 173
Ballet, 15, 19, 22, 24, 34, 36, 42, 46, 47, 84, 89, 90, 104, 120, 122, 127, 129, 137, 141, 144, 162, 164, 171, 173, 180, 189, 192, 202
Ballets Russes, 19, 84, 90, 103, 113, 116, 120, 123–33, 145, 156, 165, 173, 176
  L'Après-midi d'un faune, 126, 129
  Cléopâtre, 104, 149n85
  Jeux, 125, 126
  Parade, 19, 112
  Petrouchka, 90
  Le Rossignol, 126
  Le Sacre du Printemps, 125–6
  Schéhérazade, 139, 149n85
  La Tragédie de Salomé (1913), 24, 66, 123–33, 180
Banes, Sally, 23, 35
Bara, Theda, 5, 114, 124–5
Barnes, Djuna, 24, 25, 70n80, 114, 115–19, 206
Barthes, Roland, 22, 62
Baudelaire, Charles, 28n11, 118, 207
Bean, Jennifer, 113
Beardsley, Aubrey, 6, 24, 73, 75, 76, 78, 91, 93, 99–101, 103, 117, 125–9, 161, 162
Beckett, Samuel, 5, 25–6, 27, 75, 84, 88, 89, 162, 183, 191–207
  Dream of Fair to Middling Women, 192, 195–200, 201, 202, 208n39
  Footfalls, 204
  and French Symbolism/Decadence, 193–5

Beckett, Samuel (*cont.*)
  and the Joyces, 197–200
  More Pricks than Kicks, 208n33
  Not I, 5, 26, 29n20, 192, 200–2, 209n48
  and Peggy Sinclair, 195–6
  Play, 200, 201
  Quad I + II, 26, 192, 198, 201–4, 205
  That Time, 200
  The Unnamable, 195
Bennett, Vivienne, 175
Bergson, Henri, 15–16, 45, 134, 135, 177
Berkoff, Steven, 27
Bernhardt, Sarah, 5, 23, 24, 56–9, 60, 62, 71n109, 75, 76, 80, 95–9, 102, 112, 124, 161, 206
Berryman, John, 5
Blackton, James Stuart, 5, 123, 145
Blanchot, Maurice, 8–9, 14
Bland, Lucy, 65, 71n117
Bloom, Harold, 157
Bolm, Adolf, 116
Botticelli, Sandro, 86, 164, 196, 197
Bouchor, Maurice, 82, 88
Bourgeois, Louise, 54
Braidotti, Rosi, 21
Brancusi, Constantin, 18, 197
Brandstetter, Gabriele, 13–14, 15, 21, 22, 45, 46, 137, 204–5
Brooke, Van Dyke, 145
Brooks, Louise, 112
Browning, Tod, 145–6
Bryant, Charles, 125
Burke, Edmund, 23, 44–5

Cambridge Festival Theatre, 173–5
Cantor, Eddie, 66
Caravaggio, 5, 26, 200, 201
Carrillo, Gomez, 74, 90, 101, 102
Caselli, Daniela, 116
Casement, Roger, 64
Castle, Terry, 35, 151n140
Cecchetti, Enrico, 155, 173, 176
Celticism, 160, 162, 174; *see also* Irish Literary Revival
Chaplin, Charlie, 17, 116, 208n30
Charcot, Jean-Martin, 15, 16, 53, 54, 79, 107n29; *see also* Salpêtrière; hysteria
Chat Noir, 86
Chéret, Jules, 36
Chicago Tribune, 50

Chopin, Frédéric, 144, 175
Chopin, Kate, 140
cinématographe/cinematographic, 6, 14, 15, 24, 25, 35, 76, 88, 106n9, 111, 112, 113, 114, 121, 130, 134, 135, 141, 142 ; *see also* silent film
Claretie, Jules, 51–2, 54, 56
Cleopatra, 3, 52, 92, 124
closet drama, 80
Cocteau, Jean, 112
Comédie Parisienne, 50
Cooper Albright, Ann, 46, 52, 53, 70n79
Cornalba, Elena, 36, 38, 40
Crary, Jonathan, 115
Crowell, Ellen, 158
Cuchulain, 169, 170, 171, 182–3, 199
Cucullu, Lois, 58

D'Annunzio, Gabriele, 104
D'Humières, Robert, 51, 126
Danius, Sara, 18
Darragh, Florence, 102, 156, 161
De Chavannes, Puvis, 4, 83
De Lauretis, Teresa, 48, 118
De Valera, Eamon, 183
De Valois, Ninette, 25, 26, 155, 167, 170, 173–80, 181
Debey, Jacques, 126
Debussy, Claude, 104, 105, 144
Decadence, 5, 25, 27, 41, 44, 50, 52, 54, 62, 67, 74, 76–8, 79, 84, 93, 94, 104, 117, 118–23, 125, 126, 153, 154, 160, 161, 162, 164, 190, 191, 193, 194, 195
degeneration theory, 54, 60, 77, 82, 119, 163
Deleuze, Gilles, 192
Delibe, Léo, 171
Delluc, Louis, 136, 141
Delsartism, 45, 59, 121–2, 127, 163
Denishawn School, 112, 127
Després, Suzanne, 81, 136
Diaghilev, Sergei, 15, 19, 66, 84, 103, 110n131, 120, 126, 127, 156, 165, 173, 174, 180, 189, 196; *see also* Ballets Russes
Didi-Huberman, Georges, 11–12, 13, 14, 70n104
Dierkes-Thrun, Petra, 6, 49, 94, 123, 190
Dieterle, William, 190
Dietrich, Marlene, 114

Dionysus/Dionysian, 7–9, 14, 15, 21, 53, 88, 164, 174; *see also* maenads
Donohue, Joseph, 80, 99
Doody, Noreen, 157, 178
Dorn, Karen, 166
Douglas, Lord Alfred, 65, 73, 89, 191
Dowden, Edward, 156
dress reform, 91, 96–7
Dulac, Edmund, 171
Dulac, Germaine, 25, 111–15, 134–46
  on dance, 111–12, 114–15, 134–5, 141–5
  Disque 957, 144
  Étude cinégraphique sur une Arabesque, 144–5
  feminism, 112–15, 135, 139, 140, 142
  film aesthetics, 111–12, 134–6, 140–5
  'From Sentiment to Line', 134–5
  Malencontre, 141, 145
  'The Music of Silence', 141–2
  'Photographie-Cinégraphie', 142
  queerness, 114, 137, 140
  Thèmes et variations, 142–4
  'Trois Rencontres avec Loïe Fuller', 111, 136
  Vénus Victrix, 139, 141, 145
Duncan, Isadora, 15, 16, 17, 20, 84, 89, 115, 120, 181, 189
  Dance Idylls, 156
  and Edward Gordon Craig, 163–6
  feminism, 16, 163
  Greek dance, 8, 14, 45, 46, 59, 163–5
  influence on modernism, 19, 163–6
  natural movement, 22, 34, 44, 102, 137, 163–4
  on Salome, 163–4
Duncan, Raymond, 197
Dürer, Albrecht, 9, 11, 101
Duse, Eleanora, 75, 124
Duthuit, Georges, 193–5
Dwan, Lisa, 204

Easter Rising, 64, 182–3
Eliot, T. S., 19, 162, 183
Ellis, Havelock, 54
Ellis, Sylvia, 154, 155
Ellmann, Richard, 85, 93
Eltis, Sos, 91
Emmanuel, Maurice, 53
Epstein, Jean, 134
Euripides, 8, 174
Exposition Universelle, 45, 159

Expressionism, 53, 112, 136, 174, 180, 181

Farber, Yaël, 175, 191
Farfan, Penny, 48
Farr, Florence, 174
Fascism, 176
Felski, Rita, 16
feminism, 22–3, 35–6, 46, 48, 52, 54–7, 59–60, 62, 69n66, 75, 90, 91, 96, 97, 112–13, 121, 125, 135, 139, 142, 163, 190
femme fatale, 3, 14, 24, 28n10, 41, 42, 52, 54, 79, 109n88, 119, 148n38, 158
Fenollosa, Ernest, 167
Flaubert, Gustave, 4, 15, 28n11, 50, 76, 104
Fleischer, Mary, 156, 165
Flitterman-Lewis, Sandy, 113, 145, 152n168
Fokine, Michel, 103, 120, 139
Folies Bergère, 23, 34, 36, 38, 57, 74
Fort, Paul, 81
Foucault, Michel, 6, 13, 79
France, Anatole, 36
Franko, Mark, 42, 89
Freud, Sigmund, 110n123, 152n168, 179
Fuller, Loïe, 5, 9, 14–15, 33–67, 68n30, 69n66, 74–8, 95, 97, 154, 170, 205–7
  biography, 33–4
  and cinema, 25, 35, 36, 47, 69n62, 76, 112–15, 123, 132, 133, 136, 142–5
  costumes/ veils, 34, 36, 42, 45, 74, 171
  as director-choreographer, 22, 23, 47, 50
  Fire Dance, 48, 50, 132
  influence on modernism, 17, 19, 23, 24, 42, 46, 84, 158–9
  in Mallarmé's essays, 19, 36–42, 121, 205
  and modern dance, 9, 14–15, 19, 22, 34–6, 43–8, 56–7, 181, 189, 198
  as Nympha, 14–15, 23, 45
  queerness, 35, 48–9, 58, 70n74, 70n79, 129, 140
  reviews, 46–7, 51, 52
  and Salome (figure), 42, 50, 67n8, 78
  Salomé (1895), 48, 50–1, 52, 54
  Serpentine Dance, 33–5, 38–40, 43–5, 47–8, 69n41, 124, 132, 137

Fuller, Loïe (*cont.*)
  stage technology, 33–6, 42, 50–1, 54–6, 74, 86, 167, 171, 198
  torsion, 45–6, 57, 116, 144
  La Tragédie de Salomé (1907), 51, 54–5, 66, 103, 125
Futurism, 19

Garafola, Lynn, 120
Garber, Marjorie, 65, 73–4, 108n7
Garelick, Rhonda, 36, 70n81, 98
Gay, Peter, 4
Ghirlandaio, Domenico, 12–13
Ginner, Ruby, 46
Glenn, Susan, 22
Goody, Alex, 117–18
Gordon Craig, Edward, 17, 19, 25, 81, 89, 97, 155, 162–7, 169, 170, 171, 175, 178, 192
Gosse, Edmund, 102
Graham, Jorie, 5
Graham, Martha, 5, 137, 189–90
Gray, Terence, 174–5, 178, 180
Greek dance, 7, 9–15, 21, 23, 25, 45, 46, 49, 53, 59, 92, 105, 163, 164, 189, 197
Greek tragedy, 7–8, 92, 105, 171, 174, 180
Gregory, Lady Augusta, 153, 166, 175
Grein, J. T., 58, 63, 64
Griffith, D. W., 127, 135
Guardian, The, 98
Gunning, Tom, 69n62, 111, 115, 144, 145
Guszalewicz, Alice, 93
Gyles, Althea, 86–8

Hari, Mata, 90
Harrison, Jane Ellen, 92
Haughton, Hugh, 102
Hayworth, Rita, 5, 190
Heine, Heinrich, 28n17, 148n38, 176
Hellenism, 14, 23, 86, 91, 163, 189
Herodias, 2, 3, 4, 15, 28n17, 60, 78, 96, 126, 148n38, 157, 159, 160, 161, 170, 172, 194, 201
Hillel-Erlanger, Irène, 114, 136, 137
Hoffmann, Gertrude, 26, 66, 117, 124
Hoffmann, E. T. A., 16, 53
Hogarth, William, 43–4, 84, 98
homosexuality, 24, 49, 63, 64, 91, 93, 129, 191

Horsley, Owen, 191
Huysmans, Joris-Karl, 4, 50, 60, 77, 78–9, 80, 94, 101, 193, 198
Huyssen, Andreas, 18
hysteria, 15, 16, 53–4, 70n104, 79–80

Ibsen, Henrik, 113, 115, 119–20, 121, 125, 136, 148n45
Imagism, 19
intertextuality, 3, 8, 127, 177, 179, 198
Irish Literary Revival, 162
Irish Times, 179
Irving, Henry, 162
Ito, Michio, 25, 155, 167–72, 173, 174, 181, 196

Jacobs, Karen, 9
Japonisme, 81, 127
Jaques-Dalcroze, Émile, 168, 175, 196, 197
Jarry, Alfred, 24, 75, 81, 82–3, 84, 162
Järvinen, Hanna, 126, 129
Jolles, André, 12
Jones, Susan, 20, 38, 47, 141, 192, 207n3, 207n6
Josephus, Flavius, 3
Joyce, James, 195, 197, 198, 199–200, 208n36
Joyce, Lucia, 195, 197, 208n30
Judith and Holofernes, 3, 12, 13, 21, 49, 92–3, 179

Kabuki, 155, 168
Kandinsky, Wassily, 17
Karsavina, Tamara, 26, 66, 120, 125–8, 132, 180
Kaun, Axel, 205
Keaton, Buster, 124
Kemp, Lindsay, 26, 93
Kermode, Frank, 20–1, 38, 154
kinaesthetics, 23, 25, 27, 42, 46, 56–7, 59, 66, 98, 112, 113, 114, 115–16, 119, 121, 122, 130, 131, 136, 137, 139, 140, 141, 145, 147n14, 155
Knowlson, James, 26, 29n20, 200
Koritz, Amy, 20, 21
Kristeva, Julia, 146

Laforgue, Jules, 4, 5
Lane, John, 101
Larche, Françoise-Raoul, 36

Legat, Nicholas, 173, 176
Léger, Fernand, 121, 193
lesbianism, 35, 48, 49, 64, 65, 70n74, 92, 118, 151n140, 151n141
Lewis, Wyndham, 83
lighting, 34, 42, 49, 50, 51, 86, 91, 111, 112, 114, 134, 135, 136, 140, 144, 145, 159, 161, 166, 168, 182, 198, 201, 202
Lilith, 3
line of beauty/ grace, 23, 43–4, 84, 98
Lorrain, Jean, 23, 52–4
Lugné-Poe, Aurélien Marie, 75, 81–2, 83, 86, 136
Lumière, Auguste and Louis, 14, 19, 47, 76, 111, 123

maenad, 8, 9–15, 21, 41, 49, 53, 59, 92, 105, 160, 164
Maeterlinck, Maurice, 17, 24, 75, 81, 82, 107n39, 129, 136, 139, 161, 162, 184n39, 192
magic lantern, 36, 53–4, 88, 112, 136, 167
Mallarmé, Stéphane, 4, 8, 14, 19, 20, 23, 25, 26, 35, 36–40, 42, 44, 50, 60, 67n13, 68n32, 74, 77, 80, 82, 83, 84, 94, 121, 145, 179, 189–90, 193, 194, 195, 204, 205, 206, 208n39
  'Another Study of Dance', 38–40, 67n13
  'Ballets', 36
  Hérodiade, 4, 50, 60, 68n32, 80, 82, 94, 189–90, 194
Manning, Susan, 57
Marcus, Jane, 80, 148n45, 148n61
Marcus, Laura, 112
Marey, Étienne-Jules, 14
Marinetti, Filippo Thomas, 83
marionettes, 16, 47, 81, 82, 83, 84–90, 105, 118, 163, 170, 171, 178, 207n6; *see also* puppets
Maude, Ulrika, 192
Maule, Rosanna and Catherine Russell, 112–13
McAteer, Michael, 161, 184n39
McCarren, Felicia, 39, 47, 106n9
McGuinness, Patrick, 81, 106n19
McMullan, Anna, 200, 203
Medusa, 52, 101, 110n123, 206
Meltzer, Françoise, 3
Mills, Dana, 46, 48, 67n7

mime, 24, 104–5, 180, 181, 193, 203, 208n30
modern dance, 5, 8–9, 13–16, 19, 21, 23, 24, 33–72, 77, 84, 89, 95, 102, 111, 116, 120, 135, 137, 140, 163–4, 171, 189–90
modernism
  and aesthetic forms, 17–18, 22, 43, 46, 113, 136
  and the body, 19–20, 27, 42, 162
  and impersonality, 47, 89, 178
  and mass culture, 18
  and movement, 18–20, 42, 112, 121
Mondrian, Piet, 17
Moore, Thomas, 199
Moreau, Gustave, 4, 9–11, 40, 50, 60, 78, 79, 80, 83, 193–5, 198, 200
Morin, Emilie, 201
Morris, Margaret, 46, 197
Moulin Rouge, 41, 50, 104
Munte, Lina, 82
muse, 9, 21, 27, 36, 38, 39, 40, 65, 78, 92, 94, 97, 104, 125, 160
Myers, Kimberley, 179

Nalpas, Louis, 112
Napierkowska, Stasia, 25, 114, 137–40, 144
Nautch dance, 45, 54
Nazimova, Alla, 6, 24–5, 112–33, 141, 145, 206
  biography, 114
  career in theatre, 115–16, 119–20, 148n45
  career in silent film, 112–14, 124–5
  dance training, 113, 121, 122–3
  press, 115–16, 118, 119–20, 137
  queerness, 70n80, 114, 118, 129–31
  Salomé: An Historical Phantasy by Oscar Wilde, 24, 113, 123, 124–5, 127–33, 134, 136, 146
Negri, Pola, 112
'new modernist studies', 18–20
New Woman, 4, 16, 51, 58, 75, 91, 93, 113, 119, 140
New York Press, 116
New York Times, 50, 63, 72n137, 132
New York Tribune, 98, 118, 124
Nietzsche, Friedrich, 6, 7–8, 11, 15, 159, 174
nihon buyō, 168, 171
Nijinska, Bronislava, 173

Nijinsky, Vaslav, 84, 89, 90, 125, 126, 129, 165, 196
Nō Theatre, 163, 167–70
Noguchi, Isamu, 190
Noguchi, Yone, 169
Nordau, Max, 53
Nympha, 12–15, 21, 23, 41, 45, 86, 92, 157, 158, 189, 206; see also Warburg, Aby

O'Brien, Victoria, 176
Observer, The, 126
orientalism, 4, 9, 13, 14, 45, 50, 58, 59, 104, 109n101, 115, 126, 129, 139–40, 149n85, 164, 174
Orpheus, 8–12, 21
Overton Walker, Aida, 26, 32n104, 66
Ovid, 9

Pall Mall Gazette, 137
Pater, Walter, 77, 165
Pavlova, Anna, 125
Pemberton Billing, Noel, 63–6, 72n145
Perret, Léonce, 145
Petrescue, Eugenie, 104, 110n136
photogénie, 136
Picasso, Pablo, 112, 193
Pigott, Edward, 76
Pollock, Lady Juliet, 92
pooka, 171
Pound, Ezra, 5, 18, 84, 167–8, 169
Pre-Raphaelites, 9, 91, 160, 161
Preston, Carrie, 31n83, 45, 85, 121–2, 168, 170, 171
primitivism, 2, 8, 89, 92, 127, 135, 164, 199
Prins, Yopie, 92
puppets, 16, 75, 82, 83–90, 108n62, 162, 208n30; see also marionettes

Quattrocento, 9, 12, 14, 156, 205
queerness, 24, 35, 40, 63, 194
Quinn, John, 153, 154

Rambert, Marie, 196
Rambova, Natacha, 114, 125, 127, 129
Rancière, Jacques, 17–18, 23, 34–5, 43, 47, 48, 67n6–7, 140
Ray, Man, 121
Regnault, Henri, 4, 40
Reinhardt, Max, 59, 125, 169
Retté, Adolphe, 99, 106n20

Rice, David Edgar, 1–2
Ricketts, Charles, 80, 81, 92, 99, 161, 165, 178
Rilke, Rainer Maria, 14, 205
Rimbaud, Arthur, 77, 198, 208n36
Rivière, Henri, 86
Robertson, W. Graham, 96, 98
Robinson, Lennox, 175
Rodenbach, Georges, 23, 40–2, 206
Rodin, Auguste, 19, 36, 68n30
Romanov, Boris, 126–7
Romanticism, 20, 48, 84, 118, 174
Ross, Robert, 33, 80
Rossetti, Dante Gabriel, 3, 157, 160
Royal Ballet, 155, 173
Rubinstein, Ida, 5, 24, 25, 26, 103–5, 114, 139, 145, 190, 206
Ruprecht, Lucia, 84
Russell, Ken, 6, 190, 191

Saint John the Baptist, 2, 3, 5, 9, 12, 26, 28n17, 50, 51, 52, 78, 117, 118, 123, 146, 158, 194, 199–200, 201, 203, 208n44
Saliot, Anne-Gaëlle, 6–7
Salome
  in the Bible, 3–4, 50, 123, 190
  as *femme fatale*, 3, 14, 24, 28n10, 42, 52, 79, 119
  in medieval sources, 4, 15, 104
  as political figure, 23, 63–4, 122, 137, 172
  and popular culture, 1–2, 5, 26, 42, 58, 117
  and the Renaissance, 4, 12, 200–1
  and striptease, 22, 42, 62, 64, 101
Salpêtrière (hospital), 15, 53, 79
Savage, Roger, 165
Savoy, The, 162
Sawdust and Salome, 145
Schiller, Friedrich, 84
Schlemmer, Oskar, 88
Schmitt, Florent, 15, 51, 66, 125, 126
Schneider, Alan, 201
'School for Salomes', 58
Schwartz, Hillel, 23, 46, 116, 120
Sedgwick, Eve Kosofsky, 49
serpentine, 17, 23, 25, 33, 34, 36, 42–6, 47, 49, 50, 52, 76, 84, 86, 96, 97, 111, 113, 114, 115, 116, 119, 120, 122, 123, 132, 133, 137, 144, 145, 206

severed head, 2, 3, 5, 7, 9, 23, 51, 52, 54, 56, 76, 79, 92, 126, 146, 157, 158, 172, 179, 180, 181, 182, 199, 201, 203, 204, 205
Shaw, George Bernard, 103, 156
Shawn, Ted, 112
Sherry, Vincent, 4, 77, 106n16, 195
Show, The, 145–6
Showalter, Elaine, 93, 110n123
Shteir, Rachel, 60–2
Sidhe, 25, 155, 159–60, 170, 171, 172, 180
silent film, 5, 19, 24, 105, 111–46; *see also cinématographe/* cinematographic
Silvestre, Armand, 50
Simonson, Mary, 22, 60
Simpson, Hannah, 202
Sinclair, Peggy, 195–7
Smithers, Leonard, 162
Solano, Solita, 118–19
Sommer, Sally, 34
Sontag, Susan, 129
Sorère, Gab (Gabrielle Bloch), 35, 49, 112
Soudeïkine, Serge, 126–7
Sperling, Jody, 46
St Denis, Ruth, 15, 34, 45, 53, 55, 57, 84, 112, 120, 137, 156, 184n15
Stebbins, Genevieve, 45, 163
Stein, Gertrude, 205
Stoker, Bram, 97, 115
Strauss, Richard, 5, 6, 15, 29n19, 59, 98, 109n114, 139, 191
Stravinsky, Igor, 126
striptease, 22–3, 42, 50, 60–2, 64, 98, 101, 102, 199
Sturge Moore, Thomas, 153, 156
Stuttgart Preparatory Ballet School, 202
Sudermann, Hermann, 123
suffrage movement, 58, 62, 65, 66, 163
Sunset Boulevard, 190–1, 194
Surrealism, 72n137, 118, 123, 135, 146, 152n168
Swanson, Gloria, 191
Symbolism, 6, 9–11, 14, 21, 23, 25, 26, 34, 36, 38, 40–2, 48, 50, 65, 67, 74, 75, 76–81, 83, 91, 93, 94, 95, 98, 104, 112, 113, 115, 129, 133, 134, 135, 136, 145, 155, 157, 158, 160, 161, 169, 174, 190–5, 198, 199, 205, 208n39

Symons, Arthur, 41, 68, 77–8, 79, 80, 94, 106n16, 155, 156, 157–9, 162, 176
Taxidou, Olga, 20, 83, 85, 164
technē, 62, 72n133
Terry, Ellen, 24, 71n109, 75, 97, 109n100, 162
Théâtre d'Art, 81
Théâtre de l'Oeuvre, 24, 75, 81, 83, 86
torque/ torsion, 15, 23, 46, 49, 57, 116, 122, 144, 145, 159
Toulouse-Lautrec, Henri de, 36, 41
Towsend, Julie, 39, 46, 48
transvestism, 65, 73–4
Trouhanowa, Natalia, 15

Valentino, Rudolph, 125
Valéry, Paul, 84, 205
vamps/ vampires, 4, 54, 114,115–16, 118, 119, 123, 124, 164
Veil, 5, 8, 12, 14, 22–3, 24, 25, 33–49, 51, 52, 62–4, 66, 73–6, 78, 80, 93, 95, 98, 99, 101–5, 114, 115, 124, 129, 130, 131–3, 136, 139, 144–6, 159, 160, 169–70, 171, 175, 179, 182, 189, 190, 191, 194, 198, 200, 202, 204, 205, 206–7
Verlaine, Paul, 25, 77,80, 83
Villiers de l'Isle-Adam, Auguste, 16
Vogue, 120
Von Kleist, Heinrich, 16, 24, 84–5, 88, 89–90, 105, 118, 192
Von Laban, Rudolf, 112
Vorticism, 19
Vuillard, Édouard, 193–4
Vuillermoz, Émile, 135–6, 141

Walkowitz, Judith, 62
Wall-Romana, Christophe, 121
Warburg, Aby, 1, 9–15, 21, 23, 45, 86, 92, 156, 157, 159, 189, 192, 205, 206
Washington Post, 1–2, 139
White, Patricia, 124, 129
Whitelaw, Billie, 200, 201, 204
Wigman, Mary, 53, 112
Wilde, Constance, 92
Wilde, Lady Jane, 92

Wilde, Oscar, 25, 26, 48, 51, 60–6, 67,
    72n137, 113, 117, 206
  and Aubrey Beardsley, 24, 73, 76,
    99–101
  'Camma', 109n100
  and Decadence, 76–8
  'The Decay of Lying', 74, 102
  and Diaghilev, 103
  'The Harlot's House', 85–8, 90, 103
  and Loïe Fuller, 42–3, 73, 75
  'The Philosophy of Dress', 91
  The Picture of Dorian Gray, 27, 79
  Salomé, 2, 4, 5, 6, 8, 16, 24, 33, 41,
    56, 58, 59, 65, 66, 73–105, 109n88,
    116, 124, 125, 130, 131, 134, 136,
    138, 153, 154, 156–8, 161, 162,
    163, 170, 171, 174, 176–9, 181
  and Sarah Bernhardt, 95–7
  and sexuality, 6, 27, 49, 58, 63, 64,
    65, 73, 190–1
  and Symbolism, 76–9, 81, 82, 83
  trials, 81, 106n6
  'The Truth of Masks', 74
  'Woman's Dress', 91
Wilder, Billy, 190–1
Williams, Tami, 139, 140, 146n7
Williams, Vaughan
Woman's World, 24, 91–3, 96
Wood, Thelma, 118
Woolf, Virginia, 141–2, 145
World War I, 19, 65
Worth, Katherine, 43, 161, 193

Yacco, Sada, 159
Yeats, W. B., 5, 18, 20, 21, 25, 81, 84,
    88, 89, 146, 153–83, 189, 192, 193,
    197, 203, 206
  'Among School Children', 20, 155
  At the Hawk's Well, 5, 156, 157,
    167–72, 177, 179, 181, 186n94
  and ballet, 156, 173, 175–6
  The Cat and the Moon, 173

Cathleen Ni Houlihan, 174
'The Celtic Element in Literature', 160
Certain Noble Plays of Japan, 167–9
Countess Cathleen, 165, 166
'A Cradle Song', 162
The Death of Cuchulain, 5, 170,
    181–3, 199
Deirdre, 160–1
and Edward Gordon Craig, 162–3,
    165–7
*Fairy and Folktales of the Irish
    Peasantry*, 160, 171
The Green Helmet, 162
and the Irish Blueshirts, 176–7,
    187n131
and the Irish Literary Revival, 153,
    162, 174
The King of the Great Clock Tower,
    156, 157, 176–80, 182
'Leda and the Swan', 179, 183n9
and Michio Ito, 168–72
and modern dance, 156, 163, 166, 181
'Nineteen Hundred and Nineteen', 5,
    157, 158–9, 161, 191
and Ninette de Valois, 173–6, 179–80
and Nō theatre, 167–9
Oedipus the King, 175
The Only Jealousy of Emer, 173
and Oscar Wilde, 153, 156, 176–7
The Player Queen, 173, 174
The Resurrection, 157
'The Second Coming', 159
'The Statues', 18
and Symbolism, 25, 80, 160–1
'The Theatre', 157
'The Tragic Theatre', 165
The Trembling of the Veil, 76, 80,
    82–3, 156
'The Valley of the Black Pig', 162
A Vision, 5, 153–4, 155, 157
The Wind Among the Reeds, 159
Yellow Book, The, 73, 162

EU representative:
Easy Access System Europe
Mustamäe tee 50, 10621 Tallinn, Estonia
Gpsr.requests@easproject.com

www.ingramcontent.com/pod-product-compliance
Lightning Source LLC
Chambersburg PA
CBHW071203240426
43668CB00032B/2048